THE SOVEREIGNTY OF PARLIAMENT

THE SOVEREIGNTY OF PARLIAMENT

History and Philosophy

JEFFREY GOLDSWORTHY

CLARENDON PRESS · OXFORD

This book has been printed digitally and produced in a standard specification
in order to ensure its continuing availability

OXFORD
UNIVERSITY PRESS

Great Clarendon Street, Oxford OX2 6DP

Oxford University Press is a department of the University of Oxford.
It furthers the University's objective of excellence in research, scholarship,
and education by publishing worldwide in

Oxford New York

Auckland Bangkok Buenos Aires Cape Town Chennai
Dar es Salaam Delhi Hong Kong Istanbul Karachi Kolkata
Kuala Lumpur Madrid Melbourne Mexico City Mumbai Nairobi
São Paulo Shanghai Singapore Taipei Tokyo Toronto

ISBN 0-19-826893-9

For Helen

Preface

I am a constitutional lawyer whose interest in the history of the doctrine of parliamentary sovereignty was aroused by some critics of the doctrine. They argue that it was invented in the late eighteenth and nineteenth centuries by academic lawyers such as Blackstone and Dicey, influenced by Hobbesian political theory, who persuaded gullible judges to discard a much older common law tradition in which Parliament's legislative authority was limited. Their argument implies that judges today might justifiably reject the doctrine, on the ground that it is a comparatively recent error, contrary to deeper and more venerable constitutional principles. Indeed, they invite judges to do so, for philosophical as well as historical reasons, and an increasing number of judges find the invitation attractive.

Given the fundamental importance of the doctrine in the constitutional law of the United Kingdom and many Commonwealth countries, I was surprised to find that its origins have never been the subject of a comprehensive historical study. Parts of the story have been told by historians interested in the constitutional developments of particular centuries, or in related subjects such as the concept of fundamental law. It is also discussed in scattered sections of works of general legal history that are now rather dated, such as those of Plucknett and Holdsworth. In investigating the origins and development of the doctrine, I found it necessary to consult so many different sources, and came across so much recently discovered evidence, that it seemed worthwhile to gather the pertinent information together in one volume.

I am not a professional historian, and have neither the expertise nor the opportunity to attempt a painstaking study of primary sources. In what follows I rely heavily on the work of historians who have investigated different aspects of the subject, and attempt to integrate their findings. Moreover, on the assumption that a consensus among contemporary historians is itself evidence of the historical facts they have investigated, I often rely not only on the information they have assembled, but also on their interpretations of it. I therefore include more than the usual amount of quotations from secondary sources. The extent of my indebtedness to their work is, I hope, fully disclosed in my footnotes.

This study covers more than six centuries of developments in English and British constitutional thought and practice. Although I have read a large amount of material, I am only too conscious of the fact that it is only the tip of a huge iceberg. Historical research is potentially endless, and a halt must be called well before all possible avenues of inquiry have been exhausted. Every chapter of this book could, after further research, be expanded into a book of its own. Consequently, readers more familiar than I am with particular periods of British history will inevitably discover gaps, unanswered questions, and mistakes of fact and interpretation. I can only hope that the main outlines of the story I tell will not be disturbed by such discoveries.

In quoting primary sources I have followed the common practice of modernizing archaic spellings, and some aspects of style such as capitalization and punctuation. This seems no more questionable than quoting translations of texts written in other languages for the benefit of readers unfamiliar with them. I doubt that most of my readers will be professional historians.

As an amateur historian with no prior acquaintances among professionals, I contacted a number of distinguished historians to ask if they would be willing to comment on drafts of various chapters of this book. All of them very kindly agreed to assist. My warm gratitude is due to Professors Charles T. Wood, John Guy, Johann Sommerville, Howard Nenner, Harry Dickinson, and John Philip Reid, and to Dr Glenn Burgess. Professor Wood and Dr Burgess, in particular, went far beyond the bounds of generosity in providing assistance to a complete stranger. Of course, none of them is in any way responsible for the errors and omissions in this final version of my work, which includes new material that they did not read. Indeed, one of them strongly disagrees with my analysis of the evidence.

A condensed version of the final chapter was discussed at the Workshop on Judicial Activism and Judicial Review in Australian Democracy, held in Canberra in July 1998, and I thank participants for their comments. James Allan, Michael Detmold, and Gerald Postema kindly read a draft of this chapter, and provided me with very useful comments. I owe Michael a special debt for the support he has given me throughout my academic career, first, as a teacher, and subsequently as an adviser and referee. I have learnt an enormous amount from his jurisprudential writings, even though our legal philosophies are now so different.

Keith Akers, Gretchen Kewley, Becky Batagol, and Albert Dinelli provided invaluable research assistance. I was able to obtain their assistance through the generosity of the Australian Research Council, which awarded me a Small Grant in 1996. I am grateful to Ian Paterson for kindly translating some Latin passages for me. I would also like to thank several of my colleagues. Professor Enid Campbell provided comments on a very early draft that led to many improvements, as well as many helpful references later on. Peter Balmford showed me how to find old texts on microfilm, which proved extremely useful. Nick Pengelley, our Law Librarian, was unfailingly willing and able to obtain relevant material that the Library did not already possess. More generally, all my colleagues in the Faculty of Law at Monash University have helped to sustain a very congenial environment for the writing of this book.

My greatest debt is to my wife Helen, to whom this book is dedicated. Her love and support were essential to its completion.

Jeffrey Goldsworthy

Faculty of Law,
Monash University

Contents

1

Introduction

The doctrine of parliamentary sovereignty has long been regarded as the most fundamental element of the British Constitution. In his classic exposition of the doctrine, A.V. Dicey described it as 'the dominant characteristic of our political institutions', 'the very keystone of the law of the constitution'.[1] It is said that Parliament is able to enact or repeal any law whatsoever, and that the courts have no authority to judge statutes invalid for violating either moral or legal principles of any kind.[2] Consequently, there are no fundamental constitutional laws that Parliament cannot change, other than the doctrine of parliamentary sovereignty itself. As a political scientist has put it, 'there is a sense in which the British Constitution can be summed up in eight words: What the Queen in Parliament enacts is law'.[3]

A similar doctrine has traditionally been thought to describe the power of parliaments in New Zealand and Australia, although in the latter case, only in a heavily qualified form. In the late nineteenth century, the Judicial Committee of the Privy Council held that, when the Imperial Parliament granted power to colonial legislatures to make laws for 'the peace, welfare and good government' of their colonies, it granted them power of the same nature, as plenary and absolute, as its own power.[4] As a result of this and subsequent developments, the Parliament of New Zealand is now generally thought to be as fully sovereign as that of the United Kingdom.[5] In Australia, where legislative powers are divided and distributed between national and state parliaments, it has often been said that there are no limits to what they can do, other than those expressly or impliedly imposed by the constitutional instruments that define their powers. They are legally bound by written constitutions, but not by moral rights or common law principles, and therefore within their respective constitutional boundaries, they are as sovereign as the Parliament of the United Kingdom.[6]

---

[1] Dicey (1964: 39, 70).

[2] See Chapter 2 for detailed elaboration. How the United Kingdom's membership of the European Community affects this proposition is briefly explored in Chapter 10, text to nn. 36–7, below.

[3] Bogdanor (1996: 5).

[4] *R v Burah* (1878) 3 A.C. 889; *Hodge v R* (1883) 9 A.C. 117; *Powell v Apollo Candle Company* (1885) 10 A.C. 282.

[5] Joseph (1993: 2, 12, 399–403, 418, 430–1). On the dubious origins of this sovereign power, see Brookfield (1995: 42–52).

[6] Goldsworthy (1992: 152). The same position obtained in Canada, at least until 1982, when the Charter of Rights was adopted; indeed, technically, it still obtains: Hogg (1992: 12.2).

Whether or not the doctrine of parliamentary sovereignty prevents the United Kingdom and New Zealand Parliaments from prescribing binding requirements as to the procedure and form by which they must enact future legislation, is a question that has given rise to considerable debate.[7] But until recently, there has been little doubt about the core of the doctrine, that the courts have no legal authority to invalidate statutes on the ground that they are contrary to fundamental moral or legal principles. As a leading critic of the doctrine concedes, among English lawyers 'it is hard to question his [Dicey's] doctrine without appearing to lose touch with practical reality. Until very recently, it was almost unthinkable that the courts would ever refuse to apply an Act of Parliament.'[8]

But recently the doctrine has been challenged, by judges and academic lawyers in the United Kingdom, New Zealand, and Australia. Sir Robin Cooke, the President of the New Zealand Court of Appeal, was the first eminent judge to do so publicly. After initially expressing 'reservations' about the sovereignty of the New Zealand Parliament, he came to the view that '[s]ome common law rights presumably lie so deep that even Parliament could not override them'.[9] Since then, some other judges in New Zealand, Australia, and Britain have either endorsed that view, or agreed that it is arguable.[10] Recently, the High Court of Australia expressly deferred judgment on the issue: whether the exercise of legislative power by a State Parliament 'is subject to some restraints by reference to rights deeply rooted in our democratic system of government and the common law . . . is another question which we need not explore'.[11] In Britain, several senior judges have explored the question, in extra-judicial speeches. The Master of the Rolls, Lord Woolf of Barnes, has asserted that there are 'limits on the supremacy of Parliament which it is the courts' inalienable responsibility to identify and uphold'.[12] Sir John Laws has argued that true sovereignty belongs not to Parliament, but to the 'unwritten constitution', which includes fundamental principles, such as democracy and freedom of expression, that the judiciary can enforce, if necessary, by invalidating statutes.[13] Without going that far, Sir Stephen Sedley has suggested that the doctrine of parliamentary sovereignty has been replaced by 'a new and still emerging constitutional paradigm', consisting of 'a bi-polar sovereignty of the Crown in Parliament and the Crown in the courts'.[14]

---

[7] See Joseph (1993: ch. 15) on the New Zealand Parliament, and Bradley and Ewing (1997: 64–79) on the United Kingdom Parliament, although the debate there would now appear to be settled: see Chapter 2, nn. 32–3, and Chapter 10, text to nn. 36–7, below. Australian State Parliaments can undoubtedly bind themselves in this way: Goldsworthy (1987).

[8] Allan (1993: 16).

[9] *Taylor v New Zealand Poultry Board* [1984] 1 NZLR 394, 398; see also Cooke (1988: 158–65), Rishworth (1997*b*) and Kirby (1997). The relevant cases are discussed in Joseph (1993: 444–5).

[10] See Joseph (1993: 445) and Winterton (1996: 124–6).

[11] *Union Steamship Co of Australia v King* (1988) 166 C.L.R. 1, 10.

[12] Woolf of Barnes (1995: 69). But he has subsequently stated that 'the courts accept the sovereignty of Parliament', and that 'the vast majority, if not possibly all, the senior judiciary'—himself included—think it undesirable for the judiciary to be given power to invalidate statutes: Woolf (1998: 581, 592).

[13] Laws (1995: 87, 92); see also Laws (1996: 635).

[14] Sedley (1995: 389; 1997: 26–7). Sedley's views are criticized in Mullender (1998).

Growing doubt about parliamentary sovereignty among New Zealand, Australian, and British judges has coincided with increasing judicial activism in all three countries. In public law, this has mostly involved the invalidation of actions of the executive government, but also, in Australia, the purported discovery of 'implied rights' in the written Constitution. For causes that are obscure, an increase in both the ability and willingness of judges to control the other organs of government appears to be a worldwide phenomenon.[15] Despite occasional complaints, parliaments and executives in Britain, Australia, and New Zealand have generally acquiesced in, or even tacitly approved of, the expansion of judicial review of executive actions, which does not fundamentally threaten their powers as long as the parliaments retain their capacity to control or even reverse it.[16] But that depends on continued acceptance of the doctrine of parliamentary sovereignty. When judges question the doctrine, the potential threat posed by judicial activism to the powers of the legislature and executive is much more serious.

What is at stake is the location of ultimate decision-making authority—the right to the 'final word'—in a legal system. If the judges were to repudiate the doctrine of parliamentary sovereignty, by refusing to allow Parliament to infringe unwritten rights, they would be claiming that ultimate authority for themselves. In settling disagreements about what fundamental rights people have, and whether particular legislation is consistent with them, the judges' word rather than Parliament's would be final. Since virtually all significant moral and political controversies in contemporary Western societies involve disagreements about rights, this would amount to a massive transfer of political power from parliaments to judges. Moreover, it would be a transfer of power initiated by the judges, to protect rights chosen by them, rather than one brought about democratically by parliamentary enactment or popular referendum. It is no wonder that the elected branches of government regard that prospect with apprehension.

This apprehension has been voiced in the United Kingdom Parliament. In 1996, Lord Irvine of Lairg, at that time the Shadow Lord Chancellor, initiated a debate in the House of Lords concerning the relationship between the three branches of government.[17] In the presence of Lord Woolf and Lord Cooke of Thorndon (formerly Sir Robin Cooke of New Zealand), he criticized statements by senior judges challenging the doctrine of parliamentary sovereignty as 'unwise', and disparaged the alternative they advocated as 'obsolete'.[18] The Lord Chancellor, Lord Mackay, and Lord Wilberforce also strongly affirmed Parliament's sovereignty.[19] When the Human Rights Bill was introduced into the House of Lords in 1997, the accompanying White Paper stated that a power to invalidate Acts

---

[15] Tate and Vallinder (1995).   [16] Forsyth (1996: 135).

[17] *Parliamentary Debates, Fifth Series*, vol. 572, House of Lords, 5 June 1996, 1254–1313. See also Irvine of Lairg (1996*a*: 75–8; 1996*b*).

[18] *Parliamentary Debates, Fifth Series*, 1255.

[19] ibid. 1310 and 1268 respectively. Neither Lord Woolf nor Lord Cooke put up much opposition. Lord Woolf expressed confidence that the judges would faithfully obey every statute that he could contemplate Parliament enacting: ibid. 1273.

of Parliament is something 'which under our present constitutional arrangements they [the judges] do not possess, and would be likely on occasions to draw the judiciary into serious conflict with Parliament. There is no evidence to suggest that they desire this power, nor that the public wish them to have it.'[20]

The doubts expressed by judges such as Lord Woolf and Sir Robin Cooke are strongly supported and, no doubt, partly inspired by the work of some academic lawyers who have criticized the doctrine of parliamentary sovereignty on both historical and philosophical grounds.[21] 'Modern assertions of unlimited sovereignty', says one leading critic, 'rest on a misunderstanding of constitutional history'.[22] The main historical criticism is that the doctrine is a relatively recent invention of academic lawyers, particularly Sir William Blackstone, John Austin, and Dicey, influenced by the tradition of legal positivism founded by Thomas Hobbes, who erroneously argued that there is necessarily a sovereign law-maker at the foundation of every legal system. The doctrine was successfully foisted upon a gullible legal profession, which abandoned the traditional common law understanding that law-making was subject to fundamental legal principles.[23] Or so it is alleged, by critics who disparage the doctrine as an authoritarian, legal positivist 'dogma' that misconceives the real foundations of the British constitution.[24]

The critics attempt to clarify those real foundations through philosophical as well as historical analysis. The doctrine of parliamentary sovereignty maintains that Parliament has ultimate authority to determine what the law shall be. It is the responsibility of judges to declare what the law is, but in doing so, they are bound to accept every Act of Parliament as valid law. They can change the common law, but because it is subordinate to statute law, their decisions are always liable to be overturned by Parliament. The critics reject this doctrine as a misunderstanding of the relationship that must logically hold between statutory and common law. They argue that since it is the responsibility of judges to declare what the law is, the extent of Parliament's lawful authority to legislate is necessarily a matter for the judges to determine. In other words, it is necessarily a matter of common law, which is a body of judicial decisions based on fundamental principles such as justice and the rule of law. It follows that Parliament is entitled to override much of the common law, but not its most fundamental principles, because they are the ultimate source of its own authority.[25] Moreover,

---

[20] *Rights Brought Home: The Human Rights Bill, Presented to Parliament by the Secretary of State for the Home Department* (October 1997), 2.13.

[21] Sir John Laws has praised the work of one of these academic lawyers, Trevor Allan: Laws (1996: 631 n. 10).

[22] Allan (1993: 269). See also Detmold (1989*b*: 451), and Edwards (1996: 67).

[23] An argument along these lines is made at length by Walker (1988: ch. 5), much of which was previously published in Walker (1985). Walker's argument has influenced Allan (1993: 18 n. 74, 269) and Edwards (1996: nn. 14, 19, 137, 140). Fragments of the argument can also be found in Jennings (1959: 321), Heuston (1979: 1), and Allott (1979: 79, 102–13).

[24] See e.g. Allan (1993: 1–2, 16, 18, 69, 135, 239, 269).

[25] For citations and further discussion, see Chapter 10, Sections 3 and 4, below.

the same must be true of parliaments in Australia and New Zealand. They were originally established by the United Kingdom Parliament, which could not have granted them any power that it did not itself possess. Whatever the intended meaning of the constitutional formulas that define their powers, they too must be incapable of overriding fundamental common law principles.[26] The critics go so far as to assert that even the power to amend the Australian constitution, which is exercised by the national Parliament and the electorate voting in a referendum, is incapable of overriding those principles.[27] One critic claims that the very idea of wholly unlimited law-making power is irrational and absurd.[28]

The critics' philosophical and historical criticisms neatly dovetail. If they are right to argue that the doctrine of parliamentary sovereignty is a matter of common law, dependent on judicial recognition, then it is to be found in judicial decisions. But although it has been frequently affirmed by judges since 1871, it was rarely mentioned in judgments before then.[29] That might seem to corroborate the critics' historical argument, that judicial acceptance of the doctrine was a consequence of the conversion of academic lawyers and judges to legal positivism in the late eighteenth and nineteenth centuries.

In this book, these historical and philosophical criticisms are subjected to critical scrutiny. After the doctrine of parliamentary sovereignty is defined and clarified in the second chapter, the subsequent seven chapters are devoted to a detailed examination of its historical development. In the final chapter, the philosophical criticisms are shown to be based on a defective understanding of the foundations of legal systems, and consequently of the relationship between parliamentary authority and the common law. Readers more interested in the philosophical than the historical issues can go directly to that chapter, which can be read independently of those that precede it.

The nature of the doctrine of parliamentary sovereignty determines the nature of a proper historical study of its development. If its critics are justified in regarding it as a common law doctrine, then its history must be that of judicial recognition, recorded in the law reports. But if Sir William Wade was right to suggest that it is as much a political fact as a rule of law—and H. L. A. Hart's theory of law suggests that he was—then a proper history of its development must be a political rather than a narrowly 'legal' history.[30] Hart argues that the existence of the most fundamental rules of a legal system depends not on judicial acceptance alone (which in any event may exist well before it is explicitly acknowledged), but on a consensus among the most senior officials of all branches of government, legislative and executive as well as judicial.[31] If so, then a history

---

[26] Detmold (1985: 254–5).   [27] Detmold (1996: 35), Allan (1996: 158–9).
[28] Allan (1996: 156).
[29] It was affirmed in 1871 in *Lee v The Bude and Torrington Junction Railway Company* (1871) L.R. 6 C.P. 576, 582, *per* Willes J.
[30] Wade (1955: 188–97); Hart (1961: ch. 6).
[31] ibid. This claim is defended in Chapter 10, text to nn. 17–21, below.

of the development of parliamentary sovereignty must be a history of the development of that kind of consensus. Partly for this reason, my historical inquiry draws
heavily on the work of historians concerned more with political history, or the
history of political thought, than legal history in a narrow sense of the term.

Two mistakes are sometimes made when parliamentary sovereignty is thought
to rest on judicial acceptance alone, rather than a consensus among senior legal
officials in general. First, it is sometimes argued that Parliament's legal authority to alter a truly fundamental constitutional principle, or to enact a very unjust
law, has not yet been directly tested in the courts. Therefore, judicial opinions
to date are mere obiter dicta, and the doctrine of parliamentary sovereignty is
not as well established in strict law as most lawyers assume.[32] Secondly, it is
sometimes argued that even if the doctrine is well established, it remains subject to judicial law-making, precisely because it is a common law rule, established by judicial decisions. Therefore, today's judges have legal authority to modify
or reject it.[33]

Both these arguments are erroneous if the doctrine of parliamentary sovereignty is a fundamental rule whose existence is constituted by a consensus among
senior officials in all three branches of government. As for the first argument,
such a consensus may exist, and may have existed for centuries, without ever
having been laid down in the ratio decidendi of any judicial decision. As for the
second, a rule of that nature changes only if the consensus that constitutes it
changes, and such a change is beyond the authority of the judges alone. While
they can attempt to initiate such a change, they may or may not succeed. If they
were unilaterally to reject the rule then, according to Hart, the consensus that
previously constituted its existence, and therefore the rule itself, would be
destroyed. But the judges could not replace the rule with a different one, without the acquiescence of the other branches of government. In other words, unilateral judicial action could destroy part of the existing consensus on which the
legal system rests, without being able to replace it. That would be extremely
hazardous, to say the least. Judicial acceptance of a Bill of Rights, enacted by
Parliament after receiving popular endorsement in a referendum, would be an
entirely different matter, amounting to judicial participation in the formation of
a new consensus.

As well as correcting these essentially philosophical errors, this book will expose
several historical myths that remain popular among lawyers despite being discredited by modern historians. This is particularly true of the myth that Sir Edward
Coke's famous (but perhaps only apparent) denial of parliamentary sovereignty
in *Dr Bonham's* case was the culmination of a tradition in which judges could
declare statutes void for violating fundamental and unalterable laws.[34] Another,
possibly incompatible, myth is that before the mid-seventeenth century, the

---

[32] See Chapter 10, text to nn. 15–16, below.   [33] See Chapter 10, Section 3, below.
[34] Figgis (1922: 228–33); Pollock (1923: 165); Wright (1942: 12); Scarman (1974: 16–17); Mount
(1992: 22); Walker (1985); Walker (1988: ch. 5); Caenegem (1995: 27, 159–60, 173).

English did not clearly understand that their Parliament was a legislature as well as a 'high court'—that it made new laws rather than merely declaring and enforcing pre-existing natural and common law. According to this second myth, when Parliament's authority was described as 'absolute', as it often was during that period, it was being treated as a supreme court from which there was no appeal, rather than as a sovereign legislature in anything like the modern sense of the term.[35]

A third myth, closely associated with the first two, portrays the doctrine of parliamentary sovereignty as a development of the late eighteenth and nineteenth centuries, which radically transformed the earlier 'common law constitution' that had limited Parliament's authority.[36] It has been argued that the doctrine was relatively new even in the 1760s, and not generally adopted by British lawyers until the middle of the nineteenth century.[37] This book demonstrates that the doctrine is considerably older than that: it has been accepted by a large majority of English lawyers since the 1640s at the latest, and by the central institutions of English government since the Henrician Reformation of the 1530s.

The book also exposes a fourth myth, that the supposed common law constitution that 'controlled' statutes was eroded mainly by erroneous philosophical theories of sovereignty beginning with that of Hobbes. It must be admitted that those philosophical theories are erroneous, and that they influenced the evolution of British constitutional thought.[38] But the doctrine of parliamentary sovereignty has other and much deeper roots than Hobbesian political pseudo-science, whose influence was relatively minor. As Dicey rightly said, those roots 'lie deep in the history of the English people and in the peculiar development of the English constitution'.[39] The historical chapters of this book are intended to uncover them.

Prominent among the roots of the doctrine are the reasons that persuaded statesmen, lawyers, and political theorists to accept it. These reasons are of more than merely historical interest. In deciding whether or not the doctrine deserves continued acceptance today, it is useful to consider whether they are of continuing relevance. The opinions of classical writers such as Blackstone and Dicey should not be cited to support the doctrine today, without considering whether their underlying reasons are defunct owing to intervening social and political changes.[40] For example, Blackstone lauded parliamentary sovereignty partly because he believed that the King, Lords, and Commons were able to 'check and balance'

---

[35] See e.g. Walker (1988: 147); Detmold (1989*b*: 443–51); Allan (1993: 269); Edwards (1996: 67); Allott (1979: 112).

[36] This myth has been propagated by numerous writers, especially some American constitutional historians whose work is surveyed in Greene (1986: 56 ff.).

[37] Reid (1991: 6).

[38] H. L. A. Hart has demonstrated their errors to the satisfaction of most legal philosophers: see Hart (1961: ch. 4; and 1982: ch. 9).

[39] Dicey (1964: 69 n. 1). Dicey explicitly distinguished his own thesis from the philosophical claim that every state must contain a sovereign: ibid. 61, 72. See also Pollock (1929: 278–9).

[40] See Craig (1993: esp. 307–8, 313–24).

one another, but that is no longer the case. On the other hand, that was not Blackstone's only reason for endorsing the doctrine. In the final chapter of this book, it will be argued that some historically influential reasons are still sound, and help to provide a reasonable justification of the doctrine. It is far from irrational or absurd, as some of its critics allege.[41] But no attempt will be made to defend the doctrine against the proposal that it should be overturned by the formal adoption of a judicially enforceable Bill of Rights. The argument that it can still be given a reasonable justification will be aimed only at rebutting the claim that it is so irrational that it cannot really be part of the contemporary constitution. If that claim were sound, no Bill of Rights would be needed, because judges would already have authority to invalidate statutes that they regard as contrary to fundamental rights.

It should be clear by now that this book is intended primarily for lawyers. The major themes of the historical chapters will not be news to historians of British government, although given their usually limited specializations, the way in which I trace the development of Parliament's authority through seven centuries may be of some interest even to them. Some will regard it as largely irrelevant to their work, which involves attempting to understand earlier societies and modes of thought in their own terms, without reference to modern concerns and ideas. Historians are suspicious of attempts to locate the roots of modern ideas or institutions in the distant past, because of the danger of 'whig interpretations' of past arrangements as imperfect prototypes of present ones, which by some queer teleological process the former were fated to become.[42] I hope that no historian will attribute such an interpretation of the past to this book. It will not be suggested here that the doctrine of parliamentary sovereignty represents an essential or ideal arrangement of governmental authority, which was only imperfectly realized in earlier periods, or that the developments that led to its general acceptance were in any sense inevitable.

It should also be clear that the book is not directly concerned with all of the potential challenges confronting the doctrine of parliamentary sovereignty in the United Kingdom today. It is directly concerned with only one of them: the criticisms of the doctrine that I have mentioned, which put in question the relationship between judges and the common law, on the one hand, and parliaments and statute law, on the other. It is not directly concerned with two other potential challenges, posed by Britain's growing engagement with the European Union, and by its establishment of a new Scottish Parliament.[43] Both developments might reasonably be expected to be dealt with in a history of parliamentary sovereignty, but histories have to finish somewhere, and it is sufficient for my purposes to finish at the end of the nineteenth century.

[41] Allan (1996: 156, 160; and 1993: 18, 77).   [42] Butterfield (1931).
[43] The question of Britain's engagement with the European Community is very briefly discussed in Chapter 10, text to nn. 36–7, below.

2

Defining Parliamentary Sovereignty

1. 'Parliament' and 'Sovereignty' Defined

The words 'Parliament' and 'sovereignty' can have different meanings when used for different purposes, and therefore it is necessary to stipulate the meaning that they will have here. 'Parliament' will be used in its usual legal sense, meaning 'the King [or Queen] in Parliament'.[1] The subject of this investigation is the legislative sovereignty of Parliament considered as a whole, including the Crown as well as both Houses, and not the political sovereignty of the two Houses of Parliament or the House of Commons. Some historians who refer to parliamentary sovereignty mean the power of the two Houses to control the exercise by the Crown of its prerogatives. But that pertains to what is now called 'responsible government', which is conceptually and practically different from parliamentary sovereignty. The legislative sovereignty of the Crown in Parliament is compatible with the Crown having unquestioned authority to reject Bills passed by both Houses, and to exercise prerogative powers regardless of their approval. It follows that parliamentary sovereignty might in principle have existed well before the nineteenth century, when responsible government became firmly established.

In the sixteenth and seventeenth centuries, 'the King in Parliament' was an ambiguous expression. To some, it meant 'the King, in Parliament', because they believed that new laws were made by the authority of the King alone, even though he acted with the advice and consent of the two Houses. To others, it meant 'the King-in-Parliament', a composite institution of three partners who shared the authority to make laws. Both views are compatible with the King in Parliament having possessed sovereign law-making authority at that time.

The word 'sovereignty' is much more difficult to define, partly because it depends on the meaning of 'law', which is notoriously problematic. Dicey defines the sovereignty of Parliament in terms of two criteria, one positive and the other negative. The positive criterion is that Parliament has 'the right to make or unmake any law whatever'; the negative one is that 'no person or body is recognised by the law of England as having a right to override or set aside the legislation of Parliament'.[2] But the positive criterion is superfluous given Dicey's definition of 'law'. By the 'right' to make or unmake law he means a legal rather than a moral right. But since he defines 'law' as 'any rule which will be enforced by the courts',

---

[1] This seems to have been its meaning since the 1530s: Elton (1974*b*: 32–5).

[2] Dicey (1964: 40).

if the negative criterion is satisfied then the positive one is too.[3] If no person or body, including the courts, can override or set aside legislation, then Parliament's legislative authority is not restricted by any rule that the courts can enforce— and that is to say that it is not restricted by any law, which amounts to saying that Parliament has the legal right to make or unmake any law whatever. This is confirmed by Dicey's restatement of both the positive and negative criteria of sovereignty in terms of the legal duty of courts:

The principle then of Parliamentary sovereignty may, looked at from its positive side, be thus described: Any Act of Parliament, or any part of an Act of Parliament, which makes a new law, or repeals or modifies an existing law, will be obeyed by the courts. The same principle, looked at from its negative side, may be thus stated: There is no person or body of persons who can, under the English Constitution, make rules which override or derogate from an Act of Parliament, or which (to express the same thing in other words) will be enforced by the courts in contravention of an Act of Parliament.[4]

The positive and negative criteria are merely different formulations of the same principle. For Dicey, to say that Parliament is sovereign is to say that no other human agency possesses legal authority to override or hold invalid any statute that Parliament enacts. He goes too far in stating that parliamentary sovereignty requires that whatever statutes Parliament should enact 'will be obeyed' by the courts. What it does require is that the courts recognize the legal validity of those statutes, even if in an extraordinary situation they should decide to disobey one of them, on the ground that their legal duty to obey is overridden by a moral duty to disobey.[5]

Dicey's understanding of parliamentary sovereignty, clarified so as to accommodate this distinction between legal and moral duty, was by no means novel. Blackstone's was essentially the same. He acknowledged that all human laws were subordinate to, and would be invalid if they transgressed, the natural law prescribed by God, but also insisted that every government necessarily included a 'supreme, irresistible, absolute, uncontrolled authority, in which . . . the rights of sovereignty, reside'.[6] He was not guilty of inconsistency because he understood sovereign authority to be the one authority in the state whose misconduct could not be remedied by legal means, which is to say, by the courts. '[I]t would be a great weakness and absurdity in any system of positive law, to define any possible wrong, without any possible redress', he said.[7]

[W]herever the law expresses its distrust of abuse of power, it always vests a superior coercive authority in some other hand to correct it; the very notion of which destroys the idea of sovereignty. . . . The supposition of *law* therefore is, that neither the king nor either house of parliament (collectively taken) is capable of doing any wrong; since in such cases the law feels itself incapable of furnishing any adequate remedy.[8]

---

[3] ibid.   [4] ibid.   [5] This point is discussed further in Chapter 10, Section 7, below.
[6] Blackstone (1765: 41, 49).   [7] ibid. 237.   [8] ibid. 237–8.

Private injustices 'may be remedied by legal means', but against public wrongs contrary to the fundamentals of government 'the only tribunal to which the complainants can appeal is that of the God of battles, the only process by which the appeal can be carried on is that of a civil and intestine war'.[9]

In John Austin's definition of sovereign power, the crucial element is the absence of any superior authority that is habitually obeyed, which entails the absence of any legally recognized body able to provide a remedy for abuses of power.[10]

Dicey's definition of 'law' is that of a practical lawyer, not a legal philosopher, and is not entirely satisfactory. But apart from two qualifications, to be explained shortly, recent philosophical analysis suggests that it is basically sound. As Joseph Raz has explained, as we conceive of law, what distinguishes legal norms from purely customary or moral norms is that the former belong to a system of norms that is administered by governmental institutions. Not all of these norms have been deliberately created by a law-making institution: for example, we regard customs as laws if they are enforced by courts.[11] Moreover, some norms that are deliberately created by a law-making institution may be held invalid by courts, when they have legal authority to do so. Therefore, Raz proposes enforcement by courts, rather than enactment by law-making institutions, as a necessary condition for a norm to be classified as a law of the legal system in question.[12] He regards it as a necessary, but not a sufficient, condition, because courts sometimes enforce norms that are not laws of their own legal system: for example, when they apply the laws of another legal system in a case involving international transactions.[13]

But it may be going too far to regard judicial enforcement as a necessary condition for a norm to be classified as a law. Some legal systems include constitutional rules that are 'non-justiciable'—not enforceable by their courts—but are nevertheless generally regarded by legal officials as laws binding other institutions of government.[14] For that reason, Arthur Goodhart once suggested that 'any rule is to be regarded as a part of state law if it is recognized as being obligatory by any one of the three branches of government'.[15] He then concluded that Parliament's law-making authority was limited by fundamental legal principles, even though no other institution was authorized to enforce them.[16] But this definition of 'law' is too broad, because it could include purely customary or moral rules that are recognized as obligatory. Non-justiciable rules should be

---

[9] ibid. 186.   [10] Austin (1954: 194).

[11] For convenience, I will use 'courts' to mean what Raz calls 'law-applying institutions'.

[12] Raz (1979: ch. 5, esp. 87–8, 93, 97, 101; and 1980: 189–200). This oversimplifies Raz's position, which recognizes as laws the norms that authorize the courts to act, which they do not really 'enforce'. The law consists of the norms that authorize the courts to act, and the norms that they enforce.

[13] Raz (1979: 97–8).

[14] See Wheare (1966: 101–4), and for general comparative studies, Cappelletti (1971) and Brewer-Carias (1989).

[15] Goodhart (1958: 954).   [16] ibid.

regarded as laws only if, other than not being judicially enforceable, they are indistinguishable in form and function from other rules that are unquestionably laws. That condition is satisfied if they are expressed in written, canonical form, in formally enacted legal instruments, such as constitutions; are expected to be obeyed by legal institutions other than courts; are in fact generally obeyed by those institutions; and, despite borderline problems of vagueness and ambiguity, are sufficiently clear that some possible actions of those institutions would plainly be inconsistent with them. Provided that the rules satisfy these criteria, there is no good reason to refuse to call them laws. They belong to the system of norms that is administered by legal institutions as a whole.

Dicey's definition of sovereignty should be qualified accordingly: law-making authority is sovereign if it is unrestricted by norms that either are judicially enforceable, or satisfy the criteria just listed. But this qualification is of little importance for our purposes because, with the possible exception of the Acts of Union of 1707, no such norms are regarded as binding the United Kingdom Parliament.[17] Purely customary or moral norms, which are neither enforced by the courts nor incorporated in any formally enacted legal instrument, do not count.

This first qualification to Dicey's definition of sovereignty helps to explain why we do not describe the highest court in a judicial hierarchy as sovereign merely because its decisions are not subject to appeal to a higher court or, therefore, to norms that are enforced by a higher court. We say that such a court is bound by law, even though the mistakes it makes in applying the law are not subject to correction, and its decisions are therefore legally conclusive.[18] This is because it is generally regarded as bound by, and does generally obey, laws that are written, incorporated in formally enacted legal instruments, and relatively clear. The first qualification to Dicey's definition merely applies the same principle to the other branches of government. It invites a comparison between the authority of Parliament and that of the courts. The medieval Parliament was known as 'the High Court of Parliament', and regarded as the highest court in the land, whose actions were not subject to appeal to any other court.[19] But, as we will see, it was never like a modern Supreme Court. It was acknowledged to have authority to change not only the common law, but also its own statutes, in the interests of justice or 'reason'. Like Parliament today, it was bound only by purely customary and moral norms.[20]

The highest courts in most common law systems, such as the House of Lords and the High Court of Australia, are now regarded as having power to change the common law. This raises the difficult jurisprudential question of whether they are genuinely bound by the common law. Ronald Dworkin argues that they are bound by the deepest and most abstract principles of the common law, because they can legitimately overrule previous decisions and doctrines only in order to

---

[17] These Acts are discussed in Chapter 7, Section 2, below.
[18] See Hart (1961: 138–43).   [19] McIlwain (1910: *passim*).
[20] See Chapter 3, Section 4, and Chapter 5, Section 4, below.

maintain consistency with those principles.[21] But his argument is debatable, partly because those principles seem indistinguishable from the abstract principles of justice by which even Parliament is believed to be bound. Arguably, the most fundamental principle of the common law is something as abstract as 'justice'. Lord Esher once said that 'any proposition the result of which would be to show that the common law of England is wholly unreasonable and unjust, cannot be part of the common law of England'.[22] If so, then the ultimate criteria that guide the highest courts in deciding what the common law 'really is', are indistinguishable from those that guide Parliament in making new laws. That is why the traditional lawyers' creed, that even when overruling earlier decisions or doctrines, superior courts are merely declaring what the common law 'really is', rather than changing it, is now often disparaged as a 'fairy tale'.[23] Today, those courts are widely believed to exercise a discretionary, law-making power to change the common law in the interests of justice. But they do not possess a sovereign law-making power, because they cannot repeal statutes, and can only decide particular disputes brought to them, rather than act on their own motion and enact whatever laws of general application they please. The law-making power of the High Court of Parliament was not limited in those ways.

I have said that Dicey's definition of sovereignty should be qualified in two respects. The second qualification follows from criticisms that have been made of Hobbesian theories of law.[24] A Hobbesian theory holds that in every legal system, all laws owe their existence and validity to the explicit or implicit commands of a 'sovereign', a person or group of people that is habitually obeyed by the rest of the population and does not habitually obey the commands of anyone else. The sovereign and its authority are, by definition, above all laws, and therefore not susceptible to legal limitation.[25] In criticizing this kind of theory, Hart shows that it is unable to accommodate familiar legal phenomena, such as the continuity of legal authority between the demise of one putative 'sovereign' and the succession of another, the existence of rules governing such successions, and in many legal systems, the existence of constitutional laws limiting the authority of all governmental institutions. Hart argues that legal rules, and in particular 'rules of recognition', constitute the foundations of legal systems, and he explains the existence of these rules in terms of their being accepted as binding, at least by senior legal officials, rather than in terms of the commands of legally transcendent 'sovereigns'.[26] But Hart's theory is compatible with the existence of legislative sovereignty as it has been defined so far, because the ultimate rule of recognition in a particular legal system might recognize that some person

---

[21] Dworkin (1977: Chs. 2–4, esp. 37–8).
[22] *Emmens v Pottle* (1885) 16 Q.B. 354, 357–8.   [23] Reid (1972: 22).
[24] This is a reference to the seventeenth century political philosopher Thomas Hobbes: see Chapter 5, n. 403, below.
[25] This is essentially the theory attributed to John Austin by Hart (1961).
[26] ibid., chs. 2–6: *passim*. For further discussion, see Chapter 10, Section 2, below.

or institution possesses that kind of sovereignty.[27] Indeed, if it recognizes the existence of what Hart calls an 'all embracing' rather than merely a 'continuing' sovereign power, then the rule of recognition itself is subject to alteration by the exercise of that power. Hart explains the sovereignty of the British Parliament in this fashion, and argues that it is continuing rather than all-embracing: in other words, the one thing that the British rule of recognition does not permit Parliament to do is limit its own sovereign power.[28]

On this view, rather than being a transcendent creator of all laws, a sovereign law-maker is itself created by fundamental laws. These identify the law-maker, and if it is not a natural person, may determine its 'constitution', in the sense of its composition. 'Parliament', for example, is not a natural person, but a complex artificial institution that is defined and structured by law. Fundamental laws may also prescribe the procedure that the law-maker must follow, and the form in which it must express itself, if it is to exercise its law-making authority successfully. Laws of these kinds provide criteria that determine whether or not its deliberations have resulted in laws.

Fundamental laws governing these matters of composition, procedure, and form are consistent with an institution possessing sovereign law-making authority, as long as they do not unduly impair its ability to change the substance of the law in any respect and at any time it chooses. An impaired ability to act may be due to internal as well as external constraints: just like a natural person, an institution may be severely handicapped by its own character or anatomy. For example, a bicameral legislature that can only enact laws with the unanimous assent of all members of both chambers might be unable to enact any laws at all. Admittedly, this means that sovereignty is a question of degree.[29] In *Bribery Commissioner v Ranasinghe*, the Judicial Committee of the Privy Council discussed a requirement that the Constitution of Ceylon could be changed only by a two-thirds majority of the Ceylonese Parliament. 'No question of sovereignty arises', said the Committee. 'A parliament does not cease to be sovereign whenever its component members fail to produce among themselves a requisite majority.' The requirement limited lesser majorities, but 'does not limit the sovereign powers of parliament itself which can always, whenever it chooses, pass the amendment with the requisite majority'.[30] The premise is sound, but the conclusion debatable, given that a two-thirds majority requirement can in practice make it very difficult, if not impossible, for a legislature to act.[31]

It may be reasonable to regard a law-maker as sovereign even if it cannot change all the laws that govern its own composition, and the procedure and form by which it must make laws. That is how some British lawyers regard Parliament:

---

[27] For convenience, I will follow Hart in assuming that every legal system includes a single rule of recognition. It does not matter for my purposes if legal systems can include more than one such rule, or principles or practices, rather than rules, of recognition.
[28] Hart (1961: 145–6).   [29] Goldsworthy (1987: 420–2).
[30] *Bribery Commission v Ranasinghe* [1965] A.C. 172, 200.
[31] Goldsworthy (1987: 417–23, 425).

they deny that it can effectively prescribe the procedure or form that it must thereafter follow in order to enact valid legislation. This is presumably because, if it could do so, the courts would be bound to invalidate subsequent legislation passed by a contrary procedure or form, and then Parliament would no longer be sovereign in Dicey's sense.

But a legislature able to change its own composition, procedure, and form of legislation, is surely more rather than less sovereign. Moreover, its ability to do so may be consistent with its possessing 'continuing' sovereignty, which it cannot limit or fetter. The power of a legislature to change its own composition is consistent with its possessing continuing sovereignty provided that the power cannot be used to abolish the legislature or irrevocably transfer its powers to a quite different body. For example, a parliament could have power to change its own composition while also having continuing sovereignty provided that it must always remain recognizably a 'parliament'.[32] The power of a legislature to change its procedure, or form of legislation, is consistent with its possessing continuing sovereignty provided that it must always remain free to change the substance of the law however and whenever it chooses. Consider, for example, a procedural law requiring bills of a certain kind to be introduced and passed in the House of Commons before being considered in the House of Lords, or a law as to form providing that some existing statute can be amended or repealed only by express words, and not mere implication. If the courts were prepared to enforce those laws, by invalidating any statute enacted contrary to them, Parliament might no longer be fully sovereign in Dicey's sense. But it would still be fully sovereign in the more important sense of being free to change the substance of the law however and whenever it should choose.

In this sense, a legislature is sovereign provided that its law-making authority is not limited in any substantive respect, even if it is bound to exercise its authority according to requirements of a purely procedural or formal kind. Indeed, a legislature is more rather than less sovereign if it has the ability to subject itself to such requirements. For example, if it can require that an important statute be changed only by express words, and not mere implication, it can prevent itself from changing that statute accidentally, by enacting a less important statute that its members do not realize is inconsistent with the more important one. Without restricting the ability of future legislators to change the important statute, the legislature can ensure that they must be given clear notice of any proposal to do so. This enhances rather than detracts from its ability to control its legislative agenda. That is why the United Kingdom Parliament is still sovereign today, even though the courts sometimes refuse to apply statutes that are inconsistent with the law of the European Community. It is still sovereign as long as it retains its authority to withdraw Britain from the European Community by enacting express and unambiguous words to that effect.[33]

---

[32] A completely unrepresentative body, for example, could not be called a 'parliament'.
[33] See Chapter 10, text to nn. 36–7, below.

To summarize, a legislature has sovereign law-making power if its power to change the law is not limited by any norms, concerning the substance of legislation, that are either judicially enforceable, or written, relatively clear, and set out in a formally enacted legal instrument, even if it is governed by judicially enforceable norms that determine its composition, and the procedure and form by which it must legislate. Furthermore, its sovereign power is a continuing one even if it includes power to change the norms that govern its own composition, procedure, and form of legislation, provided that it cannot use that power to unduly impair its ability to change the substance of the law however and whenever it chooses.

2. Sovereignty and 'Higher Law'

Clarity in the definition of sovereignty is crucial to our characterization of the constitutional thought of earlier times, such as the Middle Ages. Charles McIlwain argues that '[p]arliamentary sovereignty is comparatively recent in origin; nothing, for example, can be plainer than that the idea is contrary to all mediaeval notions'.[34] This is supposedly because those notions did not include that of a Hobbesian sovereign, who is the creator of, and is therefore above, all law.[35] But while it may be true that Parliament was not sovereign in medieval England, that is because the King was arguably sovereign, and not because the concept of sovereignty is inherently Hobbesian and therefore foreign to medieval notions. As previously noted, Hart has shown that legislative sovereignty can be regarded as a power constituted by rules of recognition, and therefore by fundamental laws, rather than as a power standing completely outside and above the law. McIlwain wrote at a time when John Austin's legal philosophy, which in this respect is Hobbesian, was generally accepted, and he did not have the benefit of Hart's critique. He rightly argued that the common medieval notion that the King was 'under the law, because the law makes the King' is inconsistent with sovereignty in the Hobbesian sense.[36] But it is not inconsistent with sovereignty in Hart's sense, which can be conferred by law. It is possible that when medieval law made kings, it made sovereign legislators.

In the Middle Ages, the powers of all human rulers, Pope, Emperor, and King alike, were regarded as being not only derived from but also limited by higher laws: divine and natural laws, and sometimes important customs as well.[37] On the other hand, those limits were rarely thought to be legally enforceable by any other human agency. As Maitland puts it, 'the king . . . is below the law, though he is below no man; no man can punish him if he breaks the law, but he must

---

[34] McIlwain (1910: 355–6).   [35] ibid.   [36] See Chapter 3, n. 1, below.
[37] Both divine and natural laws were regarded as prescriptions of God, but divine laws were thought to be communicated only by revelation, and therefore only to Christians, whereas natural laws were thought to be discoverable by natural reason, and therefore by infidels as well as Christians.

expect God's vengeance'. The ruler was accountable only to his own conscience and to God, but that was thought to constitute a legal obligation at a time when people 'had not clearly marked off legal as distinct from moral and religious duties'.[38]

If Maitland is right, how should we characterize the law-making powers of medieval rulers? The question is whether they were sovereign in our sense of the word: we are using our terminology and not that of the Middle Ages. We are attempting to trace the origins of our constitutional system, and it would defeat our purpose if we described our system in our terms, and the medieval one in medieval terms. To compare one with the other, to identify both similarities and differences, we must, as far as possible, use the same terminology to describe both. Indeed, we cannot hope even to understand medieval terminology without first translating it into our own. There are, of course, risks in doing so. Our terminology may express concepts and distinctions unknown to people of the Middle Ages, and vice versa. In translating what they said into our terminology, we must not attribute to them concepts that they could not have had, or overlook relevant concepts that they did have. But every attempt to translate ideas expressed in one language into another is subject to that requirement. It does not follow from the mere fact that a word was not used by our ancestors in the same way in which we use it, that we cannot use it accurately to describe their social life or even their thoughts. That is no more unacceptable than using English to describe the social life or thoughts of Germans.

McIlwain denies that the medieval ruler's law-making power was sovereign, even in our sense of the word, because it satisfied only Dicey's negative, and not his positive, criterion: it was not limited by any law enforceable by the courts or other legal organs, but was limited by law nevertheless.[39] But since our question is whether medieval law-makers were sovereign in our sense of 'sovereign', it depends on whether they were limited by law in our sense of 'law', rather than in theirs. If we classify the 'higher laws' by which they were thought to be bound as purely customary, moral, or religious, rather than legal, then our question is answered.

The doctrine of parliamentary sovereignty is perfectly compatible with the existence, and *a fortiori* with widespread belief in the existence, of a 'higher law' by which statutes are evaluated, as long as that 'law' is neither enforceable by the courts or any other human agency, nor set out in a formally enacted legal instrument. That is why Jean Bodin, usually regarded as the founder of modern theories of legislative sovereignty, was able to argue both that true monarchs

---

[38] Maitland (1908: 101). This is somewhat inaccurate in that it ignores papal claims to possess lawful authority to enforce God's laws by excommunicating or, if necessary, even deposing temporal rulers. But few if any of the Popes who made that claim would have acknowledged the existence of lawful means by which they themselves could be brought to account by any human agency.

[39] McIlwain (1910: 144). Burgess (1996: 180) says essentially the same thing about Sir Edward Coke's conception of Parliament's law-making power.

necessarily possess absolute legislative sovereignty, and that '[t]he absolute power of princes and of other sovereign lordships . . . does not in any way extend to the laws of God and of nature': it is 'nothing but the power of overriding ordinary law'.[40] His argument was logically consistent because he denied that there were, or could be, lawful means of forcing monarchs to comply with the laws of God or nature.[41] As J. P. Sommerville has explained, 'the advent of Bodinian sovereignty did not lead absolutists to abandon theorising in terms of God's laws and man's purposes. The concept of sovereignty was itself underpinned by attitudes towards human nature and needs: in order to fulfil God's purposes and his own goals, man required the protection of an absolute sovereign.'[42] Even Sir Robert Filmer and Thomas Hobbes, who propounded the most extreme theories of legislative sovereignty in seventeenth century England, conceded that the sovereign was bound by the law of nature. Hobbes, for example, insisted that every sovereign was 'obliged by the law of nature' to procure 'the safety of the people', and that 'a sovereign is as much subject, as any of the meanest of his people' to 'equity; . . . being a precept of the law of nature'.[43] But the sovereign was 'to render an account thereof to God, the author of that law, and to none but him'.[44] For the same reason, both Blackstone and Austin, two 'classical' exponents of the modern doctrine of sovereignty, were also able to accept the existence of a higher law by which human law should be evaluated: Blackstone called it natural law, and Austin, divine law.[45] If, as Franklin Baumer has argued, 'unlimited sovereignty' necessarily includes 'the power to legislate without reference to an eternal law, or code of ideal principles', then it is not a concept to be found in any historically significant political or legal theory.[46]

While most medieval theorists held that the limitations imposed on rulers by divine, natural, or human law were not legally enforceable, they recognized that public officials ('subordinate magistrates'), on behalf of the community, had a right to disobey or even resist tyrants.[47] In this respect, they differed from the more extreme defenders of monarchical absolutism in the seventeenth century, such as Filmer and Hobbes, who denied that active resistance even to a tyrannical sovereign could be justified.[48] That denial must be understood in the light of the widespread and justifiable fear of disorder and lawless violence caused by civil wars in France and England. But on this question of resistance to lawful authority, the classical exponents of the modern doctrine of sovereignty,

---

[40] Bodin (1992: book I, ch. 8, 13); see also ibid. 31–2.
[41] Franklin (1973: 79, 85–6, 92, 93).   [42] Sommerville (1991: 351).
[43] Hobbes (1968: part II, ch. 30, 376, 385). See Carmichael (1990: esp. 9–12).
[44] Hobbes (1968: 376).
[45] Blackstone (1765: introd., sect. II); Austin (1954: 5–6, 10, 34–5, 40, 123, 134, 184–6).
[46] Baumer (1940: 5 n. 5).   [47] Lewis (1954: 269–71).
[48] In the case of Hobbes, this is an exaggeration. Hobbes thought that in extremely limited circumstances—when the sovereign threatened a subject with death—that subject was at liberty to resist. It follows that if a large number of subjects were so threatened, they would be free to join forces and engage in concerted resistance: see Burgess (1994). But this aspect of Hobbes's thought was generally ignored, and is therefore of little significance in the history of the evolution of political ideas.

Blackstone, Austin, and Dicey, are much closer to medieval theorists, and for that matter to later resistance theorists such as John Locke, than to absolutists such as Hobbes. The modern doctrine is a prescription of legal validity, a legal rule of recognition, and not a recommendation of total and uncritical submission to sovereign commands. It is inaccurate and unfair to describe parliamentary sovereignty as a 'dogma' established by Dicey under the influence of 'the Hobbesian authoritarianism he learned from Austin'.[49]

Blackstone, following Locke and other Whig theorists, considered popular resistance to be the only appropriate remedy for a gross violation of natural law by the sovereign.[50] He argued that 'all oppressions . . . of the sovereign power, must necessarily be out of the reach of any *stated rule*, or *express legal* provision'.[51] But an extra-legal remedy was available. If a sovereign's 'unconstitutional oppressions' threaten desolation to a state, 'mankind will not be reasoned out of the feelings of humanity; nor will sacrifice their liberty by a scrupulous adherence to those political maxims, which were originally established to preserve it'. If the safety of the people should require it, future generations could exert 'those inherent (though latent) powers of society, which no climate, no time, no constitution, can ever destroy or diminish'.[52]

Austin insisted that all governments were bound by positive morality and divine law, and lacked moral legitimacy in so far as they failed to comply with them; moreover, the people 'would not persist in their obedience to a government that they deemed imperfect, if they thought that a better government might probably be got by resistance, and that the probable good of the change outweighed its probable mischief'.[53] He identified as one of the two main errors made by Hobbes that '[h]e inculcates too absolutely the religious obligation of obedience to present or established government. He makes not the requisite allowance for the anomalous and excepted cases wherein disobedience is counselled by that very principle of utility which indicates the duty of submission.'[54]

Dicey argued that despite being subject to no legal limits, 'the actual exercise of authority by any sovereign whatever, and notably by Parliament, is bounded and controlled by two limitations', one external and the other internal. 'The external limit to the real power of a sovereign consists in the possibility or certainty that his subjects, or a large number of them, will disobey or resist his laws. This limitation exists even under the most despotic monarchies.' The sovereignty of Parliament 'is limited on every side by the possibility of popular resistance'.[55]

Recent historians have abandoned any suggestion of a sharp break between medieval political thought and the development of modern theories of legislative

---

[49] Allan (1993: 1–2).
[50] On Locke as a theorist of parliamentary sovereignty, see Chapter 6, Section 2, and on eighteenth century Whigs, Chapter 7, Sections 1 and 3, below.
[51] Blackstone (1765: 237–8).
[52] ibid. 238. By 'unconstitutional', he did not mean 'unlawful': see Chapter 7, Section 4, below.
[53] Austin (1954: 298); see also ibid. 307, 349, 157–8.   [54] ibid. 277 n. 25.
[55] Dicey (1964: 76–7, 79).

sovereignty. For example, according to thirteenth century canonist theories of papal authority, the Pope as God's representative on earth possessed a *plenitudo potestatis* ('plenitude of power') that was humanly unlimited. Christ's words to St Peter, 'Whatsoever you will bind on earth will be bound in heaven . . .', were interpreted literally, as conferring on each Pope a supreme, omnicompetent, and inalienable power.[56] The Pope was the supreme legislator in all matters, and deny-ing his right to issue a decree or law was punishable as heresy.[57] As Ullmann puts it,

Although the term sovereign was not applied to the medieval pope, there can be little doubt that the notion of sovereignty was perfectly clearly grasped. This idea of the pope's unfettered freedom to legislate was nothing else but legislative sovereignty. Just as Par-liament today can do away with any previous law, so could the pope exercise his leg-islative plenitude of power unfettered by any previous papal law.[58]

In jurisdictional struggles between the papacy and temporal rulers, including territorial kings as well as the Emperor, the latter often asserted that by divine appointment they represented God within their realms, and rightfully possessed the supreme power which the Pope claimed. Some medieval theorists argued that this power was necessarily indivisible and inalienable. For example, Dante, Marsiglio of Padua, and William of Ockham all defended the Imperial claim against that of the Pope partly on the ground that competing systems of law and juri-diction were incompatible with the unity required for the existence of stable government: within any given territory, there could be only one supreme and omnicompetent authority, vested in one person.[59] Dante and Ockham also insisted that the Emperor could not alienate his authority.[60] Ockham probably influenced Wycliffe, who reasoned from the need for unity, and therefore a sin-gle, supreme ruler, to the conclusion that the King, not the Pope, was supreme in England.[61]

The medieval prince was frequently described as a *lex animata* or *lex loquens*, a living or speaking law, whose function was to translate the general principles of God's law into concrete rules suited to his particular community, and to exer-cise equitable judgment when those rules proved inadequate or inflexible. As such, *Princeps legibus solutus est* ('the Prince is free of the laws'): as the sole ultimate interpreter and enforcer of the law, he could not himself be subject to legal coer-cion.[62] The prince was bound by the law in the sense of being morally oblig-ated to obey it, but no legal remedy was available if he did not voluntarily do

---

[56] Ullmann (1961: 35–6, 39, 89–90); see also Wilks (1963: part II, ch. 1, esp. 173).

[57] Ullmann (1961: 89).

[58] ibid. 72; see also ibid. 143. Wilks (1963: 169) describes *plenitudo potestatis* as 'sovereignty pure and simple', and Figgis (1922: 49) says that it 'embodies the most important elements of the theory of sovereignty'.

[59] Figgis (1922: 55–7).   [60] ibid. 57–8.   [61] ibid. 68–70.

[62] Eccleshall (1978: 50–1), and see his discussion of the ideas of John of Salisbury, the twelfth century English writer at ibid. 51–3. See also Lewis (1954: 246–7), and Pennington (1993: 77–90).

so. As Aquinas put it, the ruler was subject to the 'directive force' but not the 'coercive power' of the law, because 'none is competent to pass sentence on him if he acts against the law'.[63] The only remedies for tyranny were divine intervention or retribution.[64] This has led Ewart Lewis to conclude that, even if no complete theory of legislative sovereignty appeared in the Middle Ages, some adopted 'positions that fell short of that taken by Bodin only in clarity of definition'.

The idea that the right to make law carried with it the right to alter and abrogate it ran through all scholarly theory. . . . It was agreed that no ruler could bind his successor by his legislation and that no prescriptive rights were finally valid against him in whom the supreme legislative authority was based. . . . This position did not necessarily involve a full conception of sovereignty, but when the maker of law was presented as its only competent judge, the practical result might be indistinguishable.[65]

J. W. Allen goes even further, arguing that Pope Boniface VIII, William of Ockham, and Wycliffe all propounded theories of sovereignty in more absolute and unlimited terms than Bodin's.[66] Of course, there were many changes in political thought, and considerable competition between rival theories, throughout the Middle Ages, and it cannot plausibly be claimed that there was a general commitment to anything resembling the modern concept of legislative sovereignty. The point is simply that McIlwain and other historians of his generation were wrong to suggest that the concept is alien to that period.[67]

[63] *Summa Theologica* I–II, q. 96, art. 5, Reply Obj. 3, in Bigongiari (1953: 74).

[64] Eccleshall (1978: 52–3, 76–7, 90); Lewis (1954: 248–9).

[65] Lewis (1954: 28–30); at ibid. 269, 'a doctrine of formal sovereignty' is ascribed to Bracton. See also Tierney (1963*b*: 399–400), Post (1964: 367), and Pennington (1993: 278–84).

[66] Allen (1928: 423).

[67] Wilks (1963: 151) comments that 'the more generally accepted view of modern scholars that a clear conception of legislative sovereignty was only hinted at in the medieval period and does not become fully apparent before Bodin, is quite unnecessarily cautious'.

3

From Bracton to the Reformation

1. Medieval Kingship, Law, and Politics

The first parliaments were meetings of the King and his tenants-in-chief, in which he sought their counsel, consent, and material support in discharging his principal responsibilities, the defence of the realm and the dispensation of justice within it. The acts of those parliaments were acts of the King, and their authority was his authority, fortified by counsel and consent. To trace the history of the relationship between the authority of Parliament and the law, it is therefore necessary to begin with the relationship between the authority of the King and the law.

Bracton stated that the King is 'under God and under the law, because the law makes the King'.[1] But it does not follow that in medieval England regal authority was limited by fundamental laws in our sense of the word.[2] Contemporary scholars agree that Bracton regarded the King as subject to law in the sense that he had what we would now describe as a moral duty to obey it. His compliance with that duty depended on his own goodwill, reinforced by baronial counsel and the threat of divine retribution, and not on any form of legal compulsion.[3] Bracton compared the role of the King to that of Christ, who had conformed to the law because of his humility and love of justice, rather than compulsion.[4] Influenced by Aristotelian moral psychology, he assumed that a disposition to act justly, and therefore according to law, was so deeply ingrained in the character of the properly educated King, that external constraints were unnecessary.[5]

Bracton depicted the King as the apex of the legal system, the source of all jurisdiction and judgment: 'he has in his hand all the rights belonging to the crown and the secular power and the material sword pertaining to the governance of the realm'; no right to do justice could be exercised 'unless it was given . . . from above as a delegated jurisdiction, nor can it be delegated without ordinary jurisdiction remaining with the king himself'.[6] The jurisdiction of both greater and

---

[1] Bracton (1968–77: ii. 33); see also ibid. 110, and 305–6 generally. It is no longer believed that this work was written by the judge Henry de Bracton, or indeed by any single author (see Nederman 1988: 416). But for convenience, I will refer to the work as if it were by Bracton.

[2] An example of the interpretation rejected here is Schulz (1945: 165).

[3] Eccleshall (1978: 69–70); Corwin (1955: 27–9); Richardson and Sayles (1963: 144–5); Lewis (1964: 261–8); Tierney (1963a: 303); Post (1968: 519–25, 552–4); Wilkinson (1952b: 250); Hanson (1970: 131).

[4] Bracton (1968–77: ii. 33); Tierney (1963a: 303); Post (1968: 547–52); Hanson (1970: 127).

[5] Nederman (1984: 69–77). For a discussion of the same theme in the medieval 'mirror for princes' genre, see Watts (1996: 23–31).

[6] Bracton (1968–77: 166–7).

lesser justices was derived from the King, and could not equal his own: '[for] equal will not have jurisdiction . . . over equal, much less over a superior', and the King had neither equals nor superiors.[7] It followed that the King could not be the subject of legal compulsion. 'Private persons cannot question the acts of kings . . . No one may pass upon the king's act or his charter so as to nullify it, but one may say that the king has committed an *injuria*, and thus charge him with amending it, lest he and the justices fall into the judgment of the living God because of it.'[8] Bracton denied that the justices could even discuss the meaning of ambiguous royal charters: 'the interpretation and pleasure of the lord king must be awaited, since it is for him who establishes to explain his deed'.[9] He insisted that the King 'must not be under man', although he was under God and the law: he could be beseeched by petition to correct an injustice, but because no writ could run against him, if he refused to do so the only remedy was God's vengeance.[10] Gaines Post goes as far as to say that Bracton

comes close to seeing in the public rights of king and crown the same kind of sovereignty as that defined by Jean Bodin some three centuries later . . . [O]ne can say that medieval jurists and political writers developed the theory that sovereignty is the supreme authority in the state; that the prince who recognises no superior is the sovereign even when he summons magnates, prelates and representatives of communities to an assembly to give counsel and consent to the king's transaction of *ardua negotia* touching both the *status regis* and the *status regni*. They surely anticipated Bodin if not theorists of the twentieth century.[11]

It was often said at the time that the King was above the law or free of the law. For example, William Bereford, Chief Justice of the Common Pleas under Edward II, said during argument in a case that 'if you could appeal to legal principle what you say would be well enough, but against the King, who is above the law, you cannot rely on legal principles'.[12] Such statements did not really contradict Bracton's assertion that the King was under the law. They merely emphasized a different aspect of the King's relationship with the law: his freedom from legal compulsion, rather than his obligation to conform voluntarily. As John of Salisbury, the twelfth century English writer, explained, '[t]he prince is said to be loosed from the bonds of law, not because unjust deeds are permitted him, but because he ought to be one who cultivates equity from love of justice rather than from fear of punishment'.[13] Bodin later said much the same thing: 'persons who are sovereign must not be subject in any way to the commands of someone else . . . This is why the law says that the prince is not subject to the law.'[14]

---

[7] ibid. iv. 281. [8] ibid. ii. 109–10. [9] ibid.

[10] Ibid. ii. 33. See also ibid. iii. 43, and, on the duties of kings, ii. 305–6.

[11] Post (1964: 368). See also Lewis (1954: 269), and Wilkinson (1949: 503).

[12] *Year Books, 8 Edward II (Selden Society)*, 74, quoted by Hanson (1970: 212); see ibid. 211 for other examples of such statements.

[13] John of Salisbury, *Policraticus*, book IV, ch. 2, quoted in Lewis (1964: i. 247). On the influence of John of Salisbury on Bracton, see Nederman (1984: 72–3).

[14] Bodin (1992: book I, ch. 8, 11).

Bodin acknowledged that sovereign princes were bound by the law of God and of nature.[15]

In several places, Bracton mentioned what we would now describe as a political, rather than a legal, method of restraining the King. 'The king has a superior, namely God. Also the law by which he is made king. Also his *curia*, namely, the earls and barons, because if he is without a bridle, that is without law, they ought to put a bridle on him. That is why the earls are called the partners, so to speak, of the king; he who has a partner has a master.'[16] Elsewhere Bracton also described the earls as the King's companions or partners, associated with him in ruling the people,[17] and in several places, he suggested that their counsel and perhaps even consent was necessary for new laws to be made.[18] It seems that, although no person was equal or superior to the King, the combined authority of the King and earls was superior to the authority of the King alone.[19] Bracton regarded the earls as the King's partners in some aspects of governance, and 'he who has a partner has a master' in the sense that a partner can refuse to give consent when it is needed.[20] Moreover, although the King was not subject to ordinary legal process, if he committed a flagrant injustice the earls and barons could legitimately attempt to correct it.[21]

In speaking of the King's *curia* being able to put a bridle on the King, Bracton may have had in mind the case of Gilbert Basset, decided by Henry III's great council in 1234, after Basset's patron, the Earl of Pembroke, had rebelled. The King was compelled, or at least persuaded, to confess that he had disseized Basset of land without 'lawful judgment of his peers and by the law of the land', as required by chapter 39 of Magna Carta. The council then ordered that the land be returned to Basset. Over the next two years, other cases involving similar complaints were dealt with in much the same way by the court *coram rege* ('in the presence of the King', later the King's Bench).[22] But these cases do not demonstrate that the King's courts functioned independently of his will. On the contrary, they necessarily began as petitions to the King for amendment of his unjust actions, and his court was able to provide redress only because he admitted his errors and submitted to its judgment, whether voluntarily or under pressure from his magnates.[23] What the cases do suggest is that 'the jurisdiction of the king with his counsellors is more powerful than the jurisdiction of the king alone. The former then may assess the activity of the latter, but it is the jurisdiction of the king both times.'[24] Henry refused to become involved in another case brought in 1234, denying that he was subject to the jurisdiction of his own courts: 'the lord king can neither be summoned nor submit to the command of anyone, since he has no superior in the kingdom'.[25]

---

[15] See Chapter 2, text to n. 40, above.
[16] Bracton (1968–77: ii. 110). See also ibid. iii. 43.　　[17] ibid. ii. 32.
[18] ibid. 19, 22, 305.
[19] Warren (1987: 180–1). See also Kavanagh (1995: 219–20, 239).
[20] Nederman (1988: 426).　　[21] ibid.　　[22] Carpenter (1996: 39–42).
[23] Turner (1968: 251).　　[24] Kavanagh (1995: 219–20).　　[25] Turner (1968: 264).

The notion that the magnates were the King's partners or companions in government originated in the traditional feudal relationship between lord and vassal. As Earl Warenne insisted, during Edward I's reign, 'the king [William I] did not conquer and subdue the land by himself, but our forefathers were with him as partners and helpers'.[26] That relationship involved reciprocal rights and responsibilities, including those of seeking and giving counsel concerning matters of mutual concern.[27] Henry I, in his coronation charter, indirectly acknowledged the need for baronial consent before the law could be changed, and the same requirement was referred to by the interpolator of the *Leges Edwardi Confessoris* and the author of 'Glanvill'.[28] The anonymous legal treatise known as *Fleta* held the maxim 'the prince's pleasure has the force of law' to be justified because 'his pleasure is not whatsoever is rashly supposed to be the king's wish, but what has been properly determined by the counsel of his magnates, with the king's authority, after due deliberation and discussion thereon'.[29] In the *Mirror of Justices*, written during the reign of Edward I, it was asserted that 'if the king by his fault sin against any of his people . . . it was agreed as law that the king should have companions to hear and determine in parliament all the writs and plaints concerning wrongs done by the king'.[30] Edward III declared in 1330 that 'we wish all men to know that in future we will govern our people according to right and reason . . . and that the matters which touch us and the estate of our realm are to be disposed of by the common counsel of the magnates of our realm and in no other manner'.[31] In 1399, Henry IV went further, announcing his desire to be not only 'advised' but also 'governed by the honourable, wise and discreet people of his realm, and to do what is best . . . for the government of himself and his realm by their common counsel and assent'.[32]

But neither these principles nor their application were uncontroversial. Both Edward III and Henry IV replaced unpopular predecessors (Edward II and Richard II, respectively) who were deposed partly because they were believed to have flouted them. At the time of his deposition, Richard II was accused of having 'expressly said . . . that his laws were in his own mouth, or occasionally, in his own breast; and that he alone could establish and change the laws of his realm'.[33] Moreover, it was never clear from whom, how often, or in what forum the King was obliged to seek counsel. Henry III instructed his assembled magnates that he claimed the same right enjoyed by every other head of a household, namely, to heed whatever counsel, and to appoint or depose whatever advisers, he should choose. Vassals ought not to judge their prince, he added: 'rather are

---

[26] *Hemingburgh's Chronicle* (London, 1948–9), ii. 6, quoted in Wood (1988: 8).

[27] Brown (1989: 158).

[28] Richardson and Sayles (1963: 143–6). In paragraph 13 of Henry I's coronation charter, he promised to 'restore to you the law of King Edward, together with those amendments by which my father, with the counsel of his barons, amended it': Stephenson and Marcham (1972: i. 48). See also Prestwich (1990: 17 ff.) and Wilkinson (1952b: 248–9).

[29] Quoted by Hanson (1970: 124).   [30] Quoted by Wilkinson (1952b: 250).

[31] Quoted by Wilkinson (1949: 509 n. 23).   [32] ibid.

[33] Quoted in Hanson (1970: 174, 179).

they bound to be directed by their lord's will and be set in order according to his wish, since they are accounted inferior to him'.[34]

As Gaillard Lapsley said of the time of Edward III, there was no constitution, only precedents pointing in different directions.[35] During the thirteenth and fourteenth centuries, disagreements between Kings and their barons concerning their respective rights and responsibilities were frequent, and sometimes led to violent conflict. But the barons never attempted to use regular judicial procedures to compel the King to accept their demands: they resorted to disobedience, armed rebellion, political trials, and as a last resort, deposition.[36] They knew that the common law offered them no remedy, because it was the King's law, and the judges were his judges.[37] Bracton said that in cases of treason, 'the peers [magnates] ought there to be associated with the justices, lest the king in person, or through his justices without peers be both plaintiff and judge'.[38] This implies that a judgment of the King's justices was a judgment of the King himself, and therefore in cases in which he had a personal interest, impartiality could only be guaranteed by participation of the magnates. In 1234, claiming that the King was using 'unnatural counsellors', the barons complained that 'there was nobody to give them justice'.[39] During a dispute between Edward II and disaffected barons in 1308, a parliamentary indictment of the King's closest adviser, Peter Gavaston, declared that the barons' oath of allegiance was to the Crown as an institution, rather than the King as an individual, and that 'if the king by chance be not guided by reason, in relation to the estate of the Crown, his liege subjects are bound by the oath made to the Crown to guide the King back again by reason and amend the estate of the Crown; otherwise the oath would not be kept'.

Then it is to be asked how they ought to guide the King back in such a case, whether by form of law or by violence. He [the King] cannot be directed by course of law, for there are no judges but such as are the King's. In which case, if the King's will be not according to reason, he will only have error maintained and confirmed. Wherefore it behooves, in order to save the oath, that when the King will not redress a matter and remove that which is damaging to the Crown and hurtful to the people, it is adjudged that the error be removed by violence . . .[40]

Donald Hanson argues that 'there was so little substantive law that the question of legality at the level of high politics hardly arose. The answer of the great twelfth

[34] Quoted in ibid. 147. Richard II gave a similar response to demands that he dismiss his chancellor and treasurer: see Wilkinson (1952b: 256).

[35] Lapsley (1951: 272). I am indebted to Charles Wood for this reference.

[36] Hanson (1970: 180 and see also 152–3). See Brown (1989: 14–16) for a brief summary of the use of these methods of controlling kings.

[37] Hanson (1970: 190).   [38] Bracton (1968–77: ii. 337).

[39] Quoted by Hanson (1970: 214).

[40] Wilkinson (1952a: ii. 111). The original text and an alternative translation are set out in Richardson and Sayles (1963: 468–9). They say that this document was 'probably concocted after the Ordinances and perhaps after Gavaston's death', but add that 'it was accepted in good faith by contemporaries . . . [and] there is no question of its importance': ibid. 15. The document is also discussed by Hanson (1970: 159).

and thirteenth century law books to fundamental political questions was that such matters lay with the king and the magnates of the realm.'[41] As late as 1460, the judges declined to express an opinion concerning the dispute between Richard Duke of York and Henry VI over the right to the throne, because 'they were the King's justices' and therefore unfitted to decide it; moreover, 'the matter was so high and touched the King's high estate and regality, which is above the law and passed their learning, wherefore they dared not enter into any communication thereof, for it pertained to the Lords of the King's blood, and the peerage of this his land, to have communication and meddle in such matters'.[42]

The absence of any judicial method for resolving disputes between the King and the magnates was one reason for the widespread belief that ultimate authority was the King's alone. John Watts has studied fifteenth century political thought popularized through media such as the 'mirrors for princes' literature.[43] He concludes that the idea that the King was subject to political control by the nobility, which he doubts was ever generally accepted, had certainly lost ground by the fifteenth century.[44] Although in the exercise of his authority the King was expected to heed counsel, everyone knew that he received conflicting counsel from representatives of different sectional interests. The peace and unity of the realm depended on the existence of a single, ultimate authority willing and able to take these different interests into account, and then reach a decision binding on them all.[45] 'This was the very essence of the king's function and its successful discharge ultimately depended on the inviolability of his will.'[46] It followed that even the decisions of an unjust or incompetent King could not legitimately be overruled: the royal will was so crucial to general well-being that 'it retained its sovereignty whatever the quality of its possessor'.[47] 'Royal virtue was the best— in a sense, the only—constitutional safeguard, since the royal will had to be free of temporal interference if the whole system was to work.'[48]

Opposition which stopped short of proposing a substitute monarch was, in the end, doomed to failure: laws and councils would not work. Nothing short of the suspension of the polity in civil war was sufficient to reform a king who would not reform himself.[49]

If there were no judicial means of compelling the King to observe the law when acting without the barons' consent, then it went without saying that no such means were available when he acted with their consent. After recommending that the magnates put a bridle on a King unbridled by law, Bracton suggested that if they too were unbridled, the only remaining remedy was divine retribution: 'they shall be judged because they will not judge their subjects justly . . .'.[50] As Hanson

---

[41] Hanson (1970: 180).
[42] *Rotuli Parliamentorum*, v. 375–6, quoted by Dunham and Wood (1976: 750).
[43] Watts (1996: 11).
[44] ibid. 20; for examples of the recognition of royal sovereignty, see ibid. 60.
[45] ibid. 78; see also ibid. 31, 38.   [46] ibid. 27.   [47] ibid. 30–1.
[48] ibid. 28; see also ibid. 45, 61.   [49] ibid. 80.   [50] Bracton (1968–77: ii. 110).

puts it, Bracton's 'cardinal doctrine is that law is the product of regal and baronial cooperation. . . . In thirteenth century England, then, the idea of kingly rule in conjunction with baronial counsel and consent was the center of operative political thought.'[51] The possibility of a legal challenge to the validity of laws made by the King with the consent of his barons, to be determined by judges who were essentially bureaucrats appointed by and wholly subordinate to the King, would have been unthinkable both to Bracton and later medieval thinkers.[52] As Watts describes the position in the fifteenth century, '[n]o temporal jurisdiction exceeded that of the king counselled'.

> The personal will of the king was the one essential prescription for public acts of judgement and so, by analogy, for all legitimate acts of government. This meant that there was an important sense in which the king was, like parliament today, unrestrained. Under normal circumstances, he could not be resisted within his realm, since it was only by his authority, which depended on his personal will, that acts were done while he was king. . . . [I]n the last resort, [he] enjoyed a monopoly of legitimate power. . . . [T]here was one jurisdiction, it was his, and it ranged with equal fullness over all the causes in his realm.[53]

2. Parliament and its Authority

Parliament evolved from the medieval tradition of baronial counsel and consent. The idea that the magnates could speak for the community was an ancient one, based on the feudal idea that they could speak for their tenants-in-chief, who could in turn speak for their tenants, and so on.[54] In Magna Carta (1215) the barons claimed to be 'the community of the entire country', and in the Provisions of Oxford (1258) they described themselves as 'the community of England'.[55] Assemblies of magnates, called 'parliaments', were opportunities not only for the King to seek their counsel and consent, but also for them to press their complaints, and therefore served both as instruments of royal government and as the mouthpieces of the 'community'.[56] The Ordinances of 1311, which disaffected barons forced upon Edward II, declared that the King could appoint his most important officials, undertake warfare, leave the country, make certain grants, and change the coinage, only 'by the counsel and assent of his baronage, and that in parliament'.[57] By the early fourteenth century, then, Parliament was

---

[51] Hanson (1970: 131-2).

[52] As Harding (1973: 80) explains, thirteenth century judges were 'clerks in both senses of the word', men in clerical orders who had risen through arduous work as the king's clerks, and were required to perform all kinds of non-judicial duties, such as collecting taxes, arraying troops, inspecting rivers, and conducting diplomatic missions abroad.

[53] Watts (1996: 16-17).   [54] Holt (1981: 25-6).   [55] Wood (1988: 8, 96).

[56] Harriss (1981: 30-1, 34-5, 53).

[57] Ordinances of 1311, arts. 7, 9, 14, and 30, in Stephenson and Marcham (1972: i. 193-7). The Ordinances were repealed by the Statute of York (1322), enacted when Edward II's supporters regained control of Parliament, which declared that the Ordinances had 'wrongfully limited' the royal power of the King: ibid. 204.

clearly regarded by many barons as the proper forum for making ultimate decisions concerning matters of high policy.[58] In about 1340, Walter Burley, a learned scholar who served Edward III in many official capacities, seems to have expressed the idea that the King and Parliament together were more authoritative than the King alone, when he wrote that 'the multitude constituted from the King, nobles, and wise men of the kingdom . . . rules as much or more than the King alone, and on this account the King convokes Parliament for conducting difficult affairs'.[59]

By the middle of the fourteenth century, consultation and participation in parliamentary law-making had been extended from the earls and barons to representatives of counties and towns.[60] The common petition (*commune petition*), presented in the House of Commons, became the principal means by which landowners expressed their grievances, and sought remedies through legislation.[61] As Hanson puts it, 'in their role of political opposition the baronage did not resort to the principles of the common law. On the contrary, they worked their way to the establishment of an entirely different approach, which eventuated in the political alliance between lords and commons in parliament.'[62] The magnates claimed the right to bridle a King guilty of egregious misgovernment, and there was no more reliable evidence of misgovernment than grievances voiced in the Commons.[63] In 1340–1, the Commons revived the thrust of the Ordinances of 1311, demanding that a council of magnates, appointed by and answerable to Parliament, should investigate and punish official misconduct and manage the great business of the Kingdom.[64] The King's most influential subjects looked to Parliament, rather than the courts, to remedy their most serious grievances, and this eventually led to the sovereignty of Parliament rather than that of the common law.[65]

Parliament became the most authoritative institution in the realm, apart from the monarchy itself. It was described by Chief Baron Fray in 1441 as 'the King's court and the highest court he has', and by the Bishop of Lincoln in 1483 as 'the King's most high and sovereign court'.[66] In a speech before Parliament in 1467, Bishop Robert Stillington, Edward IV's Chancellor, declared that:

Justice is every person to do his office that he is put in according to his estate and degree, and as for this land it is understood that it stands by three estates and above that one principal: that is to wit Lords Spiritual, Lords Temporal and Commons, and over that Estate Royal above, as our sovereign Lord the King.[67]

---

[58] Dunham (1987: 426).

[59] W. Burley, *Expositio in octo libros Politicorum Aristotelis* (*c.*1340), quoted in Blythe (1992: 185) and discussed in Nederman (1997: ch. XIV).

[60] See Brown (1989: 243) which summarizes the longer account of this development in ibid., ch. 8, *passim*. For a more recent account, see Carpenter (1996: ch. 19).

[61] Harriss (1981: 49–52) and Brown (1981: 111).

[62] Hanson (1970: 190).   [63] Harriss (1981: 54).   [64] ibid. 54–5.

[65] Hanson (1970: 190).   [66] Myers (1981: 149).

[67] *Rotuli Parliamentorum* (1767–77), v. 622–3, quoted by E. Powell (1994: 31).

As early as 1388, the Lords who prepared charges of treason against some of Richard II's associates, asserted Parliament's superiority to ordinary courts and the common law, in similar terms to those later adopted by the House of Commons when exercising its powers of impeachment and attainder in the seventeenth century.[68] The Lords declared 'that in so high a crime as is alleged in this appeal, which touches the person of the King . . . and the state of his realm . . . the process will not be taken anywhere except to Parliament, nor judged by any other law except the law and court of parliament'; 'the great matters moved in this Parliament and to be moved in parliaments in the future, touching peers of the land, should be introduced, judged and discussed by the course of Parliament and not by civil law nor by the common law of the land, used in other and lower courts of the land'; the ordinary courts 'are only there to execute the ancient laws and customs of the realm and the ordinances and establishments of Parliament'.[69] The implication was that 'parliament could make up the rules as it went along: which is precisely what it did'.[70] The King was informed that Parliament was 'the highest court of his realm, in which court all right and equity ought to shine as the sun being at the highest . . . where also reformation ought to be had of all oppressions, wrongs, extortions and enormities within the realm'.[71] Judges who had previously dared to answer some questions put to them by Richard II, concerning his authority to control Parliament, were impeached and banished.[72] In 1454, Chief Justice Fortescue stated that the High Court of Parliament was 'so high and so mighty in its nature' that questions concerning its privileges could not be decided by the judges.[73]

By the end of the thirteenth century, as the wording of the writs of summons to Parliament indicates, the representatives of shires and boroughs were regarded as having full power (*plena potestas*) to bind their communities to whatever decisions were made in Parliament, which were consequently regarded as being made by 'common consent'. It was assumed that the consent of every individual within each community was merged in the common consent of that community, and that the consent of every community was merged in the common consent of the whole community of England.[74] The Statute of York (1322), which repealed the Ordinances of 1311, declared that provisions regarding the estate of the King, or of the realm and the people, should be established in parliaments by the King 'with the consent of the prelates, earls, and barons, *and of the community of the kingdom*, as has been accustomed in times past'.[75] In 1365, Chief Justice Thorpe explained that the law deemed everyone to know what Parliament had decided because 'Parliament represents the body of all the realm'.[76] By the fifteenth

---

[68] See Clarke (1931: 75).
[69] Wilkinson (1952a: ii. 280, 282); see also Chrimes and Brown (1961: 146–9).
[70] Saul (1997: 192).   [71] Holinshed (1807: ii. 775).   [72] Dunham (1987: 429).
[73] Chrimes and Brown (1961: 296); Myers (1981: 150).
[74] Edwards (1970a: 145–9). See also Sommerville (1992: 61). On the influence of this theory in the fifteenth century in particular, see Chrimes (1936: 76–9) and Doe (1990: 16 n. 46).
[75] Stephenson and Marcham (1972: i. 205), my emphasis.
[76] Chrimes (1936: 76, 352).

century, standard formulas included in statutes declared that they had been enacted 'by the assent' or 'with the consent' of the community of the realm.[77] In an argument before all the judges in 1482, counsel argued that legislation passed by the Commons was binding on all subjects 'because every man is privy and party to the parliament, for the commons have one or two for each community to bind or unbind the whole community'.[78] In 1463, and again in 1506, it was said in court that an Act of Parliament was the highest record in the law, because everyone in England was deemed privy to, and therefore bound by it.[79] Chrimes points out that in this respect the High Court of Parliament was unique: the rulings of regular courts were binding only on the parties involved in the litigation.[80]

The high authority attributed to Parliament, on the ground that it represented the entire community, is evidenced by its involvement in the most momentous constitutional upheavals of the fifteenth century, the depositions of kings. Precedents had been set when Edward II was deposed and replaced by Edward III in 1327, and Richard II by Henry IV in 1399. Because there was no lawful method of forcibly removing a King, both Edward II and Richard II were 'persuaded' to abdicate.[81] Nevertheless, in both cases the responsible magnates ensured that the supposed assent of the three estates of the realm—the Lords Spiritual, Lords Temporal, and Commons—was formally recorded. Whether or not the assemblies in which this was done were technically 'parliaments' at the time, in both cases they became the new Kings' first parliaments, and attempts were made to identify their authority with that of Parliament.[82] The deposition of Richard II was particularly significant because his successor, unlike Edward II's, was not his natural heir; Henry IV's supporters therefore placed even greater emphasis on the assent and authority of the three estates.[83]

In the statute 7 Henry IV, c. 2 (1406), Parliament dealt explicitly with title and succession to the throne, declaring that the Crowns of England and France 'shall be settled upon and shall remain with the person of our said Lord the King [Henry IV] and the heirs of his body', and prescribing the order of succession as between the King's various sons and their possible progeny. In 1460, an agreement between Henry VI and Richard Duke of York that upon Henry's death Richard would succeed to the throne, was ratified 'by the King and the three estates, in this present Parliament'.[84] In 1461, after Richard had been killed, but while Henry

---

[77] Doe (1990: 15).

[78] Quoted in Fryde, 'Introduction', in Fryde and Miller (1970: 12). He seems to have assumed that the judges would unhesitatingly accept this proposition, because he used it merely as an illustration to support an argument about the powers of the convocation of clergy: see Chrimes (1936: 78–9).

[79] Chrimes (1936: 78–9); see also ibid. 269.   [80] ibid. 79–80.

[81] Plucknett (1960: 487–93); Brown (1989: 8–10, 14–15); Valente (1998: 874–7).

[82] Brown (1989: 10–15); Plucknett (1960: 487–9); Dunham (1987: 426–7, 429); Wood (1989: 476, 485); Jacob (1961: 14–17). Valente (1998: 862–4) concludes that Edward II was deposed 'in' but not 'by' Parliament.

[83] Wood (1989: 484–5); Wilkinson (1964: 2).

[84] Dunham (1987: 430), and Wood (1989: 477–8, 485). There is some confusion as to whether the agreement was ratified by statute: see Plucknett (1960: 498), Wilkinson (1964: 285), and Brown (1989: 11).

was still alive, Richard's son Edward IV was declared King with 'the advice and assent of the lords spiritual and temporal and of the commons'. His title to the throne was stated to be 'by God's law, man's law, and the law of nature', and was confirmed 'by the authority of Parliament'.[85] In 1484, Richard III sought confirmation by Parliament of his title to the throne.[86] It was declared by statute that although his title was justly grounded on the laws of God and the realm, confusion among the people at large needed to be dispelled by

the Court of Parliament [which] is of such authority, and the people of this land of such nature and disposition, as experience teaches, that manifestation and declaration of any truth or right made by the three estates of this realm assembled in Parliament, and by authority of the same, makes, before all other things, most faith and certainty, and, quieting men's minds, removes the occasion of all doubts and seditious language.[87]

It was also stated that although a previous assembly, at which the three estates had supposedly petitioned Richard to assume the throne, was not 'in form of Parliament', the declarations of that assembly shall 'be of like effect, virtue and force, *as if* all the same things had been so said . . . in a full Parliament, and by authority of the same accepted and approved'. It would seem that only the authority of 'a full Parliament' was thought to be sufficient to judge the legal validity of a claim to the throne.[88]

After Richard III was defeated and killed at Bosworth, Henry VII quickly summoned a Parliament which enacted yet another Act of Succession (1485) to resolve 'all ambiguities and questions.' It bluntly declared that it was 'ordained, established, and enacted, by authority of this present Parliament' that the Crowns of England and France belonged to Henry and his natural heirs.[89]

It would be a mistake to infer from this history that by 1485 the authority of Parliament was superior even to that of the King, because it bestowed the Crown upon him.[90] Parliament was not an institution separate from the King; it was convened by the King to advise and assist him in transacting the affairs of the realm, and its statutes were acts of the King and community jointly, or perhaps, acts of the King to which the representatives of the community had assented. It follows that Parliament's own legal legitimacy and authority depended at least partly on his, and therefore in affirming his status as the true King, it affirmed its own status as a true Parliament. This means that it could not freely bestow the throne upon the King: that would be a blatant 'bootstraps' enterprise, Parliament's own

---

[85] Dunham (1987: 430–1), and Wood (1989: 478).
[86] Dunham (1987: 431), and Wood (1989: 479).
[87] *Rotuli Parliamentorum* (London, 1767–7), vi. 241–2, quoted by Myers (1981: 153).
[88] Wood (1989: 485).   [89] Stephenson and Marcham (1972: i. 298–9).
[90] See McKenna (1979: 481–2, 505–6) who attributes this inference to the historians C. T. Wood and W. H. Dunham Jr. (ibid. 481–2). They have responded to some of McKenna's criticisms, in Dunham (1987), Wood (1989; 1982: 56–8, 60, esp. nn. 16, 19 and 20; and 1988: parts III and IV) (which consist mainly of revised versions of the other works just cited). See further nn. 95 and 129, below.

authority depending on what it purported to bestow.[91] It could, at best, affirm the existence of an independent title to the throne: in other words, in this context it could act only as a judge, and not as a legislator (as we understand that distinction today), purporting authoritatively to decide the uncertain questions of divine and customary law upon which the title to the throne was thought to depend. In this way, the authority of Parliament was enlisted to reinforce claims to the throne based primarily on other grounds, such as superior hereditary right, or God's verdict expressed through victory in battle. The object, in G. R. Elton's words, was 'to put [the] matter beyond doubt by putting it on record'.[92] Chrimes goes further, arguing that formal legal recognition of such claims was regarded as necessary in order to convert a King *de facto* into a King *de jure*.[93]

Even in this respect an element of circularity was involved, in that the King in Parliament assumed authority to judge and declare the King's authority to be valid. For that reason, it might be argued, Parliament's judgment could not have been legally conclusive. Its authority to judge the question could not have banished all doubts as to the legal efficacy of its judgment, because anyone questioning the correctness of its judgment was, in effect, questioning its authority to make it.[94]

But in reply, it can be argued that the very fact that fifteenth century Kings found it desirable to obtain parliamentary validation of their title to the throne demonstrates that Parliament's authority was not thought to derive entirely from their own. The Lords and Commons must have been regarded as possessing an authority that was at least partly independent of that of the King, because only then could it have made any sense for Parliament to judge and affirm his title. As Chrimes argues, in explaining Richard III's Act of Succession, '[t]he older royalist and legal idea of parliament as the king's court, summoned by the force of his writ, has seemingly had grafted on to it the extraneous political and social idea of the national sanction of the estates of the realm, acting—whether for themselves or through representatives—in their own name and with an authority of their own'.[95] Parliament was not a mere instrument of royal government: it was the voice of the kingdom as a whole.[96]

---

[91] Plucknett (1960: 492); Elton (1982: 1); Mackie (1952: 61).   [92] Elton (1991: 20).

[93] Chrimes (1936: 33 n. 1). This point is overlooked by McKenna (1979: 500–1), in his critique of Dunham and Wood (see n. 90, above, and nn. 95 and 129, below).

[94] Note that the same is not true of statutes such as Henry VIII's Acts of Succession. There is no reason of pure logic to doubt that a lawful King, in a lawful Parliament, can control the future succession to the throne.

[95] Chrimes (1936: 125). In this respect, Chrimes is in agreement with the main thesis defended in Dunham and Wood (1976), especially as summarized in their final paragraph at ibid. 761. See also Wilkinson (1964: 287) and Hanson (1970: 173, 175). In his critique of Dunham and Wood, McKenna (1979) pays insufficient attention to this thesis and the considerable evidence supporting it. See further n. 90, above, and n. 129, below.

[96] 'Parliament . . . has an authority of its own as the assembly of the estates, as the agent of the public weal, and perhaps of the public will, if there be any; it is entitled to speak and act for the people' (Chrimes 1936: 348).

The procedures by which fifteenth century Acts of Succession were enacted appear to have been deliberately designed to emphasize that the two Houses acted on their own initiative and authority, rather than on that of the King, who merely certified their independent judgment.[97] The statute 7 Henry IV, c. 2 (1406), for example, was not enacted in the ordinary way. The process was initiated by the Speaker's request that the Commons have communication with the Lords, and after their consultation, the Archbishop, in the name of both the Lords and Commons, presented a petition dealing with the title and succession to the throne, praying that the King would affirm it in Parliament and that it be 'held and proclaimed as a statute'. To the petition were then attached the seals of the individual Lords and of the Speaker of the Commons, in their names, as well as the King's Great Seal.[98] Richard III's Act of Succession was supposedly instigated by a 'humble petition', presented to him in June 1483, in which the three estates of the realm proclaimed his right, and beseeched him, to assume the throne. According to that Act, passed in January 1484, the petition, 'delivered to . . . the King in the name and on behalf of the said three estates out of Parliament, [was] now by the same three estates assembled in this present Parliament, and by authority of the same, . . . ratified, enrolled, recorded, approved, and authorized', and its contents declared 'to be of like affect, virtue, and force, as if all the same things had been so said . . . in a full Parliament and by authority of the same accepted and approved'.[99] The final declaration that Richard 'was, and is, very and undoubted King of this Realm of England' was 'pronounced, decreed and declared' 'at the request, and by assent of the three estates of this realm . . . assembled in this present Parliament, [and] by authority of the same'.[100] In 1485, Henry VII's Act of Succession was enacted by the same unusual procedure and in the same form as 7 Henry IV, c. 2.[101] The original bill was presented by 'the communities [*communitates*, i.e. the Commons] of the realm of England', was assented to by the Lords Spiritual and Temporal 'at the request of the said community', and then by Henry himself.[102]

This resort to the authority of the three estates in Parliament may have been logically untidy, but the law provided no alternative: there was no superior legal authority other than that of the King himself, which was the subject-matter in dispute. As the judges explained in excusing themselves in 1460, the matter was above the law and too high for their learning.[103] Moreover, there is no evidence of any objection being made to any parliamentary affirmation of royal title on the ground that it illogically assumed what had to be proved. To challenge the validity of a statute dealing with title to the throne, on the ground that it was not enacted by a true Parliament, would have been to challenge the validity of all the other legislation passed by the assembly in question, which would have

---

[97] Charles Wood suggested this interpretation to me in correspondence.
[98] Chrimes (1936: 25); Plucknett (1960: 494).   [99] Dunham and Wood (1976: 758).
[100] Quoted in Chrimes (1936: 125).   [101] Elton (1982: 1).
[102] Dunham and Wood (1976: 760).   [103] See text to n. 42, above.

threatened legal chaos. In 1460, when Richard Duke of York asserted before the Lords in Parliament that he possessed a title superior to that of Henry VI, the Lords initially replied that statutes supported Henry (they must have had in mind principally 7 Henry IV, c. 2 (1406)): 'great and notable Acts of Parliaments . . . be sufficient and reasonable to be laid against the title of the said Duke of York: the which Acts [have] been of much more authority than any Chronicle and also of authority to defeat any manner [of] title made to any person'.[104] Richard replied that no such Act could be 'of any force or effect against him that is right inheritor of the said Crowns, as it accords with God's law, and all natural laws, how[ever] it be that all other Acts and Ordinances made in the said Parliament and since, [have] been good and sufficient against all other persons'.[105] In other words, Richard questioned the validity of the previous statutes affirming the title of his Lancastrian predecessors, not on the ground that the Parliaments that enacted them were not lawful Parliaments, but instead, on the ground that those statutes in particular were null and void because they were inconsistent with divine law. He deliberately reassured the Lords that he was not challenging the validity of any other legislation.[106] The Lords then abandoned their reliance on the earlier Acts, and decided that Richard's claim was valid. But the fact that the statute 7 Henry IV, c. 2 was then repealed suggests that they did not agree that, for practical purposes, it was already null and void.[107] They disagreed with the earlier Parliament's judgment as expressed in that statute, but still thought it necessary, or at least prudent, to repeal it. Even if they regarded repeal as merely prudent, rather than necessary, in order to dispel all possible doubts, it added to the accumulation of precedents that entrenched the principle that a statute can never be made void except by a subsequent statute.

The Lords had good reason to take this approach. If they condoned a King, or his judges, ignoring an extant statute dealing with the succession, on the ground that it was contrary to divine law or immutable custom and therefore null and void, how could they complain if other statutes were overridden for the same reason? It had long been accepted that this would be contrary to law. In 1377, the King had agreed that statutes made in Parliament could only be repealed in Parliament,[108] and at his deposition Richard II was accused of violating that principle.[109] Both Henry IV, in 1409, and Henry V, in 1419, informed the Pope that even statutes condemned by the Church could be repealed only with the assent of the three estates in Parliament.[110]

In 1461, Edward IV's first Parliament enacted a statute recognizing the validity of all judicial acts taken during 'the pretended reign[s]' of Henry IV, V, and VI, whom it described as 'recently in succession *de facto* and not rightful kings of England'.[111] The statute did not deal with the validity of statutes enacted

---

[104] Quoted by Chrimes (1936: 29).   [105] Quoted in ibid., 30.
[106] Plucknett (1960: 497).   [107] But cf. Chrimes (1936: 30, 31, incl. 31 n.1).
[108] Harriss (1981: 48).   [109] Chrimes (1936: 138).   [110] ibid. 117–18.
[111] Stephenson and Marcham (1972: i. 277–8).

during those previous reigns, and Stubbs speculates that the question may have been too difficult to tackle.[112] But it seems more likely that Edward IV, like his father Richard Duke of York, simply assumed that Lancastrian legislation was valid until repealed. In *Bagot's* case (1469), the Court of King's Bench held that 'it is necessary that the Realm should have a King under whose authority laws should be held and upheld, and though the said Henry [VI] was in power by usurpation, any judicial act done by him and touching royal jurisdiction would be valid, and will bind the rightful King when the latter returns to power'.[113] The underlying principle that the Court relied on surely applied *a fortiori* to legislation. During the brief restoration of Henry VI in 1470–1, while Edward IV was absent from the realm, Henry's title to the Crown was affirmed by what purported to be a statute, and all statutes made by Edward IV were repealed.[114] This statute was, in turn, subsequently repealed by 17 Edward IV (1477), even though the repealed statute was described in the initiating petition as having been passed 'in a pretensed Parliament, unlawfully and by usurped authority summoned and called by your rebel and enemy Henry the VIth, late in deed, and not in right King of England'.[115]

Henry VII's first Parliament formally repealed the Act of Succession (1484), which had declared Edward V to be a bastard, and Richard III the rightful King, after all the judges in the Exchequer Chamber informed the new King that it could not be removed from the record without a new statute.[116] The repealed Act was condemned in the repealing Act as 'a false and seditious bill' that 'Richard, late Duke of Gloucester and after in deed and not of right king of England' had 'caused . . . to be put unto him'; nevertheless, 'by authority of Parliament held the first year of the usurped reign of the said late King Richard III', it had been 'ratified, enrolled, recorded, approved, and authorized', and so it was declared 'void, annulled, repealed, irrite [invalid], and of no force nor effect' by authority of the repealing Parliament.[117] Ricardian statutes that had attainted many of Henry's supporters were also repealed, rather than ignored on the ground that they were already null and void, and the persons concerned were not permitted to attend Henry's first Parliament until that was done.[118] In 1525, Cardinal Wolsey was advised that an extra-parliamentary tax he wanted to impose was contrary to a statute passed in 1484, and when he angrily objected that this had been enacted during the reign of the usurper, Richard III, he was informed that whatever that King's personal failings, the statute had been made by Parliament and was therefore valid.[119]

---

[112] Stubbs (1897: iii. 201–2).   [113] Quoted by Vinogradoff (1913: 279).
[114] Edward Hall's *Chronicle*, 286, extracted in Wilkinson (1964: 185).
[115] Plucknett (1960: 498 n. 18).
[116] Chrimes (1936: 266 n. 4) observes that this is a clear application of the principle that 'every statute was deemed to be effective unless and until it was repealed by parliament'. Charles Wood kindly translated for me the law French which Chrimes quotes.
[117] The Repeal Act is set out in Levine (1973: 140), and discussed at ibid. 36.
[118] Vinogradoff (1913: 276).   [119] Elton (1977: 91); Baumer (1940: 175–6).

No doubt when its authority was enlisted in order to settle a dynastic dispute, Parliament had little choice but to affirm the title of the most powerful, or victorious, claimant. But the very fact that its affirmation was so frequently sought suggests that it was not generally regarded as merely a pliant tool of whoever held *de facto* power.[120] A completely transparent fig-leaf is not worth wearing. Moreover, there is evidence that Parliament's judgment was accorded considerable weight. First, there is the initial reliance by the Lords in 1460 on 7 Henry IV, c. 2, and, when they decided that it had settled the Crown wrongly, their belief that it had to be repealed. Secondly, there is a statement made by counsel in argument during *Bagot's* case (1470), concerning the validity of judicial acts taken during the reign of the supposed 'usurper', Henry VI, that 'the King Henry was not merely a usurper, for the Crown was entailed on him by Parliament'.[121] Thirdly, Charles Wood has argued that organized opposition to Richard III initially crumbled after Parliament's endorsement of his title to the throne, and revived only after the death of his son, which was widely interpreted as a sign of God's wrath.[122] Finally, there is the report that the Earl of Surrey, captured after fighting for Richard III at the battle at Bosworth, defended himself by explaining to Henry VII that '[h]e was my crowned King, and if the parliamentary authority of England set the Crown upon a stock, I will fight for that stock. And as I fought then for him, I will fight for you, when you are established by the said authority.'[123]

To sum up, whenever in the fifteenth century there were serious doubts about their right to the throne, *de facto* kings gave a high priority to obtaining both statutory confirmation of their title and the repeal of any previous statute inconsistent with it. That it was believed to be necessary to repeal even statutes thought to affirm the title of usurpers suggests that they, like all other statutes, were regarded as legally binding and conclusive as long as they remained in force. Other evidence confirms that they were accorded great weight. In strict logic, and apparently in fact, this understanding of the matter depended on the assumption that Parliament derived its authority from the community as a whole, as well as from the King who summoned it. The statutes in question were enacted by a procedure and in a form that seem to have been deliberately chosen to emphasize that independent authority.

It does not follow that in enacting these statutes, Parliament acted as a sovereign law-maker, assuming unfettered authority to bestow the Crown at will. Instead, it purported to provide authoritative legal recognition of titles justly acquired on independent grounds. But by the 1530s, it did come to be widely accepted that Parliament possessed unfettered authority to dispose of the Crown. Even Sir Thomas More, who sacrificed his life rather than acknowledge Parliament's authority to terminate papal jurisdiction over spiritual matters, agreed that 'a King can

---

[120] Wood (1982: 57–8, 60 n. 19).   [121] Quoted by Chrimes (1936: 32).
[122] Wood (1988: 195–9). But this is, admittedly, rather speculative.
[123] Camden (1984: 247).

be made by Parliament and deprived by Parliament',[124] and assented to the proposition put by Sir Richard Rich, Henry VIII's Solicitor-General, that Parliament could validly make even Rich the King.[125] In this respect More must have been influenced by Parliament's role in the making and breaking of kings during the previous century. In his *The History of Richard III*, he discussed the parliamentary settlement of the dispute between Richard Duke of York and Henry VI, and noted that the Crown was entailed on the Duke 'by authority of Parliament'.[126] In the Latin version of the work, intended for a European audience, More added by way of explanation that the legal power of Parliament was, in England, 'supreme and absolute' ('*summa atque absoluta*').[127] In 1587, William Harrison argued in his *Description of England* that Parliament 'has the most high and absolute power of the realm, for thereby kings and mighty princes have from time to time been deposed from their thrones'.[128] The conclusion is inescapable that those events played a significant role in the development of the doctrine of parliamentary sovereignty.[129]

3. Parliament as a Law-Maker

It has been argued, most notably by C. H. McIlwain, that nothing resembling the modern doctrine of parliamentary sovereignty was conceivable before the mid-seventeenth century, because the medieval mind regarded law as immutable, and Parliament as a court that expounded but did not change it.[130] But this argument has long been discredited. Parliament was often called 'the High Court of Parliament', but in medieval England the word 'court' was not restricted to institutions in which judges determined pre-existing legal rights and duties. To 'hold court' was to govern, and the entire kingdom was governed through 'courts' that actively engaged in administration as well as adjudication.[131] Even courts that

---

[124]   Harpsfield (1932: 274–6), translated and quoted by Pickthorn (1934*b*: 260 n. 5).

[125]   Roper (1935: 85). For further discussion, see Chapter 4, text to n. 71, below.

[126]   In More (1963–87: ii. 6, line 19).   [127]   ibid. ii. 6, line 14.

[128]   W. Harrison, *Description of England* (1587), i. 291, quoted in Patterson (1994: 103).

[129]   McKenna (1979) criticizes Dunham and Wood for supposedly arguing that as a consequence of the developments just discussed, Parliament acquired sovereignty in the fifteenth century. By 'parliamentary sovereignty' McKenna means the superiority of the two Houses of Parliament over the King (see ibid. 481–2, 505–6), and he rightly says that in the fifteenth century this was inconceivable. But our concern is with the legislative sovereignty of the King in Parliament. Moreover, Dunham and Wood never asserted that the medieval Parliament was 'sovereign' in McKenna's, or for that matter in any other, sense of the word. The closest they came to doing so was to observe that statutes such as Richard III's Act of Succession 'put parliament well on the road toward supremacy or sovereignty' (Dunham and Wood 1976: 758), which in itself is entirely justified. Chrimes (1936: 126) also took the view that the understanding of parliamentary authority which underpins Richard III's Act of Succession 'gradually worked that transformation in parliamentary theory which appeared during the three centuries from 1399 to 1688'. See also Wilkinson (1964: 2, 284–5).

[130]   McIlwain (1910: esp. 355–6, 44–7); see also Baumer (1940: 157–63) and Kern (1939: 184 ff.).

[131]   Martin (1992: 74–5); McIlwain (1910: 29–30).

were primarily adjudicative also had legislative or administrative functions.[132] According to A. L. Brown, 'the phrase "the High Court of Parliament" . . . was not a phrase with a precise significance; its most obvious meaning was that parliament made and unmade laws . . . It had the merit of conveying in traditional rather than political terms a sense of the authority and status which parliament now undoubtedly possessed'.[133] Sir Goronwy Edwards concludes that:

The evidence as a whole indicates that the functional 'essence' of the pre-representative parliaments, so far from being 'judicial', consisted rather in *not being* 'judicial'. Important 'judicial' functions could be, and often were, performed in parliament, but the essence of its functions was not specifically judicial, any more than it was specifically legislative, or specifically taxative, or specifically anything. The essence of its function consisted in being *unspecific*, in being *omni*competent, in ranging over the whole field of lay government . . . It seems, then, that if we are to understand the medieval English parliament as it really was, we must regard it as having been in origin not 'a high court of justice', not a high court *of* anything, but simply a high court. The medieval king, in England as in some places elsewhere, was deemed to act always (as the phrase went) 'with counsel'. . . . In England it was in parliament that the king found counsel at its amplest, so it was in parliament that his power was legally at its highest. That was why parliament was a 'high court' and why king in parliament was omnicompetent.[134]

G. O. Sayles, one of the most eminent recent historians of medieval parliaments, believes that they were originally concerned more with dispensing justice to individual petitioners than with legislating or taxing. But he acknowledges that they also routinely dealt with public affairs in general, including diplomacy, war and peace, legislation, and taxation. After 1327, their judicial functions began to diminish in importance, and political business assumed greater prominence. Sayles, like Edwards, describes medieval parliaments as 'omnicompetent'.[135] According to Chrimes, while the legal profession in the fifteenth century may have conceived of Parliament as the highest court of law in the realm, at the same time Parliament came to be regarded as a representative political assembly, with attributes and powers far exceeding those of an ordinary law court. These judicial and political notions were combined, and '[b]efore the century was over, it was clearly understood that parliament was the place of worldly policy, the place where laws were made and where that which was amiss was amended'.[136] Statutes continued to be drafted in the form of declaratory statements of what the law was

[132] Pickthorn (1934*a*: 142). See also Harding (1973: 80), and for the continuing administrative role of courts in the early seventeenth century, W. J. Jones (1971: 17–19).

[133] Brown (1989: 233).

[134] J. G. Edwards (1960: 23–4, 41–2), extracted in Spufford (1967: 201–2), emphasis in original. See also Edwards (1970*b*: 297), Wilkinson (1952*b*: esp. at 54), Plucknett (1960: 150–1), Dunham (1987: 425), and Elton (1986: 20–1).

[135] Sayles (1974: 75, 84–5, 109–12). See also Elton (1982: 233–4; 1974*b*: 20–2, 28), and Harriss (1981: 29, 35, 37).

[136] Chrimes (1936: 140–1); see also ibid. 75–6 and 79–80, and Holdsworth (1946*b*: 63–5; 1946*c*: 80–1).

supposed to be, but as Penry Williams puts it, '[t]his was a polite and fairly obvious fiction, which was dropped in Edward [VI]'s reign'.[137]

It is puzzling that McIlwain himself partly acknowledges this. 'When we thus speak of Parliament as a "court of justice" and designate its actions as "judicial"', he says,

> it will be remembered that 'court' and 'judicial' are not to be used in their modern definite sense. We can never understand the institutions of mediaeval England if we consider Parliament as a 'court of justice' which *in addition* exercised other distinct powers, or as a legislature with an addendum of other duties. It is the *fusion* of indefinite powers which is the most fundamental fact . . .[138]

What is puzzling is that McIlwain often seems to ignore his own advice. To take just one example, he argues that the Court of Parliament described in Sir Edward Coke's *Fourth Institute* was 'supreme' in the sense that today's American Supreme Court is supreme, rather than in the sense that today's British Parliament is supreme.[139] In other words, it was supreme in the sense that its decisions could not be reviewed by any higher court, but not in the sense that its authority was legally unlimited. But that argument is undermined by his admission that Parliament in Coke's day exercised a fusion of both adjudicative and legislative powers. If it is a mistake to think of that Parliament as a court in our modern sense, then it must also be a mistake to think of it as 'supreme' only in the sense that a modern court is supreme.[140] If it exercised a fusion of judicial and legislative powers, and was supreme with respect to both, then it possessed a fusion of what we now regard as two kinds of supremacy.

McIlwain denies this partly because he denies that the existence of law-making, in the modern sense, was recognized in the Middle Ages, notwithstanding the 'fusion' of powers exercised by medieval Parliaments.[141] 'So long as the law was a thing fundamental and immutable', he argues, 'Parliament's functions must have been conceived to be in large part merely the enforcing and applying of this law: Parliament must have been thought of first as a court rather than as a legislature.'[142] But the inference that Parliament must have been regarded as primarily a court is unwarranted, because the premise, that Parliament was believed merely to enforce an immutable pre-existing law, is false. It has been emphatically rejected by most recent historians.[143] Plucknett describes it as 'a paradox

---

[137] Williams (1995: 136).

[138] McIlwain (1910: 119). On the fusion of judicial and legislative powers in the medieval Parliament, see also ibid., ch. I, *passim*, 30, 290–1, and 323–8.

[139] ibid. 142–3.

[140] McIlwain is somewhat unclear on this point. His initial claim, that 'we may say roughly that Parliament was more a court than a legislature' (ibid., p. viii, and also 109–10) is in tension with his subsequent admission that '[w]e have not accepted the fact that in the middle ages Parliament *really was* primarily a court, and only incidentally a "legislature"': ibid. 197–8. But even on the former view Parliament was not a court in the modern sense.

[141] e.g. ibid. 42–3, 46–7, and 70–2.   [142] ibid. 110.

[143] See generally Hanson (1970: 202–11) and references cited therein, Chodorow (1972: 133–4 n. 1), Sayles (1974: 85–6), and Harriss (1963: 21). The history of legislation in late medieval England is summarized in Brown (1989: 218–24).

brilliantly sustained', and Morris Arnold concludes that 'supporting evidence is embarrassingly absent' for it.[144]

Whether the premise is true of most law-making in the early medieval period is itself debatable.[145] Even then, customs were not venerated as infallible and immutable. In 1100, Henry I in his coronation charter promised to 'remove all the bad customs through which the kingdom of England has been unjustly oppressed', which he proceeded to enumerate.[146] A thirteenth century coronation oath, possibly that of Edward I, included the promise to 'put out all bad laws and customs'.[147] At that time, according to Brian Tierney, '[e]very lawyer and administrator with a smattering of civilian learning was familiar with the idea that new law could be created by deliberate legislation'.[148] Bracton wrote that English laws and customs 'cannot be changed without the common consent of those by whose counsel and consent they were promulgated. They cannot be nullified without their consent, but may be changed for the better, for to change for the better is not to nullify.'[149] In 1291–2, an assembly styled a parliament ruled that 'the lord king . . . can and should establish new law (*condere novam legem*) by the counsel of the nobles, prelates, great men, and magnates of his realm'.[150] A contemporary chronicler reported that at Westminster, Edward I had 'established very many new laws'.[151]

At least by the late Middle Ages, the requirements of divine and natural law were believed to be sufficiently abstract to permit choices to be made between alternative specifications of them. Different communities, with different traditions and practices, were therefore permitted to legislate differently. Parliament was not regarded as merely a mouthpiece for pre-existing standards.[152] Plucknett reports that in the early fourteenth century 'contemporaries . . . frankly faced the fact that special law—"novel law"—was being "made" and that it "defeated" the common law'.[153] In 1334, Chief Justice Herle explained that although the judges could not change a rule of long standing, the party if he wished could 'sue in parliament to make a new law',[154] and Chief Justice Fortescue declared in 1453 that 'this high court of parliament . . . is so high and so mighty in its nature that it may make law, and that that is law it may make no law'.[155] Sir Geoffrey Elton comments that '[i]f medieval Parliaments did not legislate, much in the *Rolls of Parliament* becomes incomprehensible'.[156] Fifteenth century writers and judges

---

[144] Plucknett (1949: 6 n. 1); Arnold (1977: 343).

[145] Hanson (1970: 192 ff.) disputes the declaratory theory even with respect to the early Middle Ages.

[146] Stephenson and Marcham (1972: i. 46). I owe this point to Charles Wood.

[147] Maitland (1908: 99).   [148] Tierney (1963a: 305 n. 25).

[149] Bracton (1968–77: ii. 21).   [150] Quoted in Dunham (1987: 425).

[151] Powicke (1962: 369), quoting the Norwich chronicler.

[152] Eccleshall (1978: 101–2); see also Lewis (1954: i. 18–20) and Finnis (1980: 28).

[153] Plucknett (1922: 31); see also ibid. 30, esp. n. 2, and 166; Allen (1964: 445); and Gough (1955: 27).

[154] Y. B. Mich. 8 Edw. III, fo. 69, pl. 35, cited in Baker (1990: 239.)

[155] *Re Thomas Thorpe* (1453) *Rot. Parl.* v. 239–40, quoted in Myers (1981: 150). For other examples of such statements, see Hanson (1970: 210).

[156] Elton (1982: 234).

used the term 'positive law' to distinguish laws made by men from the law of God, and developed an incipient positivist theory of the former in terms of the will of the law-maker and the coercive sanction attached to the law.[157] Sir John Fortescue and Reginald Pecock, for example, advanced 'a thoroughly earth-bound conception of *human law*, shaped purely and simply by the human will. Law is *made* by people, it is not found or given by God.'[158] During the same period, the courts routinely distinguished between statutes that declared old law, and those that made new law, a distinction that determined how they were to be interpreted.[159] Chrimes concludes that '[w]e can thus be quite confident that the fact of law-making by statute was recognised during the [fifteenth] century. The ancient notion that law to be good must be old was not merely decayed; it was dead.'[160]

To defend McIlwain's thesis it is necessary to argue that although medieval parliaments were said to 'make new law', they did not really do so in the full modern sense of that expression. Kenneth Pickthorn takes this approach. He acknowledges that by 1485 'statute was already supreme . . . in this sense, that it pronounced the last word, from which there was no appeal, on what was lawful and unlawful in all secular transactions within the realm of England'.[161] But even though '[t]his looks much like what the nineteenth century has called legislative sovereignty', he insists that it was actually very different.[162] Before the sixteenth century, law-making took place only in an attenuated fashion, so-called 'new laws' being procedural rather than substantive, concerned with proclaiming and enforcing customary principles and practices (which he calls 'Law' with a capital 'L') rather than changing them.[163] The medieval mind was not attuned to social change, and assumed that those principles and practices were timeless and immutable. Parliament could change 'laws' but not 'Law'.[164]

But Pickthorn exaggerates the difference between medieval and modern attitudes to law-making. Even today there are principles and practices that the community would not regard as legitimately changeable. In arguing that one of Henry VII's statutes was 'only just on the border line' between adjudication and legislation, and would not have seemed to contemporaries to involve law-making in the modern sense, he comments: 'It was not like saying that murder should cease to be punishable or land to be heritable'.[165] But who today would think that Parliament could legitimately legalize murder! Constitutional doctrine may hold that Parliament has legal authority to do so, but that is just the modern way of expressing what was already largely true in the fifteenth century—the fact that Parliament's decisions, even if morally wrong, are for legal purposes final and unappealable. Apart from terminology, the difference between medieval and modern attitudes to law-making is one of degree rather than kind: in the fifteenth century, far more principles and practices were regarded as not legitimately

---

[157] Doe (1990: 34–7).   [158] Doe (1989: 264); and see ibid. 264–7 generally.
[159] Chrimes (1936: 254–8).   [160] ibid. 254.
[161] Pickthorn (1934a: 141); see also ibid. 89–90.   [162] ibid. 141.
[163] ibid. 141–57.   [164] ibid. 156–7.   [165] ibid. 150.

changeable. In other words, the difference is that people then were much more conservative than we are, and not that they were bound by constitutional constraints from which we have been liberated.[166] The formal structure of legislative authority for changing what is believed to be legitimately changeable, and for proclaiming and enforcing what is not, remains largely the same.

Pickthorn's attempt to show that no substantial legislative changes were made to 'Law' during the reign of Henry VII is strained.[167] Even he concedes that '[i]f statute could deprive subjects of one of their main guarantees against oppression, could treat corporations as the merest underlings, could grant wholesale dispensation for negligence of God's royal viceregent, if statute could do, could even seem to do, such things, then it became hard to know what things statute could not do'.[168] Later he acknowledges that

the very sort of law which was generally assumed to be most important and most conclusive had, to the eye of common sense, suffered great changes; the law about property in land. Men who were conscious of the Statutes of *Mortmain* (1279), *de Donis Conditionalibus* (1285), *Quia Emptores* (1290), conscious of the development of a whole system of rules about trusts, of Taltarum's Case (1472) which made or marked the inefficacy of *de Donis*—men who were conscious of all this, as was every Englishman with the least education or with the least interest in landed property (which meant every Englishman individually considerable in any sort of politics), men so conscious could not be very far from the capacity of conceiving . . . not only that law could be changed but even that there was more than one way of changing it: and if law about land were not Law, what was?[169]

But surely such men must already have acquired just that capacity, and meant exactly what they said when they spoke of Parliament 'making new laws'. *De Donis* and *Quia Emptores* have been cited by other historians as examples of deliberate and innovative law-making. *De Donis* effectively created a new estate in land, known as 'fee tail' or 'estate tail', by preventing a donee of a conditional fee simple from alienating the land contrary to the will of the donor. It enabled landowners to create a virtually inalienable estate, which the common law had not allowed. This has been described as 'a legislative feat worthy of the most powerful sovereign in the most sovereign of ages'.[170]

In a thorough demolition of McIlwain's thesis, Hanson insists not only that new laws were regularly made in medieval England in order to bring about social and political change, but that there were no fundamental laws regarded as immutable.

---

[166] Arnold (1977: 342–3).
[167] See in particular Pickthorn's discussion of the so-called 'De Facto Act' of Henry VII (1934a: 151–6), and the comments of Chrimes (1936: 254 n. 1).
[168] Pickthorn (1934a: 156).   [169] ibid. 165–6.
[170] Arnold (1977: 332), where he also observes that 'the possibility of successfully arguing that this statute [*Quia Emptores*] was merely declaratory is remote'. See also Milsom (1956: 393).

Conscious legal change, often touching the most important affairs of the realm and its people, is revealed in legal and political writings, year books, rolls of parliament, and chronicles. In framing a theory which accounts for the thought and practice of this period, the thesis that political life was governed by an ancient and immutable body of custom must be abandoned. To insist that these ideas were central to the period produces a paradox of colossal proportions. It introduces a disjunction between the theoretical account and the available facts which is too wide to be serviceable. Everything that the observer can learn of the operative beliefs and practices of this period runs contrary to the fundamental law thesis. To be sure, the celebration of that thesis has been nothing short of astonishing. But the confidence with which it has been reiterated is inversely proportional to its evidential basis.[171]

4. Parliament and the Courts

In *Dr Bonham's* case, Chief Justice Coke cited various medieval precedents to support his claim that 'it appears in our books' that the common law would control, and adjudge void, an Act of Parliament contrary to common right and reason.[172] Whether or not Coke was suggesting that the courts could invalidate statutes is debatable, but if he was, the relevance of those precedents is doubtful.[173] Modern scholars generally agree that they do not support such a suggestion.[174] Maitland doubted that medieval judges considered themselves free to question the validity of a statute on such grounds: 'The vigorous legislation of our medieval parliaments had rendered any theory of law above king, above king and parliament, an unworkable doctrine'.[175] Holdsworth thought it 'quite impossible' to suppose that medieval lawyers believed they could refuse to obey a statute on the ground that it was contrary to the common law.[176]

Subsequent historical research has vindicated these doubts. In his study of statute law in the first half of the fourteenth century, Plucknett found only a few decisions in the Year Books in which pertinent statutes were not applied, and those decisions were not based on any jurisprudential principle that subordinated parliamentary authority to fundamental principles of natural or common law. The judges simply applied what they regarded as the best law for the circumstances.[177] As Thorne explains, statutory provisions were 'merely suggestions of policy to be treated with an easy unconcern as to their precise content'; judges freely extended and restricted statutes as a routine part of their duty to administer justice between litigants.[178] This approach reflected the different relationship

---

[171] Hanson (1970: 215); see also ibid. 36–7, 93–5, and 189–216 *passim*.
[172] (1610) 8 Co. Rep. 113b, 118; 77 E.R. 646, 652.
[173] Coke's meaning is discussed in Chapter 5, Section 4, below.
[174] For an early denial, see Campbell (1874: i. 341). For more detailed criticism, see Plucknett (1926: 35–45), Gray (1972: 47–9), MacKay (1924: 223–7), Boudin (1932: i. 498–502), Stoner (1992: 54–8). See also Allen (1964: 448), and Gough (1955: 33–4).
[175] Maitland (1908: 301).   [176] Holdsworth (1925: 43–4).
[177] Plucknett (1922: 70–1).   [178] 'Introduction', in Thorne (1942: 42, 47, 70–1).

between legislation and adjudication that prevailed at that time. The powers of the King's council, courts, and Parliament were not clearly differentiated: all wielded the authority of the King, and all participated in both legislation and adjudication, which were not clearly distinguished from one another. The council and Parliament often engaged in statutory interpretation and adjudication, the judges regularly helped draft legislation, and judicial interpretation was acknowledged to be virtually legislation. Judges therefore did not think of statutes as the commands of an external authority, requiring strict construction: as royal servants administering the King's justice, they simply exercised the fusion of legislative and judicial powers at his disposal.[179] In other words, when they extended or restricted, or even, in a few cases, ignored the words of a statute, they saw themselves as giving effect to, rather than as opposing, the underlying policies of the King and Parliament. It is most unlikely that they would have done so otherwise. During the reign of Edward III, when it was argued that the King, even with the consent of Parliament, could not quash a previous judgment concerning title to land, the Court 'declared its inability to correct a decision given by Parliament, the latter being the Supreme Court of the kingdom'.[180]

By the fifteenth century, legislation was much more clearly distinguished from adjudication. Chrimes studied the relationship between statutes and common law in that century, and concluded that the supremacy of statutes over the common law 'appears to have been unquestioned . . . No one, the judges held, could prescribe against statute.' He could not find a single case in which a judge nullified a statute on the ground that it was contrary to natural or divine law.[181] His conclusions are confirmed in Norman Doe's more recent study of law and legal theory in the fifteenth century. Doe shows that both legislators and judges at that time treated morally abhorrent statutes as valid law, operative until repealed by subsequent legislation. Their approach, he says, seems to have been 'based on an incipient idea of parliamentary sovereignty.' The judges did invalidate local customs, which would otherwise have enjoyed legal status, if they offended against 'reason' or 'common right'. But they did not claim a similar authority to invalidate statutes. Doe confirms Chrimes's conclusion that there is not a single example in the fifteenth century Year Books of judges questioning the validity of statutes on such a ground.[182] A. R. Myers concludes:

By the end of the fifteenth century judicial opinion had established that statutes could override rules of common law, that statutes were superior to ordinances, that statutes could bind all the king's domains and all the king's subjects, that statutes would be upheld even if they conflicted with royal prerogative, that statutes could override the law merchant and define the limits of canon law.[183]

---

[179] Plucknett (1922: 20–22, 25, 168); see also 'Introduction', in Thorne (1942: 44–5). McIlwain (1910: 290–1, 323–8) had previously made this argument himself.

[180] Vinogradoff (1913: 278).   [181] Chrimes (1936: 284–5, 290–1).

[182] Doe (1990: 55–9, 79–82, 178).   [183] Myers (1981: 182–3).

5. Parliament in Legal Theory

Few English theorists gave much attention to questions concerning the nature
and source of law until the fifteenth century.[184] By then, according to Doe, the
prevailing view among lawyers and political theorists was that the authority of
law rested on the consent of the community as well as that of the King.[185] Theorists
such as Reginald Pecock and Sir John Fortescue drew upon civilian, canonist, and
Thomist writings to explain English law and government, combining the European
idea that political authority was derived from the community with the feudal understanding of counsel and consent that had long prevailed in English practice.[186]

Reginald Pecock (*c.*1395–*c.*1460), an Oxford Fellow, Bishop, Privy Coun-
cillor, and member of Lincoln's Inn, described secular law as 'the commands
and ordinances of *princes and of their commonalty together*'; in England, the
'act and decree of the whole parliament of England . . . is the very ground to all
the laws of England'.[187] According to Doe, Pecock held that a secular law contrary to natural law was 'unlawful, and not worthy to be had and used', but not
null or void: 'for Pecock natural law remains an extraneous morality with which
human law ought to agree'.[188] Pecock made no mention of judges having authority to hold statutes void; on the contrary, judges were appointed by the King 'to
judge all causes after the law which he and his Parliament make'.[189]

Sir John Fortescue (*c.*1395–*c.*1477), who served as a Member of Parliament,
Chief Justice of England, and Lord Chancellor, wrote several influential books
that have established his reputation as 'undoubtedly the major English political
theorist of the fifteenth century'.[190] *De Laudibus Legum Angliae* ('In Praise of
the Laws of England') and *The Governance of England* have been described as
'the first treatises on the English constitution, as distinct from the more purely
legal expositions of Glanvill and Bracton', and as 'the fullest statement of operative political thought in late medieval England'.[191]

In an earlier work, *De Natura Legis Naturae*, Fortescue expounded a
Thomistic natural law philosophy according to which man-made rules did not
deserve to be called laws if they were inconsistent with natural law.[192] But elsewhere he appeared to accept that even iniquitous rules enacted by an absolute
monarch were laws.[193] Be that as it may, he stressed that in England the monarch
was not absolute: the King could neither impose taxes on his subjects 'nor change
their laws, nor make new ones, without the concession or assent of his whole

---

[184] Doe (1990: 3, 7).   [185] ibid. ch. 1, esp. 31.   [186] ibid. 4, 7, 8, 12.
[187] Quoted by Doe (1989: 260), emphasis in original.   [188] ibid. 272–3, and 268.
[189] ibid. 260.   [190] S. Lockwood, 'Introduction', in Lockwood (1997: p. xv).
[191] Shepard (1936: 290) and Hanson (1970: 252). See also ibid. 216.
[192] Fortescue (1980: part I, ch. x); see also ibid., chs. iv, v, and xxix. These passages are all quoted
in Hanson (1970: 220).
[193] See the discussion in Doe (1990: 53–4), and Hanson (1970: 222, 224–5, 231). Doe argues that
Fortescue was simply inconsistent on this question (1990: 78; and 1989: 268–9, 271–2).

realm expressed in his parliament'.[194] Moreover, 'the whole body of the realm according to the laws of England is represented' in Parliament,[195] and this virtually ensured that unjust or tyrannical laws would never be enacted. Fortescue conceived of the law of nature as the 'truth of justice' disclosed by human reason, and agreed with Aristotle that the reason of many men in combination was superior to that of one or a few.[196] It followed that Parliament was, in effect, infallible: that the collective wisdom of able men drawn from all parts of the realm could never devise rules contrary to the common good.[197] In *De Laudibus*, after observing that rules enacted solely by a King are frequently corrupted by selfishness or carelessness, he said:

But the statutes of England cannot so arise, since they are made not only by the prince's will, but also by the assent of the whole realm, so they cannot be injurious to the people nor fail to secure their advantage. Furthermore, it must be supposed that they are necessarily replete with prudence and wisdom, since they are promulgated by the prudence not of one counsellor nor of a hundred only, but of more than three hundred chosen men ... with such solemnity and care.[198]

He added that if statutes happen not to give full effect to Parliament's intention 'they can speedily be revised, and yet not without the assent of the commons and nobles of the realm, in the manner in which they first originated'.[199] Later he argued that all laws, 'if they are defective in any respect, can be amended in every parliament. So it can be rightly concluded that all the laws of this realm are the best in fact or potentiality, since they can easily be brought to it in fact and actual reality.'[200] He insisted that English judges 'are all bound by their oaths not to render judgement against the laws of the land (*leges terre*), even if they should have the commands of the prince to the contrary'.[201]

Fortescue's reasoning led R. W. K. Hinton to attribute to him 'something quite close to nineteenth century ideas', while acknowledging that he did not use nineteenth century words.[202] Although Fortescue believed that Parliament was subject to divine law, it should not be forgotten that Blackstone and Austin both believed the same thing, even though they accepted the doctrine of parliamentary sovereignty. For them, the enactment of a statute established its validity as a law of the land, because its compatibility with divine law was not in that respect a relevant consideration. Arguably for Fortescue, the enactment of a statute established its validity because its compatibility with divine law was for legal

---

[194] Fortescue (1949: 87; ch. 36), also in Lockwood (1997: 78). For Reginald Pecock's similar ideas, expressed forty years earlier, see Doe (1990: 13–14).

[195] *The Works of Sir John Fortescue*, ed. Lord Clermont (London, 1869), 514–17, quoted by Doe (1990: 8).

[196] Fortescue (1980: 233; Part 1, ch. 37).   [197] See Eccleshall (1978: 103, 108–9).

[198] Fortescue (1949: 41; ch.18); also in Lockwood (1997: 27–8).   [199] ibid.

[200] Fortescue (1949: 135; ch. 53); also in Lockwood (1997: 78).

[201] *De Natura Legis Naturae*, in Lockwood (1997: 128); see also Fortescue (1980: 205).

[202] Hinton (1960: 414–17).

purposes conclusively settled by the judgment of Parliament. As Hanson puts it, Fortescue's argument is that 'what is enacted by the conjunction of regal will and parliamentary advice and consent is, ipso facto, an embodiment of justice'.[203] If so, then Fortescue no less than Blackstone regarded Parliament as sovereign in our sense, although for a different reason. In Eccleshall's words, Fortescue's was 'a doctrine of parliamentary omnicompetency but grounded on the assumption that the monarch in parliament was the communal embodiment of an objective reason'.[204] That assumption seems to be expressed in the parliamentary declaration, previously quoted, affirming Richard III's title to the throne.[205]

6. Parliament and the Church

A. L. Brown argues that between the years 1300 and 1461 '[s]tatutes had become recognised as the supreme form of man-made law in England and their relationship to the law of God or the law of nature was not a practical issue'.[206] But this is an exaggeration, because Parliament was not yet generally recognised as having unlimited authority to legislate with respect to spiritual affairs. It was supreme in all other matters, but not, as yet, omnicompetent. Fifteenth century discussions of the authority of parliaments, including Fortescue's, must be understood against a backdrop of assumptions that it would not have seemed necessary to express. One of these concerned papal jurisdiction in matters of religion and the Church. The papacy claimed supreme authority throughout Christendom with respect to the Church, its laws, and its courts, and also authority to punish temporal rulers who violated divine law by excommunication or, as a last resort, deposition.[207] Those claims, especially the last, may largely have been rhetorical and impractical, but none the less they were made, and widely accepted even in England. Reginald Pecock, for example, acknowledged that the Church possessed a divinely ordained power to legislate in ecclesiastical matters, and Fortescue stated that the Pope, as God's vicar on earth, was 'possessed of the highest power, to whom all earthly power is made subject'.[208]

---

[203] Hanson (1970: 230).

[204] Eccleshall (1978: 99). Hanson (1970: 416 n. 35) says that '[i]f any modern idea were to be read into Fortescue, that of parliamentary sovereignty would be most plausible. But . . . this is to make him hold an opinion on a subject which he did not confront'; see also ibid. 224 and 233.

[205] See text to n. 87, above.

[206] Brown (1989: 223); see also ibid. 219–20. See also Gunn (1995: 184): parliamentary statutes were 'recognised from at least the mid-fifteenth century as new law able to override common law custom, to bind all the king's subjects . . . and to be impervious to judicial nullification'. See also Harriss (1963: 21–2).

[207] Elton (1974d: 208–9). In 1538, Paul III excommunicated Henry VIII and attempted to instigate a crusade to depose him (Guy 1988: 134–5, 184). In 1570, Pius V excommunicated Elizabeth, the 'so-called' Queen of England, and declared that her subjects were released from their allegiance to her (Cross 1969: 39).

[208] Fortescue (1980: 263).

By the early sixteenth century, friction between Church and State in England had long been minimized by compromise, mainly on the part of the Church, which had been bullied and bribed into conceding to the Crown predominant influence over ecclesiastical appointments and many other aspects of Church govern-ance.[209] The English Church had for a long time 'been growing king-centred rather than pope-centred'.[210] But it had never surrendered its claim to supreme jurisdiction over exclusively spiritual matters. When its jurisdiction intruded into that of the King or Parliament, statutes could be enacted capable of overriding canon law. Nevertheless, canon law was regarded as supreme within its clearly exclusive sphere of jurisdiction: 'The proper sphere of statute-law did not include undoubted *spiritualia*.'[211] These could be argued to include not only the interpretation of scripture, but consequential matters of vital importance to the Crown, such as matrimonial causes, which could affect the royal succession. The potential for serious conflict remained.[212]

Arguably the only statute prior to the Henrician Reformation that purported to determine a purely spiritual matter was the Act of Succession (1484), which declared Richard III to be the rightful King. It expressly endorsed his claim that Edward V (probably, by then, already murdered) had been a bastard because his parents' marriage was invalid, and in doing so it purported to judge the validity of a sacrament, something that previously only an ecclesiastical court had re-cognized authority to do.[213] But the Parliament that passed that Act did so re-luctantly, no doubt fearful of Richard's wrath: according to one account, 'that lay court found itself (at first) unable to give a definition of his [Richard's] rights, when the question of the marriage was discussed', but eventually 'in consequence of the fears entertained . . . it presumed to do so'.[214] The statute constituted a pre-cedent for the extension of parliamentary authority to spiritual affairs in the 1530s,[215] but until then it may well have been regarded as a bad precedent, the kind of unjustified exception that proves the rule.[216] It certainly did not put an end to doubts about Parliament's authority in such matters.

In a case heard by the Court of Common Pleas in 1506, it was argued that 'the King cannot be called parson by act of Parliament, for no temporal act can . . . make a temporal man have spiritual jurisdiction', and Chief Justice Frowicke agreed: 'a temporal act, without the assent of the Supreme Head [the Pope], cannot make the King a parson'.[217] In 1529, the courts doubted Parliament's

---

[209] Harriss (1963: 13–20); Haigh (1993: 6–7); Griffiths (1984: 241–2).

[210] Harriss (1965: 89).   [211] Chrimes (1936: 286); Elton (1964: 36–7).

[212] See the disagreement between Harriss (1963), who argues that the Church had already con-ceded so much to the English Crown that the Henrician Reformation made no profound change, and Elton (1964: 32–6), continued in Harriss (1965), and Elton (1965: 104).

[213] A point stressed in Wood (1989: 485; 1982: 58; and 1988: 194–5).

[214] *Ingulph's Chronicle of the Abbey of Croyland* (1893: 495–6).   [215] Wood (1975: 285).

[216] Helmholz (1986: 99) argues that Parliament's assumption of jurisdiction to determine the ques-tion was contrary to English practice as well as canon law at that time.

[217] Quoted in Myers (1981: 144).

authority to legislate with respect to spiritual matters,[218] and at a meeting of leading clergy and lawyers in October 1530, a majority advised Henry VIII that Parliament could not authorize the Archbishop of Canterbury to grant Henry's divorce in the face of papal opposition.[219] Later, doubts were raised in Parliament itself as to its competence to legislate with respect to spiritual matters.[220] In 1536, the conservative lawyer Robert Aske, who helped lead the rebellion known as the Pilgrimage of Grace, which was pledged to defend Roman Catholicism, complained that 'spiritual matters should always be referred to the Convocation house and not discussed in Parliament'.[221] The idea that there existed a human agency with authority to invalidate legislation and other acts of the King, was not expunged until after the 1530s, when the Reformation Parliament transferred supreme authority over the English Church from the Pope to the King. This was the culmination of the expansion of parliamentary authority throughout the previous two centuries. Nevertheless, only thereafter was the King in Parliament 'truly omnicompetent and in manner omnipotent'.[222]

---

[218] Elton (1986: 34), citing Baker (1978: ii. 44 n. 2).

[219] Guy (1985a: 24) and Russell (1997:179).   [220] Elton (1973: 67).

[221] Quoted by Guy (1988: 369), and ibid. 149–52, on the Pilgrimage generally. On the influence of conservative London lawyers, see Elton (1977: 264).

[222] Elton (1977: 199).

4

The Sixteenth Century

1. The Authority of Parliament Extended

Parliament had not acquired full legislative sovereignty by the beginning of the sixteenth century. But this was not because of the medieval belief that human laws are subordinate to God's law. In the absence of any institutional means of enforcing God's law, there is no relevant difference between that belief, and the modern conviction that Parliament is morally bound to act justly. The real reason why Parliament was not yet fully sovereign was the existence of a rival institution, the papacy, which claimed, and was widely acknowledged to possess, an independent and superior authority to enforce God's law, at least with respect to exclusively spiritual matters.

In 1515, the Abbot of Winchcombe asserted that a recently enacted statute, which deprived clerics in minor orders of benefit of clergy, was contrary to the law of God and therefore void, and that the Members of Parliament who had passed it could be punished by the Church under canon law.[1] When Dr Henry Standish publicly defended the validity of the statute, he was summoned to appear before Convocation, the supreme assembly of the Church in England, on a charge of heresy. The charge assumed that, at least in some cases, the authority of canon law was superior to that of statute.[2] At a specially convened conference attended by Henry VIII, his Council, his judges, and both Houses of Parliament, Cardinal Wolsey requested that the controversy be referred to Rome for papal determination. Henry rejected the request, on the ground that 'we are king of England, and the kings of England in time past have never had any superior but God alone'.[3] The clerics who had charged Standish with heresy were threatened by Henry's judges with praemunire, a serious charge of recognizing a foreign (usually papal) jurisdiction inconsistent with that of the Crown, and the proceedings against Standish were then dropped.[4] It had been demonstrated that the only institution in England that was partly independent of the King could challenge the validity of his statutes only by exposing its officials to considerable personal risk.[5] But even that independence was subsequently extinguished, after the Church refused to annul Henry's marriage to Catharine of Aragon.

In 1532, the implicit threat of praemunire helped to induce the 'Submission of the Clergy' to Henry's demand that the Church surrender its legislative

---

[1] Haigh (1993: 81); see also Derrett (1979), Gwyn (1990: 46–51), and Baker (1978: ii. 333–4; 'Introduction').
[2] Haigh (1993: 81–2).   [3] ibid. 82.   [4] ibid. 83.   [5] Derrett (1979: 232, 236–7).

independence. The clergy agreed that all future ecclesiastical legislation would be subject to royal veto, and that all existing canons would be reviewed, and subject to repeal, by royal authority.[6] The Submission cleared the way for the enactment of statutes abolishing papal jurisdiction in England: the clergy had in effect conceded the principle underlying them, since the control of canon law had previously been a matter of papal jurisdiction.[7] In 1533, the Act in Restraint of Appeals declared that England was an 'empire', whose King possessed full and plenary jurisdiction in all causes, both secular and spiritual, and it prohibited appeals to Rome in ecclesiastical matters. In 1534, the Act of Supremacy declared that the King, and not the Pope, was the supreme head of the English Church, and the Treasons Act made any denial of the royal supremacy punishable as high treason. The Act against the Pope's Authority (1536) removed the remnants of papal authority in England, including the right to decide disputed questions of scripture. The Act of Six Articles (1539) went beyond questions of jurisdiction, and legislated upon religious doctrine, imposing heavy penalties for denying six prescribed articles of faith. This Act was doctrinally conservative and consistent with Catholic teachings, but under Edward VI and Elizabeth, Parliament used its newly won authority to prescribe Protestant beliefs and observances, in the Acts of Uniformity of 1549, 1552, and 1559. Tudor Parliaments also dealt with other matters of fundamental constitutional importance, including the succession to the throne.

Maitland dated the sovereignty of Parliament from these radical changes to the fundamental structure of the English Church and State. He concluded that the Tudors 'laid a terrible emphasis upon the enormous powers of parliament—there was nothing that parliament could not do . . . I think that the statesmen of Elizabeth's reign, witness Sir Thomas Smith, had distinctly held that king in parliament was absolutely supreme, above the king and above the law'.[8] For Holdsworth, the practical success of the Reformation Parliament demonstrated that neither the morality of a statute, nor Parliament's motives in enacting it, were matters that ordinary courts could consider. The judges, in effect, admitted this, and 'the last remnants of the idea that there might be fundamental laws, which could not be changed by any person or body of persons in the State, necessarily disappeared'.[9] A. F. Pollard agreed, as have more recent historians.[10] Throughout his long career, Sir Geoffrey Elton, the most eminent recent historian of Tudor government, argued that the Reformation Parliament staged a constitutional revolution by sweeping aside the only remaining limit to its authority, and that

    [6] Haigh (1993: 114–15).   [7] Nicholson (1988: 28–9); Elton (1982: 340–1).
    [8] Maitland (1908: 298), and ibid. 252–5, for more detailed discussion; see text to nn. 75–82, below for the views of Sir Thomas Smith.
    [9] Holdsworth (1946*b*: 65–6).
    [10] Pollard (1926: ch. XI, esp. 226–32). T. F. T. Plucknett says that Henry VIII used 'the omnipotence of the crown in parliament' to cut through papal claims (Plucknett 1960: 285). For disagreement, see Judson (1949: 80–5) and Baumer (1940: 153–63). But Baumer agreed that 'in actual practice' the King in Parliament was 'emancipated from the control of fundamental law': ibid. 154–5. See Chapter 2, text to n. 46, for criticism of Baumer's conception of legislative sovereignty.

for all practical purposes this amounted to an assumption of legislative sovereignty.[11] Although it took some time for theory to catch up with practice, after 1540 'the legislative supremacy and omnipotence of the king-in-parliament remained beyond contesting'.[12]

These developments left unresolved, questions concerning the nature of Parliament and its authority. Parliament was the King in Parliament, but was its authority that of the King alone, which he chose to exercise only in Parliament, or that of a composite institution, the 'King-in-Parliament'? Were statutes made by the King alone, with the assent of his subjects, or by the King, Lords, and Commons exercising a shared legislative power? This issue provoked continuing debate, which contributed to civil war in the 1640s, and was not finally resolved until 1689.[13] But both sides of the debate agreed that no other human institution, including the Church, could authoritatively judge any statute to be invalid. That possibility was eliminated, for all practical purposes, in the 1530s.

Many of those who retained their allegiance to the Pope must have secretly agreed with Sir Thomas More's opinion that the Act of Supremacy was 'directly repugnant to the laws of God and His Holy Church, the supreme government of which, or any part whereof, may no temporal prince presume by any law to take upon him . . .'.[14] But few were willing to follow More's example, and risk their lives by failing to conceal that opinion.[15] When Lord Chancellor Audley asked the judges who tried More for treason whether they agreed that the indictment against him was valid, Lord Chief Justice Fitz James replied equivocally 'that if the Act of Parliament be not unlawful, then is not the indictment in my conscience insufficient'.[16] Nevertheless, the judges proceeded as if the legislation, and therefore the indictment, were valid: More's conviction and execution 'finally and terribly demonstrated the legal omnipotence of the king in Parliament'.[17] The ultimate rule of recognition in any legal system is whatever rule its most senior officials do in fact apply in administering it, as evidenced by their actions and public pronouncements.[18] By enforcing the most radical Reformation statutes, without questioning their legal validity, English judges conceded the authority that the King in Parliament had asserted by enacting them.

Until Mary's reign, Roman Catholic dissenters had little influence in government circles, and therefore their doubts were mostly irrelevant to the nature of the rule of recognition at the foundation of the English Constitution.[19]

---

[11] Elton (1992: esp. at 44–5). See also Elton (1991: 168; 1982: 233 ff., 345; 1986: ch. 2, *passim*), Graves (1985: 4, 78–9, 121, 157), and Baker (1978: ii. 44; 'Introduction').

[12] Elton (1992: 55). On 'theory', see Elton (1982: 14, 236).

[13] See Section 3, below, and Chapter 5, Section 1.

[14] Roper (1935: 92). For examples of others who expressed similar doubts, see Elton (1964: 35).

[15] Elton (1982: 238).

[16] Derrett (1964: 473–4); this incident is reported in Roper (1935: 96).

[17] Baker (1978: ii. 44; 'Introduction').

[18] Hart (1961: 96–107), discussed in Chapter 2, Section 1, and Chapter 10, Section 2.

[19] See text to n. 18, above.

Objections raised in Parliament were quickly suppressed. When some bishops opposed the first Act of Uniformity (1549) in the House of Lords, arguing that Parliament had no authority to alter the traditional mass, most were deprived of office or imprisoned.[20] By 1553, 'there was no substantial body of lay opinion, inside parliament or outside it, which denied the authority of statute law to regulate the affairs of the church'.[21] Moreover, statutes once passed were regarded as binding until formally repealed. Lord Chancellor Gardiner emphasized this point in 1547, when he concluded that new royal edicts concerning Church services were contrary to the Act of Six Articles.[22] Shortly after Mary's accession, Sir James Hales, a judge of the Court of Common Pleas, insisted that the statutes penalizing nonconformity had to be enforced against Roman Catholics until they were formally repealed.[23] In restoring papal jurisdiction in England, Mary herself did not attempt to ignore her father's and brother's statutes dealing with the matter, even though she believed them to be contrary to divine law; instead, she accepted legal advice that they had to be formally repealed.[24] When she explained to a papal emissary that it was necessary 'to repeal and annul by Act of Parliament many perverse laws made by those who ruled before her', she assumed that they were legally valid irrespective of their compatibility with the law of God.[25] This was despite the strong disapproval of her kinsman Reginald Pole, subsequently Cardinal Pole, who insisted that repealing the statutes was unnecessary because they were ultra vires.[26]

When Elizabeth succeeded Mary, she acted on legal advice that only very limited changes to the recently restored Roman Catholic mass could legally be made without Parliament's consent, and she went to great lengths to secure the enactment of statutes reinstating royal supremacy over the Church as well as Protestant doctrines and observances.[27] Opposition within Parliament, which strenuously denied that it could legislate with respect to such matters, succeeded in delaying these reforms, but was eventually overcome and ultimately crushed.[28] At one stage, difficulties in enacting the requisite legislation inspired a proposal that Parliament should simply acquiesce in a unilateral declaration by Elizabeth of her supremacy, but she declined to act without a more positive parliamentary

---

[20] Loades (1979: 42–3).   [21] ibid. See also Loades (1997: 14, 44).

[22] Baumer (1940: 61).

[23] ibid. 189–90. In 1564, Royal Commissioners sent to negotiate a trade agreement with the Low Countries were told to explain to their hosts that 'laws are made in this realm by the assent of three estates, and are not to be made void but with their assent . . . the laws cannot be utterly abrogated without the like authority where with they were made': quoted in N. L. Jones (1995: 227–8).

[24] Elton (1992: 53; and 1982: 238). This point seems to have been first made by Richard Hooker in *Of the Laws of Ecclesiastical Polity* (R. Hooker 1888: iii. 408–9; ch. vi. 11). See also Guy (1993: 29).

[25] Quoted by Loades (1979: 43), and discussed at ibid. 276–7.

[26] Loades (1997: 45, esp. n. 40).

[27] N. L. Jones (1982: 10, 24–5, 46, and chs. 4–6, *passim*).

[28] ibid. 99–100 and 145–6, on the Catholic opposition, and as to its defeat, ibid., chs. 6 and 8, *passim*.

mandate.[29] Further testimony to the transcendent authority of Parliament is the fact that the Act of Uniformity of 1559, unlike its Henrician and Edwardian predecessors, was enacted despite being opposed by Convocation, and without the consent of a single prelate in Parliament.[30] Parliament demonstrated that it could change the religion of the realm regardless of the views of the clergy.

Sometimes radical puritans also denied that Parliament could authoritatively settle questions of Christian faith or practice. They became increasingly disillusioned with what they saw as a failure to reform the Church thoroughly, as scripture required, and some refused to accept the validity of the statutes they condemned as especially deficient.[31] Two of them, Henry Barrow and John Greenwood, were executed in 1587.[32] But in the sixteenth century radical puritans formed a small minority of the population and had little power.[33] They became more numerous and influential in the following century, but, in opposing the High Church policies of Archbishop Laud and Charles I, they also became supporters of Parliament, and many of them then endorsed its claim to legislative sovereignty.[34]

The authority of Tudor Parliaments to govern the succession was seldom disputed. Even Sir Thomas More conceded that Parliament could bestow the Crown at will.[35] Henry VIII's second Act of Succession (1536) declared his daughter Mary to be illegitimate, exercising a function which, with the exception of Richard III's Act of Succession, had previously been left exclusively to ecclesiastical courts.[36] In addition, after entailing the Crown on his future and as yet unborn children, it gave him unprecedented authority to designate a further succession by letters patent or will, unfettered by custom or common law, and to determine the form of government after his death, should his successor be a minor.[37] This has been described as 'a unique demonstration of the virtual omnicompetence now attributed to statute'.[38] The enactment of this statute was one of the grievances of the rebellion of 1536, called the Pilgrimage of Grace. But although the rebels demanded the repeal of the provisions bastardizing Mary, and authorizing Henry to entail the succession by will, they explicitly conceded Parliament's power to regulate the matter.[39] Henry's third and final Act of Succession (1543) reinstated Mary and Elizabeth in the order of succession after Edward and his heirs, ignoring the fact that legally they were still bastards; Parliament apparently presumed that it could order the succession regardless of questions of legitimacy.[40]

---

[29] ibid. 101, 118. On the other hand, it has been argued that Elizabeth made the same claim as her father, and denied that she owed her authority over the Church to Parliament: see Cross (1969: 23), Elton (1982: 343), Guy (1996: 226–7, 236–7; and 1988: 375). Perhaps, as Guy suggests, her advisers took the opposite view, and they prevailed.

[30] N. L. Jones (1982: 150).   [31] J. W. Allen (1928: 214, 230).

[32] Cross (1969: 54–5).   [33] Elton (1982: 443, 445).

[34] The leading example is William Prynne: see Chapter 5, nn. 181 and 373, below.

[35] See n. 71, below, and Chapter 3, n. 124.

[36] Levine (1973: 67). See Chapter 3, text to nn. 213–16, for a discussion of Richard III's statute.

[37] Levine (1973: 67).   [38] ibid.   [39] ibid. 68–9.   [40] ibid. 71.

The only serious challenge to the authority of statute in this respect occurred at the end of Edward VI's brief reign, when he was persuaded to attempt to override his father's final Act of Succession, by issuing letters patent entailing the Crown on Jane Grey and the Suffolk line instead of Mary and Elizabeth.[41] Edward was warned by his judges that a statute could not be repealed by royal decree, and after his death, the rapid collapse of the attempt to install Jane on the throne must have been partly due to its obvious illegality.[42] Mary based her successful claim to succeed not on hereditary right, but on her father's final Act of Succession and will.[43] Moreover, she secured the enactment of a statute to reverse both her bastardization by his second Act of Succession, and the earlier judgment of Archbishop Cranmer's court that her parents' marriage was invalid. Her repealing statute did not cite any ecclesiastical authority, such as the papal decision of 1533 in favour of that marriage, but simply declared that it 'shall be definitively, clearly, and absolutely declared, deemed, and adjudged to be and stand with God's law and His most holy word'.[44] This confirms Mary's acceptance of Parliament's supreme authority in spiritual matters.[45]

The Act of Succession of 1559 expressly based Elizabeth's legal right to the throne on the Act of Succession of 1543.[46] During her reign, it was generally accepted by participants in the interminable debates concerning who should succeed her, including Mary Stuart and her supporters, that Parliament could authoritatively settle the question.[47] Many challenged the validity of Henry VIII's final will, but only on the ground that it was not properly signed; they conceded the validity of the statute that authorized its making.[48] Elizabeth resisted repeated and insistent requests that the succession after her death be firmly settled in advance by Parliament, but not because she doubted its authority to do so. To the contrary, she assented to the Treason Act (1571), which made it high treason to affirm that the Queen, 'with and by the authority of the Parliament of England, is not able to make laws and statutes of sufficient force and validity to limit and bind the crown of this realm and the descent, limitation, inheritance, and government thereof'.[49] Doubting the authority of Parliament was argued to be treasonable because it was tantamount to doubting Elizabeth's own title.[50] In 1584, Lord Burghley and Attorney-General Popham went so far as to prepare a bill providing that, after the Queen's death, the Privy Council should summon a Parliament to determine the succession 'in the form of an act of parliament'. But the idea that a Parliament could lawfully meet and transact business without being summoned, and its Acts assented to, by the Crown, was too much for Elizabeth, who apparently stifled the bill.[51]

---

[41] ibid. 83–4.
[42] ibid. 83–4, 87. One of those judges was Sir James Hales: see Baumer (1940: 174).
[43] Levine (1973: 88, 170).   [44] The statute is set out in ibid. 171, and discussed at ibid. 90.
[45] ibid. 90.   [46] ibid. 98–9, 176; Elton (1986: 175–6).
[47] Levine (1973: ch. 5, *passim*, esp. 109, 110 n. 56, 114 n. 75, 120 n. 91).
[48] ibid. 111–12.   [49] Set out in ibid. 183, and discussed at ibid. 119–20.
[50] Elton (1986: 355).
[51] Guy (1988: 332–3); the background to this bill is discussed by Collinson (1997: 125–9).

As for the authority of statutes to control or diminish the royal prerogative, evidence is scarce, but Elton argues that it must have been accepted. He argues that the prerogative was generally believed to be defined by the common law, which Parliament was free to change.[52] This view was taken, for example, in William Staunford's *An Exposition of the Kinges Prerogative*, written in 1567, and Elton reports that he knows of no decision taken under the Tudors that contradicts it.[53] Not even Elizabeth, who took a high view of her prerogatives, and often shielded them from parliamentary scrutiny, ever suggested that they were beyond the reach of statute.[54] When her prerogative of granting monopolies was threatened by reforms mooted in the House of Commons, the Lord Keeper, Sir Thomas Egerton, told Parliament that the Queen 'hoped that her dutiful and loving subjects would not take away her prerogative, which is the chiefest flower in her garland, and the principal and head pearl in her crown and diadem; but that they will rather leave that to her disposition'.[55] Elton overlooks the Crown's 'absolute' prerogative to override the law in order to preserve the realm in an emergency.[56] This power was not regarded as a creature of common law.[57] Nevertheless, there is no direct evidence that at this time Parliament was regarded as incapable of controlling it. According to Holdsworth, the idea that the Crown possessed certain 'inseparable' prerogatives, which not even Parliament could abolish or restrict, was a development of the early seventeenth century.[58] Before then, there was little reason to doubt Parliament's authority to control the Crown's prerogatives, given that its authority to control the descent of the Crown itself was accepted. In the seventeenth century, Parliament's authority with respect to both matters was often denied, as a consequence of the greater emphasis placed by the Stuart kings on the indefeasibility of their supposedly divine, hereditary rights.

Other examples of Parliament's freedom from limitations can be cited. In 1527, Thomas More's father, Justice John More, firmly denied that Parliament could alter established customs such as gavelkind.[59] That he was mistaken was demonstrated twelve years later, when Parliament passed a statute entitled 'An act for changing the custom of gavelkind'.[60] Sir Edward Coke reported that Henry VIII once asked his judges if Parliament could attaint a man without allowing him to defend himself, and that they reluctantly admitted that if it did so, 'it could not come into question afterwards'. Coke conceded that their opinion 'was according to law', and that when such an Act was passed, it 'did bind, as they resolved'.[61]

---

[52] Elton (1986: 37–8; and 1972: 270–7).
[53] (London, 1567), fol. 5, quoted in Elton (1972: 271), and discussed at ibid. 271–5.
[54] Elton (1986: 37–8).
[55] S. D'Ewes, *Journals of All the Parliaments . . . of Queen Elizabeth* (1682), 547, quoted by Gough (1962: 88).
[56] Guy (1992: 66–7).   [57] ibid.
[58] Holdsworth (1903–72: iv. 205–6); see also Holdsworth (1921: 560).
[59] Elton (1986: 35), citing *Spelman's Reports* (ii. 44–5).
[60] Baker (1978: ii. 44; 'Introduction'), and Elton (1986: 35), citing 31 Henry VIII c. 3.
[61] Coke (1644: 37–8); for the events which Coke may have been reporting, see Pickthorn (1934*b*: 431–3).

This is confirmed by a statement of the Court of Queen's Bench, in 1571, that a writ of error was normally available with respect to a judgment of treason, but not if the judgment were confirmed by Act of Attainder: 'that which is confirmed by Parliament is made indefeasible, although it were defeasible before'; the Act 'takes away all error that was in the attainder'.[62] According to another report of the same case, 'a recital in an Act of Parliament is an estoppel to all men'.[63] Finally, the Reformation Parliament frequently overrode title to property, which was universally regarded as one of the most precious and inviolable of all the rights that subjects possessed. Elton argues that this 'came as near as no matter to asserting omnicompetence, a universal claim to obedience, and therefore full legislative sovereignty'.[64] The Statute of Uses in 1536, and the Statute of Wills in 1540, brought about a fundamental change to the law of real property.[65] Parliament also enacted legislation appropriating the lands of the monasteries. Even Charles McIlwain agreed that '[t]he act of 1536 transferring to the King the lands of the lesser monasteries . . . seems the most revolutionary act in the whole statute book, without clear precedent before 1536. More clearly than any other single act, it seems to mark the transition from medieval to modern notions of Parliament's powers and functions'.[66]

As David Loades has put it, '[i]n theory it was still possible to challenge a statute on the grounds that it transgressed some fundamental or divine law, but in practice such a possibility had become unreal'.[67] This was partly because the King in Parliament now prescribed not only the ecclesiastical organization and sacraments of the Church in England, but also its fundamental doctrines. It had become the 'High Court for the definition of Christian faith', with supreme authority to interpret scripture, and therefore the requirements of divine law.[68] How could divine law possibly be pleaded against it?

2. The Supremacy of Parliament Recognized

Parliament's supremacy was often commented on in the sixteenth century. In 1542, Henry VIII declared that 'we be informed by our judges, that we at no time stand so highly in our estate royal, as in the time of Parliament', whose prerogative 'is so great (as our learned counsel informs us) as all acts and processes coming out of any other inferior courts must for the time [being] cease and give place to the highest'.[69] It is significant that his judges and learned counsel gave him

---

[62] *The Earl of Leicester v Heydon* (1571) 1 Plowden 384, 594; 75 E.R. 582, 597.

[63] Baker (1994: i. 191).

[64] Elton (1982: 237). The 'therefore' may be a *non sequitur*, as Burgess (1996: 179 n. 68) suggests, but Elton's point is still clear. On the importance of the right to property, see Judson (1949: 35–6), and Sommerville (1986: 145–60).

[65] Buck (1990: 214).   [66] McIlwain (1942: 148).

[67] Loades (1979: 43). For agreement, see Williams (1979: 34; and 1995: 136).

[68] J. W. Allen (1928: 179).   [69] Quoted in Lehmberg (1977: 170).

that advice. Thomas Audley, Lord Chancellor from 1533 until 1544, is reported
to have said 'that he never knew or read of any act of Parliament in this realm
broken till the same had been by like authority of Parliament repealed'.[70] The
attitude of Henry's lawyers is conveyed in a well-known passage in Roper's biography of Sir Thomas More, recording an exchange between More and Sir Richard
Rich, the King's solicitor. According to Roper, Rich asked whether, if an Act
of Parliament declared that he, Rich, was King, More would accept that he was
King. More replied that he would, conceding that Parliament could control the
succession to the throne. Rich then asked whether More would also accept an
Act of Parliament declaring that Rich was the Pope, but More responded by
asking whether Parliament could declare that God was not God.[71] Although
Rich agreed with More that Parliament could not go that far, his position is consistent with the modern understanding of parliamentary sovereignty, which is that
Parliament can do anything except that which is impossible, such as changing a
man into a woman. More himself, in his *The History of Richard III*, had earlier
described the authority of Parliament as 'supreme and absolute' in England.[72]

The Act of Dispensations (1534) declared that:

In all and every such laws human made within this Realm . . . your Royal Majesty and
your Lords Spiritual and temporal and Commons, representing the whole state of your
Realm in this your most high Court of Parliament, have full power and authority . . . the
said laws . . . to abrogate annul amplify or diminish . . .[73]

Elton comments that this 'could hardly have expressed more plainly the principle of an absolute legislative power vested in the tripartite Parliament and
extended to all spiritual as well as secular concerns'.[74]

Between 1562 and 1565, Sir Thomas Smith, a statesman and civil lawyer
who served as Master of Requests under Edward VI, wrote in *De Republica
Anglorum* that '[b]y order and usage of England there is three ways and manners, whereby absolute and definite judgment is given', and that 'by Parliament . . . is the highest and most absolute'.[75] In Parliament, '[t]he most high and
absolute power of the realm of England', the prince, with the consent of the
whole realm, gives 'the last and highest commandment', which 'is called firm,
stable and *sanctum* [sacred], and is taken for law. The Parliament abrogates old
laws, makes new, gives orders for things past and for things hereafter to be followed, changes rights and possessions of private men, . . . establishes forms of
religion, . . . gives forms of succession to the Crown'; 'to be short, all that ever
the people of Rome might do either in *Centuriatis commitiis* or *tributis*, the
same may be done by the Parliament of England, which represents and has the

---

[70] S. Gardiner (1933: 369–70).
[71] Roper (1935: 84–6); this book was written during the reign of Mary I, sometime before 1557: ibid., p. xlv.
[72] More (1963–87: ii. 6, line 14) ('*summa atque absoluta*').
[73] 25 Henry VIII, c. 21 (1534), quoted in Elton (1974e: 233).
[74] Elton (1992: 48).   [75] Sir T. Smith (1583: 64; 2nd bk., ch. 5).

power of the whole realm, both the head and the body'.[76] What Parliament does 'is the Prince's and whole realm's deed: whereupon justly no man can complain, but must accommodate himself to find it good and obey it'.[77]

It used to be argued that Smith was not asserting any kind of legislative sovereignty. Leonard Alston, in his introduction to the 1906 edition of *De Republica*, maintained that Smith meant only that Parliament was the highest court in the land, whose judgments were not subject to appeal, an interpretation endorsed by McIlwain.[78] But Maitland disagreed, as did Pollock and Holdsworth, and more recent historians have almost all followed suit.[79] Elton asserts that it is now 'certain' that Smith was referring to legislative sovereignty, and in doing so was expressing 'a commonplace of Tudor political thinking and experience'.[80] Smith was much more aware than earlier legal theorists, such as Fortescue, of the phenomenon of social and economic change, and the need for legislative responses to it. In *De Republica*, Smith observed that 'never in all points one commonwealth does agree with another, no nor long time any one commonwealth with itself. For all changes continually . . . and the mutability of men's wits does invent and essay new ways, to reform and amend that wherein they do find fault.'[81] Arthur Ferguson observes that Smith's recognition of the need for legal change is even clearer in his *Discourse of the Common Weal*: '[i]n that enlarged context, government becomes a positive thing . . . capable of establishing policy . . . and, when necessary, of translating policy into law by statute', and 'unlimited authority to meet change with change had for practical purposes to reside somewhere'.[82]

In 1587, William Harrison inserted into his *Description of England* a new chapter, entitled 'Of the High Court of Parliament and Authority of the Same', in which he stated that it 'has the most high and absolute power of the realm, for thereby kings and mighty princes have from time to time been deposed from their thrones, laws either enacted or abrogated, offenders of all sorts punished, and corrupted religion either disannulled or reformed'.[83]

The second edition of *Holinshed's Chronicles*, to which Harrison contributed, appeared in the same year. It included the statement that

in such decrees (established by the authority of the Prince, the Lords Spiritual and Temporal, and the Commons of this realm thus assembled in Parliament) consists the whole force of our English laws. Which decrees are called statutes, meaning by that name, that the same should stand firm and stable, and not be repealed without the consent of another Parliament, and that upon good and great consideration.[84]

---

[76] Ibid. 48–9; 2nd bk., ch. 1.   [77] ibid.

[78] 'Introduction' to Sir T. Smith (1583, pp. xxvii–xxxiv); McIlwain (1910: 124–30).

[79] Maitland (1908: 254–5, 298); Pollock (1907: 221–2) (a particularly scathing rebuttal of Alston's thesis); Pollock (1929: 262–5, esp. 263); Holdsworth (1903–72: iv. 182–4, 211 n. 5). See also Pollock (1894: 244–5). Alston's argument is rejected by Hinton (1960: 419–20), Dewar (1982: 4), and Ferguson (1965: 387–91, esp. 390–1), but accepted by Burgess (1996: 179).

[80] Elton (1981: 95 n. 3).   [81] Sir T. Smith (1583: 33; 1st bk., ch. 18).

[82] Ferguson (1965: 388, 390).

[83] W. Harrison, *Description of England* (1587), i. 291, quoted in Patterson (1994: 103).

[84] Holinshed (1807: ii. 66).

The great Elizabethan statesman, Lord Burghley, is said to have often remarked that 'he knew not what an Act of Parliament could not do in England',[85] and that it could turn a man into a woman.[86] The anonymous author of *A Discourse upon the Exposicion & Understandinge of Statutes* (probably Sir Thomas Egerton, later Lord Chancellor Ellesmere) wrote that '[t]he most ancient court and of greatest authority is the king's high court of Parliament, the authority of which is absolute and binds all manner of persons'.[87] The distinguished antiquary William Camden stated that it 'has the sovereign and sacred authority in making, confirming, repealing and expounding laws . . . in all causes which may concern either the state or any private person whatsoever'.[88]

In 1578, James Morice, an influential parliamentarian who was considered one of the best lawyers of his day, wrote that the King in Parliament 'has authority to make new laws or ordinances touching the life, lands, goods or inheritances of the subjects', an authority which 'ever have been in all civil policies . . . appertaining to such as have sovereign rule and possess chief authority in the realm'.[89] Henry Wotton is reputed to have said in 1594 that although princes could be 'constrained to submit themselves' to the High Court of Parliament, 'it cannot justly or truly be said, that that is against a law or without law which is done by an high Court of Parliament, from whence all or most laws have their beginning, their foundation, their strength'.[90] In the same period, Arthur Agarde, a Deputy Chamberlain in the Exchequer and founding member of the Society of Antiquaries, stated that 'of such force is an act of Parliament here in the governance of the state of the realm, that it is deemed as an oracle from heaven, and rests only in the kings and queens power to qualify and mitigate the severity thereof [by use of the dispensing power]'.[91]

William Lambarde wrote during the 1590s that

the judgment of our Parliament [is] of as ample authority, as the sentence of any, or all other courts whatsoever; for it delivers laws, that do bind all persons, in all causes, as well ecclesiastical, as temporal . . . It has also jurisdiction in such cases which have need of help, and for which there is no help by any law, already in force; and whereas the erroneous judgments of any other courts must be reversed by a higher authority; this court does not only reverse the errors of the King's Bench, which is superior to all the other;

---

[85] James VI and I (1994: 209).

[86] Russell (1997: 235–6). He probably meant that Parliament could require a man to be treated as a woman for legal purposes. In the late seventeenth century, Burghley was reputed to have said that Parliament could do anything except turn a man into a woman: Sidney (1704: 412).

[87] Thorne (1942: 108). Egerton is identified as the author of this text by Plucknett (1944: 244–5).

[88] *Britannia* (1586), 83, quoted by Elton (1986: 22).

[89] J. Morice, *Readings on the Statute of Westminster the First* (1578), quoted by Mosse (1968: 17). The high estimation of Morice is that of Guy (1995c: 132).

[90] *The State of Christendom [etc.]* (London, 1657, but written in 1594), 205 and 207, quoted by Sommerville (1983: 243–4). It is generally thought that the author was Henry Wotton (1568–1639), but this remains unproven: ibid., 243.

[91] Thomas Hearne (ed.), *A Collection of Curious Discourses* (London, 1775: i. 304), quoted in Peck (1993: 97).

but it may also amend the errors committed in the Parliament itself, if any such shall at any time appear.[92]

McIlwain comments on this passage that 'the great antiquary and legal writer' clearly regarded Parliament mainly as a court, and did not separate its legislative from its judicial functions.[93] But although Lambarde regarded Parliament as a 'court' in the sixteenth century sense, he plainly did not regard it as a court in our modern sense.[94] He pointed out that the English Parliament's French counterpart was the 'Assembly des Estates', and not the 'parlements', which were 'but ordinary courts of justice'.[95] He emphasized the English Parliament's law-making function, explaining that it 'is summoned to devise laws, both ecclesiastical, civil, criminal, and martial, it ministers the matter whereupon all the rest of the courts do work, and it has in some cases, an ordinary jurisdiction also'.[96] Moreover, he attempted to disprove, at great length, the suggestion 'that these estates were called together more for their advice and counsel to be given to the King, than for any authority or interest they had in making the law',[97] leading to the conclusion, in the long passage quoted, that Parliament was of such high authority precisely because 'it delivers laws that do bind all persons'.[98] The significance of McIlwain's comment is in any event obscure, given his acknowledgement that, in Lambarde's day, 'courts' were agencies of government that often exercised a fusion of judicial, legislative, and administrative powers, and that the words 'jurisdiction' and 'judgment' were understood accordingly.[99]

In 1594, the prominent parliamentarian Peter Wentworth wrote that Parliament was 'most sacred, most ample and large and has prerogatives and preeminences far above any Court whatsoever, which is established by God under the heavens'. It was 'the Court of most pure and exquisite judgment', 'appointed by God, as the power next to himself to reform and redress wrongs and outrages which can not be helped by any other means'. He acknowledged that it was limited by 'justice and equity', but said that the remedy for any transgression lay in its accountability to God.[100] One of the limits that he believed was imposed by justice and equity was the future James I's divine hereditary right of succession, which Wentworth described as 'impregnable by any Parliament'.[101] He criticized those of the contrary opinion, who 'stand so precisely for the absolute power and sovereignty' of Parliament, as opportunists who would change their minds if Parliament named as King someone not to their liking.[102] But J. E. Neale

---

[92] Lambarde (1957: 140–1). The text was completed in 1591: see ibid., p. vii.

[93] McIlwain (1910: 124).   [94] See also Chapter 3, Section 3.

[95] Lambarde (1957: 123).   [96] ibid.   [97] ibid. 129.

[98] Ibid. 140, quoted at n. 92, above.

[99] On 'court', see McIlwain (1910: 29–30, 119–20, 134–6, 197–8); on 'jurisdiction' and 'judgment', ibid. 169–72, 195.

[100] P. Wentworth, *A Discourse containing the Author's Opinion of the True and Lawful Successor to Her Majestie* (1594), quoted by Neale (1924: 289).

[101] Wentworth, *A Discourse*, quoted by Allen (1928: 258).

[102] Wentworth, *A Discourse*, quoted by Neale (1924: 290).

suggests that Wentworth's own position was opportunist, and inconsistent with his general political philosophy.[103] He had previously been the most outspoken advocate of a parliamentary settlement of the succession, and an opponent of the claim of Mary Stuart, James's mother; only after her execution was he converted to her son's cause.[104] In any event, it is clear that 'the absolute power and sovereignty' of Parliament was a popular doctrine.[105]

3. Two Theories of the Authority of Parliament

Despite general agreement as to the supreme authority of the King in Parliament, there were two different kinds of theories of its nature and source.[106] According to theories of the first kind, statutes were made by the King alone, albeit with the advice and consent of the Lords and Commons in Parliament, and the High Court of Parliament possessed absolute authority because it was the King's highest seat of judgment. The Houses of Parliament merely assisted the King in his exercise of law-making power, which was conferred on him by God and not by the community. According to theories of the second kind, statutes were made by the King, Lords, and Commons in Parliament as, in effect, three partners sharing the legislative power, whose absolute authority was due to their collectively representing the entire community.[107] For convenience, I will call theories of the first kind royalist theories, and those of the second, parliamentarian theories. I refer to kinds of theories because there were different versions of each, some more extreme than others.

Henry VIII and some of his leading clerics subscribed to royalist theories, but other influential supporters of his reforms, such as Thomas Cromwell, Thomas Audley, and Christopher St German, subscribed to parliamentarian theories.[108] Consequently there was, as J. J. Scarisbrick puts it, an 'ideological ambiguity in the core of Henricianism': 'English monarchy was, so to speak, amphibious; a creature of man and God; *"politicum et regale"*; a *via media* which held in unity the opposed principles of Divine Right and the populist doctrines of thoroughgoing Aristotelians' (who held that political authority derived from the community).[109] Many apologists for the royal supremacy, such as Stephen Gardiner, prudently adopted both theories, a position that has been compared with

---

[103] Neale (1924: 290). Wentworth's understanding of Parliament's authority over the succession is discussed by Nenner (1995: 11, 14–15, 32, 55–6, 63).

[104] Neale (1957: 262).

[105] The question of Parliament's authority with respect to the royal succession is discussed at nn. 35–50, above.

[106] Baumer (1940: 57–62).   [107] Elton (1992: 46–57; 1974d: 210–13).

[108] Elton (1992: 43–56), Guy (1988: 133–4, 233, 370–5; and 1993: 26–9). See also Slavin (1992: 226–7), Skinner (1978: ii. 95, 104). The writings of Gardiner and other clerics are discussed in Figgis (1922: 93–9).

[109] Scarisbrick (1968: 393–4). See also Guy (1997b: 88–9).

'someone who fits two locks, each by a different manufacturer, to his front door. The locks have incompatible mechanisms and different keys, but when used in combination they double the level of security!'[110] The combination undoubtedly helped to strengthen the authority of Tudor statutes: who could question the validity of laws enacted by both the representative of God on earth and the representatives of the entire community?[111] Indeed, it seems likely that this dualism was 'due less either to confusion or latent theoretical disagreement between the chief architects of nationhood than to the fact that both theories, if carefully manipulated, could be rendered ideologically serviceable'.[112] But it did involve a tension between the two theories, which continued through the sixteenth and into the seventeenth century.[113] According to Scarisbrick, 'the crux of English politics' was to satisfy the proponents of both, to prevent the potential disagreement between them from emerging into the open and escalating into conflict.[114] A century after the Henrician Reformation, when the disagreements between Charles I and his House of Commons became irreconcilable, the two theories were split apart, and a choice had to be made between them. The 'little-understood mythic accommodation that the English called "King-in-Parliament"', says Gordon Schochet, 'was a fused bomb waiting to be ignited'.[115]

The primary motivation behind both royalist and parliamentarian theories was religious. In his classic study of the theory of the divine right of kings, Figgis argued that it was promoted in sixteenth century England in order to defend the English Reformation against both Roman Catholic and Presbyterian opposition.[116] His argument should be extended to include, *mutatis mutandis*, parliamentarian theories of sovereignty in England.[117] To counteract the claims of dissident clerics that the new ecclesiastical arrangements were contrary to the law of God, it was necessary to assert that either the King, or the community, or both in tandem, possessed a divine authority superior to that of any clerical organization, even with respect to religion. Furthermore, that authority had to be complete and absolute, or the dissidents' claims would find a foothold. As J. C. D. Clark observes, 'it was the headship of the Church which gave a peculiar sanctity to the monarchy . . . [and] which proved ideologically effective against the right of rebellion which continued to threaten the Roman law monarchies of continental Europe'.

Whether the Church was henceforth ruled by a caesaropapist monarchy or by the King-in-Parliament, the sovereignty of the kingdom was sanctified by the Church; and whether

---

[110] Guy (1997*b*: 89).

[111] Elton (1974*d*: 210, 213) agrees that statute law was based on both the divine right of the King and the common consent of the realm: 'it carried both common consent and executive sanction— was both "norm" and "command". By anybody's standard, the Tudor king-in-Parliament was a true sovereign'. See also Eccleshall (1978: 39–43).

[112] Eccleshall (1978: 33–4 n. 1).   [113] Guy (1985*b*: 22).

[114] Scarisbrick (1968: 394, 397), and D. L. Smith (1994: 19–20). See also Dunham (1964: 56).

[115] Schochet (1992: 10).   [116] Figgis (1922: 90–2, 100, 196–208, 257–63).

[117] At ibid. 91–2 and 257, Figgis denies this, but not convincingly given the evidence examined below.

Henry VIII's caesaropapist version of the monarchy was in the ascendant, as under the Stuarts, or Christopher St German's and Thomas Cromwell's model of the King-in-Parliament, as after 1660, the Church of England equally credited the sovereign power with a divine (though differently limited) mandate.[118]

Royalist theories were not necessarily incompatible with parliamentary sovereignty.[119] It was possible for theories which held that the King alone was sovereign, but also, as Henry VIII conceded, 'at his highest' in Parliament, to recognize no limits to the sovereignty of the King in Parliament, other than those inherent in the illimitable and inalienable nature of his sovereignty.[120]

4. Royalist Theories

According to royalist theories, the King of England within his 'empire' possessed the same authority as the Emperor Constantine, including the *plenitudo potestatis* in spiritual matters that had previously been claimed on behalf of the Pope.[121] The King controlled the laws, courts, appointments, revenues, and doctrines of the English Church.[122] His supremacy was conferred by God, not Parliament: statutes were required merely to ensure that it could be enforced in the secular courts, for example, through the statutory recognition of new forms of treason.[123]

The King's authority was admittedly subordinate to divine law, but no human agency was authorized to enforce that law against him. As God's vice-regent on earth, his authority to interpret God's law was superior to that of all but God himself, and he was therefore accountable for any error or abuse of his powers only to God. Henry VIII himself declared that '[b]y the ordinance and sufferance of God we are king of England, and the kings of England in time past have never had any superior but God alone'.[124] The preamble to the Act of Appeals claimed that the King was 'furnished by the goodness and sufferance of Almighty God with plenary, whole and entire power, preeminence, authority, prerogative and jurisdiction'.[125] This authority was believed to extend to the interpretation of scripture. In 1545, Henry advised Parliament that '[i]f you know surely that a bishop or a preacher errs or teaches perverse doctrine, come and declare it to some of our council or to us, to whom is committed by God the high authority to reform and order such causes and behaviour: be not judges yourselves'.[126] He exercised his authority to define doctrine on several occasions, acting with the advice of his clergy and without the participation of Parliament: the Act of Six Articles (1539) was enacted to help enforce the royal will, by imposing criminal penalties on dissenters.[127]

[118] Clark (1994: 78–9).   [119] Contra Guy (1988: 371).   [120] See n. 69, above.
[121] Elton (1974*d*: 201–2; 1992: 44); see also Chapter 2, text to nn. 56–8.
[122] Elton (1982: 341–2).
[123] Elton (1992: 44–5; and 1982: 242–3), quoting St German in *Doctor and Student* (*c*.1528).
[124] Quoted by Guy (1993: 24–5).   [125] Quoted by Elton (1982: 353).
[126] Quoted by Allen (1928: 164–5).   [127] Elton (1982: 396).

The *Collectanea satis copiosa*, a collection of biblical passages, precedents, and other historical evidence, compiled in order to justify royal supremacy over the Church, stood Bracton on his head by asserting that the king was 'under God but not the law, because the king makes the law'.[128] Henry himself once told the Irish that 'of our absolute power we be above the laws'.[129] He boasted to Thomas Cranmer that he recognized 'no superior in earth but only God', and that he was not 'subject to the laws of any earthly creature'.[130] In a very influential book published in 1528, William Tyndale took this view to extreme lengths when he said that 'God has made the King in every realm judge over all, and over him is there no judge. He that judges the King judges God . . . [t]he King is, in this world, without law; and may at his lust do right or wrong, and shall give accounts but to God only'.[131] Although many contemporaries would have found this way of expressing the point too blunt, they would have conceded that the King's power was 'self-limiting' in the sense that he was subject only to the 'directive', and not the 'coercive', power of law.[132] At the time, that kind of moral constraint, reinforced by religion and tradition, was no doubt 'much more powerful than we can easily imagine' in preventing abuses of power.[133] Nevertheless, it was perfectly consistent with the existence of legal sovereignty in our sense of the term.

The English remembered the civil wars of the fifteenth century, and feared the possible consequences of conflicting religious loyalties at a time when foreign invasion on behalf of the Pope was a constant threat. Consequently, the governing classes yearned for order and stability. 'All through the [sixteenth] century', says J. W. Allen, 'one finds people expatiating on the horrors that follow rebellion'.[134] Widespread agreement that the anarchy which rebellion could unleash was worse than tyranny led to a repudiation of political theories which held that rulers could in some circumstances legitimately be resisted.[135] According to Allen, this repudiation was 'axiomatic' among 'thinking Englishmen of the sixteenth century'. There was 'little question that obedience was always due, except when it conflicted with positive commands of God', and even then, the ruler could be disobeyed but not actively resisted: any punishment imposed had to be passively accepted.[136] No one had the right to judge that the ruler's

[128] Quoted by Guy (1988: 371).   [129] Quoted by Elton (1974*b*: 32).
[130] *State Papers Published under the Authority of His Majesty's Commission, King Henry VIII* (London, 1830–52: i. 392), quoted by Dunham (1964: 34).
[131] Tyndale (1848: 177–8).
[132] Daly (1979*a*: 30, 26). For the medieval origins of that distinction, see Chapter 2, text to n. 63, and Greenleaf (1964: 47–8).
[133] Daly (1979*a*: 29–31).
[134] Allen (1928: 129); see also Baumer (1940: ch. 4, esp. 86–8, 91, 106).
[135] William Tyndale, for example, argued that '[i]t is better to suffer one tyrant than many, and to suffer wrong of one than of every man. . . . For a tyrant, though he do wrong to the good, yet he punishes the evil, and makes all men obey . . . A king that is as soft as silk, and effeminate . . . shall be much more grievous to the realm than a right tyrant' (Tyndale 1848: 180). This was one reason why he held the extreme view of monarchical authority previously noted (text to n. 131).
[136] Allen (1928: 130, 128), and see ibid. 127–31 generally. See also Williams (1979: 351–9), and Hanson (1970: 253).

actions should be resisted, neither ordinary subjects, nor any class of subordinate officials.

Under Henry VIII it is constantly and emphatically declared that such rights of rule and jurisdiction as are possessed by subordinate magistrates or by landlords, are rights created by the King or by the law. 'They rule but by law', wrote Cheke; 'if otherwise, the Law, the Council, the King takes away their rule ... There can be no just execution of laws, reformation of faults, giving out of commandments, but from the King. For in the King only is the right hereof, and the authority of him derived by his appointment to his ministers.'[137]

Cheke wrote these words well before Bodin insisted that 'all power and authority to command' derives from the prince, who at any time 'can revoke all the power of his magistrates,' and therefore cannot be subject to any 'right of jurisdiction'.[138] The status of subordinate officials and judges was later described in the same terms by Richard Hooker, although he subscribed to a parliamentarian rather than a royalist theory. Given that the 'kings of England are within their own dominions the most high, and can have no peer', he asked, 'how is it possible that any, either civil or ecclesiastical person under them should have over them coercive power, when such power would make that person so far forth his superior's superior, ruler and judge?'[139]

5. Parliamentarian Theories

Parliamentarian theories held that the King in Parliament, representing the entire community, possessed a law-making authority that was legally supreme and beyond challenge. Elton has suggested that Thomas Cromwell, the principal architect of the Henrician Reformation, was a follower of the fourteenth century political philosopher Marsiglio of Padua.[140] Marsiglio had opposed the papacy's claim to possess a sovereign power superior to that of temporal rulers, and attempted to prove the opposite, that the authority of the Pope and clergy was subordinate to that of the state.[141] Moreover, he maintained that the source of the state's authority was the citizenry, who also constituted the whole body of the faithful—of the Church within their community—and therefore had ultimate authority in spiritual as well as temporal matters.[142] Marsiglio's ideas must have seemed almost tailor-made for Cromwell's programme of amalgamating State and Church in England, by parliamentary statutes to which the community supposedly

[137] Allen (1928: 130), quoting Sir John Cheke, tutor to Edward VI, in *The Hurt of Sedition: How Grievous it is to a Commonwealth, or The True Subject to the Rebel* (1549).
[138] Bodin (1992: bk. II, ch. 5, 115).
[139] *Of the Laws of Ecclesiastical Polity*, in R. Hooker (1888: iii. 455; bk. VIII, ch. ix, 6).
[140] Elton (1974e: 228–30). See also Stout (1974).   [141] Watt (1988: 416–21).
[142] ibid.; Quillet (1988: 558–61); Black (1988: 577); Lewis (1954: i. 25–7, 155–6, 159, 255–7, and ii. 391, 540–5.)

assented.[143] In 1535, Cromwell financed the publication of an English translation of Marsiglio's *Defensor Pacis* (first published in Italy in 1324), in which parts of the original were amended or omitted because they contradicted royal propaganda.[144] In attributing law-making power to the people, Marsiglio was represented as speaking 'not of the rascal multitude but of the Parliament': 'the lawmaker or chief and proper cause effective of the law is the people . . . by their election or will by words expressed in the general congregation Parliament . . .'.[145]

Marsiglio also tended towards a positivist conception of law, and is said to have come closer than any other medieval writer to a theory of legislative sovereignty.[146] He analysed human law in terms of legislative will and coercive sanction, and suggested that neither divine nor ecclesiastical law were, properly speaking, law at all, because the former had effect only in the next world, and the latter lacked coercive sanction. He therefore conceded the legal validity of unjust laws.[147] Cromwell, too, spoke dismissively of the relevance of divine law to legal affairs in England, and appears to have believed that Parliament possessed legislative sovereignty.[148]

The English did not need Marsiglio to tell them that the people were represented in Parliament. Even in the fifteenth century, it was widely believed that all members of the community were present in Parliament, either in person or by proxy, and therefore were 'privy and parties' to its decisions.[149] That idea became a commonplace during the sixteenth century.[150] Sir Thomas Smith said that in Parliament 'every English man is understood to be there present . . . [a]nd the consent of Parliament is taken to be every man's consent',[151] and similar statements can be found in the writings of Christopher St German, Thomas Egerton (later Lord Ellesmere), William Lambarde, John Hooker, Francis Bacon, and Richard Hooker, among others.[152] Peter Wentworth put the point succinctly by describing Parliament as 'the mouth of all England'.[153] In *Chudleigh's* case (1595), Chief Justice Popham argued that, for this reason, Parliament's authority was superior to that of any judge: 'the statute itself . . . is of greater authority than

---

[143] On Marsiglio's likely influence, see Baumer (1940: 53, esp. n. 57). Pollard (1926: 223) says that Marsiglio 'provided Cromwell [and his successors] . . . with the best part of their programme'.

[144] Lockwood (1991: 89–90).

[145] ibid. 95–6. Marsiglio's text was also changed to remove any suggestion that in exercising his executive powers, the King was subordinate to the people and subject to correction. The translation attributed supreme coercive jurisdiction to the King, who could do no wrong, rather than to the people: ibid. 97–100.

[146] Lewis (1954: i. 30).

[147] Canning (1988: 460–1); cf. Lewis (1954: i. 17, 20, 30, 217–18).

[148] Elton (1974e: 216–17, 232–5).   [149] Elton (1982: 236).

[150] Williams (1995: 135).   [151] Sir T. Smith (1583: 49; 2nd bk. ch. 1).

[152] St German (1974: 279); Egerton, in Thorne (1942: 108); Lambarde (1957: 126); J. Hooker (1977: 182); F. Bacon, *A Brief Discourse upon the Commission of Bridewell* (1587), in Bacon (1858–74: vii. 509); R. Hooker, in the text to n. 197, below. See also the speech of Elizabeth I, in Hartley (1981: i. 94). For other expressions of this old idea, see Elton (1974b: 36–7), and Baker (1978: ii. 44 n. 4; 'Introduction').

[153] Quoted in Nenner (1995: 56).

the particular opinion or conceit of any judge whomsoever, for it is the judgment of all the judges, and all the realm also, which ought to bind all, and to which all ought to give credit'.[154] (It was a 'judgment of all the judges' because they were required to attend, and advise, Parliament.)[155]

It is worth noting that although the claim that medieval parliaments represented the whole community may seem absurd, when measured by our standards, they did provide reasonable representation of the 'political nation', comprised of those with sufficient social standing to play an active role in the politics and government of the day.[156] Compared with other European states, the English political nation was extremely large, and the House of Commons by far the largest representative assembly, both absolutely and in proportion to population.[157] It should also be noted that the Elizabethans' conception of representation differed from ours: they thought that members of the Commons gave consent on behalf of those *for* whom, rather than *by* whom, they were sent. Supposedly elected for their superior wisdom, they were to be guided by their own judgments, after full discussion in Parliament, rather than by the preferences of those they represented.[158]

It was because of this belief that Parliament represented every subject in the realm that it could, in effect, override title to property. The right of subjects to their property was regarded as inviolable, but they were free to consent to its transfer. The fiction that the consent of Parliament was tantamount to the consent of every subject meant that property rights could be transferred or altered by the King in Parliament, but not by the King alone.[159] It seems not to have been feared that Parliament would unjustly violate those rights, because every member of Parliament owned property.[160] In the reign of Edward VI, Chief Justice Montague justified the way in which the Statute of Uses altered property rights by reasoning that 'when a gift is made by Parliament, every person in the realm is privy to it, and assents to it, but yet the thing shall pass from him that has the most right and authority to give it'.[161]

The notion that taxation was only lawful if the 'common consent' of the realm was obtained in Parliament was almost universally accepted from at least the mid-fifteenth century onwards. Sir John Fortescue stated that the King could not impose any burdens on his subjects 'without the concession or assent of his

---

[154] *Dillon v Fraine* (1595) *Popham's Reports* 70, 79; 79 E.R. 1184, 1192 (reported as *Chudleigh's* case in 1 *Coke's Reports* 120a; 76 E.R. 270).

[155] Jay (1994).   [156] Elton (1974b: 47, 58–9); Sommerville (1983: 95).

[157] Elton (1972: 290).

[158] N. L. Jones (1995: 230, 236–7, 242). See also Sacks (1992: 86–93).

[159] Wormuth (1939: 12–14); Judson (1949: 35, 39 n. 81, 80 n. 40); Mosse (1968: 24, 85–6, 101–6).

[160] In the seventeenth century, Oliver St John explained that Parliament was 'fittest for the preservation of that fundamental propriety which the subject has in his lands and goods, because each subject's vote is included in whatsoever is there done': S. R. Gardiner (1906: 114).

[161] *Wimbish v Tailbois* (c.1533) 1 Plowden 39, 59; 75 E.R. 63, 95. Although Montague depicts the statute as a piece of conveyancing, rather than as genuine legislation, on another occasion, he clearly thought of Parliament as a legislator with respect to rights in land (Elton 1964: 39). See also Lampson (1941).

whole realm expressed in his Parliament'.[162] As Sir George Croke put it in 1638, the common law required that property not be taken from subjects 'without their consent, (that is to say their private actual consent or implicity in Parliament)'.[163] If this was true of property rights, why not of other rights as well? Indeed, the concept of proprietary right was sometimes applied to the law as a whole: Sir Edward Coke said that 'the law and custom of England is the inheritance of the subject, which he cannot be deprived of without his assent in Parliament'.[164] As Charles Gray explains, 'Englishmen were encouraged to think of their legal rights as heirlooms of guaranteed value, which they *could* consent to part with, but hardly would except in small ways and on very good consideration'.[165]

The notion that everyone was represented in Parliament was widely held to ensure that its decisions embodied not only the consent but also the combined wisdom of the community. According to Robert Eccleshall, the most influential legal theorists of the time agreed with Fortescue that Parliament was virtually infallible.[166] This overcame a possible objection to royalist theories, namely, that although kings were notoriously fallible there were no legal means to enforce their obligation to obey divine and natural law. The King could hardly fail to comply with that obligation if, as parliamentarian theories maintained, in exercising his law-making power he was necessarily guided by the combined wisdom of the whole community.[167] As Christopher St German put it, the prince could make laws binding his subjects only 'by their assent . . . so that the laws that he makes be not against the law of God nor the law of reason'.[168]

St German's *Doctor and Student*[169] has been described as 'the most famous legal treatise composed between the time of Fortescue and that of Sir Edward Coke', and as 'a standard law text for English legal students in the sixteenth century' which continued to be 'the basic handbook for law students up to the time of Blackstone'.[170] In this and subsequent writings, including several polemical exchanges with Sir Thomas More, St German provided the Henrician Reformation with its most legally persuasive defence, based firmly on a parliamentarian rather than a royalist theory of the royal supremacy.[171] Probably influenced by

---

[162] Fortescue (1949: 87). The history of the requirement of 'consent' to taxation is summarized in Brown (1989: 224–30).

[163] 'Notes of the Judgment delivered by Sir George Croke in the Case of Ship-Money', in W. J. Jones (1971: 188).

[164] *Of Oaths Before an Ecclesiastical Judge ex Officio* 12 Co. Rep. 26, 29; 77 E.R. 1308, 1310.

[165] Gray (1992: 186), emphasis in original.

[166] Eccleshall (1978: ch. iv, *passim*); see also Hinton (1960: 420–1), Baumer (1940: 76). For the views of Fortescue, see Chapter 3, Section 5.

[167] Eccleshall (1978: 40).

[168] St German, *An Answer to a Letter* (1535), quoted by Guy (1986b: 209).

[169] St German (1974); first published in 1523; 2nd edn., 1530; 3rd edn., 1532.

[170] Guy (1986a: 99–100), and Baumer (1937: 631).

[171] Guy (1987b: 395–8, 402). From 1531 until mid-1534, St German's writings were published by the King's printer, as part of the government's propaganda campaign. But he was a respected, independent scholar, not a hired hack: Guy (1987a: pp. xxi–xxii, xxviii, xxix, xlvi).

Marsiglio of Padua,[172] he argued that the King in Parliament represented the Church as well as the temporal realm: 'the parliament . . . gathered together represents the estate of all the people within this realm, that is to say of the whole catholic church thereof'.[173] It followed that Parliament was omnicompetent, possessed of full power to legislate with respect to both temporal and spiritual matters, including power to settle disputes concerning the interpretation of scripture.[174] '[S]hould not the Parliament', he asked, 'which represents the whole Catholic Church of England expound scripture rather than the convocation which represents only the state of the clergy?'[175] 'The King in his Parliament', therefore, has 'the high sovereignty over the people which has not only charge on the bodies, but also on the souls of his subjects'.[176] Furthermore, '[i]t is held by them that are learned in the law of this realm, that the parliament has an absolute power as to the possession of all temporal things within this realm, in whose hands soever they be, spiritual or temporal, to take them from one man, and give them to another without any cause or consideration. For if they do it, it binds in the law. And if there be a consideration, that it binds in law and conscience.'[177] (An early recognition of a distinction between legal and moral obligation.)

St German's declaration that human law is subordinate to natural law has too often been overemphasized.[178] After all, eighteenth and nineteenth century writers such as Blackstone and Austin said the same thing, but still accepted the doctrine of parliamentary sovereignty.[179] St German found it inconceivable that statutes enacted by those representing the collective wisdom of the entire realm and church of England would 'recite a thing against the truth'.[180] In *Doctor and Student*, he argued that it was 'not best to reason or to make arguments whether they [the King, Lords, and Commons in Parliament] had authority to do that they did or not. For I suppose that no man would think, that they would do any thing, that they had not power to do.'[181] In a later text, he stated that 'it is not to presume that so many noble princes and their counsel, nor the lords and the nobles of the realm, nor yet the Commons gathered in the said Parliament, would from time to time run in to so great offence of conscience as is the breaking of the law of God'.[182]

For practical purposes, then, the fact that Parliament's authority was limited by natural law could be disregarded, because of the assumption that Parliament

---

[172] Guy (1987*b*: 398 n. 3; 1985*a*: 40).

[173] St German, *An Answer to a Letter* (1535), quoted by Guy (1987*b*: 403).

[174] Guy (1987*b*: 402, 403). But note that St German later changed his mind on this last point: ibid. 413. See also Guy (1985*a*: 43–4).

[175] *An Answer to a Letter* (1535), quoted in Baumer (1940: 59).

[176] St German (1974: 327).   [177] St German (*c*.1532: 194).

[178] e.g. by Baumer (1937: 639–40, 643–4), Hanson (1970: 257), and even Elton (1982: 237).

[179] See Chapter 2, text to n. 45.

[180] *Doctor and Student*, quoted by Eccleshall (1978: 111).   [181] St German (1974: 317).

[182] *Treatise concerning the Power of the Clergy and the Laws of the Realm* (1534/5), quoted in Guy (1985*a*: 41). See also Guy's discussion of St German's *An Answer to a Letter* (1535): ibid. 41–4.

would never violate it.[183] Moreover, even if Parliament did err, it was legally unchallengeable: divine and natural law were not enforceable by inferiors against the acts of their superiors, and the King in Parliament had no superior.[184] St German insisted that 'there lies no subpoena directly against a statute . . . for [if] it should lie, then the law should be judged to be void, and that may not be done by no court, but by the Parliament. . . . [I]f the statute be not good, it must be broken by Parliament as it was made'.[185] Leading historians therefore seem justified in describing him as the first English writer to propound a comprehensive theory of parliamentary sovereignty.[186] As J. W. Allen points out, it is one thing to say that human laws contrary to God's law are not binding, but 'since Parliament can decide authoritatively what the law of God is, the restriction becomes unreal'.[187] The same point is made by A. F. Pollard: 'the crown in parliament was the interpreter of the extent of the powers it exercised; it was judge, jury and criminal all combined, so far as its offences against fundamental law and medieval liberties were concerned . . .'[188]

St German was not alone in rejecting the possibility of Parliament acting unjustly. Dr Nicholas Hawkins thought it impossible to believe that 'a Parliament would err in a manifest truth'.[189] When John Mores was asked why an Act of Parliament ought to be obeyed, rather than a papal decree affirmed by a General Council of the Roman Catholic Church, he replied that 'the Holy Ghost is as verily present at such an act as it ever was at any General Council'.[190] This suggests that in some minds, the old idea of a 'corpus mysticum', an assembly of the faithful helped by the presence of the Holy Spirit to arrive at the truth, had been transferred from the Roman Catholic Church to the English Church represented in Parliament.[191] In 1542, Henry Brincklow, who believed that the English Church had not been sufficiently purged of papist elements, described as 'the thirteenth article of our creed added of late, that whatsoever the Parliament does, must needs be well done and the Parliament, or any proclamation out of the parliament time, cannot err'. He went on to complain that 'if this be so, it is all in vain to look for an amendment of anything, and we be in as evil a case as when we were under the Bishop of Rome'.[192] This attests to the influence that the notion of parliamentary infallibility had acquired.

When Sir Thomas Smith wrote that the King in Parliament was 'the most high and absolute power of the realm', which could change both laws and private rights

---

[183] Elton (1964: 39).   [184] Elton (1986: 39; and 1982: 238).

[185] St German, *A Little Treatise Concerning Writs of Subpoena*, in Guy (1985a: 116), discussed in ibid. 87.

[186] Guy (1988: 374), and Baumer (1937: 651). See also Guy (1988: 127, 133; 1986a: 111, 101–2, 169; 1985a: 23–5, 32), Baumer (1940: 76–7, 156), and Allen (1928: 167).

[187] Allen (1928: 167).   [188] Pollard (1926: 230–1).

[189] J. S. Brewer, J. Gairdner, and R. H. Brodie (eds.), *Letters and Papers Foreign and Domestic, of the Reign of Henry VIII* (London, 1882), vi. 94, quoted by Wood (1982: 58).

[190] Elton (1973: 67).

[191] Wood (1982: 52–3, 57, 58). This idea had been applied to secular institutions in other times and places: see Kantorowicz (1957: 218–28).

[192] *Complaynt of Roderyck Mors*, quoted by Allen (1928: 211).

and possessions, he made no mention of a higher law that confined its legislative authority.[193] This omission has been taken to reflect a waning in natural law thought.[194] But it is more likely to indicate that for Smith, like Fortescue and St German, it was unthinkable that Parliament would violate God's law. He stated that an Act of Parliament 'is the Prince's and whole realm's deed: whereupon justly no man can complain, but must accommodate himself to find it good and obey it'.[195] As Eccleshall explains, 'Smith was so sure that a representative body of the nation could not enact unjust laws that he felt no imperative to spell out the fact that its determinations were subject to a higher standard. This was simply assumed.'[196]

The best-known sixteenth century parliamentarian theory is Richard Hooker's, expounded in his *Of the Laws of Ecclesiastical Polity*.

The parliament of England together with the convocation annexed thereunto, is that whereupon the very essence of all government within this kingdom does depend; it is even the body of the whole realm; it consists of the king, and of all that within the land are subject unto him: for they all are there present, either in person or by such as they voluntarily have derived their very personal right unto.[197]

Following many earlier apologists for the royal supremacy, including Whitgift, Jewel, Gardiner, and St German, Hooker regarded the 'body of the whole realm' as equivalent to the Church in England, which included not only the King, as its head, and the clergy, but all lay believers as well.[198] '[W]ith us', he explained, 'one society is both Church and commonwealth'.[199] It followed that only Parliament could represent the whole Church, and in that capacity, make laws concerning religion, 'even laws concerning the most spiritual affairs of the Church'.[200] By arguing along these lines, Hooker hoped to show that criticisms of the structure and practices of the Elizabethan Church, made by dissident presbyterians, were inconsistent with their own populist assumptions.[201] Because Parliament spoke for everyone, everyone was obligated to obey its statutes.

A law is the deed of the whole body politic, whereof if you judge yourselves to be any part, then is the law even your deed also. And were it reason in things of this quality to give men audience, pleading for the overthrow of that which their own very deed has ratified? Laws that have been approved may be (no man doubts) again repealed, and to that end also disputed against, by the authors thereof themselves. But this is when the

---

[193] Sir T. Smith (1583: 48–9; 2nd bk., ch. 1).   [194] Mosse (1968: ch. 1).
[195] Sir T. Smith (1583: 49; 2nd bk., ch. 1).   [196] Eccleshall (1978: 117).
[197] R. Hooker (1888: iii. 408–9; bk. VIII, ch. vi, 11). Hooker exaggerated the role that Convocation played in making new laws concerning religion (Faulkner 1981: 177–8). But even he acknowledged that it could do no more than propose new laws: 'it is the general consent of all that gives them the form and vigour of laws ... thus to define of our own church's regiment, the parliament of England has competent authority' (Hooker 1888: iii. 410–11).
[198] For Jewel's earlier advocacy of this idea, see Cross (1969: 30); for Gardiner and Whitgift, see Allen (1928: 163 and 174 respectively); for St German, see text to n. 173, above.
[199] Hooker (1888: iii. 340; bk. VIII, ch. i, 7).
[200] ibid. iii. 412; bk. VIII, ch. vi, 11. See Faulkner (1981: 153–4); Lake (1988: 207–8).
[201] Lake (1988: 212–13).

whole does deliberate what laws each part shall observe, and not when a part refuses the laws which the whole has orderly agreed upon.[202]

Hooker also believed that statutes reflected a wisdom superior to that of any other person or institution: 'our laws made concerning religion, do take originally their essence from the power of the whole realm and church of England, than which nothing can be more consonant unto the law of nature and the will of our Lord Jesus Christ'.[203] He held this to be a matter of probability, rather than certainty: 'the public approbation given by the body of this whole church unto those things which are established, does make it but probable that they are good'. Nevertheless, that probability was sufficient to enjoin acquiescence and obedience: 'of peace and quietness there is not any way possible, unless the probable voice of every entire society or body politic overrule all private of like nature in the same body'.[204]

Hooker maintained that a sovereign power necessarily existed at the apex of any legal system. In an argument that became a commonplace in the following century, he explained that jurisdiction

must have necessarily a fountain that derives it to all others, and receives it not from any; because otherwise the course of justice should go infinitely in a circle, every superior having his superior without end, which cannot be: therefore a well-spring it follows there is, and a supreme head of justice, whereunto all are subject, but itself in subjection to none.

[T]here is required an universal power which reaches over all, importing supreme authority of government over all courts, all judges, all causes . . . [and over whom] no man can have lawfully power and authority to judge. If private men offend, there is the magistrate over them, which judges. If magistrates, they have their prince. If princes, there is Heaven, a tribunal, before which they shall appear; on earth they are not accountable to any.[205]

Hooker referred to 'sovereign and supreme power in the making of laws, either civil or ecclesiastical', and 'supreme power of making laws for all persons in all causes'.[206] He acknowledged that 'there is not any positive law of men, whether it be . . . received by formal express consent, as in councils, or by secret approbation, as in customs it comes to pass; but the same may be taken away if occasion serve'.[207] He sometimes spoke of the King as supreme, because he could veto proposed laws and was not subject to human judgment.[208] But he clearly attributed legislative sovereignty to the King only in Parliament, as the representative of the community.[209]

---

[202] Hooker (1888: i. 164; 'Preface').   [203] ibid. iii. 412; bk. VIII, ch. vi, 11.
[204] ibid. i. 170–1; 'Preface'.
[205] ibid. iii. 445–6; bk. VIII, ch. ix, 2 and ibid. iii. 433; bk. VIII, ch. viii, 4.
[206] ibid. iii. 413; bk. VIII, ch. vi, 12 and ibid. iii. 415, bk. VIII, ch. vi, 14.
[207] ibid. iii. 484; bk. IV, ch. xiv, 5).   [208] Hanson (1970: 277); Lloyd (1991: 282–3).
[209] Lake (1988: 201–2, 209–11, 224).

What power the king has he has it by law, the bounds and limits of it are known; the entire community gives general order by law how all things publicly are to be done . . . The whole body politic makes laws, which laws give power unto the king, and the king having bound himself to use according unto law that power.[210]

Which laws being made amongst us, are not by any of us so taken or interpreted, as if they did receive their force from power which the prince does communicate unto the parliament . . . but from power which the whole body of this realm being naturally possessed with, has by free and deliberate assent derived unto him that rules over them.[211]

Confidence that Parliament would not abuse its great powers was not based on its representative element alone. The Commons, Lords, and Crown were thought to make very different, but equally valuable, contributions to good government. Their collaboration, according to William Lambarde, created a perfect harmony: 'from such, and so well-tuned a base, mean, and treble, there proceeds a most exquisite consent, and delicious melody'.[212] England was sometimes said to enjoy a felicitous combination of all three kinds of government, monarchy, aristocracy, and democracy, the virtues of each one compensating for the vices of the others. The monarchical element suppressed the vices of faction and anarchy, the democratic element that of tyranny, and so on. When Elizabeth ascended the throne, John Aylmer, Bishop of London, dismissed fears that the reign of a woman might ruin the nation, on the ground that '[t]he regiment of England is not a mere monarchy . . . nor a mere oligarchy, nor democracy, but a rule mixed of all these . . . the image whereof, and not the image but the thing indeed, is to be seen in the Parliament House . . . If the Parliament use their privileges, the King can ordain nothing without them.'[213] This argument, in effect, attributed what we now call 'checks and balances' to the English system of government. It was not until the late seventeenth century that this understanding of the constitution became commonplace, but it enjoyed some currency even in the sixteenth.[214]

6. Prelude to the Seventeenth Century

Elton argues that under Edward VI, Mary, and Elizabeth I, royalist theories were eclipsed by parliamentarian ones.[215] Although Henry VIII believed that his supremacy over the Church was conferred directly by God, and not Parliament, legislation passed during the reigns of his children appears to have been based on the opposite assumption. For example, according to the Act of Supremacy of 1559, the Marian reaction was reversed, and royal supremacy over the Church

---

[210] Hooker (1888: iii. 443; bk. VIII, ch. viii, 9).

[211] ibid. iii. 412; bk. VIII, ch. vi, 11.   [212] Lambarde (1957: 126).

[213] J. Aylmer, *An Harborowe for Faithful and True Subjects* (1559), extracted in Elton (1982: 16).

[214] The sixteenth century versions of this theory are described in Weston (1965: ch. I, esp. at 15–23); see also Blythe (1992: 272–7).

[215] Elton (1992; and 1982: 343–4); see also Guy (1988: 233).

restored, 'by the authority of this your high court of Parliament with the assent of your Highness'.[216] Although Elizabeth held the same view as her father, until the 1590s her powerful Privy Council, led by Lord Burghley, seems to have subscribed to a parliamentarian theory.[217] But according to John Guy, royalist theories made a comeback in the 1590s, and became generally accepted in government circles because they provided a stronger defence of the Elizabethan Church against both Roman Catholic and Puritan attacks.[218] The core of that defence was the supposed existence, 'in both secular and ecclesiastical affairs, of an authority objectively limited by the laws of God and nature and yet, in this life and in its own dominions, sovereign and supreme'.[219]

In 1591, in *Caudrey's* case, the judges of the Court of Queen's Bench stated that 'by the ancient laws of this realm, this kingdom of England is an absolute empire and monarchy', and that the Queen possessed 'plenary and entire power, prerogative and jurisdiction, to render justice and right to every part and member of this body [politic] . . . in all causes ecclesiastical and temporal'.[220] The judges' use of the same language as the Act in Restraint of Appeals (1533) suggests a return to the elevated view of the royal supremacy held by Henry VIII and his principal clerics.[221] In 1592, the Queen's Printer published an influential defence of divine right kingship by Hadrian Saravia, a theologian who had emigrated to England.[222] He argued that every state was ruled by a sovereign, appointed by and subordinate only to God, with an absolute power to make or change the law. In England, the Queen was sovereign: she alone made the laws, the Houses of Parliament acting in a purely advisory capacity.[223] Influential bishops such as Richard Bancroft, Richard Cosin, John Bridges, and Thomas Bilson moved closer to absolutism, and such views were 'increasingly voiced in pulpit and press after 1589'.[224] These men were intent on defending the episcopacy against presbyterian claims that it was contrary to God's will, and should be abolished by Parliament. The Queen supported the bishops, and resisted attempts in Parliament to interfere with her governance of the Church. It is therefore not surprising that some bishops were attracted to royalist theories, which held that the Church was governed by the Crown alone, acting through their agency, rather than by the Crown in Parliament.[225] It has been suggested that the eighth book of Hooker's *Laws*, although completed by 1593, was not immediately published because it

---

[216] Cross (1969: 23–4); Act of Supremacy (1559), in Stephenson and Marcham (1972: i. 344). See also Elton (1982: 344, 396–7), on the difference between the Act of Six Articles (1539), and the Edwardian Acts of Uniformity.

[217] Guy (1997*b*: 83, 98–100). [218] Guy (1995*b*: 11–13; 1995*c*: 127–8; and 1997*b*: 100–2).

[219] Lake (1988: 100).

[220] *Caudrey's* case (1591) 5 Co. Rep. 1*a*, 8*b*; 77 E.R. 1, 10–11. [221] Guy (1995*c*: 133).

[222] H. Saravia, *De imperandi authoritate et christiana obedientia* (1692), discussed in Sommerville (1983), and Lake (1988: 135–9).

[223] Sommerville (1983: 239–42).

[224] Guy (1995*b*: 12; and 1995*c*: 126–7); Lake (1988: 129–35, 212, 219).

[225] Cross (1977: 28–30).

expounded a parliamentarian theory inconsistent with the views of the Queen and her advisers.[226] Disputes over religion, not finance, were the initial stimulus of the reassertion of royal absolutism, and 'in this respect Elizabeth's last decade may be interpreted as the first of the early Stuarts'.[227]

[226] Cross (1969: 35–7).
[227] Guy (1995c: 149); see also Lake (1988: 64–5, 131, 212). On the shift from parliamentarian or 'mixed government' thinking, prevalent in the mid-sixteenth century, to royalist or divine right thinking, at the beginning of the seventeenth, see also Eccleshall (1978: 36), Wootton (1986: 29–30), and Allen (1928: 263).

5

From James I to the Restoration

1. Political Theories in Early Stuart England

Religious and political disagreements in early Stuart England caused more attention to be given to the nature and location of the highest powers of government. But this tended to deepen rather than resolve the disagreements, as disputants developed political theories vindicating their own positions. Everyone agreed that God was the ultimate source of governmental powers. But when, how, and to whom God had conferred them were all subjects of debate. It is convenient to divide the competing theories into three kinds.[1]

Royalist theories maintained that God had conferred those powers directly on the King alone, despite the fact that in making new laws he was assisted by the two Houses of Parliament.[2] Parliamentarian theories held that the powers were originally conferred on the community as a whole, subsequently represented by the King, Lords, and Commons in Parliament, who could use the law-making power to control other powers that the community had delegated to the King. Common law theories held that both the King and the Parliament derived their powers from a kind of 'ancient constitution', comprised of the most fundamental principles of the common law, which maintained a proper balance between the two, and were therefore legally antecedent and superior to both.[3]

There were different versions of each kind of theory, some more moderate than others, and moderate versions of all kinds often had more in common with one another than with their more extreme versions.[4] But disagreements were possible even among those who accepted moderate theories. Whether consensus or conflict was more characteristic of political thought at the time is still a subject of debate. Those who emphasize conflict are criticized for neglecting the existence of a shared framework of beliefs and values, within which disagreements were negotiated. They reply that even if there was such a framework, it was an unstable compromise, as demonstrated by its catastrophic collapse in 1642.[5]

---

[1] Sommerville (1986: part one) divides the political thought of the period into something like these three kinds of theories. Christianson (1993) adopts an alternative tripartite division.

[2] The labels 'royalist', 'parliamentarian', and 'common law' are used to indicate where ultimate legal authority was located, according to each kind of theory, and not to describe the people who endorsed them; in other words, not all the King's officials subscribed to a royalist theory, nor all Members of Parliament to a parliamentarian theory, nor all common lawyers to a common law theory.

[3] Sommerville (1986: 95–100); Christianson (1993: 97–102; 1991: esp. 72 and 78–80).

[4] See Kishlansky (1996: 36–7); Peck (1993: 83).

[5] Sommerville (1986) is the leading study of disagreement. His views are criticized in Russell (1990a: ch. 6; 1993), and Burgess (1992b; 1996), to which he has responded in Sommerville (1996b; 1996a). See also Sanderson (1993).

The political disputes that occasionally flared up, even before the 1640s, usually concerned the nature and scope of the prerogative powers exercised by the King outside Parliament, especially those concerned with religion and finance.[6] There was little cause for disagreement concerning the legislative power of the King in Parliament. Because it could be regarded as belonging either to the King alone, or to the community as a whole, royalist and parliamentarian theories could agree that it was sovereign, or at least very close to it. Moreover, common law theories could also accept this, on the ground that the common law restricted the prerogatives of the King outside Parliament, in order to protect the rights of his subjects, but did not restrict the powers of the King and his subjects when they joined forces in Parliament. In other words, the sovereignty of the King in Parliament could be regarded, as it often is today, as one of the most fundamental principles of the common law itself.

A more detailed examination of each of the three kinds of theories will reveal how Parliament and its law-making authority were generally regarded in this period.

2. Royalist Theories of the Authority of Parliament

The idea that the King's authority was conferred on him directly by God, rather than by the community or the common law, was the foundation of royalist theories.[7] The King was often described as God's vicar, vice-regent, or lieutenant on earth.[8] James I himself told the House of Commons that '[t]he state of monarchy is the supremest thing upon earth; for kings are not only God's lieutenants upon earth, and sit upon God's throne, but even by God himself they are called gods . . . for that they exercise a manner or resemblance of divine power upon earth'.[9] Roger Maynwaring, an extreme royalist who was one of Charles I's favourite preachers, declared that the 'sublime power . . . which resides in earthly potentates, is . . . a participation of God's own omnipotency'.[10]

Royalists sometimes suggested that God endowed kings not only with authority to rule, but also with divine qualities of love and wisdom to guide them in exercising it.[11] Maynwaring praised 'the high discourse and deep counsels of kings, seeing their hearts are so deep, by reason of their distance from common men, even as the heavens are in respect of the earth'.[12] Lord Chancellor Ellesmere argued that the King had 'a discretion, judgment, and feeling of love towards those over whom he reigns, only proper to himself'; 'he cannot into others infuse the wisdom, power, and gifts which God in respect of his place and charge has enabled

---

[6] See the remarks in Powell (1995: 189–90).   [7] Sommerville (1986: 12, 32–3).

[8] Judson (1949: 17–20); Sommerville (1986: 33); Daly (1979*a*: part 7, 10).

[9] 'Speech to Parliament' (21 March 1610), in Kenyon (1986: 11–12).

[10] *Religion and Allegiance* (London, 1627), 10–11, quoted in Peck (1993: 103).

[11] Eccleshall (1978: 93–6).

[12] 'A Sermon Preached Before the King' (4 July 1627), quoted in Kenyon (1986: 13). That kings were widely thought to be semi-divine is demonstrated by the popular belief that they could heal scrofula, a skin disease, by touching the sufferer (Walter 1996: 203).

him with all'.[13] It followed that the King's right to exercise certain 'absolute' prerogatives according to his 'private will and judgment' could not be delegated to subordinate judges; they were bound to act according to the law, 'which is the King's own will', rather than their own private consciences.[14]

Religious, social, and political thought was dominated by the conviction that the Universe was a 'great chain of being', a hierarchy in which everyone under God had superiors and inferiors, and consequential rights and responsibilities. The refusal of an inferior to respect and obey a superior was condemned as a grave threat to this natural order.[15] These ideas were central to royalist theories. James I, for example, once admonished his subjects to 'invert not the order of nature, by judging your superiors'.[16] Thomas Morton, the Bishop of Durham, said that for subjects to attempt to overrule the King would be as 'unorderly and ugly a confusedness, in the body politic, as it would be in the body natural to stand on its head with the heels upwards'.[17] Dudley Digges the younger argued that God 'has appointed a convenient subordination in all authorities':

[A]s a private man must not oppose a Constable, nor a Constable a Justice of the Peace, nor he a Judge, so common soldiers cannot punish a Lieutenant . . . nor a Colonel the General, they being but private men in reference to one above them . . . so Kings in Monarchies . . . are not judicially accountable to any, because they are the highest.[18]

As Sir Roger L'Estrange put it much later, '[c]onsider how ridiculous it were to *appeal downward*; or from sovereign princes, to any other power, than to the *King of Kings*, who alone is above them'.[19]

Royalists were adamant that subjects could not even question, let alone attempt to overrule, the King's actions. He was accountable only to his own conscience, and to God, and not to any human tribunal or power.[20] James I condemned as 'presumption and high contempt in a subject, to dispute what a King can do, or say that a King cannot do this, or that';[21] it was 'sedition in subjects

---

[13] 'A Copy of a Written Discourse by the Lord Chancellor Ellesmere Concerning the Royal Prerogative' (1604: 3r–3v), quoted in Knafla (1977: 197–8).

[14] ibid. Sir Francis Bacon expressed the same opinion: see Wormuth (1939: 58–9). On the King's 'absolute' prerogatives, see text to n. 28 ff., below.

[15] Daly (1979*a*); Greenleaf (1964: ch. 2, esp. 49 ff.); Eccleshall (1978: 9, 18, 22, 33, 47–9, 56–9); Oakley (1984: ch. 4); Dickinson (1977: 25–6).

[16] James I (1616: 41).

[17] 'Sermon preached Before the Kings most Excellent Majestie, in the Cathedrall Church of Durham' (5 May 1639), 10, quoted in Judson (1949: 206).

[18] Digges (1643: 47). Digges was a leading royalist polemicist during the civil war. For a very similar passage by another prominent royalist writer, the clergyman Peter Heylyn, see Heylyn (1643: 16).

[19] L'Estrange (1679: 3). L'Estrange was Charles II's chief propagandist.

[20] James I and Charles I both said this: James I, 'Speech to Parliament' (21 March 1610), in Kenyon (1986: 12–13); Charles I, 'His majesties declaration to all his loving subjects, of the causes which moved him to dissolve the last Parliament' (1628, 9), quoted in I. Harris (1994: 194–5). See, in general, Judson (1949: 151–2), and D. L. Smith (1994: ch. 7).

[21] 'Speech in the Star Chamber' (20 June 1616), in James I (1616: 333).

to dispute what a king may do in the height of his power'.[22] It followed that rebellion against the King could never be justified, not even as a remedy for tyranny. At most, the subject was entitled passively to disobey a command manifestly contrary to divine law, but not actively to resist the King or any punishment he might impose. If the King acted as a tyrant in violation of God's laws, God could be relied on either to remove or punish him.[23] The popularity of these ideas is demonstrated by the fact that in the early stages of the civil war, even those who supported the parliamentary cause denied that they were rebelling against the King; they claimed, instead, to be defending the King against evil advisers.[24]

It also followed that the King's actions were not to be questioned by judges, unless he authorized them to do so. The King appointed them to administer his justice: to be 'lions under the throne', as Sir Francis Bacon put it.[25] They were accountable to the King, and not vice versa. Lord Ellesmere wrote in 1604 that 'though the King be not bound to render any account to the law for the justice which in person he does administer, yet every subordinate judge must render account to the King (by his laws) how he has administered Justice'.[26] In 1616, James I instructed the judges that

Kings are properly judges, and judgement properly belongs to them from God: for Kings sit in the throne of God, and thence all judgement is derived. In all well settled monarchies . . . judgement is deferred from the King to his subordinate magistrates; not that the King takes it from himself, but gives it unto them . . . As Kings borrow their power from God, so judges from Kings: and as Kings are to account to God, so judges unto God and Kings. . . . It is the King's office to protect and settle the true interpretation of the law of God within his dominions: And it is the judge's office to interpret the law of the King, whereto themselves are also subject . . . Keep you therefore all in your own bounds . . . As for the absolute prerogative of the Crown, that is no subject for the tongue of a lawyer, nor is lawful to be disputed . . . [R]est in that which is the King's revealed will in his law.[27]

The concept of the King's 'absolute prerogative' is crucial to this passage. The word 'absolute' was usually applied to authorities or decisions that were not subject to legal challenge or review.[28] The absolute prerogative of the Crown was really a number of prerogatives, or powers, whose exercise by the King was discretionary, in that it was not governed by legal requirements or subject to legal challenge. Those powers were uniquely governmental, and possessed only by the

---

[22] 'Speech to Parliament' (21 March 1610), in Kenyon (1986: 13). For other statements of a similar kind, see Sommerville (1996b: 168, 183 n. 48).

[23] For different variations on this theme, see Sommerville (1986: 34–5; 1992: 87–8).

[24] Ashton (1989: 183–4).

[25] *Of Judicature*, in Bacon (1985: 169). See also *De Rege Inconsulto* (1616), quoted in Coquillette (1992: 174).

[26] *Concerning the Royal Prerogative* (1604), in Knafla (1977: 199).

[27] 'Speech in the Star-Chamber' (20 June 1616), in James I (1616: 326–7, 332–3). Much of the speech is extracted in Kenyon (1986: 84–6).

[28] See Burgess (1996: 31–4); Judson (1949: 111–16, 144); Henshall (1992: 81–2, 123–4, 132); Zagorin (1954: 193–4); Holdsworth (1903–72: iv. 206–7).

King, whereas in his private capacity he had ordinary rights and powers no different in kind from those of his subjects.

According to James, and other royalists, all the laws of the realm owed their original existence and continued maintenance to the absolute prerogatives of the Crown. All laws, including the whole of the common law, were originally made by kings, rather than (as Bracton had put it) the kings by the law.[29] God had made the kings, and they had then made laws for the benefit of their subjects. But having made laws, kings were bound by solemn oaths to abide by them. Sir John Davies explained that, by the law of nations, the King had 'an absolute and unlimited power in all matters whatsoever'; but 'by the positive Law the King himself was pleased to limit and stint his absolute power . . . in common and ordinary cases'.[30] For example, it would be quite wrong for the King arbitrarily to take property from a subject, for his own enjoyment or that of a favoured courtier. Indeed, the law presumed that the King would never intentionally do such a thing. An unlawful royal command was deemed to be void, because the King could not have intended to break the law: he must have been misled by his advisers, who could be prosecuted or sued. In cases where actions against the King's servants could not remedy the wrong done, the King graciously allowed aggrieved subjects to submit a 'petition of right', asking him to correct it. Judges determined the merits of these petitions, and the King was bound to accept their decisions because of his oath to do justice. James I asked his judges 'to give me no more right in my private prerogative, than you give to any subject; and therein I will be acquiescent'; 'whenever any decree shall be given against me in my private right, between me and a subject, I will as humbly acquiesce as the meanest man in the land'.[31]

Royalists did not concede that the King reduced his power or freedom by making such promises. To be guided by reason rather than irrational passion is to be more rather than less free. The King ensured that he was guided by reason in making laws by acting with the advice of the two Houses of Parliament, the most reliable sources of public deliberation and counsel.[32] He also enhanced his freedom by subjecting the exercise of his other powers to the guidance of the common law. Even royalists, who regarded the common law as having been originally established by the King's courts, could agree that it was the embodiment of reason, tried and tested by the experience of centuries, through the evolution of precedents whose longevity attested to their reasonableness.[33] The King could confidently assume that if he complied with the common law his actions would

---

[29] As James himself said, in *The Trew Law of Free Monarchies*: 'the kings were the authors and makers of the laws, and not the laws of the kings' (James I 1616: 62).

[30] *The Question concerning Impositions* (1656: 29–30), quoted in Judson (1949: 167). Sir John Davies was a distinguished common lawyer who died shortly before he could take up his appointment by James I as Chief Justice of England. The same assumption was made by James I, in his 'Speech to Parliament' (21 March 1610), in Kenyon (1986: 12).

[31] 'Speech in the Star-Chamber' (20 June 1616), in James I (1616: 333, 337).

[32] Goldie (1991: 598).   [33] Burgess (1992*b*: ch. 2)

be reasonable, except in very unusual circumstances when his absolute prerogatives might need to be invoked.

For royalists, the King's voluntary submission to law, and its enforcement by his judges, meant that he was subject only to the 'directive', and not the 'coercive', force of the law.[34] Moreover, this did not and could not extinguish or override his absolute prerogatives, which remained the foundation on which the administration of all law and justice rested. His paramount duty in exercising those prerogatives was to preserve the peace and safety of the realm, from both external and internal threats. Sometimes, in order to fulfil that duty, he might have no alternative but to act outside or even contrary to law.[35] Extraordinary dangers might require extraordinary remedies, incompatible with procedural or even substantive legal rights. Just as equity could sometimes override the common law, in the interests of justice, so 'reasons of state' could sometimes override particular laws, in the interests of public safety and the survival of law as a whole. As the Earl of Strafford argued during his impeachment, '[t]he prerogative must be used as God does his omnipotency, upon extraordinary occasions; the laws . . . must have place at other times'.[36]

For many royalists, it logically followed that the King could not be truly bound by the law. Some of them did not hesitate to say so. Henry Peacham argued that since the King had made the laws, his will should be obeyed even if it conflicted with them: 'if therefore we must live under and obey the law, how much more the Prince, that made and established it, yea who gives vigour and life unto the law?'[37] Even when moderate royalists spoke of kings binding themselves by law, their position was often ambiguous.[38] Was a King, who was bound to obey the law because he had promised to do so, really bound by the law as such, or only by his own conscience? Even if he was bound by the law in ordinary cases, for most royalists he certainly was not when exercising his absolute prerogatives. They did not agree with the opinion of Sir Edward Coke, and many other lawyers, that 'the king has no prerogative, but that which the law of the land allows him'.[39] Instead, they agreed with Sir Francis Bacon, that 'the king holds not his prerogatives of this kind mediately from the law, but immediately from God, as he holds his crown'.[40] James I seems to have expressed this opinion when he said

[34] For references to this distinction in the works of many royalist writers, including Spelman, Maxwell, Goodwin, Ellesmere, and Filmer, see D. L. Smith (1994: 227, 244–5), Judson (1949: 200), and Sommerville (1996*b*: 181 nn. 43, 44).

[35] Sommerville (1986: 37). See also Sommerville (1991) and Weston and Greenberg (1981: ch. 2).

[36] 'Trial of the Earl of Strafford for High Treason' (1648), in Howell (1816–28: iii. 1464).

[37] H. Peacham, *The Duty of all Subjects to their King* (1639), quoted in Sommerville (1986: 43).

[38] Sommerville (1986: 133).

[39] *The Case of Proclamations* (1611) 12 Co. Rep. 74, 76; 77 E.R. 1352, 1354. For the widespread acceptance of this view, see Sommerville (1986: 100–4).

[40] Bacon (1861–74: iii. 371). John Cowell, Attorney-General Hobart, Sir John Davies, William Lambarde, Serjeant Ashley, Lord Keeper Coventry, and many other royalists agreed with Bacon: Sommerville (1986: 36, 122, 160, 163, 164–5, 167, 168, 170, and 171–2). See also Wormuth (1939: esp. chs. 4, 5, and 6).

that 'the absolute prerogative of the Crown ... is no subject for the tongue of a lawyer'.[41] This may be why, although James I once acknowledged that every 'just king' in a 'settled' kingdom, with long-established laws, is bound by his oath to comply with them, on another occasion, according to Sir Edward Coke, he denounced as 'treason' the proposition that the King was 'under the law'.[42]

The claim that legal remedies were available in the event of unlawful royal conduct must therefore be heavily qualified. It is true, as Glenn Burgess has emphasized, that although the King himself was not subject to legal compulsion, unlawful royal commands could be declared null and void, and the King's officials punished for carrying them into effect.[43] But in doing this, the judges were regarded as giving effect to the King's own will, by exercising a jurisdiction that he himself had conferred on them, in order to help him keep his voluntary undertaking to comply with the law in ordinary cases. It was the King's own prerogative that made his unlawful commands void.[44] All available judicial remedies for official misconduct were based on that assumption. Complaints against the Crown itself were brought by a petition of right, which really was a petition, in the sense that it was an appeal to the goodwill of the King, who could at any time order the proceedings to be stopped.[45] The assumption that the King wished justice to be done also underpinned the issue of prerogative writs to control unlawful conduct on the part of subordinate courts or officials. Coke's successor, Chief Justice Montague, responded to criticisms that the writ of habeas corpus was being used to obstruct the King's prerogatives, by pointing out that the writ itself was 'a prerogative writ, which concerns the King's justice to be administered to his subjects; for the King ought to have an account why any of his subjects are imprisoned'.[46] When the subject's right to equitable relief against the Crown was first established by the Court of Exchequer, in 1668, Baron Atkyns offered a similar justification: the King's honour required the presumption that he intended justice and equity to be done as between him and his subjects.[47]

It might be argued that this invocation of royal authority, in order to justify judicial remedies for executive misconduct, was a mere formality, and that in reality, those remedies were entirely independent of royal command. But when the King's absolute prerogatives were involved, this was not necessarily the case.[48] Most royalists insisted that the absolute prerogatives were not proper subjects

[41] 'Speech to the Star-Chamber' (20 June 1616), in James I (1616: 333).

[42] 'Speech to Parliament' (21 March 1610), in Kenyon (1986: 12); *The Question of Prohibitions* (1607) 12 Co. Rep. 64, 65; 77 E.R. 1342, 1343.

[43] Burgess (1996: 139–40, 146–7, 153–4, 158–9). Sommerville (1986: 75–6, 101, 157) previously noted this point.

[44] Glanvill, the Speaker of the Short Parliament, said that if commands of the King were contrary to law, they were 'made void by just prerogative', and 'the King innocent, even in his very person, defended by his prerogative': *Lords Journals*, 4: 51, quoted in Wormuth (1939: 110 n. 6).

[45] Holdsworth (1903–72: ix. 23).

[46] *R v Lord Warden of the Cinque Ports, ex parte Bourn* (1619) Cro. Jac. 543, quoted by Baker (1990: 168).

[47] *Pawlett v Attorney-General* (1668) Hardres 465, 469, quoted in Holdsworth (1903–72: ix. 30).

[48] Jaffe and Henderson (1956: 345, 361).

for judicial scrutiny except with the King's permission. James I instructed the judges to refuse to permit his absolute prerogatives to be disputed, and threatened to punish them if they did not.[49] He maintained that a subject was entitled to complain about any hardships resulting from the exercise of his absolute prerogatives, but not to question their existence.[50] In both *Bate's* case, concerning impositions, and the *Five Knights'* case, concerning imprisonment without cause stated, it was noted that the King had graciously consented to his prerogatives being examined.[51] When Charles I imposed the levy known as 'ship money' by prerogative power, he ordered his judges to provide him with their opinion as to its legality. This was for public relations purposes: the King was confident that he would be supported by his judges, whom he 'doubt[ed] not are all well studied and informed in the right of our sovereignty'.[52] The Lord Keeper told the judges that they had cause to rejoice that 'in so high a point of his sovereignty, he has been pleased to descend, and to communicate with you his judges'. He also instructed them that in requiring their opinion, the King did not intend to stop or check any proceedings that might be brought by individuals seeking to challenge the levy: 'it is his majesty's command, that all have equal and meet justice, and that they be suffered to proceed in course of law', provided that the King's counsel be forewarned.[53] It seems that in all these cases, the judges would not have dared to examine the legality of the King's actions if he had forbidden them to do so.

In the *Five Knights'* case, Attorney-General Sir Robert Heath, a future Chief Justice of England, conceded that the King could not order the judges to proceed contrary to the laws of the land which they were sworn to enforce. However,

there is a great difference between those legal [illegal?] commands, and that *absoluta potestas* that a sovereign has, by which a king commands; but when I call it *absoluta potestas*, I do not mean that it is such a power as that a king may do what he pleases, for he has rules to govern himself by, as well as your lordships, who are subordinate judges under him. The difference is, the king is the head of the same fountain of justice, which your lordships administer to all his subjects; all justice is derived from him, and what he does, he does not as a private person, but as the head of the common wealth, as *justiciarius regni*, yea, the very essence of justice under God upon earth is in him; and shall we not generally, not as subjects only, but as lawyers, who govern themselves by the rules of the law, submit to his commands, but make enquiries whether they be lawful, and say that the king does not this or that in course of justice? . . . [W]ho shall call in question the actions or the justice of the king, who is not to give any account for them?[54]

---

[49] James I (1616: 333, 337).
[50] See his speech to the House of Commons on 21 May 1610, in Foster (1966: ii. 101–2).
[51] *Bate's* case (1606), in Howell (1816–28: ii. 382 (Baron Clark) and 387–8 (Chief Baron Fleming)); *Five Knights'* case (1627), in ibid. iii. 32 (Attorney-General Heath).
[52] *The Ship-Money* case (1637) in Howell (1816–28: iii. 843).   [53] ibid. 825, 845.
[54] The *Five Knights'* case (1627), in Howell (1816–28: iii. 37). Sir Robert Berkeley in his judgment in the *Ship-Money* case (1637) said 'I never read nor heard that *lex* was *Rex*; but it is common and most true that *Rex* is *lex*, for he is *lex loquens*, a living, a speaking, an acting law': quoted in Gardiner (1906: 122).

From this perspective, the King could legitimately refuse to permit any judicial examination of his or his servants' actions, if he deemed them justified by an absolute prerogative. After Sir Edward Coke had threatened to charge the Court of Chancery with praemunire, James I instructed the judges that 'no praemunire can be sued but at my suit: and I may justly barr myself at my own pleasure'.[55] He claimed the same right to prevent interference by common law courts with the activities of his other prerogative courts, such as Star Chamber, and the Privy Council. Charles I initially denied that his servants, especially those closest to him, could be impeached in Parliament, and he sometimes ordered judges to abandon 'unjust' proceedings against them.[56] Maitland discusses several earlier instances when officials or tribunals were given sweeping powers that were either clearly or arguably unlawful, but no questions were raised in the common law courts.

The king was the fountain of all justice; they [the judges] were but his deputies . . . To hold, not that some isolated act of royal authority was illegal—but that the government of the country was being regularly conducted in illegal ways—this would have been a hard feat for the king's servants and deputies.[57]

This raised a serious objection to royalist theories: that they offered no practical means of either preventing or remedying gross misconduct on the part of the King. What if, for example, he pretended that an emergency existed that justified him requiring urgent financial assistance from his subjects without their consent in Parliament? Parliamentary propagandists made much of this objection in the 1640s. Henry Parker, the most influential of them, sneered that royalists who held that the King was subject only to the directive, and not the coercive, limits of the law, were 'almost as stupid' as those who held that he was without any limits, because 'a dry right without all remedy' is no right at all.[58]

Royalists offered several responses. Sir Robert Heath considered the possibility that the King might abuse his prerogative of pardon by pardoning all traitors and felons in the kingdom, and replied, in the same terms used, *mutatis mutandis*, by many defenders of parliamentary sovereignty today: 'shall we say, the King cannot do this? No: we may only say, he will not do this.'[59] The same example had previously been discussed by Chief Baron Fleming, in his judgment in *Bate's* case (1606), who reasoned that 'many things are left to his [the King's] wisdom for the ordering of his power, rather than his power shall be restrained. . . . [T]o argue *a posse ad actum*, to restrain the King and his power because that by his power he may do ill, is no argument for a subject.'[60] This was a common royalist argument, which James I himself employed. In 1610, he advised the

---

[55] James I (1616: 334–5).   [56] Holdsworth (1903–72: vi. 26).
[57] Maitland (1908: 267–8).
[58] Parker (1642: 44). Much of this tract is also extracted in Erskine-Hill and Storey (1983).
[59] The *Five Knights'* case (1627), in Howell (1816–28: iii. 45).
[60] *Bates'* case (1606), in Howell (1816–28: ii. 391–2).

Commons to 'beware of such arguments' as that 'because a king may do in excessive manner, therefore he shall not do it at all. Because he may pardon all offenders, which were inconvenient, therefore he shall pardon none.' It could just as speciously be argued, he warned them, that because 'heady and ill-disposed men' might abuse the privileges of the Commons, the Commons should not have them. 'Deal with me as you would be dealt with. You cannot so clip the wings of greatness.'[61] In this respect, he said, a king was like God: he necessarily had power to do what, in his goodness, he could be trusted not to do.[62]

Royalists also argued that it would be unwise to limit the King's powers in order to prevent him from harming his subjects. As John Bramhall put it, powers that could be abused to the detriment of subjects could also be used for their benefit: to take away a power to prevent its abuse would also prevent its being used for good. To want the benefit of protection without the risk of oppression was as irrational as wanting fire for warmth without the risk of being accidentally burnt, or bees to produce honey without the risk of being stung. To render the King powerless to oppress his subjects would expose society to 'a hundred hazards and blows' for the sake of only occasional benefits. It would be like cutting down every vine in the country to prevent drunkenness, or cutting the wings of a hawk to prevent it from flying too far away.[63]

Royalists insisted that it was necessary to trust somebody with supreme political authority, and there was no more suitable candidate than the King. Dudley Digges the younger explained that in every state, appeals had to come to an end, or there would be no final and peaceful resolution of disagreements: grievances would be taken from one authority to another, *ad infinitum*, or else settled by violence.[64] Since by definition there could be no appeal from whoever had 'supreme jurisdiction' to decide the final appeal, that person was necessarily beyond the coercive power of the law.[65] '[T]hat the King is *sub lege*, under the law, has this sense, that he ought to govern according to those standing rules'; however, 'if he should swerve from these rules, he is not liable to any punishment, nor compellable by strong hand; not for want of sin . . . but for want of a superior jurisdiction'; the subject therefore possessed 'no legal remedy'.[66] It followed that he had to be trusted. '[W]e cannot have any absolute security; in all governments it is necessary to trust somebody. For if we should retain a liberty to right our selves . . . the decision of controversies would be writ in blood.'[67]

Parliamentarian theories agreed that there had to be a final and supreme decision-maker, who was by definition above the coercive power of the law and

[61] Foster (1966: ii. 103).

[62] Daly (1979a: 11). As the cleric John Rawlinson put it, 'a king in his absolute and unlimited power is able to do more than a good king will do': Rawlinson, *Vivat Rex* (1619: 6), quoted in Daly (1978: 233).

[63] Bramhall (1643: 149). In the fifteenth century, Sir John Fortescue wrote that 'although an unjust king may unjustly use that power, power itself is always good, nor can it be defiled by the use made of it': Fortescue, *On the Law of Nature*, quoted in Pickthorn (1934a: 163 n. 4).

[64] Digges (1643: 31–2, 84).   [65] ibid. 83–4.   [66] ibid. 77.   [67] ibid. 71.

therefore had to be trusted to govern justly.[68] But they preferred to trust Parliament. '[A]n absolute indisputable power of declaring law', said Henry Parker, the principal parliamentary spokesman during the 1640s, 'must rest in them [Parliament], or in the King, or in some inferior court, or else all suits must be endless, and it can nowhere rest more safely than in Parliament'.[69] Digges replied as follows:

It is no discretion to prevent a possible mischief by probable inconveniences; if you will not trust one, you must trust more, that is, if you are weary of monarchy . . . you know the way to cast it off by placing so many guardians over your Prince, but have you any greater assurance than before? *Quis custodiet ipsos custodes?* They have as great temptations to fail their trusts as he [the Prince] had.[70]

Royalists also argued that it was better to trust one man rather than many, because the many might disagree among themselves, leading to violence and the collapse of law and order.[71] This could not happen if the King alone were recognized as having sovereign power that could never legitimately be resisted. Furthermore, as Digges reminded his readers, 'the hearts of Kings are in the hands of the Lord, he will put a hook into the nostrils of tyrants, and . . . will not permit them to bruise his children to pieces'.[72] In 1628, Sir Robert Heath opposed proposals to limit the King's absolute prerogatives on the ground that it was unnecessary, because the King 'is set over His people for their good; and, if He do transgress, and do unjustly, there is a greater power than He, the King of Kings: *Respondet Superiori*'.[73]

It was well established that the King could enact statutes only with the consent of the two Houses of Parliament, but many royalists maintained that even this restraint was self-imposed. Digges, for example, insisted that the power to make laws belonged to the King alone, and it was irrelevant 'that He restrains Himself from exercising some particular acts without consent of Parliament, for it is by virtue of His own grant, that such after acts shall not be valid. He has not divided His legislative faculty, but tied himself from using it, except by the advice and consent of the Peers, and at the request of the Commons.'[74] It might seem to follow that the King was legally free to retract his grant and rid himself of this restraint, and a few royalists may have thought so.[75] On the other hand, it has been forcefully argued that hardly any did take this view, and there-

---

[68] See Sections 3 and 5, below.   [69] Parker (1642: 45).   [70] Digges (1643: 69).

[71] R. Filmer, *The Anarchy of a Limited or Mixed Monarchy*, in Filmer (1991: 131–71); Hobbes (1968: 243).

[72] Digges (1643: 119).

[73] *Journals of the House of Lords*, 3: 757–8, quoted in Judson (1949: 145).

[74] Digges (1643: 107, 140). See also Sir Francis Kynaston's somewhat similar remarks, in his 'A True Presentation of Forepast Parliaments' (1629), quoted in Burgess (1996: 39).

[75] In 1610, Richard Martin indignantly reported to the Commons that 'a man in a high place' had said that 'if the King take anything without Parliament, 'tis his right, if in Parliament, 'tis his grace' (Foster 1966: ii. 328).

fore that there were very few genuine absolutists in early Stuart England.[76] This argument has been disputed.[77] But we do not need to resolve this dispute, because all royalists agreed that the King's law-making power was absolute in another sense, namely, that provided the two Houses assented to its exercise, it could not be legally challenged. The King may have subjected his law-making power to a procedural restraint, but not to a substantive one.

Statutes were frequently said to be enacted by the exercise of the King's 'absolute' authority. This is hardly surprising, at a time when the power to make laws was widely regarded as higher than, or even as encompassing, all other powers of government.[78] Dr John Cowell, a civil lawyer, wrote that 'all learned politicians do range the power of making laws *inter insignia summa et absolutae potestatis* [among the highest insignia of absolute power]'.[79] In the *Ship-Money* case, Justice Crawley drew a distinction between the King's 'regal' and 'legal' prerogatives, and stated that '[t]he first regal prerogative is this, that contains all the rest, that the king may give laws to his subjects: and this does not detract from him, when he does it in Parliament'. Among the other 'regal' prerogatives, which the law-making power 'contained', were the powers to make war and peace, to appoint judges, to pardon offenders, and to coin money.[80] On this view, the legislative power was the first and foremost of the King's absolute prerogatives.

Royalists acknowledged that the consent of the community, expressed in Parliament, fortified the King's legislative power.[81] Henry VIII had said that 'we at no time stand so high in our estate royal as in the time of parliament', and by the seventeenth century this had become a platitude, frequently reiterated on both sides of the political spectrum.[82] James I announced that '[a] Parliament is the most honourable and highest judgment in the land, (as being the King's head Court)'.[83] Royalists and parliamentarians agreed that the King was 'never so magnificent',[84] and 'never so high in point of state',[85] as in Parliament, where he was 'in the exaltation of his orb',[86] 'in the fullness of his majesty and

---

[76] Burgess (1992*a*: esp. at 840–3; 1996: esp. at 90 and 98). Sir John Spelman argued that although kings were originally bound in this respect only by their own good wills, 'constant custom becoming a law made that which was at first at their will . . . an absolute and inevitable limitation of their power' (Spelman 1644: 4–5).

[77] The debate about the prevalence of 'absolutism' is pursued in Sommerville (1996*a*, 1996*b*).

[78] This was one of Jean Bodin's most original and central theses: see Bodin (1992: 56, 58–9, 104).

[79] J. Cowell, *The Interpreter* (1607), quoted in Weston and Greenberg (1981: 20).

[80] The *Ship-Money* case (1637) in Howell (1816–28: iii. 1083).

[81] See Sir Francis Bacon in Howell (1816–28: ii. 399) and Sir Francis Kynaston, 'A True Presentation of Forepast Parliaments' (1629), quoted in Burgess (1996: 39).

[82] Cobbett (1806–20: i. 555). Sommerville describes such statements as 'hackneyed': Sommerville (1986: 154). See also Judson (1949: 69 and 235).

[83] Quoted in Hawkins (1973: 40). On another occasion James described Parliament as 'the Supreme Court of Justice': 'King's Speech to Parliament' (26 March 1621), quoted in Kenyon (1986: 92).

[84] Notestein *et al.* (1935: iv. 256).

[85] Littleton, in *Rolle's* case (1628) in Cobbett (1806–20: ii. 479).

[86] Sir Francis Bacon, quoting the Speaker of the House of Commons (Bacon 1861–74: vii. 177).

power',[87] 'in the altitude of his glory, in the highest state royal',[88] and 'in his zenith'.[89] Sir John Spelman, a leading royalist spokesman in the 1640s, said nothing controversial when he wrote that the King in Parliament stood 'in his highest estate royal, and . . . more freely and absolutely working there, than in any other time and place he can do', and therefore possessed 'the highest, most absolute, and most sovereign power in the kingdom'.[90]

It is no wonder, then, that the power to make laws in Parliament was so often described as 'absolute', meaning that it was not subject to legal challenge or review.[91] In the previous century, Sir Thomas Smith and others had described the judgments of Parliament not only as absolute, but as the most absolute in the realm.[92] James I announced that 'the King with his Parliament here are absolute, (as I understand) in making or forming any sort of laws'.[93] William Dickinson referred to 'that majesty and architectonical power, which out of its own absoluteness sets down a law, a public measure . . . whereby all men's actions are to be squared and adjudged'.[94] And in 1660, Roger Coke asserted that '[i]t is as clear as the sun at noonday, that a King of England . . . is as free and absolute in the session of Parliament, as out. And the act of a King in Parliament, is the free and voluntary act of an absolute monarch.'[95] This use of the word 'absolute' was not confined to royalists. The so-called Commons' Apology of 1604 acknowledged that the King had 'absolute power' even to make or change laws concerning religion, provided that he did so 'as in temporal causes by consent of parliament'.[96]

For royalists, therefore, the King's 'absolute' power to make laws, fortified by the consent of the whole realm, stood at the very pinnacle of his divinely ordained authority. Given their understanding of the relationship between the

[87] Petyt (1739: 8); Lord Chancellor Sir Heneage Finch in 1679, quoted in Nenner (1995: 145). See also Sir P. Warwick, *A Discourse of Government* (1694: 45), quoted in Weston and Greenberg (1981: 95).

[88] J. Howell, *The Preheminence and Pedigree of Parlement* (1644: 10), quoted in D. L. Smith (1994: 241).

[89] Sir P. Warwick, *A Discourse of Government* (1694: 45), quoted by Weston and Greenberg (1981: 95).

[90] Spelman (1644: 8 and 4).

[91] See e.g. W. Raleigh (1628), *The Prerogative of Parliaments in England*, quoted in Sommerville (1986: 43); Spelman (1644: 9 and 5); G. Williams, *Jura Majestatis, the Rights of Kings both in Church and State* (1664: 149), quoted in D. L. Smith (1994: 246); Digges (1643: 146); Knafla (1977: 73); Daley (1978: 232); Weston and Greenberg (1981: 4, 18–20); and Sommerville (1986: 99–100).

[92] See Chapter 4, text to nn. 75 and 83, and F. Bacon, *A Brief Discourse Upon the Commission of Bridewell*, in Bacon (1858–74: vii. 509).

[93] 'A Speach to the Lords and Commons of the Parliament at White-Hall' (21 March 1609), in James I (1616: 311).

[94] W. Dickinson, *The Kings Right* (1619: B3r), quoted by Judson (1949: 213).

[95] R. Coke, *Justice Vindicated* (1660), quoted in Goldie (1991: 600). See also Goldie's discussion at ibid. 596–602.

[96] Prothero (1913: 291), 'so-called' because although the Apology was drafted by a large committee appointed by the House of Commons, it was never formally endorsed by the House: see Elton (1974c: 176). See also the contemporary statement of the Speaker, Sir Edward Phelips, in Cobbett (1806–20: i. 989), and Anonymous (1642c: A4).

King and his judges, they could not have countenanced the idea that the King's laws could be held to be void by those he had appointed to administer them. If the exercise of his other absolute prerogatives was a matter for his unfettered discretion, then *a fortiori*, so was the exercise of his power to make laws with the consent of his subjects in Parliament. In the penultimate section of this chapter, more direct evidence will be provided to confirm that this was precisely how royalists understood the matter.

But an important qualification must be noted. Despite all that has been said, many royalists denied that the law-making authority of the King in Parliament was completely unlimited. Throughout the seventeenth century it was sometimes argued that, because God appointed kings and conferred their powers upon them, Parliament had no authority to control either the royal succession, or various 'inseparable' powers that constituted kingship. In these respects, royalists retreated from the position that seemed to have been settled during the previous century.[97]

The Stuart Kings and their supporters had a very practical reason for insisting that, according to God's law, the royal succession was indefeasibly hereditary. James I succeeded Elizabeth contrary to the terms of Henry VIII's will, and therefore the statute of 1536 that purported to make the will binding. To accept that the succession could legitimately be controlled by statute was implicitly to question his title to the throne, and that of the entire Stuart line.[98] James I's first Parliament was loath to have that question raised, and therefore happily passed an Act of Recognition confirming his right to succeed. Since it was arguable that he could lawfully assent to that Act only if he were already the lawful king, Parliament based his title on his 'inherent birthright', according to 'the laws of God', rather than on its own authority.[99]

Even Jean Bodin held the law of primogenitive succession to be fundamental and unalterable, yet clearly believed this to be consistent with the incumbent monarch possessing sovereign law-making power.[100] James I asserted that kingdoms were disposed of by God, each king being merely a 'life-renter', having a right to wear the Crown during his lifetime but not to bequeath it, no more entitled than the people to dispossess his rightful heir.[101] Lawyers such as Sir Edward Coke and Sir John Finch agreed that divine right, rather than common law, governed the succession to the crown.[102] In 1621, Edward Alford stated that '*Parliamentum omnia potest* except altering the right line of the crown'.[103] Sir John Spelman insisted in the 1640s that the King possessed an absolute and

---

[97] See Chapter 4, text to nn. 35–51.

[98] Russell (1993: 117); see also Russell (1990*b*: 212–13), Loades (1997: 3–4), Wootton (1986: 30), and Tanner (1930: 7).

[99] Russell (1993: 117). This point was made by the anonymous author, E. F. (1679: 6).

[100] Franklin (1973: 70–1). Franklin's explanation for this is that a sovereign's power need not be regarded as capable of controlling events after his demise: ibid.

[101] *Basilicon Doron*, in James VI and I (1994: 42); and see also *The Trew Law of Free Monarchies*, in ibid. 82.

[102] Russell (1993: 118); Howell (1816–28: iii. 1235).   [103] Quoted in Russell (1993: 118).

indisputable power to make laws in Parliament, but expressly exempted the royal succession: 'no Act of Parliament . . . can disable the right heir to the Crown, because the descent of the Crown upon him purges him of all disabilities whatsoever, and makes him capable of it'.[104] Not all royalists agreed: Sir Robert Filmer, for example, believed that a reigning King could alter the succession.[105] But according to Howard Nenner, the accession of James I made the doctrine of indefeasible hereditary right 'an orthodoxy that would last for more than another eighty-five years'.[106]

For many royalists, it logically followed that some of the King's absolute prerogatives were 'inseparable' from his Crown, and could not be removed or restricted by statute. If God had conferred the kingship directly on the King and his natural heirs in perpetuity, then any attempt to limit the powers that constituted kingship would be nullified by God's law.[107] The indefeasible hereditary right of kings was to kingship, and not an empty title from which the essential powers had been detached.

It was often argued that a number of powers were constitutive of kingship, all equally essential to genuine monarchical government. The power to make laws was one; others included the powers to conduct foreign affairs, to make war or peace, to appoint judges, and to grant pardons.[108] All were inseparable from the King's office, 'so inherently a part of kingship that a ruler, even if he would, could not dissociate them from himself'.[109] This idea had deep roots. Bracton had stated that certain rights and jurisdictions 'belong to no one save the crown alone and the royal dignity, nor can they be separated from the crown since they constitute the crown'.[110] William Camden explained that all kings necessarily possessed 'some general privileges without which there can be no king'.[111] In *Bate's* case (1606), Baron Clark said that 'the revenue of the crown is the very essential part of the crown, and he who rends that from the king pulls also his crown from his head'.[112] Justice Crawley reasoned in the *Ship-Money* case that '[y]ou cannot have a king without these royal rights, no, not by act of parliament'.[113] As Glenn Burgess puts it, the loss of certain rights would 'unking the king'.[114]

There was an alternative, somewhat different, explanation of inseparability. It was widely believed that a sovereign law-maker cannot effectively bind itself, for the same reason that no individual can do so. An individual may resolve never again to eat chocolate, but that resolution cannot prevent him from changing his

---

[104] Spelman (1644: 14).   [105] Daly (1979*b*: 42–3, 184–5).   [106] Nenner (1995: 62).

[107] Many royalists would have agreed with Sir Robert Filmer that 'kingly power is by the law of God, so it has no inferior law to limit it', and that 'the commands or laws of kings are human ordinances': (Filmer 1991: 35, 40). It followed that kings could not limit their own kingly power.

[108] Sommerville (1992: 83, 85).   [109] Judson (1949: 33).

[110] Bracton (1968–77: ii. 167).   [111] Fussner (1957: 210–11).

[112] *Bate's* case (1606), in Howell (1816–28: ii. 383).

[113] The *Ship-Money* case (1637), in Howell (1816–28: iii. 1085–6).

[114] Burgess (1996: 199). Charles I objected to the Petition of Right on the ground that any denial of his power to imprison without stating the cause meant 'the overthrow of our sovereignty': *Bibliotheca Regia* (1659: 320), quoted in Wormuth (1939: 106).

mind: it is liable to be reversed at any time.[115] The same is true of a law, passed by a sovereign law-maker, providing that he will not in the future enact some other kind of law. As Francis Bacon explained, 'a supreme and absolute power cannot conclude itself . . . no more than if a man should appoint or declare by his will, that if he made a later will it should be void'.[116] According to Sir John Davies, 'a prerogative in point of government . . . cannot be restrained or bound by Act of Parliament' because it 'is as strong as *Samson* . . . for though an Act of Parliament be made to restrain it, and the King does give his consent unto it, as *Samson* was bound with his own consent, yet if the Philistines come, that is, if any just or important occasion do arise . . . it will be as thread, and broken as easily as the bonds of Samson'.[117] (Parliamentarians replied that a King without law was as powerless as Samson without his hair.)[118]

This idea did not apply straightforwardly to the Kings of England, because it was generally accepted, even by most royalists, that statutes could be neither enacted nor repealed without the assent of the two Houses of Parliament. How, then, could anyone other than the most extreme royalists believe that the King was a sovereign law-maker, who could at any time unilaterally free himself from restrictions imposed by statute? The answer is that the King's law-making power included the power to dispense with statutes, as well as to enact and repeal them. Until the second half of the seventeenth century, it was generally agreed that the King, acting alone by the exercise of prerogative power, could dispense with the operation of statutes, except for those that prohibited what was naturally evil, or *mala in se*.[119] No statute restricting a royal prerogative could have been regarded as prohibiting actions that were naturally evil. It followed that, as Sir Edward Coke put it, 'no act can bind the king from any prerogative which is sole and inseparable to his person, but that he may dispense with it by a *non obstante* [the words used to dispense with a statute]'.[120] Furthermore, it was often said that the King could do this even if the statute in question expressly denied that he could: in

---

[115] As Thomas Aquinas put it, 'properly speaking, no man is coerced by himself': *Summa Theologica* I–II, q. 96, art. 5, Reply Obj. 3, in Bigongiari (1953: 74). For much the same reason, Jean Bodin thought that a sovereign prince could be bound by his promises, but not by his own laws (Bodin 1962: 91–2).

[116] F. Bacon, *The History of Henry VII*, in Bacon (1858–74: vi. 160); see also his *Maxims of the Law*, in ibid. vii. 370. As Hobbes explained the matter, a sovereign cannot be bound by the civil law because, 'having power to make, and repeal laws, he may when he pleases, free himself from that subjection, by repealing those laws that trouble him . . . ; and consequently, he was free before. For he is free, that can be free when he will' (Hobbes 1968: 313).

[117] *The Question concerning Impositions*, quoted in Wormuth (1939: 73). Some lawyers appear to have taken the view that a king could bind himself by statute, but not his successors: see Baron Clarke in *Bates'* case (1606), quoted in Prothero (1913: 340).

[118] See J. Milton, *Eikonoklastes*, in Milton (1953–82: iii. 545–6).

[119] More controversially, the King was also widely believed to be able to suspend the operation of statutes. I will ignore that power, which was not always clearly distinguished from the dispensing power, in what follows.

[120] *The Case of Non Obstante* 12 Co. Rep. 18; 77 E.R. 1300; see Weston and Greenberg (1981: 271 n. 12) for references to other expressions of the same opinion. Coke's early views on this subject are discussed by Burgess (1996: 198–200).

other words, that no statute could prevent the King from dispensing with it.[121] Many eminent lawyers, including Bacon, Ellesmere, Coke, and Finch, agreed that a statutory provision prohibiting the use of the dispensing power would necessarily be ineffective, and therefore void, because the King could dispense with it: he could '*non obstante . . . that non obstante*'.[122] That was why even Coke agreed that 'the King could not be restrained by any Act to make a pardon; for mercy and power to pardon is a prerogative incident, solely and inseparably to the person of the King'.[123] The same reasoning can be found in *Godden v Hales* (1686), when James II's hand-picked judges decided that his extraordinarily liberal use of the dispensing power was valid. Chief Justice Herbert stated that '[t]here is no law whatsoever but may be dispensed with by the supreme law-giver, as the laws of God may be dispensed with by God himself'; therefore 'if an act of parliament had a clause in it that it should never be repealed, yet without question, the same power that made it [the King], may repeal it'.[124]

Neither of these explanations of the inseparability of essential royal prerogatives denied that the King was truly sovereign, or asserted that his law-making power was controlled by the common law. On the contrary, both were based on the assumption that he possessed sovereign powers that are inherently perpetual and inalienable. The King, even in Parliament, could not restrict his absolute powers outside Parliament, because that would be inconsistent with his own continuing sovereignty.

Strictly speaking, both explanations were inconsistent with the idea that the King in Parliament was sovereign. The first explanation denied that the power to make law, by itself, constitutes sovereignty. It treated that power as just one of a number of powers that constitute sovereignty. The King alone, rather than the King in Parliament, was sovereign, because the King possessed all the powers of sovereignty, whereas the King in Parliament possessed only one of them, and could not use it to abolish or restrict the others. The second explanation assumed that the legislative power was superior to any other, but held that it was really a combination of powers, including the power to dispense with laws; that although the power to make laws could be exercised only in Parliament, the power to dispense with them could be exercised outside it; and that the former power could not be used to restrict the latter. This amounted to a theory of legislative sovereignty, but not parliamentary sovereignty, because it claimed that the King could exercise an essential and inalienable component of his legislative sovereignty outside Parliament. As the seventeenth century wore on, parliamentarians

---

[121] This argument had its origins in the inconclusive *Sheriff of Northumberland's* case (1485), which was dropped before the judges arrived at a decision (Plucknett 1926: 30–70). This did not deter Coke and many others from citing it as an authority.

[122] Weston and Greenberg (1981: 30, 31, 104–5, and 271 n. 12); Boudin (1932: 513); Finch (1678: 82); and for some other references, see Holdsworth (1903–72: iv. 205).

[123] *The Case of Non Obstante* 12 Co. Rep. 18; 77 E.R. 1300, 1301.

[124] *Godden v Hales*, in Howell (1816–28: xi. 1196 and 1197). For the background to this case, see Havighurst (1953).

increasingly attacked this claim. They denied that the King, being just one part of the legislature, could by an act of dispensation set aside the work of the whole. But controversies over the dispensing power concerned who the law-maker was, and not whether the law-maker was sovereign.[125]

Nevertheless, royalists who believed that some of the King's prerogatives were inseparable, for either reason, were very close to accepting full parliamentary sovereignty. They accepted that the King possessed sovereign power, and that his power was most absolute when he made laws in Parliament. They regarded his law-making power as restrained not by the common law, but only by limits inherent in his own sovereignty. This is similar to the modern theory that Parliament's sovereignty is limited only by its inability to restrict its own sovereignty.

The writings of Sir John Spelman, a prominent royalist spokesman in the 1640s, exemplify this conjunction of ideas. He asserted that the legislative power was 'the most sovereign power'; that it was necessarily 'supreme' and 'indisputable'; and that it belonged to the King who, in Parliament, 'wills and works absolutely by the power of his own inherent sovereignty'.[126] He went so far as to claim that the King in Parliament was 'above the King', because the former 'is a whole compared with some part, and the King but a part, though the most excellent part, of the whole; now, every whole is greater than any part; the head, though more excellent than all the other members, yet not more excellent than the whole man, whereof the head is but a part'.[127] So the 'indisputable' and 'most sovereign' law-making power belonged to the King in Parliament. But despite all this, Spelman denied that the King, even in Parliament, could impair his own 'regal power', which 'has always its being from God'.[128]

> And for deposing a King, or depriving him of his right and authority, or any necessary part thereof, no Act of Parliament can prevail . . . A statute that the King by no *non obstante* shall dispense with it, is void, because it would take a necessary part of government out of the King . . . [N]o Act of Parliament be of force to take away the government or any necessary part thereof from the King.[129]

In the *Ship-Money* case (1637), a number of judges asserted that statutes purporting to abolish or restrict certain prerogative powers of the Crown would be void. Sir George Vernon, Sir George Crooke, Sir Richard Hutton, Sir Humphrey Davenport, and Sir John Finch all said that a statute prohibiting the King from defending the kingdom, or from requiring aid from his subjects for that purpose,

---

[125] This is clear from the account of those controversies in Weston and Greenberg (1981: 173, 226–30, 235–8, 364–5 n. 60). Those controversies were finally settled in 1688, when the Bill of Rights effectively terminated the dispensing power: see Chapter 7, Section 1, below.
[126] Spelman (1642*b*: 19, 34); see also Spelman (1644: 8–9). For information about Spelman and his writings, see D. L. Smith (1994: 226–8).
[127] Spelman (1642*b*: 7–8). Dudley Digges said much the same thing: Digges (1643: 146).
[128] Spelman (1642*b*: 8) (the quote appears on the second of two pages both numbered '8').
[129] ibid. 8–7 (*sic*).

would be void.[130] Royalist rather than common law thinking seems to have inspired most if not all of these dicta.[131] Sir George Vernon, for example, specifically stated that 'the king may dispense with any law in cases of necessity', and Sir John Finch and Sir Humphrey Davenport insisted that statutes could not remove the King's 'regality' or '*regale jus*'.[132] However, the same may not be true of Sir Richard Hutton's dictum that statutes of the kind in question 'would not bind, because they would be against natural reason', nor Sir Edward Crooke's that they would be 'void, being against law and reason'.[133] Those statements may reflect the influence of a common law theory.

3. Parliamentarian Theories of the Authority of Parliament

Parliamentarian theories maintained that God originally conferred the highest powers of government on the community as a whole, rather than a single person. To enable those powers to be exercised effectively, the community had wisely delegated them to the King, subject to the conditions that he make laws and impose taxes only in Parliament, and exercise his other powers subject to statute and common law. Those conditions had the force and effect of contractual obligations, which were sometimes regarded as enforceable, if necessary, by active resistance on the part of the community. Some theories of this kind were based entirely on natural law reasoning, while others derived support from the research of historians such as John Selden, who claimed that from the very beginnings of civil government in England, kings, nobles, and freemen had shared the power to make law.[134]

The community participated directly in the making of laws and imposition of taxes in Parliament. James I's first statute declared that Parliament was a High Court 'where all the whole body of the realm, and every particular member thereof, either in person or by representation (upon their own free elections), are by the laws of this realm deemed to be personally present'.[135] The notion that

---

[130] The *Ship-Money* case (1637), in Howell (1816–28: iii. 1125, 1160, 1195, 1216, and 1235, respectively). Sir Edward Crawley made a similar statement, but confused the question of validity with questions of statutory interpretation: ibid. 1085–6. The case is discussed in Keir (1936).

[131] Coke had expressly included the 'sovereign power to command any of his subjects to serve him for the public weal' among the King's inseparable prerogatives: *The Case of Non Obstante* 12 Co. Rep. 18; 77 E.R. 1300.

[132] The *Ship-Money* case (1637), in Howell (1816–28: iii. 1125, 1235, and 1216, respectively).

[133] ibid. 1195 and 1160, respectively.

[134] Sommerville (1986: 62–4, ch. 2 *passim*); Christianson (1991: 83, 84–5). Selden's constitutional theory is described in more detail in Christianson (1984: 273–83; 1996).

[135] The Succession Act, 1 Jac. I, c.1, quoted in Kenyon (1986: 21). See also James I's descriptions of the Commons as the representative body of his subjects in his speeches in 1604 and 1624, quoted in ibid. 21 n. 2 and 44–5.

Parliament spoke for the whole realm was a commonplace, habitually regarded as an actual fact.[136]

The community had no corporate form apart from Parliament, and no person or group outside Parliament could speak or act on its behalf. For this reason, parliamentarian theorists generally condemned rebellion against Parliament as vehemently as royalist theorists condemned resistance to the King.[137] Charles Herle, a Presbyterian clergyman who was one of the two Houses' most effective propagandists in the 1640s, said the thesis that the people were entitled to resist Parliament was 'a position which no man I know maintains'.[138] It was impossible for the people acting collectively to defy Parliament, because that would be to defy themselves.[139] Individuals or groups who resisted Parliament would be elevating their private interests above the community's, and by doing so, threatening to unleash anarchy.[140] As William Bridge put it, when Parliament, on behalf of the community, resisted tyrannical commands of the King, the people were 'still led on by authority', but if the people were to resist Parliament, 'they should have left themselves naked of all authority and should be private men'.[141]

Parliament was described as 'not only the representative body, but the abstracted quintessence of the whole commonality . . . of England'.[142] It was like the community in miniature, encapsulating 'all the perfection and excellence' of the whole, especially its collective wisdom.[143] Since the King was part of Parliament, even royalists could accept this. In 1615, for example, Lord Chancellor Ellesmere criticized Coke's remarks in *Dr Bonham's* case for advancing 'the reason of a particular court above the judgement of all the realm'.[144] Coke himself later asserted, in his *Fourth Institute of the Laws of England*, that Parliament possessed the highest wisdom in the realm, and could never be thought to act dishonourably or, in the words of St German, 'against the truth'.[145] Henry Parker, a barrister who became the most influential writer to defend the parliamentary cause in the 1640s, wrote that 'in public consultations, the many eyes

[136] J. W. Allen (1938: 461); see also Gough (1955: 70, 225–6); and Judson (1949: 304–5).

[137] Franklin (1978: 30 n. 20 and 125–6 n. 84) states that in the first half of the century only William Ball and Samuel Rutherford accepted that Parliament could possibly be resisted legitimately. But Wootton (1990: 663–6) has identified others who argued, as early as 1643, that it could be resisted if it abused its trust. In 1647–8, Leveller and Army pamphlets argued that if Parliament became corrupt it could be resisted by the people, or by the Army on behalf of the people.

[138] Herle (1642: 20).

[139] ibid.; for Henry Parker's and William Bridge's identical views, see Sommerville (1992: 61); and Morgan (1988: 64–5).

[140] Tuck (1979: 147–51); J. W. Allen (1938: 452, 463–4). According to Franklin (1978: p. ix and 2), those who defended a right of popular rebellion against tyranny almost always meant a collective right of the community as a whole, exercisable only by its representative institutions. See also Tully (1991: 622, 639).

[141] W. Bridge, *The Wounded Conscience Cured* (1642: 36–7), in Sharp (1983: 74).

[142] Rushworth (1721: iii. 1121).   [143] Parker (1643*b*: 20).

[144] *Observacions Upon Cooke's Reportes* (1615), in Knafla (1977: 307).

[145] See text to nn. 262–4, below.

of so many choice gentlemen out of all parts, see more than fewer, and the great interest the Parliament has in common justice and tranquillity, and the few private ends they can have to deprave them, must needs render their counsel more faithful, impartial, and religious, than any other'.[146] 'That which is the sense of the whole Parliament is the judgment of the whole kingdom; and that which is the judgment of the whole kingdom, is more vigorous, and sacred, and unquestionable, and further beyond all appeal, than that which is the judgment of the king alone.'[147]

In 1640, Sir Francis Seymour said that Parliament was 'the soul of the Commonwealth, wherein one may hear and see all the grievances of the subjects and in the multitude of such counsellors is safety'.[148] Sir Roger Twysden, a moderate royalist who was punished by the two Houses during the civil war, described the Parliament as

the supreme court of judicature of the realm, and rightly so esteemed; for, as we can not suppose a supremacy of right judging can be placed where we can not possibly imagine a supremacy of knowledge, so in this assembly there cannot but be as much wisdom conceived to be gathered together as England can afford; for first, there is the king and privy council for matters of state; secondly, his judges (by whose advice he ever proceeds in business of weight moved in parliament); thirdly, the lay lords, for matters of military and civil government; fourthly, the bishops, skilled in divine, civil, and canon laws; fifthly, there are the commons, who feel and are to represent the griefs of the people, chosen out of the wisest of themselves; and therefore Sir Edward Coke well says that, when they are thus joined there, 'ultimum sapientiae.'[149]

Twysden refers to the judges because it was standard practice for them to advise the House of Lords concerning questions of law, including those relevant to proposed legislation, a practice that continued until the late nineteenth century.[150]

Parliamentary procedure was thought to guarantee that statutes would be enacted only after the most painstaking deliberation. When Justice Crawley was impeached before the House of Lords for deciding in favour of the King in the *Ship-Money* case, Edmund Waller criticized his statement that a statute taking away an essential prerogative of the Crown would be void:

And because this man has had the boldness to put the power of parliament in balance with the opinion of the judges, I shall intreat your lordships to observe, by way of comparison, the solemn and safe proceeding of the one, with the precipitate dispatch of the other. In Parliament (as your lordships know well) no new law can pass, or old be

---

[146] Parker (1642: 11). Tuck (1993: 228) says that this work 'went through many editions and was quoted extensively throughout the 1640s and 1650s as the authoritative statement of Parliament's position'. On Parker's life and thought, see Mendle (1995), Zaller (1991), and Jordan (1942).

[147] H. Parker, *Some few Observations upon his Majesties Late Answer to the Declaration, or Remonstrance of the Lords and Commons, etc.* (1642: 9), quoted in Jordan (1942: 167–8).

[148] Cope and Coates (1977: 213).

[149] Twysden (1849: 130). It is generally agreed that this work was written between 1640 and 1648: see Burgess (1996: 142 n. 60). See also the views of Thomas Hedley, text to n. 296, below.

[150] Jay (1994: 124–8). See also Coke (1644: 4).

abrogated, till it has been thrice read with your lordships, thrice in the Commons House, then it receives the royal assent; so that it is like gold seven times purified.[151]

The old idea that Parliament was virtually infallible continued to be influential. In the Apology of the Commons of 1604, it was asserted that '[t]he voice of the people in things of their knowledge is said to be as the voice of God'.[152] This was to attribute to the people what many royalists attributed to the King, although sometimes it was attributed to both: Thomas Scott described as 'common speech' the opinion that 'the voice of the people is the voice of God, if it be joined with the voice of the King'.[153] Even the royalist judge Sir Robert Berkeley said, in the *Ship-Money* case, that Parliament was 'the greatest, the most honourable and supreme court in the kingdom; that no man ought to think any dishonourable thing of it . . . and whatsoever the king does therein, is always to be taken for just and necessary . . . [T]he parliament cannot err . . .'.[154]

Henry Parker argued that '*vox populi* was ever reverenced as *vox Dei*, and Parliaments are infallible, and their acts indisputable to all but Parliaments'; Parliament 'can affect nothing but the common good'.[155] Elsewhere, in what has been described as the most influential pamphlet of the civil war, he said that the wisdom of Parliaments 'has been ever held unquestionable, and their justice inviolable'.[156] He argued that there were good reasons for this trust. 'The composition of Parliaments, I say, takes away all jealousies, for it is so equally, and geometrically, proportionable, and all the States [estates] do so orderly contribute their due parts therein, that no one can be of any extreme predominance.'[157] Parliament's absolute power over the State was therefore like a man's absolute power over himself, which need not be feared or restrained because he does not hate himself. A State can be trusted not to injure itself, and Parliament 'is indeed the State itself'.[158]

[A] community can have no private ends to mislead it, and make it injurious to itself, and no age will furnish us with one story of any Parliament freely elected, and held, that ever did injure a whole Kingdom, or exercise any tyranny, nor is there any possibility how it should.[159]

Parker later modified his position, arguing that although Parliament was not infallible, it was less likely to err than any individual.[160] Another of the two Houses' propagandists, the lawyer John Marsh, a chancellor of Lincoln's Inn, agreed that Parliaments 'can do no wrong': 'Kings seduced

---

[151] Howell (1816–1828: iii. 1302–3).   [152] Stephenson and Marcham (1972: i. 424).
[153] *High-Waies of God and the King* (1623: 68), quoted in Judson (1949: 334).
[154] The *Ship-Money* case, in Howell (1816–28: iii. 1101).
[155] H. Parker, *The Case of Shipmony briefly discoursed* (1649: 35–6), quoted in Judson (1949: 368).
[156] Parker (1642: 24). The high estimate of the pamphlet's influence is that of Tuck (1979: 146).
[157] Parker (1642: 23).   [158] ibid. 34.   [159] ibid. 22.
[160] H. Parker, *Animadversions Animadverted* (1642: 11), quoted in Judson (1932: 206).

may injure the commonwealth, but . . . Parliaments cannot'.[161] The like-minded anonymous author of an influential pamphlet, published in 1643, argued that illegal acts to which kings were prone 'cannot be suspected by a parliament, which is representatively the public, intrusted for it, and which is like to partake and share with the public, being but so many private men put into authority *pro tempore*, by common consent, for common good'.[162]

Others argued that Parliament's decisions were binding not because they were infallible—an idea that royalist writers ridiculed—but because they were necessarily final and unappealable. Parliament was 'not (as some scoff) infallibly guiding, but only inevitably suspending from all other appeals or gainsaying, as the highest court'.[163] As John Cook explained, 'it was the will of God that for the preventing of wars and bloodshed, that there should in every nation be some supreme court to whose determinations every private man is to submit'; therefore, 'though the judgment of Parliament be not unerrable because the members not impeccable, yet it is inevitable'.[164] For the same reason, Richard Hollingworth insisted that Parliament's 'ultimate and indisputable power of expounding the laws . . . [must] not be resisted or controlled by any, upon pretence of possible or actual error'.[165]

'[T]here is no law of the kingdom better known', said John Goodwin, 'than that the High Court of Parliament is the supreme judicatory of all questions and disputes in law, against and from whom there lies no appeal to any other judge or judicature but only to another of the same, I mean another Parliament'.[166] In the so-called Apology of the Commons of 1604, it was declared that 'there is not the highest standing Court in this land that ought to enter into competency [i.e. competition], either for dignity or authority, with this High Court of Parliament, which with your Majesty's royal assent gives laws to other courts but from other courts receives neither laws nor orders'.[167] The Apology later complained that James I had accepted an opinion of his judges, concerning a disputed election return, rather than a contrary determination of the House itself: 'Neither thought we that the judges' opinion, which yet in due place we greatly reverence, being delivered what the common law was, which extends only to inferior and standing courts, ought to bring any prejudice to this High Court of Parliament, whose power being above the law is not founded on the common

---

[161] J. Marsh, *An Argument, or Debate in Law* (1642: 15); quoted in Morgan (1988: 64).

[162] *Touching the Fundamental Laws or Politic Constitution of this Kingdom* (1643), in Dunham and Pargellis (1938: 614).

[163] Anonymous (1642d: 36). On this point the writer closely followed Herle (1642: 14). A similar argument appears in Hollingworth (1643: 7).

[164] J. Cook, *Redintegratio Amoris, or a Union of Hearts [etc.]* (1647), 23, quoted in Judson (1932: 369).

[165] Hollingworth (1643: 7).   [166] Goodwin (1643: 61).

[167] *The Form of Apology and Satisfaction* (20 June 1604), in Tanner (1930: 221) and Kenyon (1986: 31). A full account of the background to the Apology is provided in Hexter (1992b), incorporating his earlier discussion in Hexter (1986). The Apology was never formally endorsed by the House of Commons: see n. 96, above.

law . . .'.[168] In the 1640s, the two Houses issued similar declarations, to deter judges from heeding royal proclamations contrary to their ordinances. 'It cannot be denied but that the Parliament is the highest court of judicature in the kingdom; to it all other courts are subordinate; this court has power to question judgments given in the highest courts; . . . from judgments there had by the fundamental laws and constitutions of this kingdom there can be no appeal.'[169]

That inferiors should respect and obey their superiors was generally held to be a law of nature.[170] Just as royalists appealed to this belief to buttress the authority of the King, so did parliamentarians to reinforce that of the community represented in Parliament. Parker, for example, insisted that Parliament was the highest court in the kingdom 'and if we appeal to a lower [court], that were to invert the course of nature: and to confound all Parliaments for ever'.[171] John Pym, a leading figure in the House of Commons in the early 1640s, also said that it was 'against nature and order' that inferior courts should presume to regulate a superior, such as the court of Parliament.[172] Speaking in Parliament in 1640, Sir Francis Seymour asked '[w]hat law or reason is there, that a Parliament, which is the highest of all Courts, should be questioned by inferior Courts, and Judges: as if Common Pleas should question the King's Bench, or the Chancery be questioned by either of them'.[173] John Cook insisted that judges were obliged to obey Parliament because 'otherwise they that are at the oars should row against them that sit at the stern'.[174]

The judges themselves accepted this principle. When three members of the House of Commons were prosecuted in 1629, for making seditious speeches in the House, they objected that the charge violated parliamentary privilege, and could not be heard by any court inferior to Parliament. The judges rejected the argument because, although Parliament was indeed a higher court than all others, an individual member of Parliament was not, and was therefore subject to their jurisdiction.[175] They acknowledged that 'an inferior court cannot meddle with judgments of a superior court';[176] therefore, although the conduct of individuals could be questioned, '[w]e cannot question the judgments of parliaments'.[177]

In *Streater's* case, decided in 1653, Justice Garmond said that

God made man, and gave him a law to live by; and the laws of England are grounded on the laws of God: and in the laws of England every man is concerned. And now the

---

[168] *The Form of Apology and Satisfaction*, in Tanner (1930: 224).
[169] *An Exact Collection of the Remonstrances, Declarations [etc.]* (1643: 850); similar declarations can be found in ibid. 206–7 and 726.
[170] See text to nn. 15–19, above.   [171] Parker (1642: 43).
[172] Cope and Coates (1977: 149–50).   [173] ibid. 213.
[174] J. Cook, *Redintegratio Amoris, or a Union of Hearts [etc.]* (1647: 23), quoted in Judson (1932: 369). Cook was replying to an argument of David Jenkins, a royalist judge imprisoned by Parliament during the civil war, that judges could hold an Act of Parliament void: see n. 329, below.
[175] *Proceedings Against Sir John Elliot, Denzil Hollis, and Benjamin Valentine for Sedition* (1629), in Howell (1816–28: iii. 309, *per* Whitelocke J.).
[176] ibid. 307, *per* Hyde LJ.   [177] ibid. 306–7.

parliament of England is grounded on the whole body of the nation. Now, if one power were not above another, things would go in a circle to and fro, and have no end: now this will bring them to an end, since the whole law of the nation is grounded on the parliament laws.[178]

Justice Nichols added: 'I am of the same opinion, every thing must be done in order: and "God is the God of Order" '; therefore, 'what the parliament does, we cannot dispute or judge of'. Chief Justice Rolle agreed that 'one must be above another, and the inferior must submit to the superior; and in all justice, an inferior court cannot control what the Parliament does'.[179] As the Whig historian William Petyt put it later in the century, it was 'against nature . . . that any members of inferior courts should . . . undertake to judge of a superior court, especially the High Court of Parliament, which . . . could not be censured by any other law or sentence but its own'.[180]

The logical consequence of Parliament's status as the highest court was bluntly explained by William Prynne in 1643. Whereas errors made in inferior courts could be reversed by a higher court,

if the Parliament give any judgement, there can be no appeal to any higher tribunal, court or person, no not to the king, but only to the next or some other Parliament, as is evident by experience, by all attainders of treason, by or in Parliament, by all inconvenient and unjust Acts passed in Parliament, which concern either King or subject; which cannot be reversed nor repealed, though erroneous . . . but only by an act of repeal or restitution in another Parliament. Now this is an infallible maxim, both in common, civil, and canon law, that the court or person to whom the last appeal is to be made, is the supreme power.[181]

William Bridge went further, applying to Parliament the modern legal realist precept that 'the law is whatever the judges say it is': 'How can the people think the parliament has done anything contrary to the law of the land, when the parliament are the judges thereof?'[182] The precept was much more plausible in the case of Parliament then, than it is in the case of courts today, because Parliament was ultimately bound only by 'laws' of such abstraction and vagueness as *salus populi suprema est lex* ('the welfare of the people is the supreme law').

As Prynne's final remark suggests, many lawyers believed that a final, unappealable power to interpret laws, and *a fortiori*, to review the validity of statutes, was in practice equivalent to a sovereign power to make laws. The belief that the supreme judicial and supreme legislative powers are one and the same can be found in the writings of both royalists and parliamentarians, as well as eminent lawyers such as Sir Matthew Hale.[183] Parliamentarian theorists such as Parker and Herle were well aware that the power to interpret law could be manipulated so as to alter it, and to frustrate the will of the original law-maker. It followed

---

[178] *The Case of Captain John Streater* (1653), in Howell (1816–28: v. 387).
[179] ibid. 387 and 386, respectively.   [180] Petyt (1739: 197).   [181] Prynne (1643: 92–3).
[182] W. Bridge, *The Wounded Conscience* (1642: 43), quoted in Greenberg (1991: 219 n. 30).
[183] See the text to nn. 312–15, below.

that Parliament's supreme power to make law would be insecure unless it also possessed supreme power to interpret it: according to Parker, if it 'does not extend to the preservation of laws in their true vigour and meaning, as well as to the creation of them, 'tis empty and defeasible'.[184] 'There is in the interpretation of law upon the last appeal, the same supremacy of power requisite, as is in making it; and therefore grant the King supreme interpreter, and 'tis all one, as if we granted him to be supreme maker of law; and grant him this, and we grant him to be above all limits, all conditions, all human bonds whatsoever.'[185] Few people, if any, thought that inferior courts should possess this sovereign power.[186] It belonged to the kingdom as a whole, which was most fully represented by Parliament. Sir Edwin Sandys explained to the House of Lords in 1614 that 'some cases are above a common court and fit only for this high court, for no king will set his crown, nor subject his liberty, upon the judgment of any common court'.[187] Another Member of Parliament said in 1621 that 'the judges are judges of the law, not of the Parliament. God forbid the state of the kingdom should ever come under the sentence of a judge.'[188]

'In Parliament', declared Henry Parker, 'the Lords and Commons represent the whole kingdom, to whom so great a Majesty is due, and sit in a far higher capacity than inferior judges do'.[189] Parliament's business included the highest affairs of the realm, and it possessed judicial and legislative powers that far exceeded those of inferior courts of law, including the power to change the laws by which those courts were bound. While advocating the Earl of Strafford's attainder in 1641, Oliver St John, a prominent lawyer, declared that the 'same law gives power to the Parliament to make new laws, that enables the inferior court to judge according to the old. The rules that guide the conscience of the inferior court is from without, the prescripts of the Parliament, and of the common law; in the other [Parliament] the rule is from within, that *salus populi* be concerned . . .'[190] St John's use of this distinction to justify Strafford's attainder was controversial, but not the distinction in itself. Many people believed that Parliament should limit itself to established laws and precedents when judging individuals, but agreed that it could depart from them when dealing with the general affairs of the realm.[191]

---

[184] Parker (1643a: 7). Charles Herle made the same point in Herle (1642: 12).

[185] Parker (1642: 44). This was also assumed by Philip Hunton, who argued that to concede that the King had 'the legal power of final judging' of constitutional disputes would be to concede absolute power to him: P. Hunton, *A Treatise of Monarchy* (1643), in Wootton (1986: 209–10). Sir Robert Filmer made the same assumption: see n. 313, below.

[186] Sommerville (1986: 96).

[187] *Hastings Parliamentary Papers, Report of Sandys* (12 May 1614), quoted in Judson (1949: 294). During the debate on impositions, James Whitelocke said '[t]he commonwealth would not put any court save the high court of parliament in trust with so important a cause into which both their fortunes and liberties are involved' (Foster 1966: ii. 221).

[188] Notestein *et al.* (1935: ii. 411).   [189] Parker (1642: 9).

[190] Rushworth (1721: viii. 676).

[191] See e.g. the anonymous tract, *Touching the Fundamental Laws or Politic Constitution of this Kingdom* (1643), in Dunham and Pargellis (1938: 613), and the opinion of John Selden (n. 365, below).

John Marsh, for example, took this view, adding that it 'ought not to be conceived, or imagined' that 'this great Court, which so far transcends all others
... should be less in power ... than any other'.[192] The University of Oxford,
a royalist stronghold during the civil war, declared that whereas the judges of
ordinary courts, whose power was 'merely judicial', were 'bounded by the
present laws, and limited also by their own acts', 'the high court of parliament
having (by reason of the king's supreme power presiding therein) a power legislative as well as judicial, are not so limited by any earthly power, but that they
may change and over-rule the laws and their own acts at their pleasure'.[193]

Parliamentarian theorists sometimes agreed with royalists that, although
unlimited power was dangerous, any attempt to limit it might be even more
dangerous, because it might be disabled from being used for good as well as
evil. This was one reason why royalists believed that it was better to trust the
King with absolute prerogatives rather than to limit them.[194] Even Henry Parker
conceded that

if it be agreed upon, that limits should be prefixed to Princes, and judges appointed to
decree according to those limits, yet another great inconvenience will presently affront
us; for we cannot restrain Princes too far, but we shall disable them from some good, as
well as inhibit them from some evil, and to be disabled from doing good in some things,
may be as mischievous, as to be enabled for all evils at mere discretion.[195]

For this reason, he suggested, parliamentary rather than judicial review was
the best way to control the power of princes.

[M]ost countries have found out an art and peaceable order for public assemblies,
whereby the people may assume its own power to do itself right without disturbance to
itself, or injury to princes ... That princes may not be now beyond all limits and laws,
nor yet left to be tried upon those limits and laws by any private parties, the whole community in its underived majesty shall convene to do justice.[196]

In other words, the most prudent regimes allowed their parliaments to control
their princes, without crippling the unlimited power that enables extraordinary
measures to be taken when coping with emergencies.[197]

---

[192] J. Marsh, *An Argument, or Debate in Law: Of the great Question concerning the Militia* (1642:
40), quoted in Judson (1949: 374).
[193] *Reasons of the Present Judgment of the University of Oxford Concerning the Solemn League
and Covenant etc.* (1 June 1647), in Scott (1809–15: iv. 623). Franklin (1978: 14–15) attributes this
argument to Dr Robert Sanderson, one of Charles I's favourite preachers, who was Regius Professor
of Divinity at Oxford from 1642–7.
[194] See text to n. 63, above.
[195] Parker (1642: 14). Much the same argument can be found in John Locke's subsequent discussion of the prerogative: Locke (1690: 374–5 (II: 159–61)).
[196] Parker (1642: 14–15).
[197] This was crucial to Parker's attempt to justify the unprecedented actions of the two Houses in
1642, in assuming sole control of the militia and issuing ordinances without the King's assent. Parker's
argument was that in an emergency, the absolute powers usually exercised by the King could legitimately be exercised by the two Houses (Mendle 1995: 73–6, 84–5, 88).

In a representative parliamentary tract published in 1643, the idea that Parliament could be bound by written laws was condemned as 'destructive and absurd', because Parliament had to be free to make such new laws as public exigencies should require. The most fundamental law of all, the object of all particular laws, was '*salus populi*', the welfare of the people whom Parliament represented. Since particular laws could not adequately provide for all future exigencies, Parliament necessarily possessed a 'superlative and uncircumscribed power' to alter them whenever that fundamental law should require it. The power to make laws was 'nothing but equity reduced by common consent into polity', and the Court of Parliament 'being itself fundamental and paramount, comprehending law and equity, and being entrusted by the whole for the whole, is not therefore to be circumscribed by any other laws which have their being from it, not it from them'.[198]

Many writers agreed that the need for flexibility in response to changing circumstances meant that Parliament could not be bound by law. 'Men are not to make, nor may any entertain the laws with an oath never to change them', preached Richard Heyricke; 'none may make a perpetual marriage to their own mandates, there may be a cause for a bill of divorce, room for retractions'.[199] Charles Herle argued that since God had not ordained any particular form of government for England, it must have been originally established by 'an act of man', which was necessarily an 'act of will, and so arbitrary'.[200] Furthermore, 'it must remain somewhere arbitrary still, else our forefathers should not convey that same government to us which they began, but should bind us in that wherein they were themselves free: it is the privilege of God's laws only to bind unalterably'.[201] This element of arbitrariness resided 'where it was at first in the consent and reason of the State', which 'the law places in the votes of Parliament, where this arbitrariness [is] allayed and balanced by number, trust, self interest, 'tis best secured from doing hurt'.[202] The argument that every generation must have an equal power to determine its laws can also be found in a Remonstrance of the two Houses passed in 1642. It declared that

some precedents ought not to be rules, and no precedents can be bounds to the proceedings of a Parliament, because some are such as ought not to be followed, and all may fall short and be different from the present case and condition of things; and if this were not a truth, instead of doing what we please, we should be obliged to do whatsoever our ancestors pleased to do, whether they did well or ill, and how different or unlike soever, their case and condition should be to ours.[203]

Bulstrode Whitelocke, an eminent lawyer, later defended the necessity of Parliament's having supreme and boundless power in order to promote peace and

---

[198] *Touching the Fundamental Laws or Politic Constitution of This Kingdom* (1643), in Dunham and Pargellis (1938: 613, 610).
[199] Heyricke (1646: 7).   [200] Herle (1643: 3).   [201] Herle (1642: 13).   [202] ibid.
[203] *An Exact Collection of all Remonstrances, Declarations [etc.]* (1643: 726). A very similar statement from another Remonstrance of the two Houses is quoted in Burgess (1992*b*: 223–4).

prosperity. What might be required for that purpose could not be predicted in advance, and so nothing could be safely excluded from legislative control.

If it be demanded, what is the subject matter of that good and peace? It will be said: every thing, according as accidents, and emergencies, may make application of them, in the wisdom, and judgment, of a public council. And consequently, all matters whatsoever may be accounted legislative affairs, within the authority of parliament.[204]

Although people's lives, liberties, and estates were therefore subject to Parliament's power, it was not likely to be abused. The requirement that all three estates, King, Lords, and Commons, had to assent to any new law was the best possible security against 'the destruction of any man's life and fortune, and the public interest'.[205]

The idea that Parliament itself was the foundation of the law was a recurring theme in parliamentary propaganda during the civil war. Parker described Parliament as 'that court which gave life and birth to all laws'.[206] According to one writer, 'we have no other fundamental, but the Parliament'.[207] Charles Herle explained that 'what is meant by those fundamental laws of this kingdom . . . is that original frame of this co-ordinate government of the three Estates in Parliament, consented to and contrived by the people in its first constitution'.[208] An anonymous author drew the logical conclusion. Having described Parliament as the 'spring head' of the law, he asked: 'Orders of Parliament against law! Sure, rivers mistake their course, and rain falls to the clouds. What law, what courts, what religion have we established, but by Parliaments?'[209]

For all of these reasons, Parliament, rather than the ordinary courts, was regarded as the principal guardian of the liberties of subjects. James Whitelocke said in 1610 that 'the ancient frame of the commonwealth' was superior to that of other nations in three respects; the first two concerned the necessity for parliamentary assent to taxation and legislation, and 'the third is that the Parliament is the storehouse of our liberties'.[210] His son, Bulstrode Whitelocke, later described parliaments as 'the defenders of [the people's] liberties; and the bulwark between their rights, and all designs of oppression'.[211] People on both sides of the political spectrum, even during the civil war, agreed with this, while disagreeing as to whether or not the King in person was an essential part of Parliament. Parliament was frequently described as the 'armamentary', the 'pillars [and] bulwarks', the 'foundation' or 'fountain', of the people's liberties.[212]

---

[204] Whitelocke (1766: ii. 335); see also ibid. 185.   [205] ibid. 339–40.
[206] Parker (1642: 42).   [207] Anonymous (1643: 58).   [208] Herle (1642: 6).
[209] Anonymous (1642f: 5, 10).   [210] Foster (1966: ii. 109).
[211] Whitelocke (1766: ii. 194).
[212] Nicholas Fuller, *Debate in Committee* (22 May 1610), in Kenyon (1986: 38); Prynne (1643: page 2 of the 'Epistle Dedicatory'); Rushworth (1721: v. 583); J. Howell, *The Preheminence and Pedigree of Parlement* (1644: 10), quoted in D. L. Smith (1994: 241); J. Milton, *Eikonoklastes*, in Milton (1962: iii. 337, 578–9).

Inferior courts were ineligible to play this role because their judges were appointed and subject to dismissal by the King. In those circumstances, judicial review of the validity of statutes could easily have become a tool of royal absolutism.[213] In 1621, Edward Alford warned Parliament that 'it is dangerous that the judges, a few persons, dependant and timorous some of them, should judge between the king and the state of their liberties. . . . If this should be suffered what will become of us?'[214] In 1642, Charles Herle asked whether judges, being skilled in, and sworn to uphold, the law, could be trusted more than Parliament to protect the privileges and properties of ordinary subjects. Having explained that members of Parliament 'are subjects themselves, not only entrusted with but self-interested in those very privileges and properties', he answered:

It was the wisdom of this [form of] government, considering men's aptness rather to warp after their interests and ends, than to be kept upright by their skills and oaths, to trust it rather to the many independent men's interests, than to a few dependent men's oaths. Every day's experience tells us that interests are better state security than oaths.[215]

Judicial decisions in cases such as the *Five Knights'* and the *Ship-Money* cases were widely believed to prove Herle's point. Because they upheld the King's most controversial claims to certain absolute prerogatives, the judges were accused of having bent the law at his behest. Six judges who decided the *Ship-Money* case in his favour were impeached in Parliament.[216] Oliver St John complained that 'now the law does not only not defend us, but the law itself is made the instrument of taking all away', and Lord Falkland accused the judges of 'turn[ing] our guard into a destruction, making law the ground of illegality'.[217] The Grand Remonstrance, drawn up by the House of Commons and presented to the King in 1641, complained that '[j]udges have been put out of their places for refusing to do against their oaths and consciences; others have been so awed that they dared not do their duties', and also that 'the common law courts . . . are known frequently to forsake the rules of the common law, and straying beyond their bounds, under pretence of equity, to do injustice'.[218] William Pierrepont elaborated on the latter theme, when speaking against Sir Robert Berkeley, whose judgment in the *Ship-Money* case was widely condemned.

This judge will have the law to be what to him seems reason; the reason limited to him to judge of, is what the common law says is so, what a statute has so enacted. For him to judge this or that is law, else a mischief shall follow, because the law in such a thing is imperfect, therefore he will make a law to supply it, or because that the law written in

---

[213] Sommerville (1986: 96–7).

[214] Notestein *et al.* (1935: v. 195), quoted in Sommerville (1986: 97).

[215] Herle (1642: 13–14).   [216] See below, nn. 367–72.

[217] 'Mr. St.-John's Speech to the Lords . . . concerning Ship-Money' (1640: 31), quoted in Judson (1949: 357); John Nalson, *An Impartiall Collection of the Great Affairs of State from . . . 1639 to the Murther of King Charles I* (1682/3: i. 726), quoted in Judson (1949: 357). See also *Denzil Holles speaks against the judges*, in W. J. Jones (1971: 214).

[218] The Grand Remonstrance (1641), in Gardiner (1906: 213–14).

such particulars is against his reason, therefore his reason's to be law; then must follow, as often as a judge's reason changes, or judges change, our laws change also. Our liberties are in our laws, which a subject may read, or hear read, this is his, this he may do and be safe; and that thus the judge ought to give judgment, and then he is free. The excessive growth of courts of reason and conscience came from great and cunning persons; and though not the most sudden, yet the most dangerous and sure ways to eat out our laws, our liberties.[219]

In 1644, *The Souldier's Catechism* included in a list of the principal objectives of the parliamentary army 'the regulating of our courts of justice, which have been made the seats of iniquity and unrighteousness'.[220]

The common law itself was probably more at fault than the judges. There was much truth in Justice Berkeley's statement, in *Ship-Money*, that '[t]he law is of itself an old and trusty servant of the king's; it is his instrument or means which he uses to govern his people by'.[221] As Theodore Plucknett explains, 'the Crown had everything to gain by an appeal to antiquity . . . it was the common law itself, of which the prerogative was a part, which was the source of offence'.[222] Disillusionment caused a massive crisis of confidence in the ability of the common law to protect traditional liberties from royal encroachments.[223] Those who feared arbitrary government turned away from the common law, and attempted to use statute law to remedy its deficiencies.[224] The Petition of Right (1628) originated in a proposal to seek the King's confirmation of the common law, but when it became apparent that the common law was hopelessly unclear, the goal became that of securing a new statute giving legislative force to the interpretation preferred by the House of Commons.[225] In 1642, the Long Parliament enacted statutes prohibiting the levy of ship money, and controlling the King's discretionary power to summon and dissolve parliaments.[226]

In the debates leading to the Petition of Right, Sir Edward Coke himself said that 'a Parliament brings judges, officers, and all men into good order', and it has been suggested that even he had transferred his former faith in the common law to Parliament.[227] '[T]he sovereignty of Parliament was more tolerable than a fundamental law of which the Stuart prerogative was so legitimate a portion.'[228] According to Corinne Weston, common law theories became clearly subservient to the parliamentarian cause during the 1640s, their primary role being to prove that a sovereign parliament had existed from time immemorial. 'Despite the

[219] Howell (1816–28: iii. 1293–4).
[220] *The Souldiers Catechism, Composed for the Parliament's Army* (1644: 9), quoted in Hill (1965: 260).
[221] The *Ship-Money* case (1637), in Howell (1816–28: iii. 1098).
[222] Plucknett (1926: 54); see also ibid. 69.
[223] Glenn Burgess devotes an entire chapter, entitled 'The Crisis of the Common Law', to this thesis: Burgess (1992*b*: ch. 8). Michael Mendle describes the 'political failure of the common law' as 'spectacular': Mendle (1973: 221). See also Russell (1979: 347–52); Judson (1949: 279–80).
[224] Wootton (1986: 34).   [225] Russell (1979: 354–5).   [226] Kenyon (1986: 179).
[227] MacKay (1924: 238–9); Wormuth (1939: 66).
[228] Plucknett (1926: 54); see also ibid. 69.

seeming paradox ancient constitutionalists would now combine common-law language and reasoning with the advocacy of the modern theory of parliamentary sovereignty.'[229] The alliance between parliamentarian and common law theories will be explored in the following section.

4. Common Law Theories of the Authority of Parliament

Many lawyers believed that the common law was the immediate source and measure of the authority of both King and Parliament. As Sir Henry Finch succinctly explained, 'the common law is as the *primum mobile* which draws all the planets in their contrary course'.[230] But this belief was not in itself inconsistent with the main thrust of either royalist parliamentarian theories, because it was possible that the common law conferred sovereign power on either the King or Parliament.[231]

Many lawyers combined elements of common law and parliamentarian thinking.[232] On their view, the authority of the common law and that of Parliament were one and the same: the common law embodied the wisdom of the community, as expressed in immemorial customs, and that wisdom, as Herle put it, 'lives still in that which the law calls the "reason of the kingdom", the votes and ordinances of Parliament'.[233] Professor Pocock describes this as 'a doctrine of consubstantiality, like denying that God the Father could annihilate God the Son. ... [E]very exaltation of the antiquity of law was an exaltation of the authority of Parliament'.[234]

Henry Parker held this view. Although he insisted that Parliament possessed a sovereign, even arbitrary, power to make law, he also acknowledged that Parliament and the King were both creatures of the law.[235] John Pym believed that an ancient constitution predated both kings and statutes:

[T]he law of England, whereby the subject was exempted from taxes and loans not granted by common consent of parliament, was not introduced by any statute, or by any charter

---

[229] Weston (1991: 397–8). She disagrees with Pocock on these issues at ibid. 389. See also Weston and Greenberg (1981: 322–3 n. 28).

[230] Finch (1678: 85).

[231] This depends on sovereign power being regarded as a power conferred by law, rather than as a power standing above, and creating, all law: see the distinction between H. L. A. Hart's theory of sovereignty, and Hobbesian theories, discussed in Chapter 10, Section 2, and Chapter 2, Section 1. D. E. C. Yale contrasts the position of Sir Matthew Hale and Thomas Hobbes in something like this fashion in Yale (1972).

[232] Sommerville (1986: 108).   [233] Herle (1642: 6).

[234] Pocock (1987: 271); see also ibid. 302. On the overlap between the common law and parliamentarian theories, see Sommerville (1986: 95–100), and Christianson (1991: 86, 95). Nenner says that two themes emerged from Charles I's trial, 'parliament as keeper of the fundamental law and parliament as sovereign; and no one appeared much troubled by the possible contradictions between the two' (Nenner 1993: 194). See also Hill (1965: 253).

[235] Parker (1642: 5). For his views on the sovereign authority of Parliament, see text to nn. 302–10 and 374–7, below.

or sanction of princes, but was the ancient and fundamental law, issuing from the first frame and constitution of the kingdom.[236]

It must have been this ancient law which, he later explained, 'does entitle a king to the allegiance and service of his people; it entitles the people to the protection and justice of the king . . . The law is the boundary, the measure between the king's prerogative, and the people's liberty.'[237] But when he said this, Pym was already one of the leaders of the House of Commons whose exalted views of the authority of the two Houses helped drag a confused nation into civil war. He could not possibly have agreed that the King's judges had authority to declare statutes invalid. In an influential speech made in Parliament in 1640, he said that '[t]he Parliament is . . . the soul of the Commonwealth, that only is able to apprehend and understand all the symptoms of all such diseases which threaten the body politic'. Parliament's privileges had been violated because 'inferior courts have touched the court of parliament. It is against nature and order that inferior things should undertake to regulate superior. The court of Parliament is a court of the highest jurisdiction and cannot be censured by any law or sentence but its own.'[238] As early as 1626, during debate over the Duke of Buckingham's impeachment, he maintained that 'in a Court of Parliament . . . the proceedings are not limited either by the civil or common laws, but matters are adjudged according as they stand in opposition or conformity with that which is *Suprema lex, salus populi*'.[239]

Johann Sommerville argues that very few of the lawyers who assumed that the common law was in some sense superior to statute would have agreed that the judges had ultimate authority to decide what the common law was.

It was one thing to say that the common law was superior to statute and quite another to say that the judges were superior to Parliament. . . . The dominant legal opinion . . . was that Parliament and not the judges had supreme power to interpret the laws . . . Once Parliament had decided on a point of law, it was not open to the judges to reverse its decision. So the enactments of Parliament defined what was actually enforceable as law in the courts. Parliament was 'absolute' in the sense that there was no human authority— except a later Parliament—which could reverse its decrees.[240]

It does not follow that, even on this view, Parliament's role was limited to interpreting, declaring, and enforcing specific rules and principles of the common law. As we will see, the common law was considered a law of reason, whose most fundamental principle was the welfare of the community. In interpreting the common law, outdated rules and doctrines had to give way to that fundamental principle. In other words, Parliament's power to interpret the common law necessarily included the power to change it.

---

[236] Pym's Speech at Manwaring's Impeachment (4 June 1628), in Kenyon (1986: 15).
[237] Pym's Reply at Strafford's Impeachment (April 1641), in Kenyon (1986: 196).
[238] Cope and Coates (1977: 149–50).   [239] Rushworth (1659: i. 335).
[240] Sommerville (1986: 96–7). See also Weston (1991: 388–90); and Pocock (1987: 265, 270–1, and 302).

This was Sir Edward Coke's opinion, at least by the time he wrote his *Institutes of the Laws of England.*[241] In *Dr Bonham's* case, decided much earlier, he said that a statute contrary to common right and reason would be void,[242] but most historians deny that he meant that the courts could invalidate such a statute. In the case which he reported immediately after *Dr Bonham's* case, he said that '[t]here are divers customs in London which are against common right, and the rule of the common law, and yet they are allowed in our books, and *eo potius*, because they have not only the force of a custom, but are also supported and fortified by authority of Parliament'.[243] Several historians have argued that, in *Dr Bonham's* case, he intended to claim for the courts only a large power of equitable construction, to avoid consequences that Parliament could not have intended, or to modify provisions that were nonsensical, self-contradictory, or otherwise impossible to apply.[244] In Earl Russell's words, '[i]f Parliament . . . passed an Act dividing something into four equal thirds, the judges would not be guilty of any contempt of Parliament were they to fail to divide the thing in question into four equal thirds. That is all Sir Edward Coke was after.'[245] It has also been suggested that Coke was attempting to revive the medieval approach, which allowed judges such latitude in the application of statutes that they could sometimes decline to apply them at all, but did not recognize any judicial power of formal nullification. If that is so, Coke's position was anachronistic: the evolution of constitutional practice and theory had long made the medieval approach obsolete.[246] On the other hand, a few historians have argued that Coke did intend to assert something like a power of judicial review.[247] In the most recent assessment of the evidence, Glenn Burgess concludes that the truth probably lies somewhere in between: that Coke had in mind a power of statutory construction, but one so broad that in an extreme case it could be tantamount to a power of judicial review.[248]

---

[241] See text to n. 257 ff., below.   [242] (1610) 8 Co. Rep. 113b, 118; 77 E.R. 646, 652.

[243] *The Case of the City of London* (1610) 8 Co. Rep. 121b, 126a; 77 E.R. 658, 664. Burgess (1996: 187–8) comments that 'it seems clear from the examples given [in the case] that parliament could sanction things contrary even to some of the dearest principles (reasons) of common law'.

[244] See Thorne (1938); Gough (1955: 21–2, 30, 35–40, 48, and 57); MacKay (1924: 222–31); Plucknett (1926); Gray (1972: 35, 42 ff.); Stoner (1992: ch. 3: esp. 57–9).

[245] *Parliamentary Debates, Fifth Series, vol. 572*, House of Lords, 5 June 1996, 1303 (Earl Russell is the eminent historian Conrad Russell).

[246] Thorne (1942: 88–90); see also Plucknett (1926: 45). Holdsworth said that Coke 'was so thoroughly steeped in medieval law that he sometimes reproduced ideas which he himself would have admitted to be archaic' (Holdsworth 1946a: 67).

[247] The most thorough defence is Berger (1969); see also Corwin (1955: 48–50) and Boyer (1997: 82–9). Boyer concedes that Coke was going well beyond the precedents he cited, and 'breaking new ground': ibid. 83–4. Detmold (1989a: 444–50, esp. 449–50) argues that Coke regarded Parliament as the final court of appeal, whose statutes were binding on lower courts only if and in so far as they settled disputes between particular, named individuals; otherwise, they were liable to be overruled just as common law doctrines can be overruled if judged to be erroneous. This argument is open to the objections that (*a*) it is heavily based on McIlwain's erroneous account of Parliament's functions before the 1640s (see Chapter 3, Section 3, above), and (*b*) it implausibly attributes to Coke Detmold's own belief that an inferior court is entitled to overrule (as well as to distinguish) legal rules laid down by a superior court.

[248] Burgess (1996: 193).

It would be fruitless to attempt to settle this interpretative question here, or even to add to the debate. More important is the fact that even if in *Dr Bonham's* case Coke did advocate something like a power of judicial review, he later changed his mind. Burgess argues persuasively that by 'common right and reason', the crucial words used in that case, Coke meant the common law, not natural law. The evidence includes Coke's own statements in his *First Institute* that 'the common law of England is sometimes called right, sometimes common right' and that 'reason is the life of the law, nay the common law itself is nothing else but reason'.[249] But in the *First Institute*, Coke acknowledged that Parliament controlled, and could alter, the common law: '[t]he common law hath no controller in any part of it, but the high court of parliament; and if it be not abrogated or altered by parliament, it remains still'.[250] In *The Case of Proclamations* he said that 'the King cannot change any part of the common law . . . without Parliament'.[251]

Coke, and some other lawyers such as Sir John Davies, disapproved of Parliament changing the common law, because they believed that the wisdom of a single Parliament was unlikely to surpass the wisdom embodied in laws shaped by the accumulated experience of many generations. Sir John Davies's preface to his *Le Primer Report des Cases [etc.]* has been described as 'the classic exposition of the common lawyer's viewpoint'.[252] There, he praised the common law as 'the most perfect and most excellent, and without comparison the best' of the laws of the realm, because it had been 'tried and approved time out of mind' whereas statutes were 'imposed upon the subject before any trial or probation [is] made . . . whether they will breed any inconvenience or not'. For that reason, he thought that the common law should not be changed by statute. However, he had no doubt that it could be so changed, even in fundamental respects, and that if it was, any resulting inconvenience could be remedied only by a further statute. He said that 'when our parliaments have altered or changed any fundamental points of the common law, those alterations have been found by experience to be so inconvenient for the commonwealth, as that the common law has in effect been restored again, in the same points, by other acts of parliament in succeeding ages'.[253] Coke took the same view, warning that '[i]t is not almost credible to foresee, when any maxim, or fundamental law of this realm is altered . . . what dangerous inconveniences do follow, which most expressly appears by this most unjust and dangerous Act of 11.H.7'.[254] As Glenn Burgess points out, although Davies and Coke did their best to discourage statutory amendments of the common law, they did not suggest that it was impossible or impermissible: 'the very tone of their remarks shows their awareness of the impossibility

[249] Coke (1628: 97*b* and 142*a*).   [250] ibid. 115*b*, and see also 110*a*.
[251] 12 Co. Rep. 74, 75; 77 E.R. 1352, 1353.   [252] Wootton (1986: 129).
[253] Sir John Davies, *Le Primer Report des Cases [etc.]* (1615), in Wootton (1986: 131–2).
[254] Coke (1644: 41). Coke also told the Commons in 1628 that 'I never saw a maxim of the common law altered but much loss and harm did ensure': quoted in White (1979: 113).

of denying that the common law could be altered'.[255] They were not alone. In 1640, for example, Sir Simonds D'Ewes expressed the opinion 'that the fundamental laws of this kingdom cannot be altered but by Parliament'.[256]

In his *Fourth Institute*, Coke stated that '[t]he power and jurisdiction of the Parliament for making of laws in proceeding by bill, is so transcendent and absolute, as it cannot be confined either for causes or persons within any bounds'. He then gave some examples of statutes that seem to override basic laws of the land, for instance, a statute of attainder enacted without any trial being held.[257] 'I question not the power of Parliament', he said, 'for without question the attainder stands of force in law'.[258] There are other passages in the Institutes where he contemplated statutes contrary to Magna Carta without any hint that they would be invalid.[259] According to MacKay, nowhere in the Institutes is there 'any expression to the effect that the judges may do otherwise than put into effect the will of the framers of the statutes'.[260] In the *Second Institute*, Coke said that '[t]he highest and most binding laws are the statutes which are established by parliament', and that a resolution of all the judges was of the highest authority 'next unto the court of Parliament'.[261] Furthermore, there are passages in the *Fourth Institute* and in his *Reports* similar to those of Fortescue and St German, attesting to the superior wisdom of Parliament. For example:

And as in the natural body when all the sinews being joined in the head do join their forces together for the strengthening of the body, there is *ultimum Potentiae*: so in the politic body when the king and the Lords Spiritual and Temporal, Knights, Citizens, and Burgesses, are all by the King's command assembled and joined together under the head in consultation for the common good of the whole Realm, there is *ultimum Sapientiae* [the highest wisdom].[262]

Coke later said that 'one act of parliament is *instar omnium* [like all others], being a proof of the unanswerable and highest nature . . .',[263] and in discussing the argument that a particular statute was 'unjust and untrue', he stated:

I might answer that *le court de parliament est de tres grand honor et justice, de que nul home doit imaginer chose dishonerable*. And with the Doctor and Student [by St German] . . . that it cannot be thought that a statute that is made by the authority of the

---

[255] Burgess (1992b: 22); he adds that 'Davies and Coke were untypical in the extent to which they detested innovation'.

[256] Notestein (1923: 63–4).   [257] Coke (1644: 36).   [258] ibid. 37.

[259] Coke (1641: 51); for other examples, see MacKay (1924: 233 n. 33 and 244 n. 65); Coke (1641: Cap. 29); Coke (1644: 38–9 and 41); Gough (1955: 40–1). See also Burgess (1996: 190–2); and Stoner (1992: 43). At one point, Coke observed that 'all statutes made contrary to *Magna Charta*, which is *lex terrae*, from the making thereof until 42 E.3 are declared and enacted to be void', but this was because of the statute 42 E.2 (Coke 1641: 186); see also ibid., 'Introduction'.

[260] MacKay (1924: 237).

[261] Coke (1641: page 7 of the Preface, entitled 'A Proeme to the Second Part of the Institutes', and 218).

[262] Coke (1644: 3).   [263] ibid. 342.

whole realm as well as of the king, and of the lords spiritual and temporal, as of all the commons, will recite a thing against the truth.[264]

Coke certainly held that Parliament possessed great authority when, in the latter part of his career, he was a prominent member of the House of Commons. He accepted the orthodox opinion that the knights and burgesses in Parliament 'represent all the commons of the whole realm', and that 'parliament represents the body of the whole realm'.[265] Members of the Commons 'appear for multitudes, and bind multitudes'; they are 'the Inquisitors-General of the grievances of the Kingdom', because 'they have the best notice from all parts thereof'.[266] In discussing the legal effect of the Petition of Right, in 1628, he stated that 'whatever the Lords House and this House have at any time agreed upon no judge ever went against it, and when the judges in former times, doubted of the law they went to the parliament, and there resolutions were given, to which they were bound', and that 'a Parliament brings judges, officers, and all men to good order'.[267] It should be noted that his supposed statement, 'Magna Carta is such a fellow, that he will have no sovereign', is now regarded as a misquotation. Coke was rejecting a suggestion made by the House of Lords that the Petition of Right, in reaffirming Magna Carta, should include a qualification 'saving' the King's 'sovereign power' (or absolute prerogatives) from its reach, and what he really said was 'Magna Carta is such a fellow, that he will have no saving'. He was therefore affirming the authority of statute, which he describes in the relevant passage as 'absolute without any saving of sovereign power', to control all the prerogatives of the King.[268]

Coke's discussion in the *Fourth Institute* of the 'transcendent and absolute' power of Parliament is sometimes interpreted as being limited to Parliament's judicial power as the 'High Court of Parliament'.[269] This is not plausible. At the time, the words 'High Court of Parliament' were invariably used to denote a body to which legislative as well as judicial powers were attributed. James Howell, a Clerk of the Privy Council, expressed the common understanding of his day when he referred to it as 'this sovereign law-making court'.[270] James I said that 'this high Court of Parliament . . . is nothing else but the King's great Council, which

[264] ibid. 343. For a similar passage, see *Priddle and Napper's Case*, 11 Co. Rep. 8b, 14a; 77 E.R. 1155, 1163. Coke also said that 'an Act of Parliament, to which the Queen and all her subjects are parties, and give consent, cannot do a wrong': *Margaret Podger's* case, 9 Co. Rep. 104a, 107a; 77 E.R. 883, 889. See Cromartie (1995: 25 n. 68).
[265] Coke (1644: 1, 29).   [266] *Lords Journal*, vol. 3, 307, in Kenyon (1986: 94).
[267] The first quote is from a manuscript account of the 1628 Parliament, quoted in Judson (1949: 266); the second is in MacKay (1924: 238).
[268] See Stoner (1992: 46–7); and Burgess (1996: 208).
[269] McIlwain (1910: 140–3); Gough (1955: 42–4); Walker (1988: 147); Detmold (1989b: 449–50) (see n. 247, above). Burgess (1996: 179–81 and 187) emphasizes Coke's understanding of Parliament as a court whose acts were judgments, but also notes Coke's recognition that Parliament made new laws and in doing so, was not bound by the ordinary law of the land: ibid. 181, 193.
[270] J. Howell, *The Preheminence and Pedigree of Parlement* (1644), in Scott (1809–15: v. 47, 51, 48).

the King does assemble either upon occasion of interpreting, or abrogating old laws, or making of new, according as ill manners shall deserve . . .'.[271] In 1604, Sir Edward Phelips, the Speaker of the House of Commons, spoke of 'the jurisdiction of several courts of justice; the commanding and imperial court whereof is this your majesty's great and high court of parliament; by whose power only new laws are to be instituted, imperfect laws reformed, and inconvenient laws abrogated'.[272] Sir Henry Finch explained in 1627 that the Parliament was 'a Court . . . having an absolute power in all causes', including power 'to make laws' as well as 'to adjudge matters in law'.[273] The University of Oxford referred to 'the high court of parliament having . . . a power legislative as well as judicial'.[274] Examples of this way of speaking are legion.[275] As Charles Gray concludes,

Parliament was regularly *called* a court . . . Yet parliamentary lawyers were aware that the 'court' they sat in was a court in a rather strained sense . . . No one believed Parliament was a court in a radical sense that would truly deny or repress its legislative character—that is to say, a body incapable of making or changing law, capable only of discovering and interpreting law conceived as somehow 'already there'.[276]

Coke himself often referred to law-making as one of the main functions of the 'High Court' of Parliament: '[t]he highest and most binding laws are the statutes which are established by parliament; and by authority of that highest court it is enacted . . .';[277] '[t]he common law hath no controller in any part of it, but the high court of parliament; and if it be not abrogated or altered by parliament, it remains still';[278] the law may be changed 'only . . . by the authority of the high (that in truth is the highest) court of Parliament'.[279] In the *First Institute* he treated ordinary law-making as part of the 'jurisdiction' of the 'court' of parliament: '[t]he jurisdiction of this court is so transcendent, that it makes, enlarges, diminishes, abrogates, repeals, and revives laws, statutes, acts, and ordinances'.[280] He concluded that discussion by noting that 'this properly does belong to the jurisdiction of courts, and therefore this little taste hereof shall suffice', anticipating his

---

[271] 'Speech of 1605', in James I (1616: 287). James also said that 'Parliament is the highest court of justice, and therefore the fittest place where diverse natures of grievances may have their proper remedy, by the establishment of good and wholesome laws': 'Speech of 1609', in ibid. 314.

[272] Cobbett (1806–20: i. 989).   [273] Finch (1678: 233).

[274] *Reasons of the Present Judgment of the University of Oxford Concerning the Solemn League and Covenant etc.* (1647), in Scott (1809–15: iv. 623).

[275] J. Cowell, *The Interpreter* (1607), in Prothero (1913: 410); *The Privileges and Practice of Parliaments in England* (1628), quoted in Vile (1967: 25); Spelman (1644: 9); Twysden (1849: 173); *The Trials of Charles the First and some of the Regicides* (1649), in Howell (1816–28: iv. 999). See also Gough (1955: 100–1) (for William Prynne), and Weston and Greenberg (1981: 38) (for Charles I).

[276] Gray (1992: 182). See also Burgess (1992b: 21–3); Sommerville (1986: 99), and Weston (1991: 374, 388, and 390).

[277] Coke (1641: page 7 of the Preface, entitled 'A Proeme to the Second Part of the Institutes').

[278] Coke (1628: 115b); see also ibid. 110a.

[279] 'Preface' to 4 Co. Rep., quoted in MacKay (1924: 221).

[280] Coke (1628: 110a). In this respect Coke was simply following earlier writers: see Cromartie (1995: 53).

more detailed treatment of the topic in the *Fourth Institute*. At the time, the word 'jurisdiction' commonly meant the power of ruling in general, and not just the authority of a judge; for example, 'supreme jurisdiction' was the same as *maiestas*, which we now call sovereignty.[281] Even in the late seventeenth century, Sir Matthew Hale included legislation in the 'jurisdiction' of the 'court' of Parliament: '[T]he *commune concilium* . . . consists of both houses of parliament; which together with the king is the highest and greatest court in England, and has a plenitude of power as well legislative as deliberative and executive, or power of jurisdiction in its full comprehension'.[282]

There can be no doubt that Coke was concerned with all aspects of Parliament's activities in the *Fourth Institute*, even though that volume is devoted to 'The Jurisdiction of Courts'. Under 'The Matters of Parliament' he listed 'The state of the kingdom of England' and 'The defence of the kingdom', which hardly called for judicial treatment, and commented that 'divers laws and statutes have been enacted and provided for these ends'.[283] He discussed Parliament's distinctively judicial business in separate sections, titled 'Writs of Error in Parliament' and 'Judicature', before proceeding to consider Acts of Parliament, of which he acknowledged that 'some be introductory of a new law, and some be declaratory of the ancient law'.[284] Immediately after the chapter on Parliament, he discussed the 'Councell Board' (Privy Council), treating it as yet another 'court' although clearly regarding it as an advisory body with political rather than legal functions.[285]

MacKay argues that all the examples of Parliament's 'transcendent and absolute' power and jurisdiction that Coke provided in the *Fourth Institute* involve acts passed by Parliament in a 'judicial' capacity.[286] On the other hand, Dicey suggests that this may be because interference with the rights of nominated individuals is a more striking display of absolute power than changes to the rights of the public at large.[287] But Wormuth's opinion seems preferable to both MacKay's and Dicey's:

[Coke] was merely following his usual practice of arguing from precedent. The cases he cites are typical of bills one finds recorded as having their first or second or third reading in the Commons Journal. They are heterogeneous; they have no definite general character and one can classify them only from a preconceived theory of the nature of legislation. Coke had no clear preconceived theory of the nature of legislation, and most of his contemporaries had none.[288]

Even MacKay concludes that 'there can be little doubt but that in the Institutes Coke regarded Parliament as supreme in a much greater sense than as a court of last resort. He conceives of it as being without any limits'; 'there can

---

[281] Tierney (1982: 30; 1963*a*: 307–8); for many examples of 'jurisdiction' used in this way, see McIlwain (1910: 169–72, 195).

[282] Hale (1796: 9).   [283] Coke (1644: 9).   [284] ibid. 21–5.   [285] ibid. 53–7.

[286] MacKay (1924: 245); see also Gough (1955: 42).   [287] Dicey (1964: 48).

[288] Wormuth (1939: 62).

be little question that Coke possessed the idea, in the germ at least, of Parliamentary Sovereignty'.[289]

Glenn Burgess has recently made the most persuasive attempt to distinguish Coke's understanding of Parliament's law-making power from modern notions of parliamentary sovereignty. He argues that Coke understood fundamental law to be 'the skeleton of the entire body of the common law', the framework of abstract principles from which the rest of the law was derived. Parliament could change the common law, but only in accordance with those abstract principles: '[i]f fundamental law was like a skeleton, then parliament was like a plastic surgeon . . . [with] considerable power to mould and refashion tissue and muscle'.[290] But this analogy is misleading, for two reasons. First, there was no clear distinction between fundamental, 'skeletal' common law principles, and others. Whether or not a principle was so fundamental that it could not justifiably be changed was itself a debatable question, which was necessarily subject to the unappealable and in that sense absolute 'judgment' of Parliament. Secondly, the most fundamental principles of the common law were (and still are) as abstract as 'justice ought to be done', and 'the welfare of the community ought to be protected'. That makes it impossible, in this context, to draw any practical distinction between interpretation and legislation: the interpretation of such abstract principles is what legislation is all about, even today. As late as 1886, A. V. Dicey in his classic exposition of the doctrine of parliamentary sovereignty said that statutes 'bear a close resemblance to judicial decisions, and are in effect judgments pronounced by the High Court of Parliament'.[291] No one has ever suggested that Dicey regarded Parliament as a court rather than a genuine legislature.

These points are illustrated by the prominent lawyer Thomas Hedley's explanation of Parliament's role, in his speech on impositions in the House of Commons in 1610. He first insisted that the common law as a whole was of higher authority than Parliament:

[T]he parliament has his power and authority from the common law, and not the common law from the parliament. And therefore the common law is of more force and strength than the parliament, *quod effecit tale maius est tale.* . . . But you will say the parliament has often altered and corrected the common law in diverse points and may, if it will, utterly abrogate it, and establish a new law, therefore more eminent. I answer set a dwarf on a tall man's shoulders, and the dwarf may see further than the tall man, yet that proves him not to be of a better stature than the other. The parliament may find some defects in the common law and amend them (for what is perfect under the sun), yet the wisest parliament that ever was could never have made such an excellent law as the common law is. But that the parliament may abrogate the whole law, I deny, for that were includedly to take away the power of the parliament itself, which power it has by the common law.[292]

---

[289] MacKay (1924: 245, 242).   [290] Burgess (1996: 192).
[291] Dicey (1964: 197).   [292] Foster (1966: ii. 174).

This is not in itself inconsistent with parliamentary sovereignty, when that is understood as an authority conferred by the common law, and one which is 'continuing' rather than 'all embracing'—something that not even Parliament can abdicate or restrict.[293]

Hedley acknowledged that Parliament could change the law for the good of the commonwealth, and rejected the idea that inferior courts could overrule its legislative judgments. The common law, he explained, was 'tried reason, that is, the best reason or the quintessence of reason, reason tried and allowed by the wisdom of time for many ages together to be good and profitable for the commonwealth'. It was therefore not static, but transcended old customs and precedents:

it is a good and necessary argument to say, it is ill for the good of the commonwealth, ergo, no law, which must needs be so because the end of the laws is the good of the commonwealth. Whatsoever, then, crosses this end, the law will not digest it, but reject it as unsavoury as soon as time, the trier of truth, has found it out, and that notwithstanding any former precedents or judgments . . .

He supplied several examples of cases in which old precedents and judgments had been rejected for this reason.[294] On the other hand, he said that the common law 'cannot be proved by reason alone . . . but by custom and reason conjoined'; only parliament, by statute, could declare something to be law on the ground of reason alone. '[T]o say it is reason and good for the commonwealth ergo law is no good argument, for then . . . the parliament were in vain.'[295] In other words, the common law, understood as reason and custom combined, conferred authority on Parliament, and not inferior courts, to make new laws based on reason alone, which necessarily meant Parliament's assessment of reason. Furthermore, Parliament possessed this authority because of its superior wisdom:

I entered into consideration with myself what that was that could try reason better than the parliament. I found it could not be the judges of the law, for they are all joined to the parliament and there is besides the whole wisdom of the whole realm, the king, his nobilities, clergy and commons . . .

[T]he reason or opinion of three or four judges . . . must needs come short of the wisdom of the parliament.[296]

Judgments of great legal consequence were sometimes reached without adequate argument, because the matter in dispute was of little value or the parties too poor to retain counsel; moreover, judges were not always strictly impartial or highly competent. There was '[t]herefore no reason that a judgment should be so sacred or firm that it may not be touched or changed, for then every judgment should be stronger than an act of parliament . . .'.[297]

---

[293] See Chapter 2, text to n. 28 ff.   [294] Foster (1966: ii. 176–8).
[295] ibid. 182 and 181.
[296] ibid. 175 and 178. The judges were 'joined to the parliament' because they were required to attend and give advice on questions of law (Jay 1994: 118, 124–28).
[297] Foster (1966: ii. 179).

According to Hedley, then, the common law was ultimately concerned with the common good, and could be amended by Parliament if the common good so required. Coke would surely have agreed, since he believed that the law depended more on reason than on custom: 'how long soever it [a custom] has continued', he said, 'if it be against reason, it is of no force in law'; 'nothing that is contrary to reason, is consonant to law'.[298] But decisions about the common good are just what modern legislatures are supposed to make; they, too, are expected to be governed by fundamental, abstract principles of political morality that are not judicially enforceable.

This evidence suggests that the claim made on behalf of the two Houses in the 1640s, that Parliament had an absolute power to override any statute or precedent in order to protect the welfare of the people (*'salus populi'*), was not in itself a radical one. What was really radical was the further claim that the two Houses could exercise that power without the King's actual assent.[299] The idea that the common law was fundamentally a matter of reason directed to the welfare of the commonwealth, of which Parliament was the supreme judge, was entirely orthodox.

The extent to which those who made these claims regarded Parliament primarily as a 'court', making 'judgments' guided by 'law', is often overemphasized. Glenn Burgess errs in this respect in discussing Henry Parker's claim that Parliament possessed an 'absolute, indisputable power of declaring law'. Burgess argues, along McIlwainian lines, that Parker thought of this power to 'declare' law as judicial, not legislative, and as exercised by the two Houses of Parliament in their capacity as a court rather than as a legislature.[300] 'Parker's argument was not that every legal system needed a (legislative) sovereign, but that every legal system needed a court whose decisions were final and absolute (i.e. against which there could be no appeal)'.[301]

This dichotomy is alien to Parker's thought, and that of most of his contemporaries. It is true that Parker described Parliament as 'the supreme judicature, as well in matters of state as matters of law', which therefore 'assumes a right to judge' whether the people were endangered by the King's rejection of its advice.[302] But he made it clear that, at least in extraordinary matters of 'state', Parliament was bound not by legal precedents, but by 'right and justice', and 'the paramount law that shall give law to all human laws whatsoever, and that is *Salus Populi*'.[303] The superintending power of the 'court' of Parliament was clearly not a judicial power as we understand the concept today: its ability to override any legal precedent in the interests of public necessity made it 'arbitrary' and 'sovereign'.[304] It combined supreme powers to interpret, and also to

---

[298] Coke (1628: 62*a* and 56*b*).   [299] See the text to nn. 376 and 385, below.
[300] Burgess (1996: 177–8).   [301] ibid. 178.   [302] Parker (1642: 28, 34).
[303] ibid. 37–8 and 3; and see also 45 (Parliament is bound not by statutes or precedents but only its own 'justice and honour'). This seems to clarify what he meant by saying that '[i]n this intricacy . . . we must retire to ordinary justice': ibid. 44.
[304] ibid. 34 and 45.

make, law, which were indistinguishable: 'there is in the interpretation of law upon the last appeal, the same supremacy of power requisite, as in the making of it', whose possessor is 'above all limits, all conditions, all human bonds whatsoever'.[305] That is why 'the King . . . has in Parliament a power as extensive . . . as ever the Roman Dictator's was, for the preventing of all public distresses', a power which was 'uncircumscribed'.[306] The King 'governed his subjects by his laws, his laws by his lawyers, and . . . his subjects, laws and lawyers by advice of Parliament, by the regulation of that court which gave life and birth to all laws'.[307]

Parker acknowledged that the legislative power was 'partly in the King, and partly in the kingdom', and in 'ordinary cases, when it concerns not the saving of the people from some great danger or inconvenience', neither the King nor the Parliament could 'make a general binding law or ordinance' without the assent of the other.[308] But it is not the case that he regarded the power of the two Houses to act independently of the King, in extraordinary cases of public danger, as judicial and not legislative. By implication, they could make a 'law or ordinance' in such cases without the King's assent.[309] Indeed, Parker specifically said that the two Houses had made 'use of their legislative power' to make an ordinance to secure forts and the militia.[310] To sum up, Parker maintained that both in ordinary cases with the King's assent, and in extraordinary cases without it, the two Houses exercised a supreme power to 'judge' what the welfare of the people required, a power that would not today be called 'judicial', and that he himself acknowledged was indistinguishable from a sovereign power to make laws.

In 1644, Sir John Spelman said that

though this High Court . . . be the supreme Judicatory of the Kingdom, yet it has not that superiority of judgment ascribed to it, for any sovereign faculty it has in discerning the true dictate and result of law, no more than of other particular science . . . for the judgment of sciences belongs to the professors therefore, and the judgment of law as well as other sciences. But the High Court of Parliament is the superior judge . . . for the great power they have to bind all other judgment, and to make their sentence law, though . . . it was not law before.[311]

Parker's thesis that a supreme power to interpret law was equivalent to a supreme power to make it was popular in the seventeenth century.[312] It was endorsed by royalist writers, such as Sir Robert Filmer:

Every supreme court must have the supreme power, and the supreme power is always arbitrary—for that is arbitrary which has no superior on earth to control it. The last appeal in all government must still be to an arbitrary power, or else all appeals will be in infinitum,

---

[305] ibid. 44.   [306] ibid. 24 and 9.   [307] ibid. 42.   [308] ibid. 16.

[309] Especially given that 'where this ordinary course cannot be taken for the preventing of public mischiefs, any extraordinary course that is for that purpose the most effectual, may justly be taken and executed': ibid. The extraordinary power 'to save the Kingdom from ruin' is 'the sovereign power': ibid. 45.

[310] ibid. 42, 34, and 27, respectively.   [311] Spelman (1644: 9).

[312] Philip Hunton agreed that the powers of making laws and of interpreting them were 'in effect' the same: Hunton (1643: 26).

never at an end. The legislative power is an arbitrary power, for they are *termini convertibiles* [convertible terms].[313]

Sir Matthew Hale, the most widely respected judge of the century, later employed much the same premise to refute the claim that the House of Lords was the supreme and final court (or 'dernier resort') of the kingdom, whose judgments were not subject to appeal. In his *The Jurisdiction of the Lords House of Parliament*, written in the 1670s, Hale criticized that claim as 'extravagant' and 'untrue'.[314] If the Lords were the dernier resort, he argued,

then is the legislative power virtually and consequentially there also . . . For what if the lords will give judgment against an act of parliament, or declare it null and void? If they have the dernier resort, this declaration or judgment must be observed and obeyed and submitted unto irremediably; for no appeal lies from their judgment, if they be the supreme court.

But that would be to 'wholly dissolve the legislative power of the whole body of the parliament, king lords and commons, and put it into the house of lords; who, by their supreme decisive power without appeal, and as the dernier resort originally radicated in them, may at their pleasure render the legislative power idle vain and insignificant'. He therefore held that '[w]herever the dernier resort is, there must needs be the sovereignty; and so this word is constantly used and joined with it'; it 'is one of the greatest points of sovereignty that can be and is coincident with it'.

The truth is, it is utterly inconsistent with the very frame of a government, that the supreme power of making of laws should be in the king with the advice of both his houses of parliament, and [final] judgment should be in one of the houses without the king and the other . . . Therefore it is not only *de facto* true in our government, but it is most necessary, that the supreme decisive power or jurisdiction and the dernier resort must be where the legislative power is. And it is impossible it should be otherwise . . .

'[T]he laws of this kingdom', he added, 'have better provided for the preservation both of the king's rights and the people's, than to put them and all the laws of the kingdom into the power of the lords'.[315] This conclusion, and its basic premise—that a power to declare legislation null and void is in effect a legislative power, and if final and unappealable, a sovereign legislative power —obviously applied *a fortiori* to courts inferior to the House of Lords.

Common lawyers sometimes spoke of statutes contrary to natural law being 'void'.[316] But it does not follow that they believed that judges possessed

---

[313] *The Free-holders Grand Inquest, Touching our Soveraigne Lord the King and His Parliament* (1648), in Filmer (1991: 99–100).

[314] Hale (1796: 204–5).   [315] ibid. 205–7.

[316] In *Darcy v Allin*, Nicholas Fuller argued that if an Act of Parliament prohibited a man from living by the labour of his own trade, 'it were a void Act; for an Act of Parliament against the law of God directly is void, as is expressed in the Book of Doctor and Student . . .': *Noy's Reports* 173, 180; 74 E.R. 1131, 1137. In the debate on impositions, Fuller said 'every law against the laws of God (although it were by act of parliament) is a void law' (Foster 1966: ii. 153).

authority to declare statutes invalid. In his book *Law, a Discourse Thereof* (1627), an exposition of the common law that is reputed not to have been superseded until Blackstone's *Commentaries*, Sir Henry Finch wrote that positive laws contrary to natural law 'lose their force, and are no laws at all'.[317] This has been interpreted as a denial of parliamentary sovereignty.[318] But later in the same book, Finch asserted that Parliament had 'an absolute power in all causes', including the making of laws, and that 'if the Parliament itself do err (as it may) it can no where be reversed but in Parliament'.[319] Finch was not the only one who thought that parliamentary sovereignty was compatible with natural law. Everyone would have agreed with James I's statement, that by God's law 'all common and municipal laws must be governed: and except they have dependence upon this law, they are unjust and unlawful'.[320] James did not, of course, believe that his judges could hold his statutes to be invalid. The important questions were, first, which organ of government had ultimate legal authority to determine the requirements of God's law, and secondly, what the consequences were if it erred. The orthodox answer to the first question was the King in Parliament, and to the second, that if the King in Parliament erred, the only earthly remedy was repeal by a subsequent statute. 'It is true', Samuel Rutherford conceded, that 'the Parliament has no power to deny their voices to things just, or to cross the law of God'.

Objection: Who should then punish and coerce the Parliament in the case of exhorbitance?
Answer: Posterior Parliaments.
Objection: Posterior Parliaments and people both may err.
Answer: All is true, God must remedy that only.[321]

It was generally agreed that subjects were not morally obligated to obey a statute manifestly contrary to the laws of God, although disobedience was legally punishable and had to be submitted to.[322] That was probably what was usually meant when such statutes were said to be 'void': they were not morally binding, even though they could be repealed only by Parliament. Judges, like other subjects, might justifiably disobey such statutes, but it did not follow that they had legal authority to declare them invalid, any more than it followed that ordinary subjects had such authority. All were subordinate to the King in Parliament.

The evidence, then, strongly suggests that even among lawyers who accepted a common law theory there was very little support for judicial review of the validity of statutes. Alan Cromartie observes that Coke's dictum in *Dr Bonham's* case was 'largely ignored', for example in Ireland's and Davies's independent abridgements of Coke's *Reports*, which suggests that it was 'embarrassingly extreme'.[323] It is doubtful that the other judges sitting with Coke in *Dr Bonham's*

[317] Finch (1678: 75); for the book's reputation, see Stephen and Lee (1917: vii. 13).
[318] See Gough (1955: 34).   [319] Finch (1678: 233).
[320] 'A Speach in the Starre-Chamber' (20 June 1616), in James I (1616: 330).
[321] Rutherford (1644: 389).   [322] Sommerville (1986: 97–8).   [323] Cromartie (1995: 28).

case endorsed it. Apart from the ambiguity of his famous dictum, there is persuasive evidence that it was an embellishment he added, after judgment had been delivered, when preparing his report of the case.[324] It may have been one of those 'dangerous conceits of his own, uttered for law', which in 1616 he was ordered to remove from his *Reports*.[325] Chief Justice Hobart made comments similar to Coke's in *Day v Savadge*, but they too have been interpreted as assert- ing a power of construction rather than of nullification.[326]

The authority of Parliament was sometimes challenged during the 1640s, when the two Houses of Parliament, or their officials, were often accused of trampling on traditional rights in their desperate struggle with the King. Although it was possible to question the authority of the two Houses, without questioning that of a proper Parliament, in some minds the former seems to have led to the latter. And not without cause: if the two Houses could not be trusted to protect the rights of the people, then the main reason for trusting the King in Parliament was also put in doubt. By the late 1640s, when the Levellers and the Army advoc- ated Agreements of the People to limit Parliament's authority, confidence in the institution had clearly been damaged.[327]

As early as 1642, one author said that although the two Houses, with the King's consent, could make new laws or repeal old statutes,

the main common law, and the ancient rites, usages, and native customs of the land, they themselves cannot alter. For (as the lawyers phrase is to say) it is *oppositum in objecto* that they that sit by the common laws, and by the ancient rites, usages, and customs of the land, should alter and change that which gave them their authority to be a repres- entative body.[328]

The Welsh judge David Jenkins, an outspoken supporter of the King who was imprisoned by the Houses during the civil war, argued that Parliament was bound by Magna Carta, and cited Coke's dictum in *Dr Bonham's* case with approval.[329] Gough correctly points out that this was the first appearance of that dictum 'as a matter of public, political, and constitutional importance'.[330] The dictum was also cited by another lawyer who was punished for supporting the King, the Recorder of Lincoln, Sir Charles Dallison. In a long tract written while he was imprisoned by the two Houses, Dallison defended at considerable length the thesis that 'the Parliament itself (that is, the King, the Lords, and Commons) although unanimously consenting, are not boundless, the judges of the realm by

---

[324] This suggestion is based on a comparison of a newly discovered manuscript report of the case with Coke's official report of it: see Gray (1972).

[325] Boyer (1997: 88 n. 158).

[326] (1614) *Hobart* 85, 87; 80 E.R. 235, 237; for this interpretation, see Gough (1955: 38–9).

[327] See Section 6, below.   [328] Anonymous (1642e: 6).

[329] *A Discourse touching the Inconveniencies of a long-continued Parliament* (1647), 123 ff., quoted in Gough (1955: 104). For a discussion of Jenkins's treatment at the hands of the two Houses, see Ashton (1994: 109–13).

[330] Gough (1955: 105).

the fundamental law of England have power to determine which Acts of Parliament are binding and which void . . .'.[331] His position was quite unusual, because he denied that either Parliament as a whole, or the House of Lords, was the highest court of law. He maintained that the judges of the Courts of King's Bench, Common Pleas, and Exchequer 'are the judges of the realm, and the persons unto whom all the people of this nation are bound lastly and finally to submit themselves for matter of law'.[332] He acknowledged that '[i]t may seem strange to some' that the High Court of Parliament should be limited in power.[333]

Coke's dictum also inspired John Cleveland to state in 1649 that 'if . . . the Parliament shall enact . . . against natural equity, as to constitute a man judge in his own case, such a statute is void in itself, and shall be controlled by the common law'.[334] It was also argued by or on behalf of Sir John Maynard, an eminent lawyer and member of the House of Commons who was imprisoned by the two Houses in 1647, that Magna Carta 'has a double consideration either as it is in part a statute law, and so it is subject to the pleasure of the Parliament, to be altered, repealed or confirmed, or as it is a declaration of the common law, or common reason and equity, and thus it is not prostrate at the feet of Parliament's will'.[335]

Lord President Keble is reported to have said in 1651 that

[w]hatsoever is not consonant to the law of God in Scripture, or to right reason, which is maintained by Scripture, whatsoever is in England, be it Acts of Parliament, customs, or any judicial acts of the Court, it is not the law of England, but the error of the party which did pronounce it; and you or any man else at the bar, may so plead it.[336]

It is clear that some lawyers did advocate some kind of judicial review of the validity of statutes. But disapproval of the idea was much more common, because it was inconsistent with the prevailing hierarchy of political authority, and the principal theories—royalist as well as parliamentarian—that sought to justify that hierarchy.

5. Parliamentary Sovereignty Affirmed

Charles I claimed in 1628 that the House of Commons was attempting 'to break through all respects and ligaments of government, and to erect a universal overswaying power to themselves, which belongs only to us and not to them'.[337] The question contested in the civil war was who possessed this 'universal overswaying

---

[331] Dallison (1648: 48). Dallison and this tract are discussed in D. L. Smith (1994: 237–9).
[332] ibid. 64.   [333] ibid. 39.
[334] J. Cleveland, *Majestas Intermerata* (1649: 38–40), quoted in Gough (1955: 105).
[335] *The Lawes Subversion: or Sir John Maynard's Case Truly Stated* (1648: 13–14), quoted and discussed in Ashton (1982: 198; 1994: 116).
[336] *R v Love* (1651), in Howell (1816–28: v. 172).
[337] 'Royal Proclamation' (1628: 33–4), quoted by Mosse (1968: 137).

power'.[338] Royalist theories maintained that it belonged to the King, and parliamentarian theories, to Parliament. They also disagreed as to who made law in Parliament. Did the King alone make law, acting with the advice and consent of the two Houses, but without sharing his legislative power with them, or did all three estates, King, Lords, and Commons, share the power to make law? Were statutes enacted by the King, in Parliament, or by the King, Lords, and Commons in Parliament?[339]

Everyone agreed that the King's authority was at its highest in Parliament.[340] Even those who insisted that his authority outside Parliament was strictly limited by law agreed that it was not so limited when exercised with the assent of the two Houses. The Commons' petition of July 1610 informed James I that he could not punish his subjects except in accordance with the law of the land, but acknowledged that '[t]he policy and constitution of this your kingdom, appropriates unto the kings of this realm, with the assent of Parliament . . . the sovereign power of making laws'.[341] Richard Martin, a lawyer who was to become Recorder of London, said in Parliament in the same year that 'the King of England [is] the most absolute King in his Parliament; but of himself, his power is limited by law'.[342] James Whitelocke, a future Justice of the Court of King's Bench, made the same point in a speech in Parliament in 1610, asserting that although the King possessed sovereign power, which 'can control all other powers and cannot be controlled but by itself . . . the power of the king in parliament is greater than his power out of parliament; and doth rule and control it'. Therefore, the King's power to make Acts of Parliament, with the assent of the Lords and Commons, is 'the most sovereign and supreme power above all and controllable by none'.[343] In 1640, Lord Digby said: 'The King out of Parliament has a limited power, a circumscribed jurisdiction, but waited on by his Parliament, no monarch of the East is so absolute in dispelling grievances'.[344] Philip Hunton drew the same distinction in 1643, arguing that 'the sovereignty of our Kings is radically and fundamentally limited', but 'all three [estates of Parliament] together are absolute and equivalent to the power of the most absolute monarch', who 'has no limits or bounds under God, but his own Will'.[345]

It was often said that, just as new laws could be made only by Parliament, existing laws could be amended or repealed only by the same authority. In 1604 the Speaker, Sir Edward Phelips, said of Parliament that 'justice therein is such,

---

[338] See Judson (1949: 7).   [339] Weston and Greenberg (1981: 4).

[340] For royalist statements to this effect, see text to nn. 82–90, above.

[341] Petition of the House of Commons (7 July 1610), in Prothero (1913: 302).

[342] R. Martin, in S. R. Gardiner (eds), *Parliamentary Debates in 1610* (1862: 89), quoted in Sommerville (1986: 154).

[343] 'James Whitelocke's Speech on Impositions' (29 June 1610), in Kenyon (1986: 61).

[344] 'Speeche of the Lord Digby in Parliament concerning grievances and the Triennial Parliament' (19 January 1640/1: 24), quoted in Judson (1949: 352); see also ibid. 69.

[345] Hunton (1643: 31, 61, and 6). Elsewhere he said that 'all [estates] taken together have an unlimited power' (Hunton 1644: 23).

and so absolute, that no such laws can either be instituted, reformed, or abrogated, but by the unity of the Common's agreement, the Lord's accord, and Your Majesty's royal and regal assent'.[346] In the opinion of Lord Chancellor Ellesmere, this principle ruled out judicial nullification of statutes: 'it is *Magis Congruum* that Acts of Parliament should be corrected by the same pen that drew them, than to be dashed in pieces by the opinion of a few judges'.[347] Sir Henry Yelverton, who served as a Member of Parliament, Solicitor-General, and Attorney-General, used very similar language in criticizing Coke's remarks in *Dr Bonham's* case.[348] In his speech to Coke's successor as Chief Justice of the King's Bench, Lord Ellesmere reiterated his opinion that judges could not nullify statutes they deemed contrary to common right and reason, because such questions were for the King and Parliament to decide.[349] On another occasion, he stated that Parliament 'ought to be obeyed and reverenced, but not disputed' because it was 'the great Council of the kingdom, wherein every subject has interest'.[350]

Coke's dictum in *Dr Bonham's* case was listed among the reasons for his dismissal in 1616 as Chief Justice of the King's Bench, which Coke complained was orchestrated by his enemies, Lord Ellesmere and Sir Francis Bacon.[351] Bacon held that at the foundation of every legal system there was a 'supreme and commanding power', which could not be bound by any 'civil law'. All civil laws were changeable, although the moral or natural law was not; even 'the most ungracious and mischievous laws', which created no moral obligation, therefore created 'a civil obligation'.[352] Bacon held that in England, Parliament possessed the 'supreme and absolute' power.[353] He went so far as to assert that

if the parliament should enact in the nature of the ancient *lex regia*, that there should be no more parliaments held but that the king should have the authority of the parliament, or, *e converso*, if the King in Parliament were to enact to alter the state, and to translate it from a monarchy to any other form, both these acts were good.[354]

---

[346] Cobbett (1806–20: i. 989).

[347] *Observacions Upon Cooke's Reportes* (1615), in Knafla (1977: 297, 307). In *The Earl of Oxford's Case* (1615), Ellesmere quoted Coke's remarks in *Bonham*, but then said: 'And yet our books are, that the Acts and Statutes of Parliament ought to be reversed by Parliament (only), and not otherwise': 1 Chan. Rep. 1, 12; 21 E.R. 485, 488. Judson (1949: 98–9) omits Ellesmere's comment, and erroneously suggests that he endorsed Coke's remarks. Ellesmere is also reported to have criticized Coke for 'trampling' on an Act of Parliament, and 'blowing [it] away as vain, and of no value', in a footnote to *Dr Bonham's* case (1610) 8 Co. Rep. 113b, 118a; 77 E.R. 646, 652n.C.

[348] Quoted in Knafla (1977: 149).

[349] 'The Lord Chancellor's Speech to Sir Henry Montague' (1616) Moore (K.B.) 826, 828; 72 E.R. 931, 932.

[350] Lord Ellesmere, *Touching the Post-Nati* (1608: 108), quoted in Knafla (1977: 249).

[351] Boyer (1997: 87 n. 157).

[352] 'Aphorisms on the greater Law of nations, or of the Fountains of Justice and Law' (unpublished, *c*.1614), quoted in Coquillette (1992: 241 and 243).

[353] Bacon (1858–74: vi. 160).

[354] ibid. vii. 370 inc. n. 1. See discussion in Wormuth (1939: 59).

It is difficult to imagine more radical changes to the fundamental constitution of the kingdom.

The judges' role with respect to statutes, Bacon said on another occasion, was 'to expound them faithfully and apply them properly'.[355] He insisted that '[n]o decrees shall be made, upon pretence of equity, against the express provision of an act of parliament';[356] otherwise, 'the judge would pass into the legislator, and everything would be at discretion'.[357] He later modified this view, by suggesting that courts of equity could legitimately 'decree against laws and statutes which are obsolete, and have not lately been passed'. On the other hand,

with more recent statutes, which are found to be injurious to public justice . . . the power of giving relief . . . should be left not to the judge, but to kings, councils, and the supreme authorities of the state, who should be empowered to suspend the execution of them by Acts or Proclamations, till the re-assembling of Parliament or of that body which has the power of repealing them.[358]

During parliamentary debate in 1604, concerning the proposed union of England and Scotland, Sir Henry Spelman observed that 'some will say a Parliament can do anything. I say it may quickly change the law but not the minds of the people whom . . . we must seek to content.'[359] In 1610, the Lord Treasurer, Robert Cecil, said 'I know not what an Act of Parliament may not do'.[360] These were words previously used by Cecil's father, Lord Burghley, whom James I quoted in 1616. Criticizing some judges for erroneously advising him that Parliament could not unite his two kingdoms, England and Scotland, without first uniting their laws, James observed that 'I am since come to that knowledge, that an Act of Parliament can do greater wonders: and that old wise man the Treasurer *Burghley* was wont to say, he knew not what an Act of Parliament could not do in England'.[361]

Sir Richard Grosvenor, a prominent Cheshire gentleman, advised his fellow electors in 1624 to be very careful in electing their representative to the House of Commons, because Parliament had 'an absolute jurisdiction and an unlimited power to dispose of the lives, limbs, states, goods, honors and liberties of the subject, yea and of their religion too, so far as concerns the free public and outward profession thereof'.[362]

---

[355] *Chudleigh's* case, in Bacon (1858–74: vii. 623).

[356] *Ordinances in Chancery*, in Bacon (1858–74: vii. 760).

[357] 'Example of a Treatise on Universal Justice or the Fountains of Equity', Aphorism 44, in Bacon (1858–74: v. 96).

[358] Aphorism 58, in ibid. v. 99–100.

[359] H. Spelman, 'Of the Union', quoted in G. Burgess (1992*b*: 26).

[360] Foster (1966: i. 66).

[361] 'A Speach in the Starre-Chamber' (20 June 1616), in James I (1616: 329). James was referring to advice given to him in 1604 by judges who apparently considered this a case of Parliament being unable to do what is logically impossible: see Levack (1987: 38–9).

[362] 'Speech of Sir Richard Grosvenor' (2 February 1624), Cheshire Record Office, Grosvenor MSS, Eaton 25, quoted in Sacks (1992: 112).

John Selden, the eminent legal historian regarded by many of his contemporaries as the greatest jurist of his age, declared in 1628 that 'an act of Parliament may alter any part of Magna Carta', and anticipated the most extreme nineteenth century hypotheticals by asserting that Parliament could make it a law that anyone rising before nine o'clock should be put to death.[363] Admittedly, Selden may have believed that such a law would not be contrary to the laws of God or nature, which do not prescribe any time for rising.[364] In his *Table Talk*, he is recorded as saying that Parliament had 'arbitrary power . . . in point of making law', although not 'in point of judicature'.[365]

In a tract written in 1629, Sir Francis Kynaston criticized suggestions that the King and Parliament were separate, and that Parliament could act without the King. He insisted that Parliament included the King, and agreed that there was no limit to what it could do, provided it was understood in that sense.[366]

The common lawyers in the House of Commons expressed their understanding of the relationship between Parliament and inferior courts very clearly, when six judges who had decided for the King in the *Ship-Money* case were impeached in 1641. Many of those judges had stated that a statute prohibiting the King from defending the kingdom, or from requiring aid from his subjects for that purpose, would be void.[367] They were interpreted as denying that Parliament could take away the King's supposed right to levy ship money in the way he had done in 1637, a right whose existence was vehemently disputed by many members of Parliament. The judges were therefore accused, not only of wrongfully permitting the King to steal from his subjects, but also of denying that those subjects could ever obtain redress in Parliament. This was one of the 'treasons and misdemeanours' alleged against them.[368]

In explaining the case against the judges to the Lords at a joint sitting of both Houses, Oliver St John, a future solicitor-general, argued that

to have their judgments and their Acts of Parliament overthrown by the judges . . . makes parliaments to be nothing; this sets up the judges above the Parliament, this puts us out of hope of redress; if they may overthrow the proceedings of that Parliament of 3 Car. [which passed the Petition of Right] they may by the same reason overthrow the actions of this, and of all future parliaments . . . . The judges . . . are the executors of the statutes, and of the judgments and ordinances of Parliament; they have here made themselves the executioners of them; they have endeavoured the destruction of the fundamentals of our laws and liberties.[369]

---

[363] Johnson *et al.* (1977: iii. 439; ii. 576). On Selden's reputation, see Tuck (1982: 138).

[364] Johann Sommerville made this point in correspondence.   [365] Selden (1696: 133).

[366] F. Kynaston (1629), 'A True Presentation of Forepast Parliaments', quoted in Burgess (1996: 38–9).

[367] These statements are discussed in the text to nn. 130–3, above.

[368] *The Accusation and Impeachment of John Lord Finch* (1640), in Scott (1809–15: iv. 131–2).

[369] Howell (1816–28: iii. 1272).

Arguing for the conviction of Sir Robert Berkeley, William Pierrepont condemned his alleged statement 'that in some cases the judges were above an act of Parliament' as 'false' and 'malicious'.[370]

Unlimited power must be in some to make and repeal laws, to fit the dispositions of times and persons. Nature places this in common consent only, and where all cannot conveniently meet, instructs them to give their consents to some they know or believe so well of, as to be bound to what they agree on. His Majesty, your Lordships, and the Commons, are thus met in Parliament, and so long as we are often reduced to this main foundation our King and we shall prosper . . . . This judge . . . would pull up that root of our safeties and liberties, which whilst we enjoy, the malice and injustice of all other courts and persons can never ruin; and when near to ruin (as most near of late) this only sure remedy will help us; nothing can ruin a Parliament, but itself.[371]

Edmund Waller complained that Justice Crawley 'had the boldness to put the power of Parliament in balance with the opinion of the judges'. By denying that Parliament could abolish ship money, the judge 'did not only give as deep a wound to the commonwealth as any of the rest, but dipped his dart in such a poison, that, so far as in him lay, it might never receive a cure'. Waller suggested that Crawley could not really have believed this:

Sure he is more wise and learned, than to believe himself in this opinion, or not to know how ridiculous it would appear to a parliament, and how dangerous to himself. And therefore, no doubt, but by saying no parliament could abolish this judgment, his meaning was, that this judgment had abolished parliaments.[372]

The evidence reviewed so far suggests that the theories of parliamentary sovereignty propounded during the civil war by apologists for the two Houses were not as novel as some historians have suggested. Their novelty lay in attributing sovereignty, in extraordinary cases of necessity, to the two Houses alone. Their assumption that in ordinary cases the King in Parliament was sovereign was not new. But the propaganda campaign that accompanied the civil war did call forth more frequent and explicit discussions of the nature and location of sovereign power. William Prynne, a lawyer and Puritan polemicist who was commissioned to provide a justification of the radical steps taken by the two Houses in 1642, declared that

Parliament is the absolute sovereign power within the realm, not subject to, or obliged by the letter or intendment of any laws, being in truth the sole law-maker, and having an absolute sovereignty over the laws themselves (yea, over Magna Carta and all other objected acts) to repeal, alter, determine and suspend them when there is cause, as is undeniable by its altering the very common law in many cases . . .[373]

---

[370] ibid. 1286.   [371] ibid. 1293–4.   [372] ibid. 1301–2.
[373] Prynne (1643: Bk. iv, 15). In this passage, he meant by 'Parliament' a body which included the King.

Henry Parker, the principal parliamentary propagandist, agreed:

That there is an arbitrary power in every State somewhere tis true, tis necessary, and no inconvenience follows upon it; . . . it is no good consequence [i.e. it does not follow] . . . that the Parliament doth abuse power, because it may.

[A]n absolute indisputable power of declaring Law . . . must rest in them [Parliament], or in the King, or in some inferior court, or else all suits must be endless, and it can nowhere rest more safely than in Parliament.[374]

Parker later said that the two Houses of Parliament had an 'arbitrary power' to 'abridge the freedom of the subject', to 'enlarge the kings prerogative, beyond all measure', even to repeal 'the great Charter, the Charter of Forests, and the Petition of Right'.[375] He defended the unorthodox view that sovereign power ultimately lay in the two Houses alone, rather than in the King in Parliament, because in emergency situations the two Houses could legitimately act without the King's personal assent in order to protect the commonwealth.[376] But if ordinances passed by the two Houses in these situations were beyond legal challenge, then *a fortiori*, so were statutes passed by the two Houses with the King's assent in normal circumstances.[377]

Charles Herle stated that 'the very being' of the law depended on the King and Parliament, who could not be resisted even if they 'should enjoin us all to deny Christ, and worship the sun', or 'enact paganism itself'.[378] Lesser writers made similar comments. According to one, 'he knows nothing of parliaments, that knows not that the House of Commons is absolutely entrusted with our persons and estates, and by our laws invested with a power to dispose of them as they shall think meet'.[379] Others asserted that it possessed 'the supremacy, or the *supremum jus domini*, that is over all laws, *figere* or *refigere*, to make or disannul them at pleasure';[380] that it 'is above the law, has power of the whole realm, can question, alter, and repeal any law, when it sees just cause, and make any new laws, *pro re nata*, as new emergent occasions shall require';[381] and that it 'can take away life, liberty and estate of any man, by a legislative power, without any written law'.[382]

In 1642, the two Houses resolved '[t]hat when the Lords and Commons in Parliament, which is the supreme court of judicature in the kingdom, shall declare what the law of the land is, to have this not only questioned and controverted, but contradicted and a command that it should not be obeyed, is a high

---

[374] Parker (1642: 34, 45).
[375] H. Parker, *The Contra-Replicant* (1643: 30), quoted in Mendle (1989: 535).
[376] See Mendle (1995: 70, 119).
[377] See the text to nn. 300–10, above, for additional discussion of Parker's views.
[378] Herle (1642: 8 and 21; 1643: 14).   [379] Anonymous (1642*b*: 2).
[380] J. Geree, *A Case of Conscience Resolved* (1646: 9), quoted in Judson (1932: 320).
[381] Mocket (1644: 13).
[382] Dr Robertson, *The People's Plea* (1645/6), Preface, quoted in Judson (1932: 332).

breach of the privilege of Parliament'.[383] Their claim was supported by an old distinction between the King's 'two bodies': his 'politic body' which gave expression to his 'legal will', and his 'natural body' which gave expression to his 'personal will'. This was essentially a distinction between his official and his private capacities, his regal office and his personal affairs. It was argued that just as the King's judicial powers were exercised by the courts of Westminster, and not by him personally, so his other official powers were exercised in his regular councils and courts. It was alleged to follow that although he could remove his 'natural body' from his councils and courts, as he had done by moving to York and then to Oxford at the beginning of the civil war, he could not lawfully remove his 'politic body' from them. His 'legal will' continued to be expressed by his regular councils and courts, and since Parliament was his highest council and court, the two Houses meeting in London could continue to act in his name despite his refusal to co-operate with them. Moreover, it followed that the legal maxim 'the King can do no wrong' applied, not to his personal decisions and actions, but to their official ones, which therefore could never be unlawful.[384] As one anonymous author put it, subjects were bound to obey 'not the regal, personal, and private judgment of the king, but the politic, public, and righteous judgment of the kingdom', which was expressed by 'the high court of parliament, or the great council of the realm'. It was the latter rather than the former which could never be deemed to be legally wrong; hence, 'none is above', and no inferior court 'dares control', the Houses of Parliament.[385]

The proposition that Parliament possessed an absolute and unlimited power to make and change the law was neither new, nor disputed by the King or most of his supporters. What they vehemently repudiated was the claim that the two Houses of Parliament could exercise that power without the actual assent of the King, who could be deemed a party to their actions *ex officio*. In 1642, Charles I himself declared: 'We very well know the great and unlimited power of a Parliament, but we know, as well, that it is only in that sense, as we are a part of that Parliament. Without us, and against our consent, the votes of either, or both Houses together, must not, cannot, shall not . . . forbid anything that is enjoined by the law, or enjoin anything that is forbidden by the law'.[386] In an anonymous pamphlet purporting to be published by the King's command, a royalist writer responded to Henry Parker's argument that 'an absolute, indisputable power of declaring law' belonged ultimately to the two Houses.[387] The pamphlet complained that 'such a vast transcendency of arbitrary power . . . was never claimed by any Parliament, though in conjunction with (the head of it) the King'.[388]

---

[383] Quoted in J. W. Allen (1938: 389).   [384] Greenberg (1991: 218–20).
[385] *The Subjects Liberty*, quoted in ibid. 218–19.   [386] Charles I (1642: 1–2).
[387] See text to n. 374, above.
[388] Anonymous (1642*a*: 16) (Parker was often referred to as 'the Observator').

He [Parker] means the Parliament without the King; if he had allowed the King his place in Parliament, I know no understanding man but will easily subscribe, that the King in Parliament, or the Parliament with him, have an absolute indisputable power, both to make, and declare law; and to end all suits of what kind soever, determinable by human law within the kingdom. And here is the most safe resting of this power (and here it has ever rested) and not in the King alone (who claims not that power . . .) and much less in any inferior court.[389]

Sir John Spelman said the same thing. 'A supreme indisputable power must be somewhere, this observator [Henry Parker] acknowledges, and all must acknowledge that are not in love with anarchy: the question then is only this, where is its most safe resting?' Spelman insisted that it lay with the King in Parliament, which was more trustworthy than the Lords and Commons without the King.[390] 'Should the three Orders [King, Lords, and Commons] declare law contrary to what were law indeed, yet could not their declaration be erroneous, for that it thenceforth altered the law, and made their dictate law, though it were none before'.[391]

Other evidence confirms that in the 1640s, most royalists agreed that a true Parliament, including the King, possessed legislative sovereignty. The staunchly royalist University of Oxford published an argument purporting to prove that the King's personal assent was required for all acts of legislation. It agreed that ordinary judges did not need the King's personal assent to decide legal controversies, because their power was strictly judicial, and confined to applying laws to which the King had already assented. But parliaments, on the other hand, exercised a legislative as well as judicial power: they were 'not so limited by any earthly power, but that they may change and over-rule the laws and their own acts at their pleasure'; they could act 'beside, beyond, above, or against the laws already established'. It followed that the King's personal assent was required: 'no act of legislative power, in any community . . . can be valid, unless it be confirmed by such person or persons as the sovereignty of that community resides in'.[392]

Sir Roger Twysden, a distinguished antiquary and constitutional historian, was a moderate who emphasized 'more than any other royalist writer' the legal limitations to the King's authority.[393] But he agreed that the 'court of parliament' was 'so transcendent' and 'so high' that nothing could be 'of greater authority than what, upon mature and sound advice, passes from it'.

Yet the intent in forming of it being only the good of the people, our ancestors, finding some things unfit for that assembly to deal in, have left us their prohibitions, rather as directions not at all to meddle with them, than that if a parliament should, what was concluded by the generality in it were invalid; for no law can be so strong but that court may

---

[389] ibid. 13.   [390] Spelman (1642*b*: 34).   [391] Spelman (1644: 4).
[392] *Reasons of the Present Judgment of the University of Oxford Concerning the Solemn League and Covenant etc.* (1647), in Scott (1809–15: iv. 623).
[393] Daly (1979*b*: 175).

repeal it, and, setting themselves at liberty, deal in whatsoever they are most restrained in; as appears plainly by several records.[394]

At his trial by Parliament in 1644, William Laud, Archbishop of Canterbury and one of Charles I's most influential advisers, denied that Parliament could determine the true meaning of scripture.[395] This is not inconsistent with the orthodox understanding of parliamentary sovereignty, which concedes that Parliament cannot do what is impossible, because it is impossible to make a falsehood true by legislative fiat. On the other hand, it is possible to require people to behave as if they believe a falsehood to be true, for example, by prescribing a particular form of religious worship.[396] It is therefore very significant that Laud went on to acknowledge that Parliament could do just that: 'it is not (as I conceive) to be denied, that the King and his High Court of Parliament may make any law what they please, and by their absolute power may change religion, Christianity into Turkism if they please (which God forbid)'. He added that both King and Parliament 'must answer to God for all such abuse'.[397]

In the same year, James Howell, a Clerk of the Privy Council who was imprisoned by the two Houses, acknowledged that 'the high national court of parliament' possessed 'transcendent and uncontrollable jurisdiction' in matters of church and state, to make, alter, or repeal 'any law, statute, act, or ordinance whatsoever'.[398]

The most prominent royalist writers before 1646, such as Spelman, Dr Peter Heylyn, and Dudley Digges the younger, enthusiastically proclaimed the absolute sovereignty of the King, while conceding that he exercised his power to make laws in Parliament. The views of Digges and Spelman have already been discussed.[399] Heylyn stated that the King possessed 'unlimited power', and was owed 'absolute obedience'.[400] In a recent study, Howell, Spelman, and Digges, along with five others, are classified as moderate, 'constitutionalist' royalists. By contrast, Sir Robert Filmer, Thomas Hobbes, and the high church divines John Maxwell, Griffith Williams, and Michael Hudson, are described as absolutists, who supposedly went even further than the 'constitutionalists' in emphasizing the King's freedom from legal control.[401] Henry Parker complained that it was 'the common Court doctrine that Kings are boundless in authority'.[402]

---

[394] Twysden (1849: 173).   [395] Laud (1695: iv. 352).

[396] This point was made by Hooker (1888: iii. 401). The same kind of distinction was relied on by Judge Yelverton in *Calvin's* case, with respect to naturalization: 'A parliament may make a man to be accounted as naturalised, and conclude every man to say, but that he is so, but it can never make a man to be so indeed': quoted in Galloway (1986: 157).

[397] Laud (1695: iv. 352).

[398] J. Howell, *The Preheminence and Pedigree of Parlement* (1644), in Scott (1809–15: v. 47, 48). For information about Howell and this tract, see D. L. Smith (1994: 239–40).

[399] See text to nn. 64–72, and 126–9, above.

[400] P. Heylin, *Briefe and Moderate Answer* (1637: 156 and 179), quoted in Sommerville (1986: 37).

[401] D. L. Smith (1994: 244–53); but see the critical review of Seaward (1997: 227–30).

[402] H. Parker, *The Case of Shipmony briefly Discoursed* (1640: 34), quoted by Sommerville (1992: 17).

Hobbes's theory, that there is a sovereign in every state who is the author of all its laws, and therefore cannot be bound by them, is well known.[403] In his opinion, the common law existed only by virtue of the sovereign's will, signified by his silently permitting his judges to administer it.[404] Sir Robert Filmer argued that the supreme power in any state, which had 'no superior on earth to control it', must be an 'arbitrary' power; that this was necessarily the legislative power, because to make law according to a higher law was to be subject to a superior; and that in England the legislative power was exercised by the King alone.[405] It logically followed that no principles of the common law were so fundamental that they could not be overridden by an Act of the King made in Parliament. Arguing against Philip Hunton, the author of a moderate parliamentarian tract, *A Treatise of Monarchy*, Filmer said:

I would very gladly learn of him, or of any other for him, what a fundamental law is . . . I confess he tells us that the common laws are the foundation, and the statute laws are 'superstructive'. Yet I think he dares not say that there is any one branch or part of the common law but that it may be taken away by an act of parliament. For many points of the common law *de facto* have; and *de jure* any point may be taken away. How can that be called fundamental which has and may be removed, and yet the statute laws stand firm and stable? . . . Besides, the common law is generally acknowledged to be nothing else but common usage or custom, which by length of time only obtains authority. So that it follows in time after government, but cannot go before it and be the rule to government by any original or radical constitution. Also the common law being unwritten, doubtful and difficult, cannot but be an uncertain rule to govern by, which is against the nature of a rule—which is and ought to be certain.[406]

Filmer misunderstood Hunton, who argued that fundamental laws limited the King outside Parliament, but not the King in Parliament: 'the sovereignty of our Kings is radically and fundamentally limited', but 'all three [estates of Parliament] together are absolute and equivalent to the power of the most absolute monarch', who 'has no limits or bounds under God, but his own will'.[407]

According to Mark Goldie, '[t]he royalists all grasp the indefeasible and illimitable nature of sovereignty and locate it firmly in crown not parliament . . . There are . . . no legitimate coercive limitations upon a king, who is legislatively omnipotent'.[408] Even Charles McIlwain agrees that in the 1640s, 'there is little difference whether the writers be royalist or parliamentarian, they both accept

---

[403] Hobbes (1968: 312–13).   [404] ibid. 313–14.

[405] *The Free-holders Grand Inquest, Touching our Soveraigne Lord the King and His Parliament* (1648), in Filmer (1991: 72 ff., 100); *The Anarchy of a Limited or Mixed Monarchy*, in ibid. 132; *Observations Concerning the Originall of Government*, in ibid. 201–2. Sommerville defends the traditional attribution of *The Freeholders Grand Inquest* to Filmer: see the introduction to Filmer (1991: pp. xxxiv–xxxvi).

[406] *The Anarchy of a Limited or Mixed Monarchy*, in Filmer (1991: 131, 153). On Filmer's views regarding the nature and status of the common law, see also *Patriarcha*, in Filmer (1991: 45–52).

[407] Hunton (1643: 31, 61, and 6).

[408] Goldie (1991: 589, 596, and 598). This must be subject to reservations concerning the royal succession and inseparable Crown prerogatives, discussed in Section 2, above.

the new [*sic*] idea of legislative sovereignty. For the royalists this sovereignty lies in the king alone, for their opponents in the Parliament'.[409] As one pamphleteer described the cause of the civil war, shortly after its conclusion: 'The question never was whether we should be governed by arbitrary power, but in whose hands it should be'.[410]

6. The Interregnum

When Charles I's forces were defeated in 1646, it became necessary to determine what kind of government would rule England and Scotland thereafter. While Parliament negotiated with the King, who sought to preserve as many of his traditional prerogatives as possible, the Army grew increasingly concerned that the war might prove to have been fought in vain. In addition, there were grave fears that a majority in Parliament would subject the nation to an intolerant Presbyterian religious establishment. In that climate, the Army itself entered the political fray, although riven by disagreement between rank and file radicals, who were attracted to the policies of the Levellers, and its generally more conservative leadership. From 1648 until 1660, various constitutional experiments involving novel institutions were tried and abandoned, in almost all cases at the instigation of the Army.

The Levellers urged their countrymen to seize the opportunity to establish a new, more democratic form of government, which would better protect the rights of the common people. In 1647, they proposed that the powers of Parliament, especially to compel particular religious observances or military service, be expressly limited by an 'Agreement of the People', which would serve as a fundamental law embodying the will of the nation.[411] They recommended this strategy, rather than a petition to Parliament itself, because 'no Act of Parliament is or can be unalterable, and so cannot be sufficient security to save you or us harmless, from what another Parliament may determine, if it should be corrupted'.[412] The Levellers seem to have had no common or consistent understanding of Parliament's existing legal authority. They sometimes insisted that it was already bound by fundamental laws: for example, a pamphlet published in 1647 declared that Acts of Parliament contrary to fundamental liberties were 'null and void in law, and bind not at all, but ought to be resisted and stood against to the death', and in 1649, John Lilburne quoted Coke's dictum in *Dr Bonham's* case with approval.[413] But they did not consistently adhere to this view. Lilburne

[409] McIlwain (1910: 94).
[410] A. Warren, *Eight Reasons Categorical [etc.]* (1653: 5), quoted by Mosse (1947: 28).
[411] See *The First Agreement of the People* (28 October 1647), in Kenyon (1986: 274).
[412] 'Letter From Edmond Bear, et al. to the Free-born People of England', in *An Agreement of the People* (1647), in Wolfe (1944: 230).
[413] *England's Freedom, Souldiers' Rights* (14 December 1647), quoted in Gough (1955: 114–15); and J. Lilburne, *The Legal Fundamental Liberties of the People of England* (1649: 55), quoted in Gough (1955: 111 n. 2).

also described Parliament as 'unlimited and arbitrary', and the Leveller manifesto *The Case of the Army Truly Stated* (1647) referred to 'the nature of the legislative power . . . [being] arbitrary'.[414] Moreover, the proposed Agreement of the People presupposed that Parliament's powers were not already limited by law. In 1648, the Levellers temporarily abandoned that strategy and petitioned Parliament instead. These petitions did not include any demands that Parliament's powers be limited.[415] The Humble Petition, written by John Lilburne, stated that 'we judged this honourable House to be the supreme authority of England, as chosen by and representing the people, and entrusted with absolute power for redress of grievances and provision for safety', and that 'the safety of the people . . . [is] above law, and that to judge thereof appertained to the supreme authority', which could therefore indemnify actions 'though against the known law of the land or any inferior authority'.[416] The Petition asked Parliament itself to exempt 'matters of religion and gospel' from its 'compulsive or restrictive power', and to 'disclaim' any power to impose military conscription.[417] According to Richard Tuck, the predominant Leveller view was that abuses of power should be cured by fresh elections: they 'believed in the supremacy of Parliament, provided it was truly representative and properly elected'.[418]

The Levellers were very influential among the lower ranks of the Army, but were suppressed by Cromwell in 1649. The Army's own political agenda was to uphold the supreme authority of Parliaments, while reforming the House of Commons to reduce the risk of corruption and ensure greater accountability to the community. It assumed that a purified legislature would be the best guardian of the people's rights and liberties.[419] In June 1647, it called for frequent elections because the 'great and supreme power of the commonwealth (viz. the legislative power, with the power of final judgments)' was 'in its nature so arbitrary, and in a manner unlimited unless in point of time'.[420] Elections, it was said, would ensure that however unjust the members of parliament might be, and whatever harm they might do, 'yet they shall not have the temptation or advantage of an unlimited power fixed in them . . . to the oppression and prejudice of the community . . . but that the people may have an equal hope or possibility, if they made an ill choice at one time, to mend it in another'.[421]

In November 1648, the Remonstrance of the Army declared that 'the public interest of the nation, in relation to common right and freedom' consisted in

---

[414] J. Lilburne, *The Legal Fundamental Liberties of the People of England*, quoted in Gough (1955: 110); and *The Case of the Army Truly Stated* (October 1647), quoted in ibid. 112. This work is also reprinted in Wolfe (1944: 196–222).

[415] See the Petitions of January and September 1648 (the latter called The Humble Petition), in Wolfe (1944: 259 and 279, respectively).

[416] The Humble Petition (11 September 1648), in Kenyon (1986: 276–7).

[417] ibid. 278–9; and *The First Agreement of the People* (28 October 1647), in ibid. 275–6.

[418] Tuck (1993: 243).   [419] Kishlansky (1982: 170–81).

[420] *A Representation of the Army* (14 June 1647), quoted in Gough (1955: 112 n. 2).

[421] *Declaration of June 14, 1647*, quoted in Kishlansky (1982: 176).

having 'a supreme council or parliament', of 'deputies or representers' freely chosen by the people, invested with 'the power of making laws, constitutions and offices . . . and of altering or repealing and abolishing the same', together with 'the power of final judgment concerning . . . the safety and welfare of the people, and all civil things whatsoever, without further appeal to any created standing power, and the supreme trust in relation to all such things'. The exercise of these 'extraordinary powers' by the supreme council or parliament should 'be binding and conclusive to the people, and to all officers of justice and ministers of state whatsoever; and . . . it may not be left in the will of the king, or any particular persons standing in their own interest, to oppose, make void or render ineffectual such their determinations or proceedings'. The context makes it clear that the Army took these 'matters of supreme trust' to include 'extraordinary and arbitrary powers over the people, their laws, liberties, properties, yea, their persons and consciences too'; the Remonstrance attributed the civil war to the King's determination to exercise those powers alone, with no supreme council or parliament 'to restrain or check him'.[422] But the Remonstrance shows the influence of Leveller ideas by further demanding that the supreme council or parliament should have no power to alter 'the foundations of common right, liberty or safety contained in this settlement', which were to be 'declared and provided by this Parliament, or by authority of the Commons therein, and to be further established by a Contract or Agreement of the People'. Those 'foundations' concerned provision for a regular succession of freely elected parliaments, electoral reform to make them more representative of the people, formal recording of dissents in Parliament so that the people could know who to blame for any abuse of its powers, legal immunity for things said or done during the civil war, and the election of all future kings subject to their disavowing any power of veto over legislation.[423]

The Army's Remonstrance was never implemented, but its continuing commitment to parliamentary government was demonstrated by its decision in 1648 to purge Parliament of its Presbyterian enemies, rather than take even more radical steps to impose its will.[424] This created the so-called Rump Parliament, which declared in January 1649 '[t]hat the Commons of England, in parliament assembled, being chosen by, and representing the people, have the supreme power in this nation', and that whatever the Commons should enact 'hath the force of law; and all the people of this nation are concluded thereby'.[425] This was a modification of the traditional claim that Parliament was supreme because it represented the entire community. It amounted to the claim that only the Commons was truly representative, and therefore supreme, and that English liberties were best protected by a popularly elected legislature, unrestrained by either the Lords or the King. The House of Lords and the monarchy were abolished.

---

[422] The Remonstrance of the Army (November 1648), in Kenyon (1986: 281–3).
[423] ibid. 289–91.   [424] ibid. 252.
[425] Commons' Resolutions (4 January 1649), in Kenyon (1986: 292).

It is doubtful that many people believed the Rump's claim to represent the people. But some did. John Milton, an ardent republican employed by the new regime as its chief propagandist, asserted that whereas the King and the Peers 'represent but themselves, the Commons are the whole kingdom'.[426] He believed that Parliament, which now consisted of the (purged) Commons alone, possessed sovereign law-making power. 'Law in a free nation has been ever public reason, the enacted reason in a free Parliament', which exercised 'the plenipotence of a free nation'.[427] 'What the laws of the land are, a Parliament should know best, having both the life and death of laws in their lawgiving power', 'which laws are in the hands of Parliament to change or abrogate, as they shall see best for the Commonwealth; even to the taking away of King-ship itself'.[428] Parliament was not bound by old laws: '[i]t were a thing monstrously absurd and contradictory to give the Parliament a legislative power, and then to upbraid them for transgressing old establishments'.[429] '[A]ll human laws are but the offspring of that frailty, that fallibility, and imperfection which was in their authors . . . and no law is further good, than mutable upon just occasion . . . [we] are as free born to make our own laws, as our fathers were who made these we have.'[430] Neither the King nor the judges could frustrate the will of Parliament. 'In all wise nations the legislative power, and the judicial execution of that power have been most commonly distinct, and . . . the former supreme, the other subordinate'. The King's highest power was to execute the law, and therefore he had no more right to prevent Parliament from making any law 'than other inferior judges, who are his deputies'.[431] Parliament 'is the supreme council of the nation, set up by a completely free people and furnished with full power . . . to consult together over the most important matters', and 'the authority of parliament either sets up or removes all the courts where judgements are made'.[432]

The advocacy of frequent and freely elected parliaments became known as the 'Good Old Cause', or the 'Blessed Cause', after Cromwell expelled the Rump in April 1653 for reasons that are still debated.[433] In June 1653, he established a new legislature to provide for 'the peace, safety and good government' of the Commonwealth, which immediately assumed the name 'parliament' and came to be called the Nominated, or Barebones, Parliament.[434] The judges' acceptance of this new Parliament's authority was demonstrated when it ordered the imprisonment of John Streater, a former Army officer turned publisher of radical tracts, for allegedly publishing a seditious libel. In *Streater's* case, decided in November 1653, Justice Nichols held that 'what the Parliament does, we cannot

---

[426] J. Milton, *Eikonoklastes*, in Milton (1953–82: iii. 415).
[427] ibid. 360 and 410.   [428] ibid. 451 and 458.   [429] ibid. 530.
[430] ibid. 573. See also J. Milton, *Brief Notes Upon a Late Sermon* (1660), in Milton (1953–82: vii. 467, 481): 'how could our forefathers bind us to any certain form of government, more than we can bind our posterity?'
[431] *Eikonoklastes*, in ibid. iii. 413. See also ibid. 576.
[432] J. Milton, *A Defence of the People of England*, in Milton (1991: 218–19).
[433] See Taft (1984).   [434] Kenyon (1986: 300).

dispute or judge of: their laws are to bind all people; and we are to believe they had cause for what they did . . . [T]heir power is a law, and we cannot dispute any such thing'. Chief Justice Rolle agreed that 'in all justice, an inferior court cannot control what the Parliament does . . . Why, they have the legislative power, and may alter and order in such sort as they please . . . [I]f the cause should come before us, we cannot examine it, whether it be true or unjust.' He remarked that it was 'strange that a counsellor should say' that acts of Parliament contrary to the laws of the land were void. Justice Garmond concurred.[435]

After the Nominated Parliament was disbanded in December 1653, Cromwell ruled the country for several years as Lord Protector, and convened two 'Parliaments', pursuant to a written constitution called the Instrument of Government. Cromwell argued that '[i]n every government there must be somewhat fundamental, somewhat like *Magna Charta*, that should be standing and be unalterable'.[436] In the spirit of the old Remonstrance, the Instrument entrenched certain 'fundamentals', concerning regular elections of parliaments, freedom of religion, and control of the militia. It provided, for example, that 'all laws, statutes and ordinances . . . contrary of the aforesaid liberty [of religion] shall be esteemed as null and void'.[437] Cromwell's speech, and the Instrument itself, assumed that no fundamentals, such as Magna Carta, were already protected from alteration.[438] Indeed, he defended his dissolution of the Rump on the ground that it had exercised an unlimited power, as would any parliament able to continue in existence indefinitely: 'an arbitrary power . . . to make men's estates liable to confiscation, and their persons to imprisonments', he said, 'is incident and necessary to parliaments'.[439] Although the Instrument contained no express provision for its own future amendment, in 1657 Cromwell acceded to the Humble Petition and Advice, submitted by the 'Parliament', which requested that the Instrument be amended.[440] It was apparently assumed on all sides that the Lord Protector 'in Parliament' possessed the same absolute power that the King in Parliament previously had, to alter even the most fundamental laws.[441]

Various methods of governance were advocated during the Interregnum. James Harrington's classic work of republican political theory, *The Commonwealth of Oceana* (1656), was published in the hope that Cromwell would establish the model of government it recommended.[442] Harrington opposed proposals to restrict legislative sovereignty by an 'Agreement of the People'. He criticized

[435] *The Case of Captain John Streater* (1653), in Howell (1816–28: v. 386–7). For information on Streater, see Raymond (1998).

[436] 'His Highness the Lord Protector's Speech to the Parliament' (12 September 1654), quoted in Kenyon (1986: 320).

[437] *The Instrument of Government* (1653), in Kenyon (1986: 313).

[438] Sommerville (1990: 241).

[439] 'His Highness the Lord Protector's Speech to the Parliament' (12 September 1654), in Kenyon (1986: 318); Sommerville (1986: 255).

[440] Article 24 of the Instrument dealt with the enactment of bills, but expressly excluded bills contrary to its own provisions: see Kenyon (1986: 301 and 304).

[441] See Woolrych (1982: 370).   [442] Pocock (1977: 9–14).

the idea that the people's representatives could 'have sovereign power, save that in some things the people may resist them', as 'a flat contradiction, and . . . downright anarchy. Where the sovereign power is not as entire and absolute as in monarchy itself, there can be no government at all.'[443] Sovereign power should not be limited, but vested in a composite legislative body so carefully structured and balanced that it would never abuse that power. 'It is not the limitation of sovereign power that is the cause of a commonwealth, but such a libration or poise of orders, that there can be in the same no number of men, having the interest, that can have the power, nor any number of men, having the power, that can have the interest, to invade or disturb the government.'[444] '[T]he sovereign power of a commonwealth is no more bounded, that is to say, straitened, than that of a monarch, but is balanced. The eagle mounts not unto her proper pitch if she be bounded, nor if she be not balanced'.[445] In Harrington's ideal commonwealth, called Oceana, laws would be made by a parliament, consisting of a senate and an assembly of the people: 'the senate and the people constitute the sovereign power or parliament of Oceana'.[446] '[T]he parliament is the heart which, consisting of two ventricles . . . sucks in and gushes forth the life blood of Oceana by a perpetual circulation.'[447]

After Cromwell's death, the Rump was recalled on a wave of popular enthusiasm, and various proposals for a permanent republican constitution were canvassed, the major concern being the supremacy of representative Parliaments.[448] With the exception of religious freedom, the idea that the legislature's powers ought to be limited was abandoned. Republicans were persuaded that 'the supremacy of representative Parliaments . . . would protect the liberties they had long sought'.[449] Milton returned to the fray, arguing that 'the Parliament is above all positive law, whether civil or common, makes or unmakes them both, and still the latter Parliament above the former, above all former law-givers, then certainly above all precedent laws'.[450] Richard Baxter wrote in *A Holy Commonwealth* (1659) that 'King and Parliament conjunctly . . . have the legislative (that is, the sovereign) power', which included both 'the supreme legislative power' and 'the supreme power of judgment'. Although 'no law-giver can dispense with God's laws', '[i]t belongs to the sovereign to be judge of all inferior judges', and '[t]he last appeal is to the sovereign's judgment, and his sentence is final; so that from him there is no appeal but unto God . . .'.[451]

Proposals for a republican constitution came to nought: no consensus was achieved, and in the absence of any viable alternative, the monarchy was

---

[443] J. Harrington, *The Art of Lawgiving in Three Books* (1659), Preface to the Third Book, in Pocock (1977: 657–8).

[444] ibid.

[445] J. Harrington, *The Commonwealth of Oceana* (1656), in Pocock (1977: 230). Harrington's theory of sovereignty is discussed at length in Fukuda (1997).

[446] Pocock (1977: 245).   [447] ibid. 287.   [448] Taft (1984: 460–1).   [449] ibid.

[450] J. Milton, *Brief Notes Upon a Late Sermon* (1660), in Milton (1953–82: vii. 483).

[451] Baxter (1994: 217, 173, and 176–7).

restored, and with it the law-making authority of the King in Parliament. The failure of the various revolutionary regimes of the 1650s created a deep aversion within England to deliberate constitutional innovation and written constitutions, and a strong preference for pragmatic, incremental adaptation of customary institutions.[452] This helps explain the survival not only of the monarchy, but of the sovereignty of the King in Parliament.

On the eve of the Restoration, the distinguished lawyer and parliamentarian Bulstrode Whitelocke, a son of James Whitelocke and protégé of John Selden's, stated that

> the power of parliament . . . is too vast for a particular recital of it. Our books say, 'it may do all things': and doubtless it is the supreme power of this nation; and can bind the persons, estates, and liberties of all the people . . . . And, although each estate has its bounds, by law: yet all the three estates together, the king, lords, and commons, have no bounds; but power to do what they please.[453]

Whitelocke's argument was conventionally legalistic, not abstractly philosophical: he cited Fortescue, St German, Sir Thomas Smith, Plowden, and Coke to demonstrate Parliament's great honour and trustworthiness, and necessarily unlimited power.[454] According to Weston and Greenberg, a majority of the political nation agreed with him.[455]

---

[452] D. L. Smith (1992: 33–4).   [453] Whitelocke (1766: ii. 311).
[454] ibid. 194 ff. and 333–5.   [455] Weston and Greenberg (1981: 81).

6

From the Restoration to the Revolution

1. Monarchist Ideologies

The idea that Parliament's legislative authority was limited by unchangeable, fundamental laws was probably more influential after the Restoration than it had been before. After twenty years of unpredictable and violent social upheaval, the desire for stability and security must have enhanced its appeal.[1] Coke's dictum in *Dr Bonham's* case had gained some currency, as a result of being cited by David Jenkins and John Lilburne in civil war tracts denouncing oppressive actions of the two Houses.[2] In the 1640s, the royalist camp had attempted to turn the tables on the two Houses by claiming that they, rather than the King, had violated fundamental laws. The two Houses had responded by asserting the absolute sovereignty of Parliament. This dialectic established a pattern that to some extent continued after the Restoration. Supposedly immutable fundamental laws were appealed to more often by monarchists than anyone else, to protect the succession and prerogatives of the Crown from statutory control.[3]

Robert Sheringham, a Cambridge scholar exiled during the interregnum, is an example of this kind of monarchist. In a book published in 1660, he defended the common royalist claim that even the King, in Parliament, could not restrict the inseparable prerogatives of the Crown.[4] But he went further, arguing that this was just one example of the authority of statute being restricted by fundamental laws laid down when the English constitution was first established.[5] Those laws protected the rights of subjects as well as of the King, such as the right of every person not to be deprived of his inheritance.[6] Not only were statutes which violated these laws 'void by the common law', but 'the judges . . . are bound to declare them so, and have done it de facto upon several occasions'.[7] But Sheringham acknowledged that 'it may seem strange' that the King, Lords, and Commons, 'which are virtually the whole kingdom, should not have power to make what law they please'.[8]

---

[1] Seaward (1988: 17–18, 38, 44–8).   [2] See Chapter 5, nn. 329, 413.
[3] Gough (1955: 145).
[4] Sheringham (1660: 4, 6, 21, 29–30); this work may have been written as early as the 1640s, since it includes a lengthy response to Hunton (1643).
[5] Sheringham (1660: 30).   [6] ibid.
[7] ibid. 27. In this passage, he is referring to laws wrongfully infringing the King's rights of sovereignty, but for the reason just given, he must have believed the same to be true of laws violating the rights of subjects.
[8] ibid. 30.

Another example is the lawyer Fabian Philipps, who in 1660 denied that Parliament could alter feudal tenures, because it 'cannot enact things against right reason, or common right, or against the laws of God or nature'.[9] He agreed with those judges in the *Ship-Money* case who denied that a statute could abolish the King's duty to defend the kingdom, or his right to the assistance of his subjects in doing so. For the same reasons, he added, Parliament could not lawfully provide that a man should be judge in his own cause, or that children should not obey their parents.[10]

Monarchists of this kind can be called constitutionalists: they embraced a common law rather than a royalist theory, as these terms were defined in the previous chapter.[11] For them, the lesson to be learned from the civil war was the need for fundamental laws, protecting the rights of the King as well his subjects, to be treated on all sides as inviolable.

But this was not the only or even the most characteristic reaction to the civil war among supporters of the monarchy. For many others, the violence and disorder of those years taught the opposite lesson: the need for ultimate decision-making authority to be vested in a single, undivided, and unchallengeable authority.[12] To ensure that religious and political disagreements would never again tear the nation apart, the people had to be more thoroughly instructed that the King was invested by God with 'an absolute and uncontrollable power'.[13] 'Appeals must not be infinite', said the author of *The Royal Apology*. 'There must be some supreme power, in whose final determination (be it *right*, or be it *wrong*) all inferiors must acquiesce and submit, otherwise, no controversies could be decided; nay, there could be no government, nothing but disorder and confusion in the world.'[14] Sir Roger L'Estrange, Charles II's chief propagandist, insisted that 'all government may be tyranny. A king has not the means of governing, if he has not the power of tyrannising.'[15] He conceded that the King was limited by law, but only 'conscientiously', for in observing the law 'he does but keep his own word'; he did not forfeit his right to be obeyed if he violated it.[16] George Hickes, a well-known royalist writer, insisted that the King possessed all the 'prerogatives and pre-eminences of power and greatness, which are involved in the formal conception of sovereignty'. Among these rights was 'to have the legislative

---

[9] F. Philipps, *Tenenda non Tollenda* (1660), 251–6, quoted in Gough (1955: 146).
[10] ibid. [11] See Chapter 5, Section 1, above. [12] Dickinson (1977: 13–14).
[13] S. Parker (1671: 255), discussed in Ashcraft (1986: 47–9); Edward Bohun, *A Defence of Sir Robert Filmer, Against the Mistakes and Misrepresentations of Algernon Sidney, Esq.* (1684: 8), quoted in Daly (1979b: 129).
[14] *The Royal Apology: Or, An Answer To the Rebels Plea* (London, 1684: 35–6), quoted in Houston (1991: 79). For other examples of the same reasoning, see Houston (1991: 79 n. 46).
[15] L'Estrange (1662: ch. 10), quoted in Seaward (1988: 47).
[16] L'Estrange (1662: 119). As another writer put it, the King was restrained not 'by the efficient and compulsive part of them [the laws], but by the exemplary only': T. L., *The True Notion of Government* (1681: 26–7), quoted by Harris (1993: 97). For other examples of the directive/coercive distinction in royalist writings, see Daly (1979b: 38, esp. n. 45); and Houston (1991: 78–9).

power, or, the power that makes any form of words a law', and in exercising his rights, the King was 'accountable to none except God'.[17]

Constitutionalists and absolutists among the King's supporters sometimes disagreed with one another. Fundamental law as a restraint on legislative power was first invoked by constitutionalists during debates concerning the repeal of statutes enacted by the Long Parliament, including the Triennial Act, the Act that attainted the Earl of Strafford, and the Act that excluded bishops from the House of Lords. They claimed that Parliament had lacked authority to enact these statutes, which should therefore be declared null and void, and not merely repealed. But this claim was disputed, even among those who strongly supported repeal. The Earl of Clarendon, Charles II's principal adviser, opposed the inclusion of the words 'null and void' in the Act reversing Strafford's attainder, fearing that they might be taken to justify other controversial statutes being treated as void without formal parliamentary repeal. Eventually only the Triennial Act was declared null and void, although in the statute readmitting bishops to Parliament their exclusion was condemned as 'prejudicial to the constitution and ancient rights of parliament and contrary to the laws of this land'.[18] But in both cases, it seems that formal repeal by statute was still assumed to be necessary.

In October 1660, during the trials of the 'regicides', whom royalists blamed for the execution of Charles I, several of the accused argued in their defence that they had acted pursuant to an Act of Parliament, which no inferior court could question.[19] That argument was rejected on the ground that the 'Rump' Parliament of 1649, consisting of the remnants of the House of Commons after its purge by the Army, was not a genuine Parliament. Chief Baron Bridgeman observed that it was 'a thing never known or seen under the sun, that the Commons, nay a few Commons alone, should take upon them, and call themselves the Parliament of England'. The so-called 'Parliament' was not even a proper House of Commons.[20] Bridgeman accepted the principle that inferior courts had no authority to question statutes: 'the judges have power after laws are made to go upon the interpretation of them', but were 'not to judge of those things that the Parliament do'.[21] However, to be able to apply that principle, the judges had to be satisfied that a putative statute really was an Act of Parliament, and

it is no derogation to parliaments, that what is a statute should be adjudged by the common laws. We have often brought it into question, whether such and such a thing was an Act of Parliament, or not. . . . [I]f forty men should meet on Shooters-Hill . . . and say, 'We do declare ourselves a Parliament of England', because they do so, shall not this be judged what is a statute, and what not?[22]

[17] G. Hickes (1683), *Jovian, Or, An Answer to Julian the Apostate* (London, 1683: 200–2), quoted in Houston (1991: 78).
[18] Seaward (1988: 165); See also ibid. 47–8, 132–3.
[19] Howell (1816–28: v. 1025, 1043–4, 1053–5, and 1157–9). The case is discussed in Nenner (1997).
[20] Howell (1816–28: v. 1027, 1029); see also ibid. 1044–5, 1055–6, 1065–7, and 1159–62.
[21] ibid. 1029.   [22] ibid. 1066.

Allegedly unchangeable law was invoked during the Exclusion Crisis of 1680–1, when several attempts were made, by politicians who became known as Whigs, to enact Bills excluding James, the Roman Catholic Duke of York and brother of Charles II, from the throne.[23] Those who opposed exclusion, who came to be called Tories, were not content to rely on the royal veto, even though the King was implacably opposed to the measure. This was no doubt because the events of 1641–2 had proved that a politically weakened King, in desperate need of supply, could be forced to assent to legislation he detested. As Sir George MacKenzie put it, if Parliament were able to alter the succession, 'weak Kings might by their own simplicity, and gentle Kings by the rebellion of their subjects, be induced to consent to such Acts . . .'.[24]

Whether or not Parliament could control the royal succession was highly controversial throughout the century.[25] As previously noted, the Stuarts had every reason to deny that it could, because James I had succeeded Elizabeth contrary to the terms of Henry VIII's will, and therefore to the statute that authorized the making of the will.[26] When Charles II was restored to the throne, he stated that he owed his title solely to 'God and nature', and the proclamation that declared him King asserted his hereditary right in similar language to that used in the Act of Recognition of 1603.[27] This reinforced the theory of divine hereditary right: 'from the vantage point of 1660 it appeared that whatever the degree of difficulty, the next in blood was not to be denied'.[28]

Many Tories argued that an Act of Exclusion would be legally invalid, although not always for the same reason. Constitutionalists held that the royal succession was governed by a fundamental law protecting the rights of kings, and were prepared to concede that other fundamental laws protected rights of ordinary subjects. In 1679, for example, an anonymous author advised a newly elected Member of Parliament

that the judges of the common law (to whom alone by a deep polity the construction and superintendence of all statute-laws is entrusted) have in all ages made bold sometimes to weigh the same statute-laws in the balance, and for certain reasons appearing to them, have now and then (without deflowering their consciences and integrity) adjudged them null and void.[29]

He argued that any statute contrary to divine or natural law, or to the fundamental laws constituting the foundations of government, would be *ipso facto* null and void. The 'laws of God and nature', which 'inseparably annexed' the succession to 'proximity and nextness of blood', was one example of a law that bound even Parliament; but he also argued that no statute could validly enact 'that no man should honour the King, or love his parents or children, or give alms to the

---

[23] Gough (1955: 145–53).   [24] MacKenzie (1684: 163).
[25] The best discussion of the issue is in Nenner (1995).   [26] See Chapter 5, text to n. 98.
[27] Nenner (1995: 93–6).   [28] ibid. 96.   [29] E. F. (1679: 1); See also ibid. 7.

poor, or pay tithes to the parson of his parish, or the like . . .'.[30] He clearly possessed some legal knowledge, citing in his support St German on natural law, Coke's dictum in *Dr Bonham's* case, and Hobart's in *Day v Savadge*.[31]

Arguments of this kind were apparently not uncommon. Describing the exclusion debates, which he witnessed at first hand, Gilbert Burnett said that 'all lawyers had great regard to fundamental laws; and it was a maxim among our lawyers that even an act of parliament against Magna Carta was null of itself'.[32] This must be an exaggeration, because the maxim was certainly not accepted by the leading Whig lawyers. Burnet himself thought it a 'a wild and extravagant conceit, to deny the lawfulness of an exclusion in any case whatsoever'.[33] Nevertheless, the Whigs were compelled to rebut such arguments. William Petyt, the eminent Whig constitutional historian, devoted considerable effort to refuting the claim that judges could invalidate statutes, a claim he described as having been 'artificially spread abroad' and 'in late times made so great a noise and bustle in the world'.[34]

On the other hand, many Tories who opposed exclusion were divine right absolutists, who took a different view. They agreed that there were limits to what a King could validly do, even in Parliament, but not for the same reason as constitutionalists. In their opinion, it was because God conferred sovereign authority upon the King and his natural heirs, that he could not alienate or limit it, or alter the right of his natural heir to succeed him.[35] They opposed exclusion because they deemed it inconsistent with the source and nature of the King's sovereignty, and not because they denied that the King was truly sovereign. Upon the death of every King, full sovereign authority equal to that which he himself had inherited passed automatically to his natural heir. That authority was inalienable and perpetual, and could be neither limited nor diverted from its divinely ordained course by any temporary incumbent. This point of view was succinctly expressed in an address presented to Charles II in 1681 by the University of Cambridge, which denied both that the King could be censured or held to account by his subjects, and that he could, even by law, alter the succession:

We will still believe and maintain that our kings derive not their title from the people but from God; that to Him only they are accountable; that it belongs not to subjects either to create or to censure, but to honour and obey their sovereign, who comes to be so by a fundamental hereditary right of succession, which no religion, no law, no fault or forfeiture can alter or diminish.[36]

The King may have been 'absolute in parliament', as the politician and historian Sir Philip Warwick claimed.[37] But it did not follow that he could alter the

---

[30] ibid. 7.   [31] ibid. 7–8.   [32] Burnet (1897–1900: ii. 216).   [33] ibid. 218.

[34] Petyt (1739: 66–7); see further the text to nn. 96–9, below.

[35] See Chapter 5, text to nn. 97–132, above, on the 'inseparable prerogatives'.

[36] A. Seller, *The History of Passive Obedience* (1689: 108), quoted in Dickinson (1977: 20).

[37] P. Warwick, *A Discourse of Government* (1694: 45; but probably written in 1678), quoted in Weston and Greenberg (1981: 95).

succession. In 1686, Nathaniel Johnston insisted that the king possessed legislative sovereignty, while denying that he could alter the succession.[38] Charles Leslie, an outspoken Jacobite after the Glorious Revolution, also proclaimed the 'absolute and arbitrary' sovereignty of the King while denying that the succession could be altered.[39]

So there were two different reasons for thinking that any Exclusion Act would be legally null and void.[40] To complicate matters further, not everyone who opposed exclusion did so on that ground.[41] Many objected that it would be politically imprudent, even though legally valid.[42] That was the position of the Marquess of Halifax, for example, who led opposition to the first Exclusion Bill in the House of Lords, and whose speeches have been widely credited with inspiring its defeat. He admitted that Parliament could exclude the Duke of York if it so desired, but warned that this might lead to civil war.[43] Charles II's opinion is unclear: he was said by one contemporary to regard exclusion as 'an unlawful act', but another reported that he opposed it without doubting his power to assent to it.[44] Some Tories changed their minds on the question: Daniel Finch once claimed that an Act of Exclusion 'would be in itself invalid', but later denied having held that opinion.[45] Howard Nenner, who has made the most thorough study to date of the exclusion debates, concludes that 'the assertion that God and nature were the sole determinants of right and the denial that positive law rules had any role in the succession of the crown were essentially minority positions', and that '[b]y most readings of the Exclusion debate the real obstacle to disabling James from inheriting the throne was political, not constitutional'.[46]

Whether most supporters of the monarchy after the Restoration were constitutionalists, or absolutists, is debatable. Many of them did not clearly distinguish between the fundamental laws of the land, which only constitutionalists held to be unalterable, and the laws of God, which even absolutists held to be inviolable.[47] Sir Robert Filmer's works defending extreme monarchical absolutism were republished during the Exclusion Crisis,[48] and John Locke, who devoted his *First Treatise of Government* to refuting Filmer's theory, described it as 'the

---

[38] N. Johnston, *The Excellency of Monarchical Government* (London, 1686: 139), quoted in, and discussed by, Salmon (1959: 148).

[39] Daly (1979*b*: 135–6).

[40] In his vigorous defence of Parliament's right to alter the succession, the Whig lawyer John (later Lord) Somers distinguished between four different royalist arguments to the contrary: the second was that statutes could not override the divine right of the natural heir, and the fourth was that they could not override 'the fundamental laws of the land': J. Somers, *A Brief History of the Succession of the Crown of England* (1689), in Scott (1809–15: xiii. 664).

[41] For arguments that they would, see Daly (1979*b*: 42 and 144–5).

[42] Nenner (1995: 113 and 136).

[43] Kenyon (1969: 13–14). Halifax conceded that the King in Parliament did have an unlimited law-making power: see the text to nn. 115–20, below.

[44] Nenner (1995: 113–14, 149).   [45] ibid. 113.   [46] ibid. 114, 149.

[47] Daly (1979*b*: 144); Nenner (1995: 33). The royalist response to exclusion is also discussed in Knights (1994: 245–50).

[48] Ashcraft (1986: 187 n. 16).

current divinity of the times'.[49] Many historians believe that most monarchists after the Restoration were absolutists.[50] But some others have argued that most were moderates and legalists, and that Whig polemicists such as Locke used Filmer to caricature their opponents and set up an easily refuted 'straw man'.[51] The disagreement may be mainly terminological.[52] As Mark Goldie explains, '[t]hat English kingship was both absolute and limited was a standard Tory paradox'. The King was limited by the law of God, and such other limits as he freely chose, but since he could neither be called to account nor actively opposed for transgressing them, he was also absolute.[53] No doubt some royalists were confused or uncertain, 'torn between their profound commitment to the rule of law and the traditional constitution, and their acceptance of the logic of sovereignty'.[54] Moreover, there may have been a shift from constitutionalist monarchism, in the years immediately after the Restoration, to divine right absolutism in the late 1670s.[55]

But the important point is this. Only some Tories believed that the common law included an 'ancient constitution' of unalterable, fundamental laws. Many others were absolutists, who held that the King possessed unchallengeable, sovereign authority, which he exercised in Parliament when making laws. Some of them admitted that the King in Parliament had power to alter the succession, but opposed its use on prudential grounds. Others denied that he had such power, but only because they thought it inconsistent with the source and nature of his sovereign authority. Absolutists derided the idea that the common law preceded and governed the King as a 'wild assertion, without any just proof'.[56] As Figgis put it, the theory of divine right 'implied sheer absolutism with the exception of the succession'.[57] That exception was intended to ensure the consensual, orderly

---

[49] Locke (1690: 138; Preface). Thomas Burnet, in 1698, described Filmerism as the 'palladium' of the Stuart court (Jolley 1975: 31). Note that Filmer thought it possible for the succession to be governed by an Act of Parliament assented to by the reigning monarch: see Daly (1979*b*: 42–3, 184–5).

[50] Kenyon (1977: 63, 65); Dickinson (1977: 13–26), Goldie (1983: 69–71); (1997: 19–29); Ashcraft (1986: 187 n. 16 and 189–90 n. 26).

[51] Daly (1979*b*: 55–6, 102–3, 148, ch. 6, appendix A, *passim*); see also Harris (1993: 36–7, 82, 96–7, 119). But see the criticisms of Daly's view in Houston (1991: 93–4).

[52] Harris and Daly classify as legalists, rather than absolutists, those who believed that the King was bound by laws that were self-imposed, and therefore unenforceable against him: Harris (1993: 37, 97); Daly (1979*b*: 35–40, 50–2). This may be why Daly (1979*b*: 34–6, 50–2, 150, 165) describes Heylyn, Hickes, and Nalson as typical, moderate royalists, whereas according to J. Marshall (1994: 112), all three regarded the King as having absolute and illimitable power. Goldie (1997: 19) also describes Hickes and Nalson as absolutists.

[53] Goldie (1997: 19–28) (1991: 589, 595–602).   [54] Houston (1991: 95).

[55] J. Marshall (1994: 205; but see 112 n. 59). Goldie (1997: 19) refers to the period from 1675–85 as 'the decade of Tory absolutism'. D. L. Smith (1994: 294) argues that the publication of Sheringham's book in 1660 (see n. 4, above) indicates the currency of a moderate and constitutionalist version of royalist thought at that time.

[56] Goldie (1997: 24), quoting Francis Turner; see also Filmer's account of the common law, discussed in Chapter 5, n. 406, above.

[57] Figgis (1922: 282 and 279). Russell (1993: 119) also observes that 'the succession, however great its theoretical significance might be, was in practice an enclosed issue, and showed little sign of producing fundamental change in thinking on other issues'.

transmission of sovereign authority from each king to his successor, but not otherwise to restrict it.[58]

2. Whig Ideology

A consensus between monarchists and the so-called 'presbyterian party' made the Restoration possible, but it dissolved after 1675 owing to the latter's fear of 'popery and arbitrary government'. The 'presbyterians' inherited the ideology of those who, in the 1640s, had attempted to employ Parliament's authority to control the King.[59] By their lights, Parliament was the principal guardian of the liberties of subjects, which justified its having unlimited authority. In 1667, during debate over the Earl of Clarendon's impeachment, their leader in the House of Commons, John Swinfen, affirmed that '[t]he power of parliaments is indeed great; it has no bounds but the integrity and justice of parliaments'.[60] The presbyterians became known as Whigs during the Exclusion Crisis. The Earl of Shaftesbury, who became the Whigs' leader, referred in 1659 to the 'supremacy and omnipotency' of the people's representatives in Parliament.[61]

In the early 1670s, some Protestant nonconformists claimed that statutes penalizing their religious practices were contrary to divine law, and therefore null and void.[62] They were faced with a dilemma, because their best hope for relief from those statutes was the King's dispensing power, whose use they opposed on constitutional grounds.[63] They tended to favour parliamentary action, to suspend or repeal the oppressive statutes or to authorize dispensation by the King.[64] They never sought relief by way of judicial invalidation of the statutes, or even suggested that such relief might be available. In 1687, William Penn proposed that religious liberty be permanently guaranteed by Parliament enacting a 'Magna Carta of Religion', to be protected from subsequent amendment or repeal by a requirement that all office holders, peers, and Members of Parliament take an oath that they would not attempt to alter its provisions.[65]

As had happened before the civil war, judicial decisions undermined public confidence in the judges' willingness or ability to protect the liberties of subjects. In 1680, the House of Commons listed several controversial decisions as grounds for initiating impeachment proceedings against Sir William Scroggs, Chief Justice of the Court of King's Bench. The Commons declared that the judges of

---

[58] J. H. Franklin argues that this did not restrict the King's sovereignty at all, because any King attempting to nominate his successor would be attempting to project his sovereign power posthumously, which was impossible because his sovereignty was extinguished by his death: Franklin (1991: 308; 1973: 70–1).

[59] Goldie (1997: 17).   [60] Cobbett (1806–20: iv. 399).

[61] Speech (28 March 1659) quoted in Christie (1859: pp. lxiii–lxxiii).

[62] Harris (1990: 229–31); Lacey (1969: 63–70, 95, 184).   [63] Lacey (1969: 64–5, 66–7).

[64] ibid. 66–8, 70.   [65] J. P. Jones (1991: 59–60).

the Court were guilty of 'usurping to themselves legislative power'.[66] A leading Whig lawyer, parliamentarian, and solicitor-general, Sir Francis Winnington, complained that their decisions seized 'the legislative power out of our hands', and asked: 'Shall we have law when they [the judges] please to let us, and when they do not, shall we have none?'[67]

The two pillars of the government are Parliament and juries. It is these that give us the title of freeborn Englishmen, for my notion of freedom is this: they are properly so called who are bound by laws of their own, being tried by men of the same condition as themselves. These two great privileges of the people have of late been invaded by the judges who now sit in Westminster Hall; they have espoused proclamation against law; they have discountenanced and opposed several legal Acts . . . ; they have grasped the legislative power into their own hands . . . [and] made their private opinion to be law.[68]

The Whig historian, William Petyt, complained that important matters concerning the whole kingdom 'ought never to be intrusted in the hands of judges, chosen and paid by the Crown . . . [and who] had been awed and influenced by great men, corrupted by bribes, intoxicated with the love of power, vassals to their passions and revenge, and some groaning under the temptation of poverty'.[69] But distrust of judges was not due solely to their role as officers of the King. In 1674, a Bill to grant judges a measure of independence, by confirming their tenure and regulating their salaries, was defeated in the Commons 'by a number of backbenchers who were normally no friends of the monarchy, but who feared that . . . [the judges] would evolve into a separate species of political man, accountable to nobody'.[70]

The Earl of Shaftesbury expressed the Whig point of view when he wrote that:

The Parliament of England is that supreme and absolute power, which gives life and motion to the English Government. It directs and actuates all its various procedures, is the parent of our peace, defender of our faith, and foundation of our properties; and as the constitution of this great spring, and *primum mobile* of affairs, is in strength and beauty, so will also all Acts and performances which are derived from it, bear a suitable proportion and similitude.[71]

[66] The Resolutions of the House of Commons (23 December 1679), Article II, in Schwoerer (1995: 867).
[67] Anchitell Grey, *Debates of the House of Commons, From the Year 1667 to the Year 1694* (1763: viii. 205 and 57), quoted in Schwoerer (1995: 858).
[68] *State Tracts* (1692: 82). Winnington is identified as the speaker by Miller (1990: 200); for the reasons for his complaints, see ibid. 211–12, Havighurst (1950; 1953). On the role of juries in the seventeenth century as a more useful shield against sovereign power than judges, see Stimson (1990: 22–33).
[69] Petyt (1739: 61). This work was probably written in the 1680s: see n. 96, below.
[70] Anchitell Grey, *Debates of the House of Commons, From the Year 1667 to the Year 1694* (1763: ii. 415–20), quoted in Kenyon (1986: 394).
[71] Earl of Shaftesbury, *Some Observations Concerning the Regulating of Elections for Parliament [etc.]* (1689: 5), quoted in Schonhorn (1991: 46) and, in part, in Harris (1993: 89). When Shaftesbury was tried for treason, after the failure of the Rye House plot, his counsel argued that 'the Courts of Westminster . . . have judged of the validity of acts of Parliament', but as Nenner comments, this was 'in a circumstance of practical necessity': Nenner (1977: 218–19 n. 78).

Shaftesbury became a close friend and patron of John Locke, who served for many years as his political secretary and adviser.[72] Locke's conception of legislative authority evolved. In his *First Tract on Government*, written in 1660, he insisted that 'the supreme magistrate of every nation', by which he meant 'the supreme legislative power', 'must necessarily have an absolute and arbitrary power over all the indifferent actions of his people', that is, all actions not specifically prohibited or commanded by scripture.[73] '[I]n a pure commonwealth ... the same arbitrary power [is] there in the assembly ... wherein each particular man has no more power (bating [excepting] the inconsiderable addition of his single vote) of himself to make new or dispute old laws than in a monarchy.'[74] In England, 'it would be a strange thing if anyone amongst us should question the obligation of those laws which are not ratified nor imposed on him but by his own consent in parliament'.[75]

In his *Second Treatise of Government*, written during the Exclusion Crisis, Locke described the legitimate authority of legislatures in less generous terms. They were bound not only by the law of God, but by the limited nature of the authority that the people had conferred on them. He denied that any legislature 'can possibly be absolutely *arbitrary* over the lives and fortunes of the people'; it 'can never have a right to destroy, enslave, or designedly to impoverish the subjects'.[76] It was bound to govern by general, promulgated laws, equally applicable to all; to raise taxes only with the consent of the people; not to transfer its power to any other legislative body; and always to legislate for the good of the people.[77]

But even though he described human laws contrary to natural law as 'invalid', the remedy was not nullification by the judiciary:[78] 'The first and fundamental positive law of all commonwealths, is the establishing of the legislative power. ... [which is] the supreme power of the commonwealth'.[79]

[I]n a Constituted Commonwealth ... there can be but *one supreme power*, which is *the legislative*, to which all the rest are and must be subordinate ... In all cases, whilst the government subsists, *the legislative is the supreme power*. For what can give laws to another, must needs be superior to him ... [T]he *legislative* must needs be the *supreme*, and all other powers in any members or parts of the society, derived from and subordinate to it.[80]

The judiciary was therefore subordinate to the legislature, and it was 'impossible to conceive that an inferior power should prescribe to a superior'.[81] No 'edict of any body else, in what form soever conceived, or by what power soever backed,

---

[72] Ashcraft (1986: 83 ff.).

[73] J. Locke, *First Tract on Government* (1660), in Locke (1997: 3, 9, 11 n. 4).

[74] ibid. 11.　　　[75] ibid. 10.

[76] Locke (1690: 357 (II. 135)); see also ibid. 359–61 (II. 137–8). For a careful assessment of the evidence, which confirms Laslett's dating of this work, see Knights (1994: 250–6). See also Tully (1993: 37–9).

[77] Summarized in Locke (1690: 363 (II. 142)); and argued at length in ibid. 353 (II. 131) and 355–63 (II. 134–42).

[78] ibid. 358 (II. 135).　　　[79] ibid. 356 (II. 134).

[80] ibid. 366–8 (II. 149–50). Emphasis in original.　　　[81] ibid. 354 (II. 132).

[can] have the force and obligation of a *law*, which has not its *sanction from* that *legislative*, which the public has chosen and appointed'.[82]

It followed that there could be 'no appeal on earth', 'no *judge on earth* ... between the legislative, and the people, should ... the legislative ... design, or go about to enslave, or destroy them. The people have no other remedy in this, as in all other cases where they have no judge on earth, but to *appeal to heaven*'.[83] An 'appeal to heaven' was an extra-constitutional resort to arms: '[t]here are two sorts of contests among men: the one managed by law, the other by force: and these are of that nature, that where the one ends, the other always begins'.[84] '[T]ho' the *people* cannot be *judge*, so as to have by the constitution of that society any superior power, to determine and give effective sentence in the case; yet they have, by a law antecedent and paramount to all positive laws of men, reserved that ultimate determination to themselves, which belongs to all mankind, where there lies no appeal on earth.'[85]

And thus the *community* may be said in this respect to be *always the supreme power*, but not as considered under any form of government, because this power of the people can never take place till the government be dissolved. In all cases, whilst the government subsists, *the legislative is the supreme power*.[86]

Locke's thesis, that the supreme power recognized by the constitution, the legislature, was subject to a higher power outside the constitution, the community as a whole, became very popular in Whig circles, and was later adopted by Blackstone.[87]

Locke clearly believed that in England, the King, Lords, and Commons shared the supreme legislative power. Moreover, he seems also to have thought that this was the most desirable of all possible arrangements. Immediately after the Revolution of 1688, he recommended that the 'settlement of the nation upon the sure grounds of peace and security ... can no way so well be done as by restoring our ancient government, the best possibly that ever was if taken and put together all of a piece in its original constitution'.[88] He continued to believe that 'what is done in parliament in civil things may be truly said to be the consent of the nation because they are done by their representatives who are empowered to that purpose'.[89] Even in the *Second Treatise*, he said of 'every member of any commonwealth' that 'the judgments of the commonwealth ... are his own judgments, they being made by himself, or his representative'.[90]

---

[82] ibid. 356 (II. 134). Emphasis in original.
[83] ibid. 379–80 (II. 168). Emphasis in original.   [84] Locke (1689: 55).
[85] Locke (1690: 379–80 (II. 168)).   [86] ibid. 367 (II. 149–50).
[87] Locke was not the first to expound this thesis. Philip Hunton agreed with royalists that no one had legal authority to judge whether or not the King had transgressed the limits to his authority. The power to resist the King, to be resorted to only in extreme cases, was 'not ... Civil but moral' (Burgess 1996: 25). The thesis was also developed in Lawson (1657): for discussion, see Franklin (1978: ch. 3).
[88] *Letter to Edward Clarke*, quoted in M. Goldie, 'Introduction', in Locke (1997: p. xxiv).
[89] J. Locke, *Critical Notes on Stillingfleet* (1681), quoted in Locke (1997: 373).
[90] Locke (1690: 324–5 (II. 88)); see also ibid. 330 (II. 94). But Locke treated the consent of a majority as the consent of all: ibid. 362 (II. 140).

Peter Laslett has observed that belief in the supremacy of Parliament was typical of the body of thought that Locke represented.[91] Another leading spokesman for radical Whig ideology, Algernon Sidney, argued that '[t]he legislative power is always arbitrary', and that what characterized good as opposed to bad government was, not an absence of arbitrary power, but its use for the benefit of the people by their representatives. It was unlikely to be abused if it was vested in men who bound themselves by the laws they made.[92] Sidney argued that the variety of laws and modes of government demonstrated that they were the products of men who were 'subject to no rule but that of their own reason, by which they see what is fit to be embraced or avoided, according to the several circumstances under which they live. The authority that judges of these circumstances is arbitrary.'[93] It followed that in England, '[w]e know no laws but our own statutes, and those immemorial customs established by the consent of the nation; which may be, and often are changed by us'.[94]

William Petyt, an eminent constitutional historian and prominent Whig theorist, said that Parliament had 'absolute power in all cases, both to make laws, and judicially to determine matters in law'.[95] In the 1680s, he wrote a lengthy demolition of what he condemned as pernicious judicial pretensions, both to make new law in important cases and to invalidate statutes. Citing numerous precedents, he insisted that past practice required the courts of Westminster to refer to Parliament any important cases in which legal gaps or ambiguities seemed to require the making of new laws.[96] As for the proposition that judges 'had any such enormous jurisdiction, or boundless authority, as to declare Acts of Parliament to be void', it was 'a mere mockery' and a 'monstrous conceit': statutes were 'the highest security to Englishmen under heaven, because the King, Lords and Commons, and in them the whole Kingdom, had consented to the making thereof'.[97] It was the right of all Englishmen to be subject only to such laws as they consented to, and their Parliaments had taken extraordinary care to frame laws protecting them from slavery and oppression.

But that ancient fence they very well knew, would never be kept up, if they left it to the arbitrary discretions and dictates of the judges of Westminster Hall: and therefore, according to their duty and office, as being the supreme expounders, declarers, explainers, interpreters and judges both of the common and statute law, they in all ages provided, *Nequid absurdum, nequid illusorium, nequid perniciosum Republicae admittatur* [that nothing absurd, insulting or ruinous to the Commonwealth be done].

Away then with that apparently sophistical argument, which in late times made so great a noise and bustle in the world; namely, that the King, the Lords House, and the Commons House concurring, had not an unlimited power to make laws, it being in the breast of the judges of the realm to determine which Acts of Parliament were binding,

---

[91] ibid. 367 nn. 3–5. See also Knights (1994: 252).
[92] Sidney (1704: 455–6; ch. III, sec. 45).　　[93] ibid.
[94] ibid. 450 (ch. III, sec. 44).　　[95] Nenner (1977: 106).
[96] Petyt (1739: 7, 9, and chs. 2, 4, and 5, *passim*). The work was probably written in the 1680s: Dickinson (1976: 192 n. 11).
[97] Petyt (1739: 24).

and which void ... And that by referring this unto the judges of the realm, the people
were better secured from an arbitrary power, than by attributing it to the Parliament.

A notion which has been artificially spread abroad and industriously improved: a notion
which is equally pernicious and injurious to all kings and parliaments, whose inherent
right it ever was by joint consent to alter, amend, explain, and interpret their own statutes
as they saw cause, and according to public convenience.

But how could any thing of all be done, if the judges had ever been invested with such
a power inseparably united and annexed to their person, *quatenus* [as] judges, to invalidate, disannul, and declare but one Act of Parliament to be void? Since by the same authority they might have declared another to be so too; and by like logic, all, without ever
adjourning any case *ad proximum Parliamentum propter difficultatem* [to the next
Parliament on account of the difficulty]. And thus we see, *uno absurdo dato infinita sequ-
untur* [granted one absurdity, endless others follow].[98]

Petyt insisted that the authority of the judges at Westminster 'was always subservient to that of the supreme Court of the Kingdom'; they 'ought to be, and
never were other than executors, and not executioners, of the ancient laws and
customs of the realm, and ordinances and establishments of Parliaments'.[99]

The radical Whig lawyer William Disney, later executed for being involved
in the Monmouth Rebellion, wrote that Parliament's legislative power was
'unlimited and universal', 'above the law itself', and could be used 'to alter the
common law of England, to declare the meaning of any doubtful laws, to repeal
... [any] judgments whatsoever of the King, or any other court of justice, if erroneous or illegal'.[100] Thomas Hunt, another Whig lawyer, stated that 'the power of
a Parliament is unrestrained, and unlimited', and that 'no laws of men are so
fundamental but they are alterable'.[101] Hunt argued that it would be dangerous,
and indeed criminal, to attempt to restrict Parliament's power, because that might
'disable it to provide remedy against the greatest mischiefs that can happen to
any community. No government can support itself without an unlimited power in
providing for the happiness of the people.'[102] Hunt, like Disney, was writing to
justify the enactment of a Bill to exclude the Duke of York from the throne, which
he regarded as an extraordinary remedy required to prevent the nation's ruin.

During the Exclusion Crisis, Whigs 'repeatedly ... referred to the overriding
power of parliament in dealing with the succession to the throne'.[103] They also
repeatedly used the same argument as Hunt to justify that power. For example,
Sir Francis Winnington argued in Parliament that 'to doubt that there is not [*sic*]
an unlimited, uncontrollable power, residing somewhere in all governments, to
remedy the exigencies that may happen, is to suppose there is such a weakness
in this, or any other government, as that it must fall when a powerful faction
shall endeavour it. In this nation, this power is in the king, lords and commons.'[104]

---

[98] ibid. 66–7.   [99] ibid. 7 and 43, respectively.   [100] Disney (1681: 135).
[101] Hunt (1682: 132, 130).   [102] ibid. 41–2.
[103] Weston and Greenberg (1981: 181); see also ibid. 176 and 204 (on Petyt), 326 n. 6 and 349
n. 54.
[104] Cobbett (1806–20: iv. 1211).

John Hampden and Sir William Jones, one time Attorney-General, made almost identical remarks.[105]

The same argument was made by John Somers, later Lord Somers, an eminent friend and patron of John Locke. Somers served as Solicitor-General and Lord Chancellor of England, and was reputedly one of the ablest constitutional lawyers of his generation.[106] He insisted that there must be 'a supreme uncontrollable power lodged somewhere', and that in England it was lodged 'in the King, Lords and Commons in Parliament'. He warned that it would be dangerous if this were commonly denied, because 'it does directly tend to anarchy, and makes the government to want power to defend itself, by making such alterations as the variety of accidents of several ages may make absolutely necessary'. Responding to the argument that the royal succession was determined by fundamental laws that could not be altered by statute, he asked 'by what authority these imaginary laws were made? For if an authority equal to that which made them be still in being, that authority may certainly repeal them whenever it pleases to exert itself'.[107] Some years later, he agreed that the power of parliaments was 'tethered', because 'the law of nature or reason tells us, that there are rules and measures of right and wrong which no positive law of man can exceed'.[108] But there is no reason to think that he changed his mind about the necessary existence of a 'supreme uncontrollable power': he presumably regarded it as perfectly compatible with 'rules and measures of right and wrong'.

An equally distinguished Whig lawyer, Sir Robert Atkyns, a judge of the Common Pleas who rose to be Lord Chief Baron of the Exchequer, also proclaimed the sovereignty of Parliament in unequivocal terms. Among seventeenth century judges, Atkyns enjoyed a reputation for learning and probity second only to that of Sir Matthew Hale.[109] In 1684, while defending the Speaker of the House of Commons against a charge of publishing a seditious libel, Atkyns asserted that Parliament 'is of an absolute and unlimited power in things temporal within this nation', with 'the highest and most sacred authority of any court'.[110]

The Parliament gives law to this court of the King's Bench, and to all other courts of the kingdom; and therefore it is absurd and preposterous that it should receive law from it, and be subject to it. The greater is not judged of the less ... The judges of this, and of the other courts of common law in Westminster, are but assistants and attendants to the high court of Parliament: and shall the assistants judge of their superiors? ... [T]herefore, this court, nor no other inferior court, can, for this very reason, judge or determine of what is done in Parliament, or by the Parliament.[111]

---

[105] ibid. 1192 and 1209.   [106] Nenner (1995: 107).
[107] J. Somers, *A Brief History of the Succession of the Crown of England* (London, 1689: 14, 15–16), in Scott (1809–15: xiii. 664).
[108] [John Somers] *Jus Regium: Or, the King's Right to Grant Forfeitures* (London, 1701: 44), quoted by Hamburger (1994: 2109 n. 61).
[109] Stephen and Lee (1917: i. 704).
[110] 'Sir Robert Atkyns' Argument', in *Proceedings against Sir William Williams*, in Howell (1816–28: xiii. 1423); also published in Atkins (1689: 49–50).
[111] Howell (1816–28: 1422–3, 1425); Atkins (1689: 49–50, 52).

Atkyns was not referring to Parliament acting in a judicial capacity distinct from its legislative capacity. As he put the same point later, when criticizing the decision in *Godden v Hales*, a judgment given by 'the supremest court in the nation ... must not be contradicted by any other court, nor by all the courts of the nation put together; this supreme court exercises its legislative and judicial power both at once, and shall it all at last be lost labour?'[112]

Distinguished politicians and lawyers aligned with neither the Tories nor the Whigs espoused the same doctrine. George Savile, the Marquess of Halifax, was involved in politics at the highest levels during the last quarter of the century, without joining any political party or group.[113] He has been described as '[i]ntellectually ... head and shoulders above most contemporaries', and 'one of the few non-partisan observers of a period which was of decisive importance in the formation of the British Constitution'.[114] One of the most respected opponents of the Whigs' campaign to exclude the Duke of York from the throne, he nevertheless accepted their most fundamental legal premise. In *The Character of a Trimmer*, probably written in 1685, he argued that Parliament could make provision for 'extraordinary cases, in which there would be otherwise no remedy'. Every government needed 'a kind of omnipotence ... to be exerted upon great occasions', and this required the consent of the people, so that 'whatever sap or juice there is in a nation may be to the last drop produced, whilst it rises naturally from the root'.[115]

In a later work, he maintained that 'there can be no government without a supreme power ... [which] must be unlimited; it has jurisdiction over everything else, but it cannot have it above itself ... its very being is dissolved when any bounds can be put to it'. If the supreme power should make a law purporting to forbid its repeal in the future, it 'could bind none but the first makers of it, another generation would never be tied up by it'.[116] This was essential to the well-being of the community, because no law or constitution could survive unless it could be adapted to differing times and circumstances; therefore, none was immune from change. The most fundamental law was 'that in every constitution there is some power which neither will nor ought to be bounded', and which 'alters the Constitution as often as the good of the people requires it'.[117]

As for the notion that the common law was fundamental and unchangeable, Halifax objected that it was impossible to define the common law so that all might know it, and government could not be 'left to a thing that cannot be defined ... so that the supreme appeal is we know not what'.[118] In addition,

[i]f the common law is supreme, then those are so who judge what is the common law; and if none but the Parliament can judge so, there is an end of the controversy. There is

---

[112] Howell (1816–28: xi. 1203).
[113] J. P. Kenyon, 'Introduction', in Kenyon (1969: 7).   [114] ibid. 8.
[115] Halifax, *The Character of a Trimmer*, in Kenyon (1969: 66, 64–5).
[116] Halifax, *The Anatomy of an Equivalent*, in ibid. 135–6.
[117] Halifax, *Political Thoughts and Reflections*, in ibid. 195.   [118] ibid. 197.

no fundamental, for the Parliament may judge as they please; that is, they have the authority, but they may judge against right their power is good, though their act is ill. No good man will outwardly resist the one, or inwardly approve the other.[119]

Therefore '[t]o say a power is supreme and not arbitrary is not sense', and from Acts of Parliament 'there can be no appeal but to the same power at another time'.[120]

Sir Matthew Hale, who served on the bench both before and after the Restoration, was highly esteemed on all sides for his learning and probity. He did not ascribe to the common law a source or authority superior to that of statute. He acknowledged that all the laws of England were created by will and consent, either 'implicitly by custom and usage, or explicitly by written laws or Acts of parliament'.[121] He also held that it was impossible for an inferior court to have power to nullify laws made by a supreme legislature, because 'the supreme power of making of laws' and 'the supreme decisive power or jurisdiction and dernier resort' were necessarily vested in the same institution, which in England was the King in Parliament.[122]

Sir Heneage Finch, who served Charles II as solicitor-general, Lord Keeper, and Lord Chancellor, was 'a constitutional lawyer of the highest repute'.[123] He observed during the impeachment of the Earl of Clarendon in 1667 that '[t]he power of parliaments is double, legislative, which has no bounds, [and] declaratory, by pronouncing judgments. And . . . I know not what the legislative power of a parliament cannot do . . .'.[124]

A statement made in 1677 by Chief Justice Vaughan, in *Thomas v Sorrell*, is sometimes quoted as evidence of support for a judicial power to invalidate statutes. He said that a law making murder, stealing, perjury, or trespass lawful 'would be a void law in itself'.[125] But too much should not be made of this. He explained that such a law would be self-contradictory, because it is part of the very meaning of the words 'murder', 'stealing', and so on, that the acts denoted are unlawful. The supposed law would make 'the same thing, at the same time, . . . both lawful and unlawful, which is impossible': and 'a law which a man cannot obey, nor act according to it, is void'. He conceded, on the other hand, that

killing a man, or taking from him his lands or goods, do not import, *ex vi termini*, that which is unlawful, as murder and stealing do; for in many cases killing a man, or taking his liberty or goods from him, is lawful, and where it is not, may by a law be made so, which the other can never be . . . . But this is because a law can alter, change, or transfer

---

[119] ibid. 198.   [120] ibid. 197.
[121] M. Hale, 'Reflections by the Lord Chief Justice on Mr. Hobbes, His Dialogue of the Law', in Holdsworth (1903–72: v. 505).
[122] Hale (1796: 207). Blackstone (1765: 157) quotes Hale to support the doctrine of parliamentary sovereignty, but his source is almost certainly inauthentic: see Anstey (1867: 306–8), and Stephen and Lee (1917: viii. 907).
[123] Stephen and Lee (1917: vii. 11).   [124] Cobbett (1806–1820: iv. 375).
[125] *Thomas v Sorrell* (1677), *Vaughan's Reports* 330, 336; 124 E.R. 1098, 1102.

a mans property in life, liberty, estate, or any interest, as it will, which cannot be done without a law, and thereby nothing unlawful is made lawful . . . [T]o alter or transfer mens' properties to others, is no *malum per se*, it is daily done by the owners' express consent, and by a law without their express consent.[126]

In conclusion, the evidence reviewed in this chapter confirms Howard Nenner's account of Parliament's authority during the second half of the seventeenth century:

The rhetoric of fundamental law had only a small effect on the seventeenth-century understanding of how law was or ought to be made. For the most part, politicians and jurists alike recognised that the positive law of England, although forged in custom, could be originated, altered, and repealed in Parliament . . . By and large there was little if any question about Parliament's wide-ranging legislative function.[127]

---

[126] ibid. 336–8; 124 E.R. 1102.

[127] Nenner (1992: 99–100). See also Judson (1949: 56), on so-called 'fundamental laws'. But cf. Nenner's more cautious judgment in Nenner (1993: 194, text to n. 53) (but note that it is not clear what Pocock means by 'sovereign' in the passage that Nenner discusses).

7

After the Revolution

1. Whig and Tory Consensus

The Revolution of 1688 vindicated the parliamentarian theory of the Whigs, who held that sovereignty was vested in the King in Parliament rather than the King alone. After James II fled to France, a Convention of two Houses was convened in January 1689 to settle the terms on which the monarchy would continue. The Houses established committees to draft a Declaration of Rights, which was read to William and Mary, James's daughter, during the ceremony at which they were offered the Crown. The principal authors of the Declaration were radical Whigs in the House of Commons, whose political principles were supported by a majority of the drafting committees of both Houses.[1]

The Bill of Rights (1689), which enacted most of the Declaration of Rights, restricted many important royal prerogatives, and this 'laid the foundations for affirming, the ultimate sovereignty of Parliament'.[2] Most importantly, it controlled the royal succession, and the so-called inseparable prerogatives of the Crown, especially the disputed power to dispense with statutes. It placed the dispensing power firmly under the control of Parliament, providing that no statute could be dispensed with, except as allowed by the statute itself, or by the special provision of a bill 'to be passed during this present session of parliament'. No bill making such a 'special provision' was passed, despite some support for the idea in the House of Lords.[3] To reinforce the Crown's subjection to statute, the Coronation Oath Act (1689) was passed. In 1685, James II had sworn to 'grant and keep and by your oath confirm to the people of England the laws and customs to them granted by the Kings of England . . . agreeing to the prerogative of the kings thereof, and the ancient customs of the realm'. The new Act required William and Mary, and subsequent kings and queens 'in all times to come', to swear 'to govern the people of this kingdom . . . according to the statutes in parliament agreed on, and the laws and customs of the same'. This oath emphasized the primacy of statute law, and removed any suggestion that laws were granted by, and subject to the prerogatives of, the Crown.[4]

As for the succession, it was provided that anyone who professed Roman Catholicism, or who married a Catholic, should be forever excluded from the

---

[1] Schwoerer (1984: 107–8, 109–10, 111).   [2] ibid. 112.
[3] Weston and Greenberg (1981: 253–4).
[4] These oaths are set out in Schwoerer (1992: 128–9), and discussed in ibid. 123–4, and in Hoak (1996: 7–8).

throne.[5] This was inconsistent with the most extreme versions of the royalist theory, which claimed that hereditary divine right was indefeasible. Howard Nenner argues that

indefeasibility was dead. Notwithstanding continuing Jacobite hopes for its resurrection after the death of William, the doctrine effectively disappeared from the mainstream of English politics and political thought. . . . After 1689 it was plainly established that an hereditary expectation of the crown might be defeated or abridged by an authority other than God.[6]

The sovereignty of Parliament, 'the highest power in England', became 'one of the supreme touchstones of the ideology and language of Whiggism',[7] '[t]he starting point of Court Whig thought . . . trumpeted in unequivocal language'.[8] The Whigs described Parliament's authority as 'absolute [and] unlimited', 'unaccountable and uncontrollable', and 'as ample and extensive as that of the great Turk, over the lives, persons, and properties of men'.[9] In *Lex Parliamentaria* (1689), a representative Whig tract, George Philips comprehensively restated and defended the doctrine of parliamentary sovereignty. Quoting lawyers such as Fortescue, St German, Smith, Coke, and Atkyns, he reiterated the familiar propositions that everyone is considered to be represented in Parliament, whose consent is taken to be everyone's consent; that therefore statutes necessarily advance the well-being of the community; that Parliament is of such great honour and justice that no one ought to imagine anything dishonourable of it, on pain of defaming the entire nation which it represents; and that as the court of last resort, its actions are beyond examination or control.[10] Philips acknowledged that Parliaments could err, but added that 'the law has provided a remedy against those errors, and a way to reform them. A subsequent Parliament may reform the errors of a preceding Parliament.'[11]

Tories did not immediately relinquish their belief in divine hereditary right. Jacobitism remained a viable force for some time, and a large number of Tories, called 'non-jurors', refused to swear an oath of allegiance affirming William to be the rightful King. On the other hand, many Tories had either acquiesced in, or actively supported, the removal of James II, which was very difficult to reconcile with the theory of indefeasible hereditary succession. Many of them advanced various rationalizations of the Revolution aimed at salvaging as much as possible of that theory.[12] But further legislation reaffirmed Parliament's authority over the royal succession. In 1696, it was made an offence to assert that any person had any right to the Crown otherwise than according to the Bill of Rights; in

---

[5] Stephenson and Marcham (1972: ii. 604).
[6] Nenner (1995: 168); see also Nenner (1996: 114–15) and Hoak (1996: 7).
[7] Schonhorn (1991: 61).   [8] Browning (1982: 196).
[9] ibid., citing an anonymous author, William Hay, and William Arnall; original emphasis removed.
[10] G. P. (1690: 7, 14, 17, 19–20, 37). Weston and Greenberg (1981: 373 n. 109) describe this tract as 'representative of the ideological outlook at the Revolution'.
[11] G. P. (1690: 14).   [12] Nenner (1995: 188–90, 215–18).

1701, the Act of Settlement, passed with widespread support among Tories as well as Whigs, declared that the sovereign must belong to the Church of England, and that the Protestant House of Hanover would succeed Queen Anne if she died childless; in the same year, resolutions of both Houses, affirming Anne's and her successors' rights to the throne, referred solely to statutes as the source of those rights; and in 1706, the Regency Act declared that it was treason to deny the authority of the monarch and parliament 'to make laws and statutes of sufficient force and validity to limit and bind the Crown of this realm and the descent, limitation inheritance and government thereof'.[13] The primary purpose of the legislative union of England and Scotland was to unify the laws of succession in the two kingdoms, which logically required their subordination to statute. The second article of the Treaty of Union, ratified by the two Acts of Union (1707), provided that, if Queen Anne died childless, the House of Hanover would succeed to the throne 'of the united kingdom of Great Britain' in accordance with the Bill of Rights and the Act of Settlement. The succession of George I in 1714, pursuant to these statutes, effectively extinguished any remaining doubts about Parliament's authority in the matter, except among Jacobites, whose numbers gradually dwindled as the chances of a Stuart restoration became ever more remote, and who were finally crushed in 1746.[14]

For extreme royalists before 1689, the law governing the royal succession was by far the most important example of a law that could never be changed, even by the King in Parliament. When it became clear that it could be changed, they had little reason to insist that other laws were beyond the authority of statute. Indeed, according to H. T. Dickinson, they found good reasons to agree that Parliament's legislative authority was unlimited. Anxious to preserve as much of their ideology as possible, and to defend an authoritarian, hierarchical society in which their position and property were secure, they transferred their unconditional loyalty, and belief in divine ordination, from the King alone to the King in Parliament. 'By changing the location of sovereignty they found an absolute and irresistible power, the legislature, which was more able than an absolute monarch to protect the interests of propertied men.'[15]

Dickinson argues that, given their support for the Act of Settlement, the vast majority of Tories had made this transition by the beginning of Queen Anne's reign in 1702.[16] But R. J. Frankle has pointed out that as early as 1696, a large majority of the Members of Parliament, which was almost evenly divided between Whigs and Tories, seem to have accepted that Parliament was sovereign.[17] A Bill of Attainder against Sir John Fenwick was passionately opposed, and debated at

---

[13] ibid. 235, 226–37.

[14] ibid. 248, 254–7. See Daly (1979*b*: 11), for some examples of Jacobite writers.

[15] Dickinson (1977: 43, 28–9), and also ibid. 33–4, 46–7. See also Harris (1993: 166–7), and Schonhorn (1991: 63–6).

[16] Dickinson (1977: 39–40, 47).

[17] Frankle (1985: esp. 73, 76–9); on the political complexion of the 1696 Parliament, see Holmes (1993: 423).

great length, because it had been introduced to overcome a lack of sufficient evidence to convict him in a court of law. Fenwick was accused of participating in a Jacobite plot to assassinate King William, and one of the only two witnesses against him had been induced by his friends to flee the jurisdiction.[18] The Bill of Attainder included provisions retrospectively nullifying a recent statute requiring two witnesses to establish a charge of treason, a requirement that some believed was prescribed by divine law. Proponents of the Bill argued that it was an exceptional measure for an extreme case, justified by the need to prevent legal requirements being improperly exploited to the detriment of public safety.[19] According to Frankle, even those who opposed the Bill agreed with its supporters that Parliament was sovereign in the sense of having legal authority to enact any law whatsoever.[20] Some of them appealed to natural law, but only on moral, and not legal, grounds.[21] Despite extensive discussion of Parliament's legislative authority, several of the Bill's opponents made it clear that they were not questioning that authority, and no one suggested that the Bill would be null and void if enacted. Frankle concludes that 'the near universal agreement which existed from the very early stages of the debates indicates that by 1696 Members were already operating under the assumption that Parliament was sovereign'.[22]

In 1701 a dispute between the two Houses of Parliament arose when the Lords acquitted four members of the Whig Junto, who had been impeached by the Tory dominated House of Commons. The Lords argued that the procedures adopted by the Commons were unjust.[23] At issue was an exercise of Parliament's judicial rather than legislative authority. But that does not seem to have mattered to Sir Humphrey Mackworth, a leading Tory lawyer and member of the Commons. In his *A Vindication of the Rights of the Commons of England*, he restated the doctrine of parliamentary sovereignty in uncompromising terms:

[T]he absolute, supreme, and legislative authority (which is necessary to support all governments against contingencies) be lodged . . . in three distinct persons or bodies, united by interest in the same common end, the public good . . . [T]he king, lords, and commons, united together, have an absolute supreme power, to do whatever they shall think necessary or convenient for the public good, of which they are the only judges, there being no legal power on earth to control them . . . [T]hese supreme powers are above the jurisdiction of all inferior courts, and may be exercised according to the discretion of the respective parties.[24]

Mackworth insisted that in cases of impeachment, the Houses of Parliament were not bound by the rules and procedures that protected the rights of accused

[18] See Garrett (1980).   [19] See Anonymous (1697: 6).   [20] Frankle (1985: 76–7, 79).
[21] This interpretation is corroborated by Browning (1982: 251), who explains that Court Whigs in the early eighteenth century reconciled the doctrine of parliamentary sovereignty with theories of natural law, by treating the latter as moral rather than legal.
[22] Frankle (1985: 79).
[23] These events are described in Sachse (1975: ch. ix, 'Impeachment' and 211–12).
[24] Mackworth (1701: 2–4).

persons in inferior courts. In an argument reminiscent of that made by Whig lawyers such as John Somers during the Exclusion Crisis, Mackworth argued that 'it is absolutely necessary for the safety of England, that such large powers should be lodged somewhere, to preserve the king and people', in order to 'provide for all possible cases that may happen, and on which the happiness or ruin of a nation may depend'.[25] This was ironic, because Lord Somers was the most eminent of the four Whig Ministers who had been impeached. Mackworth reiterated a familiar theme in parliamentary apologetics when he maintained that '[i]t is not to be imagined that a majority of so numerous a body of gentlemen, can be influenced against reason and justice'.[26] Lord Somers himself had said only four years earlier that '[o]ur representatives do well to secure our Constitution, by the most effectual means they can think on: But after all, we must trust England to a House of Commons, that is to itself'.[27]

The Lords who voted for acquittal apparently agreed with Mackworth that the Houses could lawfully override normal legal procedures and rights. In a reply to his argument, it was explicitly conceded 'that the high court of parliament has a more extensive jurisdiction, and is not tied up to the formalities and strict rules of inferior courts'. The objection to the actions of the Commons was one of morality, not law: 'the more high a court is, the more just and honourable it ought to be in proceeding, and to give example in inferior courts'.[28]

The evidence strongly suggests that Mackworth's views were shared by most of his fellow Tories. Offspring Blackall, Jonathan Swift, George Berkeley, William Higden, and Samuel Dodd were among other prominent Tories of this period who expressly affirmed the sovereignty of the King in Parliament.[29] Higden's change of mind is particularly significant, because he was originally one of the 'non-jurors' who refused to take the oath of allegiance affirming William to be the rightful king. By 1709 he had changed his mind, and confidently asserted that the King and Parliament 'can by virtue of the supremacy of their power, which cannot be bound by any prior law, or settlement', extinguish old legal rights and establish new ones, even to the Crown itself.[30] In 1710, a Tory clergyman, Dr Henry Sacheverell, was impeached for denouncing the lawfulness of active resistance to the 'supreme power', and therefore, it was alleged, implicitly denying the legitimacy of the Revolution of 1688 and of Queen Anne's title to the throne. The leading Tory lawyers who defended him, including Sir Simon Harcourt, a future Lord Chancellor, argued (perhaps disingenuously) that he had meant that the King in Parliament, and not the King alone, was the 'supreme power' that could never legitimately be resisted, and therefore, that he had said

---

[25] ibid. 2, 24.   [26] ibid. 30.   [27] Somers (1697: 15).

[28] *A Vindication of the Rights and Prerogative of the Right Honourable the House of Lords* (1701), in Scott (1809–1815: i. 325).

[29] Dickinson (1977: 48–50).

[30] W. Higden, *A View of the English Constitution [etc.]* (London, 1709: 86–7), quoted in Nenner (1995: 238–9).

nothing controversial, and in particular, had not impugned the legitimacy of resistance to James II.[31]

In March of that year, Jonathan Swift reported that of all the Tories he had ever conversed with, at least nineteen out of twenty accepted the following principles: first, that every government includes 'a supreme, absolute, unlimited power', with a law-making power that is 'without all bounds'; secondly, that 'among us, as everybody knows, this power is lodged in the King or Queen, together with the Lords and Commons of the Kingdom'; and thirdly, that succession to the throne by hereditary right was 'defeasible by Act of Parliament'.[32] Swift claimed elsewhere that '[e]verybody knows and allows, that in all government there is an absolute, unlimited legislative power', which in England is placed in the two Houses of Parliament in conjunction with the King:

And whatever they please to enact or to repeal in the settled forms, whether it be ecclesiastical or civil, immediately becomes law or nullity. Their decrees may be against equity, truth, reason and religion, but they are not against law; because law is the will of the supreme legislature, and that is, themselves. And there is no manner of doubt, but the same authority, whenever it pleases, may abolish Christianity, and set up the Jewish, Mahometan, or Heathen religion. In short, they may do any thing within the compass of human power.[33]

Doubts about Parliament's legislative sovereignty did continue to surface.[34] In debates which preceded the passing of the Septennial Act (1716) and the Peerage Act (1719), for example, the doctrine of parliamentary sovereignty was sometimes questioned.[35] But as Dickinson observes, 'it always carried the day against its critics'.[36] '[I]t was repeatedly shown that the authority of the legislature knew no bounds', and that proposition 'rapidly became a constitutional maxim'.[37] Moreover, with one exception, the doubts that were expressed did not pose what we would now regard as a truly fundamental challenge to the doctrine of parliamentary sovereignty. It was rarely suggested that Parliament's authority was subject to legal limits in the modern sense of the term, which denotes limits that are either judicially enforceable or set out in a formally enacted legal

[31] *The Trial of Henry Sacheverell* (1710), in Howell (1816–28: xv. 366 (Dr Sacheverell), 196–7 (Sir Simon Harcourt), 220 (Samuel Dodd), 229–30 (Constantine Phipps)). Sir John Hawles agreed with the proposition that the Queen in Parliament had to be obeyed in all cases: ibid. 119.

[32] Swift (1966: 112–14). Similar statements can be found in Swift (1708a: 16); see also ibid. 20, 23, and Swift (1701: 83). See Blackall (1705) for a very explicit acceptance of all these propositions.

[33] Swift (1708b: 74–5). Swift went on to make much of the qualification that Parliament cannot 'alter the nature of things', such as by making a married woman into a virgin. He concluded that Parliament could not give new ecclesiastical laws to the Church, because these had been laid down by Christ and could no more be altered than 'the common laws of nature'. On the other hand, Parliament could prevent the observance of those laws: although the clergy received its authority from Christ, its liberty to exercise that authority depended on Parliament's permission: ibid. 75–8.

[34] Some examples are mentioned in Langford (1991: 150–3).

[35] See Gough (1955: ch. 11) and Kenyon (1977: ch. 10, esp. 184–5, 197–8).

[36] Dickinson (1977: 187).   [37] ibid. 147.

instrument.[38] The exception involves the limits referred to in the Acts of Union that united England and Scotland in 1707.

2. The Union of England and Scotland

Parliament was sometimes accused of exceeding its lawful powers by Scots, who maintained that it could not lawfully violate the terms of the union between England and Scotland in 1707. After intensive negotiations and, in Scotland, fierce political debate, the two kingdoms entered into a Treaty in 1706, providing for their union under a single Crown and Parliament. Many of the Articles of the Treaty were intended to preserve cherished Scottish institutions. Article 19, for example, provided that the principal Scottish Courts 'do after the union and notwithstanding thereof remain in all time coming within Scotland as now constituted by the laws of that kingdom'. In addition, the Scottish Parliament passed an Act for Securing the Protestant Religion and Presbyterian Church Government, which provided for that religion 'to continue without any alteration . . . in all succeeding generations', for the four Universities of Scotland to 'continue within this kingdom for ever', and for the Act itself to 'be held and observed in all time coming as a fundamental and essential condition of any treaty or union to be concluded between the two kingdoms, without any alteration thereof or derogation thereto in any sort for ever'. The English Parliament passed An Act for Securing the Church of England as by Law Established (6 Annae, cap. 8), expressed in similar terms.

The Scottish and English Parliaments enacted Acts of Union to implement the provisions of the Treaty and the statutes securing their two Churches. The English Act of Union With Scotland 1707 (6 Annae, cap. 11) confirmed that the provisions of those two statutes would 'for ever be held and adjudged to be and observed as fundamental and essential conditions of the said union, and shall in all times coming be taken to be, and are hereby declared to be, essential and fundamental parts of the said articles and union'. It also provided that all the Articles of Union were 'hereby for ever ratified, approved and confirmed'. The Scottish Act included similar language.[39]

Arguably, the Acts of Union extinguished the parliaments that enacted them, and replaced them with a new Parliament of Great Britain.[40] But to many observers, even (or especially) in Scotland, it seemed that in reality, the English Parliament was simply augmented by the addition of a comparatively small number of new Scottish members.[41] The third clause of Article 22 authorized Queen Anne to allow all existing members of the English Parliament to be

---

[38] See Chapter 2, Section 1.

[39] The Scottish Act of Union (1706–7) is set out in T. B. Smith (1962: 869–83).

[40] But for an argument to the contrary, see Munro (1987*b*: 65–6).

[41] Daiches (1977: 133), MacKinnon (1896: 232).

members of the Parliament of Great Britain, which she did by proclamation dated the 29 April 1707.[42] Apart from the addition of new Scottish members, an expanded territorial jurisdiction, and the limitations expressed in the Acts of Union, the Parliament of Great Britain was identical to the Parliament of England.

Nevertheless, two reasons have been given for thinking that this new Parliament did not inherit the full sovereign powers of the English Parliament. The first is that the doctrine of parliamentary sovereignty 'is a distinctively English principle which has no counterpart in Scottish constitutional law', and there is no good reason to assume that the new Parliament inherited 'all the peculiar characteristics of the English Parliament but none of the Scottish Parliament'.[43] Putting the point more strongly, it is said that the non-sovereign Scottish Parliament could not have conferred on the new Parliament of Great Britain an authority with respect to Scotland greater than it itself possessed.[44] The second reason is that the powers of the new Parliament were expressly and deliberately limited by the Acts of Union, which gave statutory force to the provisions of the Treaty of Union and of the statutes securing the established Churches of the two kingdoms.

The first reason rests on a dubious premise, that the Scottish Parliament before the union was not sovereign. Acts of the Scottish Parliament, like those of its English counterpart, were Acts of the King with the consent of the other Estates of the realm. As well as enacting laws, Parliament was the highest court of appeal.[45] No doubt partly for that reason, lower courts claimed no authority to invalidate its Acts.[46] It was said in 1627 that '[t]he said Act of Parliament could not be drawn in dispute before the [Court of] Session, if it was formally or well done or not, they not being judges thereto', and in 1683, that decrees of Parliament were not to be disputed by inferior judges.[47]

Between 1574 and 1579, Sir James Balfour, a former President of the Court of Session, with the assistance of Sir John Skene, produced a compilation of Scottish statutes and judicial decisions known as the *Practicks*.[48] They acknowledged the supremacy of Parliament, stating that only Parliament had power to make laws or statutes, and therefore that any question not decided by a clear written law must be referred by the judges to Parliament.[49] Laws made by the three Estates in Parliament were said to bind and oblige all the lieges of the realm.[50] In the early seventeenth century, both Sir Thomas Craig and Sir John Skene affirmed

---

[42] Powicke and Fryde (1961: 540).

[43] *MacCormick v Lord Advocate* (1953) S.C. 396, 411 *per* Lord Cooper.

[44] T. B. Smith (1962: 52).

[45] D. M. Walker (1995: iii. 224–6); Erskine (1777: Bk. 1, Tit. 3, 2).

[46] This is admitted even by those who deny that the Parliament of Great Britain can lawfully alter the fundamental terms of the union. T. B. Smith (1957: 113–14) confirms that '[t]he existing privileges of the courts of Scotland in 1707 . . . certainly did not include scrutiny of the legislation of the Scottish Estates'.

[47] *Stuart v Wedderburn* (1627) Durie 301, and *Murray v Bailie of Torwoodhead* (1683) Harc. 13, respectively, both quoted by Mitchell (1964: 66 n. 74; 67 n. 81), who cites other authorities for the same proposition. See also Middleton (1954: 40).

[48] D. M. Walker (1995: iii. 10–11).   [49] Quoted in ibid. iii. 363.   [50] ibid.

that Acts of Parliament were the most authoritative source of law in Scotland.[51] According to Brian Levack, '[t]he reverence paid to statute continued throughout the seventeenth century . . . It was the Scottish acts, rather than Scottish custom or common law, which formed the basis of the Scottish conception of their law.'[52] Scottish lawyers, he believes, were less apprehensive of their common law being changed by statute than were English lawyers such as Sir Edward Coke.[53] Furthermore, the popular idea that a sovereign power cannot limit itself was thought to apply to the Scottish Parliament. Viscount Stair, in his *Institutions of the Law of Scotland* (1693), stated that

the Parliament can never exclude the full liberty of themselves, or of their successors; no more than persons can by one resolution secure that they cannot resolve the contrary . . . [W]hatever a Parliament can do at one time, in making of laws, or determining of causes, may be at their pleasure abrogate or derogate.[54]

Professors Dicey and Rait argues that the Scottish Parliament was not fully sovereign before 1690, because its authority was limited by two institutions, the Lords of the Articles and the Conventions of Estates.[55] The Lords of the Articles constituted a parliamentary committee, nominated by the King and elected by Parliament, charged with preparing and submitting proposed legislation, called Articles, which Parliament then accepted or rejected, usually without debate. Dicey and Rait claim that before 1690, Parliament 'at times' had no authority to discuss or pass any Article not submitted to it in that way.[56] But even during those times, the Lords of the Articles were part of the internal procedure by which Parliament exercised its legislative authority, rather than an external limitation of that authority.[57] It is irrelevant that the Lords of the Articles were usually controlled by the King, because he himself was part of the law-making process.[58] As for Conventions of Estates, Dicey and Rait describe them as augmented meetings of the Privy Council, convened by the King when no Parliament was in session, in order to grant taxes and to pass temporary legislation, which required subsequent parliamentary recognition.[59] It is difficult to see how either institution could have detracted from Parliament's legislative sovereignty.[60] In any event, Parliament abolished the Lords of the Articles in 1690, because 'its members

---

[51] Levack (1994: 218, 228).   [52] ibid. 219.   [53] ibid. 223.

[54] Dalrymple (1693: 538; Bk. IV, tit. I, 61). This statement appeared in subsequent editions of the Institutions, notwithstanding the terms of the Union of 1707.

[55] Dicey and Rait (1920: 32–44).   [56] ibid. 14, 33–42.

[57] The Lords of the Articles are described as part of 'the machinery of Parliament' in Professor Rait's subsequent book (1924: 7–8).

[58] It is odd that Dicey and Rait refer to 'the King acting through the Lords of the Articles' as one of Parliament's 'competitors' for legislative authority (Dicey and Rait 1920: 22). The explanation of the oddity is that, by 'Parliament', they mean the House of Parliament alone, rather than the King in Parliament: ibid. 1 n. 1.

[59] ibid. 42–3.

[60] Dicey and Rait acknowledge that it was 'never disputed that a Scottish Convention acted in some sense in subordination to the Parliament': ibid.

were determined to assert their right to an authority at least equal to . . . [that] of the English Parliament', and no Convention of Estates was ever summoned after that date.[61]

Dicey and Rait also suggest that the Scottish Parliament was not generally acknowledged to possess sovereign authority with respect to the Church of Scotland.[62] But from 1689, Parliament passed many Acts dealing with the most fundamental affairs of the Church, for example, abolishing prelacy, and consequently expelling Bishops from Parliament, restoring Presbyterian ministers, abolishing Church patronage, ratifying the Presbyterian Confession of Faith, and settling the governance of the Church, which included re-establishing its General Assembly.[63] Moreover, 'the days when [the General Assembly of the Church] could nullify an Act of Parliament and prohibit all persons from obeying it . . . were past and gone'.[64]

The Scottish Act of Union was itself an extraordinary demonstration of the authority of the Parliament that enacted it: it is difficult to conceive of laws more fundamental than those it altered. The term 'fundamental laws' usually meant, in Scotland, the fundamental laws of government, such as those relating to the succession to the Crown, the royal prerogative, and the structure of Parliament, and it was precisely those kinds of laws that were changed by the Act of Union.[65] It was strenuously objected at the time that, by abolishing the Parliament and relinquishing Scottish sovereignty, the Act would violate the fundamental laws of the kingdom, and the trust reposed in Parliament by the people.[66] William Seton of Pitmedden, one of the Scots Commissioners who negotiated the Treaty of Union, replied that in Scotland, 'the sovereign and representatives are the only judges of every thing which does contribute to the happiness of the body politic, and from whom no appeal can legally be made. . . . Our law is positive, that this supreme court is subject to no human authority.' He pointed out that great changes had been made to the Scottish constitution in the past: the monarchy, previously elective, had been made hereditary during the reign of Kenneth III; representation of the clergy in Parliament was restored under James VI; the royal prerogative expanded under Charles II; and the King dethroned, and the clergy expelled from Parliament, in 1688. He challenged those who appealed to unalterable fundamental laws to explain when they had been laid down, where they were recorded, and whether all succeeding Parliaments had sworn to obey them.

In fine, I believe there are no fundamentals of government in any nation, which are not alterable by its supreme power, where the circumstances of times require . . . I do, indeed, acknowledge, there are fundamentals in nature, to wit, liberty and property, which this House can never destroy, without exceeding its utmost bounds of power, that are always

[61] ibid. 62–6.   [62] ibid. 22, 75, 78, 95.   [63] ibid. 67; Rait (1924: 106).
[64] Dicey and Rait (1920: 92).   [65] Levack (1987: 33–4).
[66] ibid. 34–5; MacKinnon (1896: 296, 305, 314).

limited to the public good; nevertheless, this honourable House is only capable to judge of the most proper means of securing these fundamentals.[67]

There were, of course, other opinions, but Seton was certainly not alone in his. The Earl of Cromarty agreed that Scottish sovereignty was reposed in the Crown and Parliament.[68] Seton spoke during debate over Article 3 of the Treaty of Union, providing that the two kingdoms be represented by a single Parliament, and consequently abolishing the Scottish Parliament. It was subsequently carried by a vote of 114 to 57.[69] Whatever the balance of informed opinions may previously have been, Seton's view carried the day.

There is more to be said for the second argument that the new Parliament of Great Britain could not have been fully sovereign, which is that the Acts of Union expressly prohibited it from altering certain clauses of the Treaty of Union and the statutes securing the two established Churches. But if this argument is sound, it is because those prohibitions are written, relatively clear, and set out in formally enacted legal instruments, and not because they were intended to be judicially enforceable.[70]

Daniel Defoe reported that when some members of the Scottish Parliament expressed the fear that the terms of the Treaty would not be binding, they were reassured that 'all subsequent power is inferior in its extent to the power which it derives from. The Parliament of Britain, being the creature of the Union, formed by express stipulations between the two separate Parliaments of England and Scotland, cannot but be unalterably bound by the conditions so stipulated, and upon which it received its being, name, and authority.' If the Parliament violated those conditions, it would pull itself up by the roots.[71] This happened to be Defoe's own opinion, but not everyone found it convincing, because no formal mechanism was provided for the practical enforcement of the conditions of the union.[72] James Hodges pointed out that a compact subject to conditions could be binding only as long as there were distinct parties; once the parties were united, '[i]t is no less ridiculous to plead any compact than to suppose that a person, society, state, can make a compact with themselves'. The articles of agreement would be 'squibs and fireworks, that must all be blown in the air so soon as the work is finished'.[73]

The plain fact was, that if a majority of the new Parliament should desire to violate those articles, the only practical impediment would be the danger that

[67] 'Speech in Parliament by Mr. Seton junior, of Pitmedden' (18 November 1706), in Defoe (1786: 360–1). For Seton's status as a Scottish Commissioner in 1706, see Dicey and Rait (1920: 383).
[68] *A Friendly Return to a Letter Concerning Sir George MacKenzie's and Sir John Nisbet's Observation and Response on the Matter of the Union* (22 August 1706: 5–29), quoted in Robertson (1995b: 220).
[69] Daiches (1977: 153).   [70] See the definition of 'sovereignty' in Chapter 2, Section 1.
[71] Defoe (1786: 357–8).   [72] Levack (1987: 134–5).
[73] Quoted in MacKinnon (1896: 254).

outraged Scottish opinion might lead to the dissolution of the union. Since judicial review of legislation had not yet been invented, no remedy other than dissolution was conceivable.[74] As a Presbyterian minister complained in 1714,

'tis a jest to imagine that the Parliament cannot . . . alter any law or article of the Union, if to them it seems proper; and although I readily grant that by law or equity they ought not and cannot do it, yet if it should so happen that they actually do it, where is our relief and how shall we help ourselves? 'What the Parliament does is law and we must either submit or rebel.'[75]

The threat of rebellion was believed by some to be sufficient. Defoe, the most prolific English propagandist in favour of the union, assured the Scots that 'to break the Treaty, is to dissolve the constitution and very being of the parliament, and overthrow the union'.[76] He predicted disastrous consequences, which no Parliament would be mad enough to risk: '[t]he fundamental is destroyed, the government dissolves, and the whole island becomes a mob, one universal rabble. . . . property ceases, authority dissolves, constitution suffocates, and the national capacity dies'.[77] The Scots natural lawyer Gershom Carmichael argued that the Treaty of Union incorporated pre-existing rights of the Scottish people, who were entitled to oppose any threatened violation of them by resistance if necessary.[78] One pro-unionist pamphleteer maintained that any contravention of the Treaty would absolve the Scottish nation from its allegiance to it, and restore the Scottish Parliament 'to resent the encroachment'.[79] He did not explain how that Parliament could be convened otherwise than by the Queen of Great Britain, but may have had in mind the ad hoc procedures adopted in 1688, when a self-styled Convention of Estates selected a new King and Queen and then purported to turn itself into a lawful Parliament.[80]

In 1713, aggrieved by various perceived breaches of the terms of union, Scots members of the Parliament of Great Britain attempted to dissolve the union by legal rather than extra-legal means. A Bill for dissolution was debated in the House of Lords, and defeated by only four votes after a count of proxies.[81] The Scots did not rely on Defoe's thesis, that any breach of its fundamental terms would automatically dissolve the union.

---

[74] Middleton (1954: 58). As Robertson (1995b: 223–4) observes, no other explanation was offered of how the new Parliament could be bound by Acts of predecessor Parliaments which would have ceased to exist. Even T. B. Smith (1957: 113–14) agrees that Scottish courts had no authority to scrutinize legislation before 1707, and '[n]o such power was conferred on the courts at the union'.

[75] *The Lockhart Papers, Memoirs and Commentaries upon the Affairs of Scotland from 1702 to 1715* (1817: i. 576–7), quoted by G. Marshall (1957: 52).

[76] D. Defoe, *An Essay at Removing National Prejudices against a Union With England, Part III* (Edinburgh, 1706: 26), quoted by Robertson (1995b: 223).

[77] D. Defoe, *An Essay at Removing National Prejudices against a Union With England, Part III* (Edinburgh, 1706: 12), quoted by Penovich (1995: 237).

[78] Moore and Silverthorne (1995: 193–6).

[79] *The Trimmer; or, Some Necessary Cautions concerning the Union of the Kingdoms of Scotland and England*, 485, quoted by MacKinnon (1896: 262).

[80] For this suggestion, see Middleton (1954: 55–6).   [81] MacKinnon (1896: 425–31).

English lawyers were well aware of the danger that insensitivity in amending the terms of the union might precipitate its dissolution.[82] They acknowledged that the Act of Union was no ordinary statute, yet still seem to have assumed that it could be altered if necessary. In 1747, Lord Chancellor Hardwicke introduced a bill to abolish heritable jurisdictions in Scotland, which was opposed by some Scots members of Parliament on the ground that it violated Articles 19 and 20 of the Treaty of Union. He claimed that '[n]obody holds those articles more sacred than I do: they are the *pacta conventa* between the two nations, to be religiously observed, inviolably maintained'.[83] He argued that the bill in question did not violate the articles, but hinted that it could be enacted even if it did. The objection that the bill violated the articles 'leads to no less a question, than that of binding the legislature of the whole United Kingdom. In all countries, the legislative power must, to a general intent, be absolute.'[84] Even the Lords who most strongly opposed the bill conceded that it would have been acceptable if 'justified by some necessity of state, or by some general, manifest, and urgent utility to the public'.[85]

The same view was taken in 1772, by several Members of the House of Commons who were considering whether or not Parliament could alter the official doctrines of the Church of England. They agreed that the Act of Union was 'fundamental' and 'sacred', but insisted that it could nevertheless be altered in circumstances of pressing necessity.[86] '*Salus populi suprema lex esto*', declaimed Thomas Townshend: 'If the state of the nation requires a change in any part, however essential, the experiment must be hazarded'.[87] '[H]ow are we to be restrained from making innovations and improvements in our own system?' asked Edmund Burke. 'Our ancestors were neither so bigotted nor so ill-informed as to leave no door open for reformation'; '[t]he Act [of Union] never meant, I am sure, any such unnatural restraint on the joint legislature it was then forming. History shows us what it meant, and all that it could mean with any degree of common sense.'[88]

This raises a problem for the argument that Parliament's law-making authority is limited by the expressly unalterable terms of the union. It would seem to follow that those terms are permanently unalterable, unless the union itself is dissolved and the Parliaments of England and Scotland re-established. But that is unlikely to have been intended by the experienced Scottish politicians and

---

[82] Blackstone (1765: 98) observed that any alteration to the constitutions of either of the two established churches of England and Scotland would 'greatly endanger the union'.

[83] Cobbett (1806–20: xiv. 11–12.)   [84] ibid. 12.

[85] *Protest Against Committing the Heritable Jurisdictions Bill*, signed by Lords Denbigh, Litchfield, Stanhope, Ward, Talbot, Oxford and Mortimer, Westmoreland, Ferrers, Shaftesbury and Beaufort, in Cobbett (1806–20: xiv. 52). The Earl of Morton was willing to 'admit that the parliament of Great Britain has a power in cases of necessity, to vary from the Articles of Union': ibid. 55.

[86] Charles Jenkinson, Lord North, Thomas Townshend, and William Burke, in Cobbett (1806–20: xvii. 269, 272, 275, 276). Only Sir Roger Newgate is recorded as disagreeing: ibid. 256.

[87] ibid. 275.   [88] ibid. 277–9.

lawyers who helped to establish the union. They must have known of the many previous Scottish statutes that had been altered or repealed notwithstanding the inclusion of clauses declaring that they were to last 'in all time coming' or 'for ever'.[89] Even Professor T. B. Smith, the most forceful recent proponent of the view that the Acts of Union were legally binding, concedes that 'those who framed the Union could not have considered that they were framing a constitution which would last till Doomsday. They might have regarded their labours as well rewarded if they had thought that it would last for fifty years substantially as they had framed it.'[90] He also acknowledges that 'it would be impracticable to regard any constitution as immutable throughout all time'.[91] He proposes that even the provisions declared to be unalterable should now be regarded as legitimately alterable with the consent of a majority of Scottish electors, ascertained in a referendum.[92] Professor J. D. B. Mitchell, another advocate of the view that the Acts of Union were legally binding, agrees that 'it is impossible, in any absolute sense, to confine the evolution of societies by the Statute Book . . . [S]ucceeding generations must have or will find opportunities of development according to their ideals'.[93] He suggests that the clearest example of a breach of the articles of union was excusable because it 'was in effect carried out at the request and with the consent of the body most able to express [Scottish] national opinion upon the topic'.[94]

The problem with these concessions is that neither the Treaty nor the Acts of Union make any allowance for amending those provisions declared to be permanent, either by referendum or by any other procedure. Any referendum would have to be authorized and organized by an Act of Parliament, which would therefore be the ultimate author of any resulting amendment. To countenance that possibility is to presuppose that Parliament is legally sovereign, while insisting that it exercise its sovereignty in a particular way in order to ensure political legitimacy.[95] A referendum cannot be a requirement of legal validity in the absence of a superior constitutional law requiring that it be held. If Parliament can amend the terms of the union after holding such a referendum, then legally it must be able to amend them without doing so. Therefore, even Professors Smith and Mitchell seem driven to the conclusion that the terms of the union amount to 'fundamental laws' only in the traditional British sense of those words. They are principles of political morality, which Parliament must take into account, as a matter of conscience and political prudence, but can legally change if there are sufficiently strong reasons for so doing. The advantage of such 'laws' is that if there are good reasons for infringing them, accepted even by those whose interests they

---

[89] Mitchell (1964: 55), and Middleton (1954: 57 n. 55).

[90] T. B. Smith (1957: 112–13).   [91] T. B. Smith (1962: 56).

[92] T. B. Smith (1987: v. 145–6, 148, 150). For his earlier, more tentative suggestion to this effect, see T. B. Smith (1962: 56).

[93] Mitchell (1964: 58–9).   [94] ibid. 58.   [95] See Munro (1987b: 70–1).

protect, they can be infringed. Criteria of political legitimacy are more flexible than those of legal validity.

For these reasons most Scottish lawyers and politicians have long held the same opinion as Lord Chancellor Campbell in the early nineteenth century. He claimed to 'entertain no doubt that by the just construction of the treaty of Union with Scotland . . . the united legislature was to be vested with supreme and absolute power over the whole empire. The fact that a proposed law repeals or alters any article of the Union is a very strong but not a conclusive objection to it.'[96]

3. Legal Sovereignty, Popular Sovereignty, and the Right of Resistance

Those who questioned Parliament's sovereignty in the eighteenth century never suggested that its authority was subject to limits enforceable by judicial review. The relationship between Parliament and 'inferior courts' was never in question. As the distinguished Whig lawyer Sir John Hawles observed, during his speech at the trial of Dr Sacheverell, 'matters determined by Act of Parliament are never suffered to be disputed afterwards' in 'any Court of Westminster-hall'; 'there being no higher power or authority to appeal to than the supreme power, that must needs be the judge'.[97] It was the relationship between Parliament and the people it claimed to represent that was in question. Its duty to act in their interests was widely thought to implicitly limit its authority. But that duty was also thought to be enforceable only by the people, at parliamentary elections or, as a last resort, by resistance or rebellion.[98]

Previously, parliamentary and popular sovereignty had rarely been considered rivals, because of the ancient fictions that Parliament represented all subjects, and was incapable of acting against their interests. Although royalists had challenged those fictions in the 1640s, when the two Houses acted independently of the King, even they accepted them in normal circumstances, when the King's veto formed part of the checks and balances of the constitution. But in the eighteenth century, those who opposed parliamentary measures increasingly attacked the two fictions.

Political divisions in the early part of the century are often described in terms of Court versus Country, as well as Whig versus Tory. The word 'Court' refers to the Crown, its ministers, and their political allies and supporters, whether Whig or Tory, while 'Country' refers to those who tended to distrust the Court and its

---

[96] Campbell (1857: vi. 251 n. e). He added that '[o]n this doctrine I acted when I supported the entire abolition of the Court of Admiralty and the subsequent abolition of the Court of Exchequer in Scotland, both declared by the articles of Union to be for ever established in that country': ibid.

[97] *The Trial of Doctor Sacheverell* (1710), in Howell (1816–28: xv. 118–19). During his career Hawles was a Member of Parliament and Solicitor-General.

[98] Dickinson (1977: 287–90).

policies, and oppose the manipulative and sometimes corrupt methods by which it attempted to maintain majority support within Parliament. The Country opposition included both Country Tories, who suspected Court Whigs of advancing the commercial interests of business entrepreneurs at the expense of the landed gentry, and 'old' or 'radical' Whigs, who championed the rights and liberties of 'the people'. Both groups insisted that Parliament must defer to the wishes of the electors, and threatened censure or even rebellion if it failed to do so. In their opinion, members of the Commons were not independent agents, trusted to exercise their own judgment concerning the welfare of the nation. Instead, they were delegates in the strict sense of the term, bound to act according to the wishes of their constituents, who could instruct them on how they should vote on particular issues.[99] This proposal, along with more radical reforms to enhance the representativeness of the House of Commons, was popular among the Country opposition.[100]

Country Tories and Whigs often argued that Parliament had no legitimate authority beyond that conferred on it by 'the people', by which they meant the men of property who constituted the electorate. They opposed the Septennial Act (1716), for example, on the ground that, since the House of Commons had been elected on the understanding that it would sit for a maximum of three years, it would be acting beyond the authority conferred on it by the electors if it passed a Bill to extend its life to seven years. (There would have been far fewer objections to such a Bill if, prior to the preceding election, the electors had been given notice that it would be introduced, and had been able to exercise their votes accordingly.) They occasionally argued that statutes such as the Septennial Act were 'unconstitutional', because they violated fundamental rights reserved by the people.

But the Country opposition never suggested that the judges could invalidate 'unconstitutional' legislation. An example is Daniel Defoe.[101] In 1702, Defoe attacked Sir Humphrey Mackworth's claim, in *A Vindication of the Rights of the Commons in England*, that it was unimaginable that the House of Commons could act 'against reason and justice'.[102] Defoe argued that, although it was not probable that the House would do so, it was undoubtedly possible, because the House was not infallible.[103] One of his deepest fears was tyrannical power exercised by a corrupt House of Commons.[104] He once ironically observed that, although its members were the 'best, ripest, ablest, wisest, and wealthiest of our gentry', they were nevertheless 'subject to mistakes, capable of acting contrary to the true

---

[99] Defoe (1702a: 23).   [100] Dickinson (1977: 116–17, 181–2); but cf. ibid. 189.

[101] Defoe's political beliefs were somewhat idiosyncratic and difficult to categorize. He is often described as a Whig, because of his opposition to the Tory dominated House of Commons in 1701–2. But in 1704, he became a lifelong supporter and client of a leading Country Tory, Robert Harley, 'with whose political ideas he could not have been more compatible', according to Schonhorn (1991: 101–2).

[102] See text to nn. 24–6, above.   [103] Defoe (1702a: *passim*).

[104] Schonhorn (1991: 69, 75, 78, 79).

nature of their Constitution, capable of abusing their trust, betraying their country, tyrannizing over the liberties of the people, ruining those they are sent there to defend'.[105] It followed that the obligation to obey Parliament could not be absolute and unconditional. The people entrusted their power to their representatives in the House of Commons, but the trust would be revoked, and the power revert to the people, if it were grossly abused.[106] Although Defoe once said that Parliament had an 'unlimited power' in law-making,[107] he usually denied that Parliament was omnipotent, and coined his own word, 'magnipotent', to describe its power.[108] Nevertheless, the remedy for any abuse was extra-judicial, as he warned the House of Commons in 1701:

tho' there are no stated proceeding to bring you to your duty, yet the great law of reason says, and all nations allow, that whatever power is above law, is burdensome and tyrannical; and may be reduced by extrajudicial methods . . . [W]hile Parliaments . . . betray their trust, and abuse the people whom they should protect: And no other way being left us, but that force which we are very loath to make use of . . . [I]t is the undoubted right of the people of England to call them to an account for the same, and by Convention, Assembly or force, may proceed against them as traitors and betrayers of their country.[109]

The same view was taken by Viscount Bolingbroke, during his Country Tory phase, when he advocated greater accountability of the House of Commons to the electorate.[110] He denied that Parliament possessed 'arbitrary power': 'the obligations of the law of nature cease not in society', and therefore Parliament could 'never have a right to destroy, enslave, or designedly to impoverish the subjects'. Furthermore, 'Parliament cannot annul the constitution'.[111] But he believed that if Parliament exceeded its legitimate authority, the only possible remedies lay in the hands of 'the people', by which he meant men of property: dismissal of those responsible at the next election, and failing that, rebellion.[112] The first of these remedies was provided for by the constitution, and was adequate in all situations except those so 'extravagant' that they were hardly within 'the bounds of possibility'.[113] '[F]reedom of elections and the frequency, integrity, and independency of parliaments . . . are the essentials of British liberty. Defects in other parts of the constitution can never be fatal, if they are preserved entire.'[114] But should an 'extravagant' case arise, in which, for example, the two Houses agreed immediately to surrender all their rights and those of the people to the Crown, this 'would break the bargain between the king and the nation, between

---

[105] A. W. Secord (ed.), *Defoe's Review* (New York, 1938), 5: 106 (30 November 1708), quoted in Schonhorn (1991: 79).

[106] Defoe (1702*a*: 22–3).   [107] Defoe (1702*b*: 9).

[108] Schonhorn (1991: 60). Exactly how Defoe thought that 'magnipotence' fell short of 'omnipotence' is not clear, but control of the succession seems to have been one example. Defoe held that Parliament could adjudicate between competing claims to the throne, but not bestow the crown at will: ibid. 59, 73–5. See also Nenner (1995: 227–8).

[109] Defoe (1701: 84).   [110] Dickinson (1977: 190).

[111] St John (1735: Letter XVII, 210).   [112] See Langford (1991: 154).

[113] St John (1735: Letter XVII, 210–11).   [114] ibid., Letter XI, 125; see also ibid. 131.

the representative and collective body of the people, and would dissolve the constitution'. '[T]he people would return to their original, their natural right, the right of restoring the same constitution, or of making a new one.' The preservation of the Constitution was ultimately up to them. '[W]ho has the right, and the means, to resist the supreme legislative power; I answer the whole nation has the right, and a people, who deserve to enjoy liberty, will find the means.' 'In short, nothing can destroy the constitution of Britain, but the people of Britain'.[115] Bolingbroke, although a Tory, was clearly influenced by Locke, and indeed quoted him twice in discussing the right of the people to 'appeal to heaven' when the constitution provides no adequate remedy against the abuse of power.[116] He never suggested that the law itself provided a remedy. To the contrary, he said that although Parliament was not an arbitrary power, it was 'a supreme, and may be called, in one sense, an absolute . . . power',[117] and elsewhere that '[t]here must be absolute, unlimited, and uncontrollable power lodged somewhere in every government'.[118]

According to Dickinson, it was 'only occasionally that the Country opposition endeavoured to limit the exercise of the legislature's sovereign authority', because even they were aware of the usefulness of the doctrine of parliamentary sovereignty 'in combating the twin dangers of absolute monarchy and popular sovereignty'.[119] Politicians such as Bolingbroke were no more attracted to genuine democracy than Court Whigs and Tories. The latter abhorred the idea that real sovereignty belonged to the people, on the ground that it was a recipe for anarchy and the destruction of property rights. The people had to be content with their representation in the House of Commons, and to respect and obey Parliament.[120]

The radical principles of the 'old' Whigs, proclaiming the ultimate sovereignty of the people and their right to resist tyrannical governments, had served them well when they were in opposition. But when Whig politicians enjoyed power themselves, particularly during their long period of ascendancy under George I, they tended to ignore, or at least de-emphasize, those principles.[121] The ideologies of Court Whigs and Tories converged: the Tories adopted the Whig theory that legislative sovereignty belonged to the King in Parliament rather than the King alone, and the Whigs agreed with the Tories that 'the people' could not be trusted with more than an indirect and strictly limited political role. Contemporaries often marvelled at this apparent convergence of party ideologies.[122] Jonathan Swift observed that he was 'not sensible of any material difference there is between those who call themselves the Old Whigs, and a great majority of the present Tories'.[123]

---

[115] ibid., Letter XVII, 210–12; see also Letter XI, 131. Original emphasis removed.

[116] ibid., Letter XI, 129 and Letter XVII, 210 (*Essays on Civil Government*).

[117] ibid., Letter XVII, 210.

[118] St John (1749: 93). Bolingbroke's constitutional philosophy is discussed in Burns (1962: esp. 271–5).

[119] Dickinson (1977: 187).   [120] ibid. 69, 101; see also ibid. 43, 46–50, 82, 147.

[121] Kenyon (1977: 197, 203).   [122] ibid. 172–3.

[123] J. Swift, *The Examiner*, 22 March 1710, reprinted in Swift (1966: 111).

The views of Francis Atterbury, a prominent Tory clergyman, and Joseph Addison, an influential Whig polemicist, exemplify this convergence. During his own impeachment in 1723, Atterbury affirmed the sovereignty of Parliament. In some respects, he said, it had a greater power than God, because He could do nothing unjust. 'But though there are no limits to be set to a Parliament, yet they are generally thought to restrain themselves . . . The Parliament may order a criminal to be tortured, who can say they cannot? But they never did, nor never will, I hope . . .'.[124] On the other hand, he complained in 1710 that 'the voice of the people is the cry of hell, leading to idolatry, rebellion, murder and all the wickedness the devil can suggest . . .'.[125] In this context, 'the people' referred to ordinary people, rather than men of property.

Addison agreed that Parliament was sovereign. Appealing to 'the first principles of government, which . . . are of no party, but assented to by every reasonable man', he asserted that '[e]very one knows, who has considered the nature of government, that there must be in each particular form of it an absolute and unlimited power; and that this power is lodged in the hands of those who have the making of its laws'. 'This is so uncontroverted a maxim, that I believe never any body attempted to refute it.'[126] But it could not be lodged in the people at large, with respect to whom he was as scathing as Atterbury: 'nothing can be more contemptible and insignificant, than the scum of a people, when they are instigated against a king, who is supported by the two branches of the legislature'. The authority of the King, Lords and Commons 'is not to be controlled by a tumultuary rabble'.[127]

Sir Robert Walpole, who led a Whig administration for nearly twenty years, warned in 1734 that 'we are to guard against running too much into that form of government which is properly called democratical', because 'faction and sedition . . . always arises from the people's having too great a share in the government'.[128] Similar sentiments were expressed by prominent Tories and Whigs throughout the century.[129] Edmund Burke condemned the doctrine of the sovereignty of the people as 'the most false, wicked, and mischievous doctrine that ever could be preached to them', which, if ever adopted as the rule of government, would spell the end of 'property . . . and religion, morality, and law, which grew out of property'.[130]

Because they distrusted popular opinion, Court Whigs and Tories agreed that the people were not entitled to any direct influence in matters of government other than by electing Members of Parliament. The people's share of the power to make laws was completely devolved upon and vested in their representatives in Parliament. 'If we don't like what they have done, we are at liberty, when the time is expired, to choose others; this, and this only is our power.'[131] On this

---

[124] Cobbett (1806–20: viii. 287–8).   [125] Atterbury (1710: 6).
[126] Addison (1716: 107, 109; no. 16, 13 February).
[127] ibid. 154; no. 28, 26 March.   [128] Cobbett (1806–20: ix. 473–4).
[129] Gunn (1983: 73–88, 299–312).   [130] Cobbett (1806–20: xxx. 554–5).
[131] *London Journal*, 26 May 1733, quoted by Dickinson (1977: 157).

view, Members of Parliament were not delegates of their electors, bound to follow their instructions. Members had a responsibility to exercise an independent
judgment as to the best interests of the nation, and should not be dictated to or
intimidated by voters.[132]

John Locke had argued that the supreme power recognized by the constitution, the legislature, was subject to a higher power outside the constitution, namely,
the community as a whole. But Court Whigs and Tories tended to view this
as a dangerous doctrine, which threatened to make government precarious and
promote civil discord.[133] A small number went so far as to deny that the people
possessed any rights at all, other than those conferred on them by positive
law.[134] A more common view was that, although there was a right to resist the
Crown in order to preserve the constitution, that right was exercisable only by
the two Houses of Parliament. There was no right whatsoever to resist Parliament itself. As Samuel Dodd said, in defending Dr Sacheverell during his impeachment in 1710,

The supreme power is the Queen and Parliament . . . and I have not heard it said by any
that it is lawful to resist the Queen in Parliament. Here is the strength of the nation, and
here there ought to be a standing obedience; otherwise it is setting up the people to be
judges, and not the collective body of the people assembled in Parliament.[135]

Another view was more subtle: there was a right of resistance, but it could
never be recognized as lawful, because it was limited to extraordinary emergencies
in which the constitution was dissolved or, at least, threatened with dissolution.[136]
Before the Revolution of 1688, royalists had strenuously denied that active resistance to the King could ever be justified, either morally or legally. The horrors
of the Civil War seemed to confirm the sixteenth century teaching that tyranny
was preferable to anarchy. But at least after 1710, only Jacobites denied the moral
legitimacy of resistance during the Revolution of 1688. The problem posed by
these conflicting precedents was to vindicate that Revolution, without encour-
aging resistance to the regime it had established, which might unleash a new civil
war. Part of the solution was to deny that resistance could ever be lawful, even
if in extraordinary circumstances it could be morally justified.

There was solid support for this position in Locke's writings. He had denied
that 'any edict of any body else, in what form soever conceived, or by what power
soever backed, [can] have the force and obligation of a *law*, which has not its
sanction from that *legislative*, which the public has chosen and appointed'.[137]
The constitution did not recognize even the people as having a power superior
to that of the legislature: their right of revolution therefore derived from a law

---

[132] See Dickinson (1977: 157–9).
[133] See e.g. ibid. 130; for the reservations which Whigs had concerning Locke's theory, see ibid.
71–8, 125–6.
[134] See ibid. 307–8, esp. n. 88.
[135] *The Trial of Dr Henry Sacheverell* (1710), in Howell (1816–28: xv. 220).
[136] Dickinson (1977: 132).   [137] Locke (1690: 356), (II: 134). Emphasis in original.

'antecedent and paramount to all positive laws of men', and was enforced not by legal methods, but by rebellion.[138] This understanding of the matter was developed in the eighteenth century, and became a standard plank in the defence of parliamentary sovereignty.

Sir Matthew Hale, in the seventeenth century, had argued that no human constitution could provide perfectly for every possible eventuality. When comparing constitutions, 'we are to weigh which answer most exigencies of human life, and though it answer not all, yet it deserves a preference before any other that answers some occasions but not so many or so well as the former'.[139]

[T]he method and modelling of governments are to be fitted to what is the common and ordinary state of things . . . And it is a madness to think that the model of laws or government is to be framed according to such circumstances as very rarely occur. 'Tis as if a man should make agaric and rhubarb his ordinary diet, because it is of use when he is sick which may be once in seven years.[140]

Hale used this reasoning to rebut the royalist argument that the authority of the King ought not to be controlled by law, because he might need to override the law in an unexpected emergency. He pointed out that such emergencies were extremely unlikely, even if theoretically possible, and therefore the desirability of the King having unlimited power in order to deal with them, was outweighed by its undesirability in the vast majority of cases that would arise. In the eighteenth century, Court Whigs and Tories used the same reasoning to argue that it was better for the law not to recognize any limits to the legitimate authority of the Crown or Parliament, enforceable by popular resistance, because in the vast majority of cases likely to arise, it was much more likely that such limits would be interpreted too broadly, and encourage unjustified resistance, than that the Crown or Parliament would exceed them.

This argument was made again and again during the trial of Dr Sacheverell in 1710. Sacheverell was a High Church Tory, who had preached '[t]hat it is not lawful, upon any pretence whatsoever, to make resistance to the supreme power'.[141] He was prosecuted by the Whig government for publishing a seditious libel, in that by denying the legitimacy of resistance to government, he had implicitly denied the legitimacy of the Revolution, and therefore of Queen Anne's title to the throne. One of his defences was that by 'the supreme power' he meant the King in Parliament, rather than the King alone, and therefore he had not said anything that any reasonable person could disagree with, let alone impugned the legitimacy of the Revolution.[142] A second defence was that, by emphasizing the obligation of subjects to obey the supreme power, without acknowledging any right of resistance, he had merely followed the examples of

---

[138] ibid. 379–80 (II: 168), and Locke (1689: 55), quoted in full in Chapter 6, n. 85.
[139] Hale (1924: 512).   [140] ibid.
[141] *The Trial of Henry Sacheverell* (1710) in Howell (1816–28: xv. 55).
[142] See text to n. 31, above.

the Bible, orthodox teachings of the Church, and the law. None explicitly recognized any right of resistance, even though such a right existed, because it was
unnecessary and imprudent, and perhaps even impossible, to do so. As Sir Simon
Harcourt argued, '[t]he general rule [of obedience] ought always to be pressed;
but the exceptions of extraordinary cases, or cases of necessity, are never particularly to be stated. To point out every such case before-hand, is as impossible,
as it is for a man in his senses not to perceive plainly when such a case happens.'[143] Furthermore,

> Such cases . . . with respect to resistance against the supreme power, are noway fit to be
> considered, but in parliament; and even the parliament itself has never yet thought fit
> otherwise to consider them than by way of retrospect, to justify what had of necessity
> been done in those cases; but never went so far as to enumerate the cases of that kind,
> which might happen for the future, wherein it might be lawful for the subject to resist;
> nothing being more evident, than that the subjects would be, some time or other, thereby
> tempted to exceed their just liberty. . . . [I]f clergymen . . . instead of preaching up the gen-
> eral rule of obedience, are permitted to state the several extraordinary cases which may
> arise, the several excepted cases which, notwithstanding the general rule, are implied; such
> exceptions will in time devour all allegiance.[144]

Harcourt cited many statutes to demonstrate 'that the law, in all cases
concerning our allegiance, lays down the general rule, without making any
exception . . . [C]ases of necessity, such as the Revolution, were implied, [but]
they are improper to be expressed'.[145] Sacheverell's other counsel made similar
arguments.[146]

The Whig lawyers who prosecuted Sacheverell did not disagree with this.
Sir Joseph Jeckyll conceded that it would indeed have been improper for Dr
Sacheverell to attempt to state the limits of non-resistance, and teach the people
when they would be justified in resisting their government.[147] It would be
equally improper for the law itself to do so, because that would tend to corrupt
or annul the law itself. 'The wisdom of the law, in not expressing the exception,
is plain: It is neither decent, nor probably would have a good effect, to put odious
cases, such as a prince's overturning the constitution. . . . Laws are framed upon
a view of ordinary and common cases.'[148] But he insisted that Sacheverell should
have acknowledged that the Revolution was an exception to the general duty
of obedience, because he was preaching on a day dedicated to its commemora-
tion.[149] The Solicitor-General said 'that the general expressions in the laws
[requiring obedience] do not extend to any such case as that of the Revolution,
which no municipal law can be supposed to include'.[150] Nicholas Lechmere asserted
that it would be 'equally absurd, to construe any words in a positive law to authorize the destruction of the whole, as to expect, that King, Lords, and Commons

---

[143] Howell (1816–28: xv. 201).   [144] ibid. 202.   [145] ibid. 208–9.
[146] See ibid. 218, 220 (Samuel Dodd), and 230–1 (Constantine Phipps).   [147] ibid. 387.
[148] ibid. 389.   [149] ibid. 387.   [150] ibid. 403.

should, in express terms of law, declare such an ultimate resort as the right of resistance, at a time when the case supposes that the force of all law is ceased'.[151] And Sir Robert Walpole agreed:

Resistance is no where enacted to be legal, but subjected, by all the laws now in being, to the greatest penalties; it is what is not, cannot, nor ought ever to be described or affirmed, in any positive law, to be excusable: when, and upon what never-to-be-expected occasions, it may be exercised, no man can foresee, and ought never to be thought of, but when an utter subversion of the laws of the realm threatens the whole frame of a constitution, and no redress can otherwise be hoped for: it therefore does, and ought for ever to stand, in the eye and letter of the law, as the highest offence.[152]

Court Whigs and Tories therefore agreed that, although there were limits to the authority of any government, they were too dangerous to be explicitly formulated, especially by law. Charles Yorke wrote in 1746 that 'every Constitution of government has its peculiar cases tending to dissolution, beyond the power of any stated remedy . . . [and] not to be subjected to the ordinary provisions of law'.[153] In such cases 'the law will not suppose the possibility of a wrong, since it cannot mark out or assist the remedy'; 'they are cases which the law will not put, being incapable of distrusting those, whom it has invested with the supreme power, or its own perpetual duration; and they are out of the reach of laws, and stated remedies, because they render the exercise of them precarious and impracticable'.[154] With respect to these cases, 'the law will make no answer, but history will give one': namely, that when an extraordinary case actually arose, in 1688, 'the remedy suggested itself, and was suited to the necessity'.[155]

Yorke's views, and indeed, some of his words, were later adopted (without attribution) by Blackstone.[156] This resolves the apparent inconsistency between Blackstone's denial that human laws contrary to the law of nature are valid, and his insistence that the British Parliament was 'absolute and without control' and could 'do every thing that is not naturally impossible'.[157] He believed that the only appropriate remedy for a legislative violation of natural law was popular resistance, which could not be countenanced by law. After referring to Locke's thesis that a legislature which abused its powers could be removed by the people, he commented that

however just this conclusion may be in theory, we cannot adopt it, nor argue from it, under any dispensation of government at present actually existing. For this . . . includes in it a dissolution of the whole form of government established by that people . . . and by

[151] ibid. 63.

[152] ibid. 115. The Whigs' prosecution of Sacheverell backfired on them. Sacheverell was found guilty, but lightly punished, because of the vociferous public support he received during his trial.

[153] Yorke (1746: 107).   [154] ibid. 108, 109.

[155] ibid. 110, 112.   [156] Blackstone (1765: 237).

[157] ibid. 1765: 41 and 156–7, respectively. For the suggestion of inconsistency, see e.g. Sheridan (1779) and Gough (1955: 189–91); for the following way of resolving it, see Stourzh (1970: 21–2 and 216 n. 49), Lieberman (1989: 52–5), and Snowiss (1990: 115–17).

annihilating the sovereign power repeals all positive laws whatsoever before enacted. No human laws will therefore suppose a case, which at once must destroy all law . . . nor will they make provision for so desperate an event, as must render all legal provisions ineffectual.[158]

Blackstone deemed it not only unwise, but impossible, for the law to attempt to enumerate the situations in which resistance to government would be justified: 'how impossible it is, in any practical system of laws, to point out before-hand those eccentrical remedies, which the sudden emergence of national distress may dictate, and which that alone can justify'.[159] It followed that any adequate remedy for an abuse of sovereign power

must necessarily be out of the reach of any *stated rule*, or *express legal* provision: but, if ever they unfortunately happen, the prudence of the times must provide new remedies upon new emergencies. . . . And therefore, though the positive laws are silent, experience will furnish us with a very remarkable case, wherein nature and reason prevailed.

The Revolution of 1688 demonstrated 'that whenever the unconstitutional oppressions, even of the sovereign power, advance with gigantic strides and threaten desolation to a state, mankind will not be reasoned out of the feelings of humanity; nor will sacrifice their liberty by a scrupulous adherence to those political maxims, which were originally established to preserve it'.[160] But the law itself remains mute, 'leaving to future generations, whenever necessity and the safety of the whole shall require it, the exertion of those inherent (though latent) powers of society, which no climate, no time, no constitution, no contract, can ever destroy or diminish'.[161] A sovereign power cannot be disobeyed 'in the ordinary course of law: I say, in the *ordinary* course of law; for I do not now speak of those *extraordinary* recourses to first principles, which are necessary when the contracts of society are in danger of dissolution, and the law proves too weak a defence against the violence of fraud or oppression'.[162]

Parliament was fully sovereign according to positive law, even though its authority was limited by the law of nature, because those limits were enforceable only by extra-legal means. 'For, whenever a question arises between the society at large and any magistrate vested with powers originally delegated by that society, it must be decided by the voice of the society itself: there is not upon earth any other tribunal to resort to.'[163] 'I know it is generally laid down more largely, that acts of parliament contrary to reason are void. But if the parliament will positively enact a thing to be done which is unreasonable, I know of no power that can control it. . . . [T]here is no court that has power to defeat the intent of the legislature, when couched in such evident and express words, as leave no doubt whether it was the intent of the legislature or no.'[164] In the ninth edition of the *Commentaries*, Blackstone added some words to this paragraph: 'if

[158] Blackstone (1765: 157).   [159] ibid. 244.   [160] ibid. 237–8; emphasis in original.
[161] ibid. 238.   [162] ibid. 243; emphasis in original.   [163] ibid. 205.   [164] ibid. 91.

Parliament will positively enact a thing to be done which is unreasonable, I know of no power *in the ordinary forms of the Constitution that is vested with authority* to control it'.[165] There was such a power outside the Constitution, but the power of Parliament was absolute and uncontrolled '[s]o long . . . as the English constitution lasts'.[166]

Three years before Blackstone's *Commentaries* were published, Adam Smith argued that the power of the King in Parliament was absolute, in the sense that it was not subject to any legal remedy, even though it was not unlimited. He differed from Blackstone in that he referred to the limits as legal: 'there are still some things which must be unlawful even for the sovereign'.[167] But he acknowledged the impossibility of clearly specifying those limits. The sovereign itself could not be expected to enumerate them: '[t]hey would never have any thoughts of making any laws which should tell us that, when they went beyond such and such limits, the people were not bound to obey them but might resist. That they should do this can not be imagined.'[168] Furthermore, there was no regular and impartial judge who could establish what the limits were.

[T]ho the sovereign may be resisted, it can't be said that there is any regular authority for so doing. The property, life, and liberty of the subject are in some measure in his power; nor is it or can it be ascertained what abuses justify resistance. No laws, no judges, have or can ascertain this matter, nor formed any precedents whereby we may judge.[169]

As for popular resistance, even if successful it could not prove that it was justified. 'All decisions on this subject have been made by the prevailing party, and never coolly by a court of justice, and can give us no light into the subject.'[170]

[T]here is no court which can try the sovereigns themselves, no authority sovereign to the sovereign, and [? which has] examined and ascertained how far the actions of the sovereigns . . . are justifiable and how far their power extends. The precise limits have been little considered and are very difficult to ascertain . . . There are without doubt certain limits, but no one has yet considered them with the same candor and composure as [a] court does the private affairs of individuals. . . . All disputes of this sort have been decided by force and violence. If the sovereign got the better of the subjects, then they were condemned as traitors and rebels; and if the subjects have got the better of the sovereign, he is declared to be a tyrant and oppressor not to be endured. Sometimes the decision has been right and sometimes wrong, but they can never be of such weight as the decisions of a cool and impartial court.[171]

During the debates concerning Britain's dispute with her American colonies, it was sometimes suggested that resistance could be lawful. Lord Abingdon, for

---

[165] The italicized words were not included in earlier editions: see the discussion in Plucknett (1926: 60–1).

[166] Blackstone (1765: 157).

[167] A. Smith (1978: 311; see also 315 and 434). Here and in what follows, I combine remarks made by Smith in his 1762–3 and 1766 lectures.

[168] ibid. 315.   [169] ibid. 325.   [170] ibid. 433.   [171] ibid. 311.

example, said that when the laws were subversive of the constitution, 'then disobedience instead of obedience is due; and resistance becomes the law of the
land'.[172] And an anonymous correspondent to the *London Evening Post* insisted
that 'if government be supreme, it is above the law . . . but if the law be paramount, then all other powers may be lawfully resisted'. To deny that a government could ever be 'lawfully resisted' would be to 'destroy the difference
between free and absolute governments . . . between a British Parliament and a
Turkish divan'.[173]

But Charles Yorke, now Attorney-General, reiterated the proposition that
'[y]ou cannot put a case for the dissolution of governments by law'.[174] And Lord
Lyttelton agreed: '[t]here cannot be two rights existing in government at the same
time, which would destroy each other; a right in government to make laws, and
a right in the people, or any part, to oppose or disobey such laws'.[175] One of the
most lucid defences of parliamentary sovereignty published at the time was written by George Chalmers.[176] He argued that the threat of rebellion effectively prevented parliamentary tyranny: to act tyrannically, Parliament 'must pass by the
scaffold on which Charles expired', and 'lift the hand of suicide against itself'.[177]
But although there were limits to Parliament's authority that the people would
not permit it to exceed, they could not take the form of legal rules. In describing them, it was impossible to be sufficiently precise: to invoke natural justice,
the welfare of the community, and the principles of the Constitution, would be
far too abstract and vague for legal purposes. Fortunately, legal rules of that kind
were unnecessary. The people had not needed them as guides when confronting
tyranny in the past: 'the country found remedies which, in similar tyrannies, it
will always find. Extreme cases point out their own remedies.' Moreover,
because rebellion signifies the dissolution of the constitution, '[s]uch rules
would be applicable just at that moment when all laws, when all rules, are at an
end'.[178]

In 1781, Dr Josiah Tucker took the same approach in his *A Treatise on Civil
Government*. Although there could be exceptional cases when it would be per-
missible to disobey or even forcefully resist the law, 'the English constitution
does not point out those cases, for fear mankind should make a bad use of such
an interpretation; for fear crafty and designing men should mislead the giddy
populace to deem that to be legal liberty, which in truth and reality is no better
than a rampant licentiousness, and lawless anarchy'.[179] In 1785, William Paley
agreed: '[n]o form of government contains a provision for its own dissolution'.[180]

Those who affirmed that Parliament was legally sovereign therefore did not
deny that, morally speaking, its authority was limited, or that in extreme cases,
the limits were enforceable by resistance or even rebellion. Another example is

---

[172] Bertie (1778: 205).   [173] Quoted by Reid (1991: 84–5).
[174] Simmons and Thomas (1982–7: ii. 139).   [175] ibid. 126.
[176] Chalmers (1777).   [177] ibid. 53, 57.   [178] ibid. 54–5, 61.
[179] Tucker (1781: 421–2).   [180] Paley (1785: 338).

Edmund Burke, whose views in this respect were shared by Lord Rockingham and his faction, for whom Burke was one of the leading spokesmen.[181] Burke emphatically denied that any person or body, including the supreme legislature, could possess arbitrary power, on the ground that all power derives from God and is bound by God's Law.[182] '[I]t is not in the power of any community, or of the whole race of man, to alter [that law]'.[183] Therefore, '[l]aw and arbitrary power are at eternal enmity . . . It is a contradiction in terms, it is blasphemy in religion, to say that any man can have arbitrary power.'[184] But he also believed that the British Parliament was legally sovereign. He referred to 'the unlimited and illimitable nature of supreme sovereignty',[185] and said that '[t]he power of rectifying the most sacred laws must, by the very nature of things, be vested in the legislature; because every legislature must be supreme, and omnipotent with respect to the law, which is its own creature'.[186] Concerning the British Parliament in particular, he said

When I first came into a public trust, I found your Parliament in possession of an unlimited legislative power over the colonies . . . Indeed common sense taught me, that a legislative authority, not actually limited by the express terms of its foundation, or by its own subsequent acts, cannot have its powers parcelled out by argumentative distinctions, so as to enable us to affirm that here they can, and there they cannot bind . . . If other gentlemen were able to see, how one power could be given up, (merely on abstract reasoning) without giving up the rest, I can only say that they saw further than I could . . . I had indeed very earnest wishes to keep the whole body of this authority perfect and entire as I found it . . . For I thought I saw, that many cases might well happen, in which the exercise of every power, comprehended in the broadest idea of legislature, might become, in its time and circumstances, not a little expedient for the peace and union of the Colonies . . . The completeness of the legislative authority of Parliament *over this kingdom* is not questioned . . . I see no abstract reason, which can be given, why the same power that made and repealed the High Commission Court and the Star Chamber, might not revive them again . . . If anything can be supposed out of the power of human legislature, it is religion: I admit however that the established religion of this country has been three or four times altered by act of Parliament, and therefore that a statute binds even in that case.[187]

He apparently believed that legislative power was omnipotent and unlimited, although not arbitrary, if it was not subject to legal challenge or correction. The 'supreme power in every country' is 'unaccountable' to any legal tribunal for its actions, and 'it is from confounding the unaccountable character inherent to the supreme power with arbitrary power that all this confusion of ideas has arisen'.[188] But he maintained that all persons exercising governmental power were accountable to God: 'they act in trust; and . . . they are to account for their conduct in

[181] Toohey (1978: 122–3).   [182] Burke (1788: 350–1); see also Burke (1765: 454–6).
[183] Burke (1765: 455).   [184] Burke (1788: 351).   [185] Burke (1774: 458).
[186] Cobbett (1806–20: xvii. 276).   [187] Burke (1777: 314–15).
[188] Burke (1788: 351–2).

that trust to the one great Master, Author, and Founder of society'.[189] He also regarded the right of rebellion as a remedy for violations of God's law:

Despotism if it means anything that is at all defensible, means a mode of government bound by no written rules; and coerced by no controlling magistracies or well-settled orders in the state. But if it has no written law it neither does nor can cancel the primeval, indefeasible, unalterable Law of Nature and of nations; and if no magistracies control its exertions, those exertions must derive prior limitation and direction either from the equity and moderation of the ruler; or from downright revolt on the part of the subject by a rebellion divested of all its criminal qualities.[190]

Burke's reference to the 'equity and moderation of the ruler' and 'revolt on the part of the subject' anticipated Dicey's acknowledgement that in practice, parliamentary sovereignty is properly controlled by both 'internal' and 'external' constraints of a political nature.[191] Burke continually insisted that although Parliament possessed sovereign legislative authority, it risked rebellion if it did not exercise that authority prudently and circumspectly. If Parliament's authority were exercised without regard to public opinion, he warned, legislative omnipotence is

a theory to entertain the mind but it is nothing in the direction of affairs . . . [M]any things indubitably included in the abstract idea of that power, and which carry no absolute injustice in themselves, yet being contrary to the opinions and feelings of the people, can as little be exercised as if Parliament in that case had been possessed of no right at all.[192]

Those who asserted that Parliament's legal authority was limited were not proposing judicially enforceable limits, while those who took the opposite view agreed that it was subject to moral limits, enforceable in extraordinary cases by rebellion. Both sides therefore agreed that Parliament's authority was subject to limits enforceable as a last resort by rebellion. They disagreed, often passionately, about what those limits were, and about whether particular measures, such the Septennial Act or the Stamp Act, exceeded them. But those disagreements were moral or political, rather than legal. In so far as there was a legal disagreement, it was one of terminology rather than substance: whether the limits to Parliament's authority, which everyone agreed existed, could properly be described as *legal* limits.

The subtleties, and potential confusions, of the eighteenth century understanding of Parliament's authority can all be found in Charles James Fox's speeches opposing the Treasonable Practices and Seditious Meetings Bills in 1795. These repressive wartime measures were put forward by the Pitt administration, which

---

[189] E. Burke, *Collected Works*, ed. Bohn (1854–6: ii. 365), quoted in Dickinson (1977: 303).
[190] Burke (1788: 469–70).   [191] Dicey (1964: 76–85).
[192] Burke (1777: 315); see also Burke (1774: 458). Charles James Fox expressed similar sentiments in 1795: Cobbett (1806–20: xxxii. 348).

feared that the burgeoning movement demanding constitutional reforms har-boured a conspiracy to subvert the constitution.[193]

Fox maintained that 'these bills attack the fundamental principles of the con-stitution'; they 'positively repealed the Bill of Rights, and cut up the whole of the constitution by the roots, by changing our limited monarchy into an absolute despotism'.[194] At one point, he went so far as to say that 'neither Lords nor Com-mons nor King, no, nor the whole legislature together, were to be considered as possessing the power to enslave the people of this country; they might separately or unitedly do such acts as might justify resistance from the people'.[195] It is clear that this denial of Parliament's power was merely a means of justifying resist-ance, because at another point, Fox conceded that Parliament had the legal auth-ority to enact the bills in question:

With respect to the right which parliament possessed, of altering the Bill of Rights, he agreed with the right hon. secretary [Henry Dundas]. He never could consent to the pro-position that there were some fundamental laws of the constitution which parliament was incompetent to alter. They certainly were competent to make any alterations in the code either of civil or criminal law, so far as their acts would necessarily be recognized in the decisions of the various courts of judicature in the kingdom. But though they might be competent in point of power . . . [t]here were many laws of the constitution which never ought to be repealed, and many privileges of the people which never ought to be invaded.[196]

If Parliament did invade those privileges, the people would be morally entitled to resist it. Indeed, Fox felt so strongly about the bills in question that he warned the Commons that if they were enacted, and rigorously enforced, 'the propriety of resistance, instead of remaining a question of morality, will become merely a question of prudence'.[197] '[H]e had no such idea of the omnipotence of the whole legislature of the country, as to suppose that it could not so conduct itself as to justify the resistance of the people. . . . Did any man say, or would any man main-tain, that they were so omnipotent that nothing which they did could justify the resistance of the people?'[198]

Henry Dundas, one of the leaders of the administration, provided Fox with the standard response:

The right hon. gentleman had put an extreme case, and had asked, whether if the King, Lords, and Commons, were united for the purpose of depriving the people of their liber-ties, the people would not have a right to resist? There could be no difficulty in answer-ing that question in the affirmative; because, in that case, there would not, in fact, exist any government at all. But he wished to put one plain question to the good sense of the right hon. gentleman; which was, whether he really thought it consistent with policy, or even with humanity, to hold such language to the people? The expediency of resistance

---

[193] See Dickinson (1985: ch. 2).   [194] Cobbett (1806–20: xxxii. 385, 383).
[195] ibid. 454.   [196] ibid. 348.   [197] ibid. 385; see also 383.   [198] ibid. 455.

was not a point which the generality of mankind could safely consider . . . Every ignorant man would conceive he had a right to resist every thing which did not accord with his opinions, and the result might be shocking to humanity. Such language tended to bring all government into disgrace, or, at least, to render it precarious.[199]

For this reason, Dundas insisted, '[n]othing could be more dangerous in a legislature, than to hold up the doctrine of resistance to the people. That it was a rule to be laid down was by no means true; as resistance never could form a part of government. It must arise from the dissolution of government.'[200] Fox seems to have agreed with this. 'No man ever supposed that the legislature should adopt the doctrine of resistance, as a direct and practical maxim.'[201] When he had mentioned resistance, 'he urged it as an advice to the governors, not an incitement to the governed'.[202]

4. Law-Making Power and Constitutional Principle

John Phillip Reid has rightly pointed out that when legislation was alleged to violate fundamental principles, parliamentary debates were often conducted in legalistic terms, with legal principles and doctrines, precedents and analogies being cited, and carefully scrutinized, on all sides.[203] But he mistakenly infers from this that the doctrine of parliamentary sovereignty was not yet generally accepted.[204] He argues that the doctrine did not become generally accepted in Britain until the middle of the nineteenth century, and that even as late as the 1760s it was rejected by many lawyers and politicians who subscribed to an older 'common law constitutionalism' of customary constraints on government.[205]

Reid's mistaken inference is due to his assumption that the doctrine of parliamentary sovereignty is naturally expressed in a 'discourse of power' rather than of 'right', and that its historical emergence is therefore marked by a shift from the latter to the former. 'In the new constitutional liturgy', he argues, 'power rather than right, expediency rather than precedent, were measures for action, and the concept of sovereignty was used to answer questions of law that usually were answered by experience, practice, precedent and history'.[206] But this argument is based on a false dichotomy. Everyone, including those who most enthusiastically proclaimed the doctrine of parliamentary sovereignty, agreed that

---

[199] ibid. 467; see also William Pitt's remarks, at ibid. 520–1.   [200] ibid. 341.
[201] ibid. 348.   [202] ibid. 456.   [203] Reid (1991: 15, 17–21, 32–3, 62–3).
[204] ibid. 21 ('the rhetoric of law [which] pervaded the politics of the eighteenth century . . . will provide much of the evidence for the subsequent chapters of this book').
[205] ibid. 4, 6, 24, 63, 78, and 81. Reid (1977: 493–6) previously argued that in the eighteenth century, Parliament was regarded as legally sovereign by 'almost everyone of importance in London', and by everyone in Great Britain 'except radical civil libertarians', and that as a matter of 'constitutional reality', Parliament had become fully sovereign in 1688. It is my contention that this earlier argument is closer to the truth than Reid's subsequent position.
[206] Reid (1991: 63).

Parliament's authority was subject both to natural law and to 'constitutional principles'. Parliament's sovereignty was invoked in political debate, not to substitute power for principle, but to remind participants of two generally accepted propositions.

The first proposition was that in every legal system there had to be an ultimate tribunal with power conclusively to resolve disagreements of principle, and that throughout the British empire that tribunal was Parliament. The point was not that debate about principle was irrelevant, but that Parliament's resolution of the debate was legally binding, and indeed, legally binding even if it were wrong. That is why Parliament was often said to possess a limited right but an unlimited power. Colonel Barré, who defended the rights of the American colonists in the 1760s, said that 'no man has the right to tax his money without his own consent or by his representative. The supreme power is uncontrollable, but it should control itself.'[207] His second point would not have been disputed by any of those who accepted the sovereignty of Parliament. Attorney-General Yorke, for example, advised Parliament that there was 'no boundary to the legislative power but . . . your wisdom and your justice'.[208]

Samuel Johnson's *Taxation No Tyranny* (1775), an officially solicited rebuttal of the disaffected Americans' constitutional arguments, reaffirmed in uncompromising terms the doctrine that the British Parliament was 'ultimately and essentially absolute', having a power 'from which there is no appeal, which admits no restrictions'.[209] Yet he conceded that what Parliament possessed was 'whether the right or not, at least the power' of legislating as it should see fit, and '[i]t is not infallible, for it may do wrong'.[210] In his opinion, the possible or even actual abuse of a power did not affect its legality: as he argued elsewhere, '[i]f the possibility of abuse be an argument against authority, no authority ever can be established; if the actual abuse destroys its legality, there is no legal government now in the world'.[211] Edmund Burke admitted that '[t]he speculative idea of a right deduced from the unlimited nature of the supreme legislative authority [was] very clear and very undeniable', but cautioned that '[t]he practical, executive, exertion of this right may be . . . inequitable and may be contrary to the genius and spirit even of the constitution which gives this right'.[212] After attributing unlimited and irresistible power to Parliament, Sir Robert Chambers, who succeeded Blackstone to the Vinerian Chair of English Law in 1767, acknowledged that he was speaking only of juridical, and not moral, power: Parliament 'though unaccountable to any sublunary tribunal may yet violate the laws of God'.[213]

---

[207] Simmons and Thomas (1982–7: ii. 144). This may have also been William Pitt's position. He said, with respect to taxation of the colonies, that 'our right is a right only to do wrong', and that '[t]he noblest exercise of power is to moderate and control itself. Power you have. I think in this case you have not the right' (ibid. 286, 150, 312, respectively).

[208] ibid. 137; see also 146.   [209] Johnson (1775: 422–3).

[210] ibid. 429, 423, respectively.   [211] Johnson (1770: 322).

[212] Quoted in Draper (1996: 280).   [213] Chambers (1986: i. 140).

The second generally accepted proposition was that although precedents and legal principles were relevant to the exercise of parliamentary power, they could not be absolutely binding, because Parliament's ultimate responsibility was to the public good, which in cases of 'necessity' could justify departures from precedent, changes to the law, and even violations of constitutional principles.[214] As Lord Grenville argued in 1795, in support of the Seditious Meetings Bill, 'new and adequate remedies' might have to be used to combat serious threats to the constitution, and it might be 'worthy of the wisdom of the legislature . . . to sacrifice a part of the constitution to preserve the whole'.[215]

The dichotomy drawn by Reid between 'the values of the seventeenth-century constitution of customary restraint' and 'the newer constitutionalism of legislative sovereignty' is therefore a false one.[216] It is true that the constitution 'of Sir Edward Coke, John Selden and Algernon Sidney'—the constitution 'that beheaded Charles I and dethroned James II'—was based on customary rights and the rule of law.[217] But it was also based on the sovereignty of Parliament. The idea that Parliament was 'the only true, great, and constitutional bulwark of our liberties' was as much a 'constitutional cliché' of the seventeenth as it was of the eighteenth century.[218] The sovereignty of Parliament itself was therefore widely regarded as a fundamental customary right of the subject. There was certainly a difference between those who justified it in those terms, and those who preferred to argue that in every state, the sovereignty of the legislature is a logical or practical necessity. But again, both views can be found in the political literature of both centuries, and so their coexistence does not justify the inference that there was a transition from one predominant conception of the constitution to another.

From the seventeenth century until today, mainstream British constitutional thought has held that Parliament is both legally sovereign and subject to customary restraints. A statute violating those restraints could, and still can, be called unconstitutional, even though its enactment would be within Parliament's sovereign authority and therefore legally valid. That distinction is found, for example, in Sir Robert Chambers's lectures. He embraced the doctrine of parliamentary sovereignty whole-heartedly: Parliament was 'supreme and absolute', its powers 'unlimited and uncontrolled' and 'irresistible'.[219] Nevertheless, he said that a statute enacted under Henry VIII

though not illegal, for the enaction of the supreme power is the definition of legality, was yet unconstitutional; being, at least in the Commons who act in Parliament as deputies

---

[214] If it were true that 'most eighteenth-century English-speaking political theorists thought the legislature restrained by the same constitutionalism that restrained the judiciary', requiring judgment to be governed by pre-existing laws (Reid 1991: 18–19), then Parliament's acknowledged power to change the law would be mysterious. John St John's statement, that Parliament sat as 'a great legislative proceeding founded on political necessity', rather than 'like judges in a court of law' (Reid 1991: 28–9), was entirely orthodox even in the early seventeenth century.

[215] Cobbett (1806–20: xxxii. 528).   [216] Reid (1991: 49).   [217] Reid (1993: 5 and 60).
[218] ibid. 161.   [219] Chambers (1986: i. 127, 137, 140).

of the people, a perfidious and cowardly surrender of their trust, contrary to the principles of the English government, and to the faith implicitly given to their constituents.[220]

This distinction between legality and constitutionality was by no means uncontroversial. William Paley objected that 'the terms *constitutional* and *unconstitutional*, mean legal and illegal', and complained that

some writers upon the subject absurdly confound what is constitutional with what is expedient; pronouncing forthwith a measure to be unconstitutional, which they adjudge in any respect to be detrimental or dangerous . . . An Act of Parliament can never be unconstitutional, in the strict and proper acceptation of the term; in a lower sense it may, *viz.*, when it militates with the spirit, contradicts the analogy, or defeats the provision, of other laws, made to regulate the form of government.[221]

But the notion that something could be unconstitutional despite being legal proved popular. In 1830, Henry Brougham criticized 'the school of Mr. Bentham' for arguing that the terms 'constitutional' and 'unconstitutional' mean 'only something which somebody, for some reason, likes or dislikes. It is not lawful or unlawful; for it is, avowedly, not to be tried by its legality. Therefore it means nothing.'

Cannot they comprehend how a thing may be wrong, as inconsistent with the spirit of our political system, which yet the law has not prohibited? . . . [I]f Parliament were to vote twice as large an army as the public service demanded, and twice as large a civil list as the dignity of the crown required, have the words no sense by which all thinking men would condemn such resolutions as contrary to the spirit, and dangerous to the existence, of the constitution—in one word, as *unconstitutional*? Yet by the supposition they would be legal; for the legislature itself would have sanctioned them.[222]

The distinction between legality and constitutionality was perpetuated by Austin and Dicey, and survives today in the language of constitutional 'convention'.[223] As Geoffrey Marshall describes the current orthodoxy, 'the most obvious and undisputed convention of the British constitutional system is that Parliament does not use its unlimited sovereign power of legislation in an oppressive or tyrannical way. That is a vague but clearly accepted conventional rule resting on the principle of constitutionalism and the rule of law.'[224] Professor Reid suggests that today '[w]e may think it odd . . . to say that an uncontrollable sovereign has no "right" because of the need for the sovereign to exercise self-control. It was, however, familiar usage in the ambiguous context of the two contemporary constitutions.'[225] In fact, to say this is no more odd today than it was in the eighteenth century, and the prevalence of such statements then had little to do with a struggle between two rival constitutional theories, one of customary constraints and the other of legislative sovereignty. Even in

---

[220] ibid. 141.   [221] Paley (1785: 372). Emphasis in original.
[222] Brougham (1830: 142).   [223] Austin (1954: 257–8), and Dicey (1964: 24–7 and part III).
[224] G. Marshall (1984: 9); see also ibid. 201.   [225] Reid (1991: 43).

1893, Erskine May's treatise on Parliament observed that '[t]here are some subjects upon which Parliament, in familiar language, is said to have no right to legislate; but the constitution has assigned no limits to its authority. . . . Parliament is not controlled in its discretion, and when it errs, its errors can only be corrected by itself.'[226] Henry Goodricke, whom Reid identifies as a 'common law constitutionalist', said that supremacy meant 'nothing more, than that . . . there is no *civil* or *legal* power in the state *superior* to it, and that its acts can not be controlled or annulled by any other *authority*. This does not preclude in the least its being limited, as to the extent of its power, either by the laws of Nature, or by rules and principles of the Constitution.'[227] But that is precisely how the doctrine of parliamentary sovereignty has been understood by British lawyers, then and ever since.

5. British Opinion during the American Crisis

When American colonists disputed Parliament's sovereignty in the 1760s, by denying that it could tax them, the overwhelming majority of the British political nation rushed to its defence. The Declaratory Act (1766) was sponsored by the Rockingham faction, which consistently advocated a conciliatory approach to the Americans.[228] That Act proclaimed that Parliament 'had, has, and of right ought to have full power and authority to make laws and statutes of sufficient force and validity to bind the colonies and people of America, subjects of the Crown of Great Britain, *in all cases whatsoever*'.[229]

William Pitt, in the House of Commons, and Lord Camden, in the House of Lords, were the leading parliamentary advocates of the minority view that Parliament did not possess unlimited authority over the American colonies. Pitt objected only to taxation, which he distinguished from legislation: '[a]ll acts must be submitted to, but taxes'.[230] He acknowledged 'the authority of this kingdom over the colonies, to be sovereign and supreme, in every circumstance of government and legislation whatsoever', but added that '[t]axation is no part of the governing or legislative power'.[231] Because taxation was a gift to the Crown made on the people's behalf by their representatives, Parliament could not rightfully tax colonists whom it did not represent.

Pitt doubted Parliament's sovereignty only with respect to taxation in the colonies, and not at all within Britain itself. Very few of the dissident Americans, or their

---

[226] May (1893: 37).

[227] H. Goodricke, *Observations on Dr. Price's Theory and Principles of Civil Liberty and Government* (York, 1776: 43–4), quoted by Reid (1991: 83).

[228] Dickinson (1977: 147); see also ibid. 79–80, 92–3, 123–7, 273, 287–90.

[229] Emphasis added.   [230] Simmons and Thomas (1982–7: ii. 286).

[231] ibid. ii. 85–6. Pitt recommended that the Stamp Act be immediately repealed, but that simultaneously 'the sovereign authority of this country over the colonies, [should] be asserted in as strong terms as can be devised, and be made to extend to every point of legislation whatsoever' (ibid. 90–1).

British sympathizers, questioned Parliament's sovereignty within Britain. In testimony given to a parliamentary committee in 1766, Benjamin Franklin said that the colonists understood that consent to taxation of subjects 'within the realm' could be given in Parliament, but did not regard themselves as being within the realm or represented in that assembly.[232] A friend of the Americans, Baron Rokeby, discussing the proposition that 'a total and absolute dependence on the British Parliament without any exception whatsoever either with regard to taxes or any other, is liberty itself', said 'I answer, who says otherwise in the case of us, who choose that Parliament; but that in some other cases, this position may perhaps be more liable to question'.[233] Major John Cartwright, a leading radical and American sympathizer, approvingly cited an argument that 'the parliament have [*sic*] a most extensive power over the subjects of Great-Britain, because every power in the state meets in that body: but considered with respect to the colonies, their pretension to such a power there clashes with the legislatures of those colonies'.[234]

Lord Camden was a protégé of Pitt's, and the two were believed to have co-ordinated their attack on the Stamp Act during the debate over its repeal.[235] While Camden agreed with Pitt that there could be no taxation without representation, he initially suggested that Parliament was limited in other respects as well: it had no right to appropriate property without compensation, or to convict someone without a hearing.[236] But he is reported to have suggested later that taxation was *sui generis*: 'the people, though they trusted the legislature with every other authority in the most unlimited manner, never gave up the dominion over their purses'.[237]

Pitt and his supporters, the only group in Parliament opposed in principle to taxing the Americans, represented a small minority.[238] No member of Parliament raised constitutional objections to the Stamp Act when it was first enacted; indeed, 'Parliament's right to tax America was affirmed even by acknowledged friends of the colonies'.[239] When Camden later raised objections he was criticized, according to his own report, for propounding 'new-fangled doctrines, contrary to the laws of this kingdom, and subversive of the rights of parliament'.[240] Lord Chancellor Northington complained that Camden's arguments were 'so new, so unmaintainable, and so unconstitutional, I cannot sit silent'.[241] Only five of the 130 Lords present voted with Camden; all the others joined Northington in supporting a resolution asserting parliamentary sovereignty over the colonies.[242] The Scottish political philosopher Adam Ferguson observed that 'till within these few years, or few months . . . Parliament was supposed omnipotent and irresistible'.[243]

---

[232] Quoted in Draper (1996: 366–7).   [233] Robinson-Morris (1774: 56).
[234] Cartwright (1776: 141).   [235] Thomas (1975: 122, 185–6).
[236] Simmons and Thomas (1982–7: ii. 127).   [237] ibid. 320.
[238] Thomas (1975: 199, 248); Toohey (1978: 114–15).   [239] Thomas (1975: 52, 61, 98).
[240] Speech of Lord Camden, in Simmons and Thomas (1982–7: ii. 321).
[241] ibid. 128.   [242] ibid. 124, 125.   [243] Ferguson (1776: 260).

Critics of Parliament's claim to sovereignty over the colonies sometimes conceded the unpopularity of their position within Britain. A newspaper correspondent wrote that '[n]either is it much to be wondered at, that the people of England are so unanimous in their opinions', because in claiming power over the colonies for the House of Commons they were claiming power for themselves.[244] Major John Cartwright agreed that it gratified the pride of Englishmen to think that their own legislature had 'the rights of sovereignty' over the Americans, and added that 'there are not wanting an *honest few* who think more justly and more generously'.[245] Benjamin Franklin had the same impression. 'Every man in England seems to consider himself as a piece of sovereign over America, seems to jostle himself into the throne with the King, and talks of OUR subjects in the colonies', he complained in 1767; 'nothing is more common here than to talk of the Sovereignty of Parliament, and the Sovereignty of this Nation over the Colonies'.[246] Jared Ingersoll, New Haven's agent at Westminster, reported to the state's Governor in 1765 that 'there are scarce any people here, either within doors or without, but what approve the measures now taking which regard America'.[247] In his thorough study of the Stamp Act crisis, P. D. G. Thomas concludes that there was an 'almost universal consensus of opinion in Britain on the question of Parliamentary supremacy over America'; '[p]ublic opinion, with hardly a dissenting voice, had no doubt of Parliament's right in the matter'; '[t]he American challenge to Parliament's sovereignty outraged the contemporary British interpretation of the constitution'.[248]

Even Pitt, Camden, and their followers soon changed their minds. Upon forming a ministry in 1766, and having to govern the colonies themselves, they argued that the Declaratory Act had established Parliament's right to tax the colonies, and set out to suppress any further resistance to British authority.[249] In 1774, Pitt denied that he had earlier questioned Parliament's right to tax America.[250]

None of those who insisted that Parliament's authority was limited ever suggested that the limits were judicially enforceable. Even Lord Abingdon, who criticized Burke's defence of parliamentary sovereignty, acknowledged that 'the Parliament is *supreme* . . . It is the *supreme court*, or *curia magna* of the Constitution.'[251] In the most influential defence of the American revolutionaries written in England, Richard Price asserted that all government was 'in the very nature of it, a trust; and all its powers a delegation for gaining particular ends . . . Nothing, therefore, can be more absurd than the doctrine which some have taught with respect to the omnipotence of parliaments. They possess no power beyond the limits of the trust for the execution of which they were formed.'[252]

---

[244] 'A. B.', Letter, *The Public Advertiser*, 22 March 1774, quoted in Cartwright (1776: 140–1).
[245] Cartwright (1776: 137; Letter II, 22 March 1774); emphasis added.
[246] Labaree (1959–97: xiv. 65 and 69).   [247] Quoted by Thomas (1975: 98–9).
[248] ibid. 364, 37, 371, respectively; see also ibid. 32.
[249] ibid. 291, 293, 299, 314, 359, 366–7.   [250] ibid. 172 n. 2.
[251] Bertie (1778: 205).   [252] Price (1776: 9–10).

But the remedy for any violation of that trust was political, not judicial. As one of Price's critics pointed out,

As an individual, I can appoint a trustee, I can prescribe to him the extent of the trust and the uses he shall make of it. If he exceeds the bounds of that trust, if he perverts it to other uses, I know where to apply for a control. The judicial power affords it—the judicial power to which I and my trustee must alike submit. But when the majority of the people have appointed this public trustee, where shall they apply for a controlling power? To themselves you [Price] tell us; there can be no power to which they ought to submit, 'for theirs is the only real omnipotence.'[253]

The idea of judicial review of the validity of statutes seldom entered the heads of British lawyers. In 1773, Londoners who objected to the expulsion of John Wilkes from the House of Commons petitioned the King to dissolve Parliament. The petition complained that

[o]ur repesentatives, who were chosen to be the guardians of our rights, have invaded our most sacred privileges . . . We therefore . . . supplicate your Majesty to employ the only remedy now left by the Constitution, the exercise of that salutary power with which you are intrusted by law, the dissolving of the present Parliament.[254]

The statement that this was 'the only remedy' provided by law was 'a recurring theme in petitions' of that period.[255] The only alternative was rebellion. As late as 1824, when his *The Book of Fallacies* was first published in English, Jeremy Bentham condemned occasional suggestions that some venerated law was immutable, partly on the ground that

[i]n speaking of a law which is considered as repugnant to any law of the pretended immutable class, the method has been to call it void. But to what purpose? Only to excite the people to rebellion in the event of the legislator's passing any such void law. In speaking of a law as void, either this is meant or nothing.[256]

But in many cases, the denunciation of legislation as 'void' or even 'illegal' was not intended to incite rebellion. Lord Camden described the Declaratory Bill as 'illegal, absolutely illegal, contrary to the fundamental laws of nature, contrary to the fundamental laws of this constitution'.[257] Yet he emphatically denied 'that the consequence of my reasoning will be that the colonies . . . have a right to oppose acts of legislature in a rebellious manner, even though the legislature has no right to make such acts'.[258] He promised that 'once the Bill should have passed into a law, he should think himself obliged to acquiesce in the same manner as he should believe himself bound to draw his sword in his country's cause,

[253] Lind (1776: 242).
[254] 'Petition of the Lord Mayor, Aldermen and Livery of London', *Scots Magazine* (1773), 35: 162–3, quoted by Reid (1993: 158).
[255] ibid. [256] Larrabee (1952: 57). [257] Cobbett (1806–20: xvi. 178).
[258] Simmons and Thomas (1982–7: ii. 127).

even though the quarrel might appear to him unjust'.[259] Camden was Chief Justice of the Court of Common Pleas: if he believed that he would be 'obliged to acquiesce' if the Bill became law, then he must have believed that other judges would be too. But if the passage of an 'illegal' statute was not properly remediable either by judicial review or by rebellion, what was the point of calling it illegal? He must have been appealing to what we now describe as moral rather than legal principles, and attempting to persuade his audience to reject a bill that he believed would violate them.[260]

Disagreements about parliamentary sovereignty were more apparent than real, and therefore counter-productive. Of course, the underlying political disputes that generated those disagreements, for example, the dispute that lost Britain its American colonies, were only too real. The point is that what seemed to be a disagreement about the legal authority of Parliament confused rather than clarified those disputes, because on that issue substantial agreement was concealed by divergent use of terminology. Almost everyone agreed that Parliament was governed both by natural law and fundamental customary principles, and also that it was not subordinate to any human authority other than that of 'the people'. It was also generally agreed that a violation of those principles might justify resistance or even rebellion, but only as a last resort in an extreme case. Disagreement concerned terminology and details: for example, whether those principles were properly regarded as 'constitutional', if not 'legal', and what an extreme case might be. The terminology that people preferred in discussing such questions depended on whether they regarded parliamentary tyranny, or unjustified rebellion, as the greater danger. Members and supporters of governments, who naturally feared rebellion more than tyranny, claimed that Parliament's authority was legally unlimited, while their opponents, who were more fearful of tyranny, denied that claim in order to emphasize Parliament's subjection to higher principles. But the disagreement about Parliament's legal authority was one of emphasis and terminology, not substance. The confusion that this generated inspired Bentham and Austin to propose a sharp distinction between legal and moral terminology.

Most recent historians agree that the doctrine of parliamentary sovereignty was firmly entrenched in British constitutional thought by the mid-eighteenth century.[261] In his recent study of the legal and religious ideologies of the period, J. C. D. Clark concludes that

[t]he Blackstonian definition of sovereignty was more than an abstraction, recently devised for theoretical purposes in an Oxford college or an Inn of Court; it was the embodiment of attitudes to authority and state formation which were of ancient origin and which

---

[259] ibid. 319. He is reported to have said elsewhere that once Parliament did declare its intention to act unjustly, 'he did not think himself, nor any man else, at liberty to call it any more in question' (Bailyn 1965: i. 413), and for Bailyn's source, see ibid. 719 n. 12.

[260] Gough (1955: 194).

[261] Perry (1990: 12), Langford (1991: 148), Pallister (1971: 55), Bailyn (1965: 115, 118), Toohey (1978: 2), Thomson (1938: 395–6).

were widespread within England on the level of popular attitudes . . . [I]t penetrated popular discourse as an assumption, a necessary truth.[262]

6. Judicial Opinion and Legal Theory

Some confused dicta, attributed to Chief Justice Holt in an unreliable report of *City of London v Wood* (1701), suggest that he may have believed Parliament's legislative authority to be limited by law.[263] But in a careful analysis of two unpublished manuscripts of Holt's judgment, one in his own hand, Philip Hamburger has shown that he actually held the opposite view.

The question Holt discussed, in dicta, was whether Parliament could make someone a judge in a case in which he was also a party. Holt was strongly influenced by recent natural law theory, which regarded any attempt to do this as an attempt to do the impossible. The primary purpose of government being to end otherwise interminable private disputes, by providing an independent arbiter, theorists such as Locke claimed that it would be contrary to the very essence of government for one party in a dispute to act as its judge. Indeed, this principle had become central to their refutation of absolute monarchy, and justification of resistance to tyranny, by supposedly demonstrating that no monarch could authoritatively judge disputes between himself and his people. Only God could authoritatively judge such disputes.[264] Endorsing these ideas, Holt said that 'it is contrary to the principles and the end of all commonwealths and civil societies for a man to be a judge in his own cause', and that an Act of Parliament purporting to authorize this 'would be an absolute contradiction' because 'a judge and a party are in their nature and institution different and distinct, for the being of the one doth necessarily exclude the other'.[265] In other words, it would be as if Parliament were attempting by statute to turn a man into a woman, which even Dicey later acknowledged to be impossible.[266] According to Holt, such an Act would have to be interpreted in some other way, either as designating someone other than the parties to adjudicate their dispute, or as allowing one of them to do whatever he wanted, in effect exempting him from legal judgment. In the latter case, said Holt, clearly influenced by Locke, the parties would be returned to the state of nature, and government with respect to the matter in effect dissolved.[267]

There is no mention in Holt's own manuscript of statutes being 'void'. On the contrary, he said that the acts of inferior bodies which 'have not a sovereign power

---

[262] J. C. D. Clark (1994: 111); see also ibid. 5–6, 7 n. 20, 89.

[263] *City of London v Wood* (1701) 12 Mod. 669, 687; 88 E.R. 1592, 1602; see Allen (1964: 449, esp. n. 1); Plucknett (1926: 55 n. 72) and Gough (1955: 10).

[264] Hamburger (1994: 2135–6, 2147–8).

[265] *City of London v Wood* (unpublished manuscript in British Library), quoted by Hamburger (1994: 2132 and 2131, respectively).

[266] Dicey (1964: 43), quoting De Lolme.   [267] Hamburger (1994: 2131–7).

... are subject to the review of the kings courts', and are 'ipso facto void' if contrary to 'law and right reason', but 'an act of Parliament ... binds absolutely without any dispute to be made of its justice or equity'.[268] That is why he said elsewhere that 'the liberty or property of the subject ... cannot be diminished or infringed by a less[er] authority than the Legislature of the kingdom, which is the Queen, the Lords and Commons assembled in Parliament'.[269] As Hamburger summarizes Holt's position, '[t]he only power to defeat an act of a body with "sovereign power" lay, not in the judiciary, but presumably in those who had originally given that sovereign power'.[270]

When the situation that Holt had discussed actually arose, the courts did not follow his cautious approach. In 1742, it was held that in some circumstances a statute could authorize someone to act as judge in a cause in which he had an interest, and that decision was affirmed in 1849, despite *Dr Bonham*'s case being cited to the contrary.[271]

David Lieberman, in his study of British legal theory in the eighteenth century, reports that although eighteenth century judges often criticized statutes for being poorly drafted or misconceived, and insisted that the courts were better qualified than Parliament to develop the law, they were careful not to claim that the courts could control Parliament's legislative will.[272] Referring to legislative sanctions against Roman Catholics, Chief Justice Mansfield said that even if the policy underlying them were unsound, they had to be applied 'according to their true intent and meaning', for 'the legislature only can vary or alter the law'.[273] In *Sommersett's* case (1771–2), he said that slavery, despite being contrary to moral reason, could be established by positive law.

The state of slavery is of such a nature, that it is incapable of being introduced on any reasons, moral or political, but only by positive law, which preserves its force long after the reasons, occasion, and time itself from whence it was created, is erased from memory. It is so odious, that nothing can be suffered to support it, but positive law.[274]

The attitude of the judges to the authority of Parliament was sometimes clearly expressed in cases involving parliamentary privilege. For example, in *Crosby's* case (1771), concerned with the power of the two Houses to punish

---

[268] *City of London v Wood* (unpublished manuscript), quoted in ibid. 2139–40. Holt is also reported to have said that the judges 'construe and expound Acts of Parliament, and adjudge them void': *R v Knollys, a.k.a. the Earl of Banbury* (1694) Skin. 517, 526–7; 90 E.R. 231, 236. Hamburger reports that 'curiously', this opinion is missing from Holt's surviving manuscript opinions (ibid. 2142 n. 162).

[269] *The Judgements Delivered by the Lord Chief Justice Holt in the Case of Ashby v White and Others, and in the Case of John Paty and Others* (1837: 43), quoted in ibid. 2145.

[270] ibid. 2142.

[271] *Parish of Great Charte v Parish of Kennington* (1742) 2 Strange 1173; 93 E.R. 1107, 1108 (K.B.) and *Grand Junction Canal Co. v Dimes* (1849) 12 Beav. 63, 77; 50 E.R. 984, 989 (Court of Chancery).

[272] Lieberman (1989: 71–2, 54).

[273] *Foone v Blount* (1776) 2 Cowper 464, 466; 98 E.R. 118, 1190.

[274] Howell (1816–28: xx. col. 82).

for contempt, Lord Chief Justice de Grey stated that '[t]he laws can never be a prohibition to the Houses of Parliament; because, by law, there is nothing superior to them. Suppose they . . . should abuse the powers which the constitution has given them, there is no redress, it would be a public grievance.'[275] Justice William Blackstone added that 'if any persons may be safely trusted with this power, they must surely be the Commons, who are chosen by the people; for their privileges and powers are the privileges and powers of the people. . . . Can any good man think of involving the judges in a contest with either House of Parliament?'[276] This reasoning would undoubtedly have applied *a fortiori* to the law-making power of the Parliament as a whole.

In 1747, Lord Chancellor Hardwicke asserted that '[i]n all countries the legislative power must, to a general intent, be absolute'.[277] In 1766, in asserting Parliament's right to tax the American colonies, Lord Chancellor Northington and Lord Mansfield both vigorously defended the doctrine of parliamentary sovereignty. Lord Northington described as 'a self evident truth' the proposition that '[e]very government can arbitrarily impose laws on all its subjects; there must be a supreme dominion in every state', and Lord Mansfield insisted that '[i]t is now settled that there is no restriction to the legislative authority of Great Britain'.[278]

In 1795, George III asked Lord Chancellor Kenyon whether he could properly consent to a bill relaxing laws against Roman Catholics, and Kenyon replied that

[i]t is a general maxim that the supreme power of a State cannot limit itself. Either of the Houses of Parliament may, if they think proper, pass a bill up to the extent of the most unreasonable requisition that can be made; and, provided sound policy, and a sense of the duty they owe to the established religion of the country, do not operate on their minds so as to prevent their doing what is improper, there is no statute law to prevent their entertaining and passing such Bill, to abolish the supremacy of the whole of the government and discipline of the Church of England, as now by law established.[279]

It is not surprising that judges took the same view of Parliament's authority as a majority of parliamentarians. British courts have never enjoyed the institutional independence they would have needed to mount a successful challenge to the sovereignty of Parliament. The courts and their jurisdictions depend on statutes, the judges are appointed by the Crown, and since 1701 they have been subject to dismissal on an address by the two Houses of Parliament. The court of final appeal is formally the House of Lords, the upper House of Parliament, and its presiding officer, the Lord Chancellor, is a member of Cabinet. As such, he 'would *ex hypothesi* be identified with the policy of any bills introduced into Parliament

---

[275] *The Case of Brass Crosby* (1771) 3 Wils. K.B. 188, 202–3; 95 E.R. 1005, 1013.
[276] ibid. 205, 1014.　　　[277] Campbell (1857: vi. 251).
[278] Simmons and Thomas (1982–7: ii. 129, 342, respectively).
[279] G. T. Kenyon (1873: 317).

by the government of the day'.[280] One of Blackstone's harshest critics alleged that 'the doctrine of the Omnipotence of Parliament is a very favorite one in the Quarter of Promotion', and insinuated that Blackstone endorsed it in order to secure judicial appointment.[281] But it is unlikely that this was the main cause of judicial deference to Parliament in the eighteenth century. The judges, like parliamentarians, were men of property, equally attached to the prevailing ideology of their social class.[282]

Writers of legal treatises often observed in passing that Parliament was a sovereign law-maker. Daines Barrington was one of many who cited Bacon's maxim in order to describe the constitutional duty of the judiciary: 'let the inconveniences of a statute be what they may, no judge or bench of judges can constitutionally dispose with them; their office is *jus dicere* and not *jus dare*'.[283] In 1763, Dr Richard Burn wrote in his *Ecclesiastical Law* that statutes, being made 'by the united suffrage of the whole kingdom, either in person or by representative', had a 'strength and superiority above all other laws in this kingdom whatsoever; by virtue whereof, they control, alter, mitigate, repeal, revive, explain, amend, both the common, canon, and civil laws, and actually have done so in abundance of instances'.[284] The author of *A Treatise of Equity*, who insisted that the court of equity must exempt cases from positive rules of law if necessary to preserve 'natural justice', added that it could not override a clear statutory provision: 'for the Chancellor to relieve against the express provision of an Act of Parliament would be the same as to repeal it'.[285]

Legal theorists unequivocally embraced parliamentary sovereignty. Blackstone, Burke, Paley, De Lolme, and many others, described the British Constitution as a well-balanced combination of the best aspects of the monarchical, aristocratic, and democratic forms of government, each of which checked the worst aspects of the others.[286] This was 'a fundamental assumption of eighteenth-century England', which 'pervaded English political life in the years from the Restoration to the passing of the Great Reform Bill'.[287] Court Whigs and Tories were united in their admiration for the almost perfect equilibrium they perceived between the powers of the King, Lords, and Commons.[288] While the Commons protected the rights of the subject against any tendency towards tyranny, the counterweights of King and Lords prevented the excesses of unchecked democracy. According to this idealized but entirely orthodox understanding of the Constitu-

---

[280] Hood Phillips (1975: 448).   [281] Sheridan (1779: 5, 23).

[282] Atiyah and Summers (1987: 227).

[283] Daines Barrington, *Observations on the More Ancient Statutes . . . With an Appendix being a Proposal for new Modelling the Statutes* (3rd edn., London, 1766: 116), quoted in Lieberman (1989: 54).

[284] Burn (1763: i. p. xviii).

[285] J. Fonblanque (ed.), *A Treatise of Equity* (London, 1793–94: i. 17–19), quoted in Lieberman (1989: 54).

[286] Weston (1965: 123–78).   [287] ibid. 142. For other references, see Jay (1994: 153–7).

[288] Weston (1965: 3).

tion, the checks and balances among the three component parts of Parliament adequately protected the rights of all sections of the community, leaving no need for anything like judicial review. As Blackstone put it, 'there can no inconvenience be attempted by either of the three branches, but will be withstood by one of the other two; each branch being armed with a negative power, sufficient to repel any innovation which it shall think inexpedient or dangerous'.[289]

Montesquieu, in the chapter of *The Spirit of the Laws* dealing with the English Constitution, emphasized the role of the executive and the two branches of the legislature as checks on one another, and dismissed the judicial power as 'in some measure next to nothing'.[290] The judges were 'only the mouth that pronounces the words of the law, inanimate beings who can moderate neither its force nor its rigour', and the legislative power would not 'bow before the tribunals of law, which are lower than it'.[291] In most theoretical writings of this period, the judicial power was treated as merely one aspect of the executive power, which was acknowledged to be vested in the Crown and subordinate to the legislature.[292]

Before Blackstone's *Commentaries* were published, Adam Smith expounded the doctrine of parliamentary sovereignty in his lectures on jurisprudence at Glasgow University. 'The sovereign power is in all governments absolute, and . . . liable to be controlled by no regular force', he argued, because otherwise the regular force able to control it would be the true sovereign. 'To suppose a sovereign subject to judgement, supposes another sovereign.'[293] As for Britain, 'the king is not here the sovereign. The sovereign power is lodged in the king and Parliament together, and no one can tell what they can not do.'[294] 'The authority of the Parliament in some things, of the king and Parliament in others . . . are incontestable, and if they act amiss there is no regular right of resisting them as sovereigns in any way'; apart from popular resistance, 'there is no remedy against a law which appears to be unjust unless it be repealed'.[295] Like Blackstone, Smith believed that Parliament's authority was subject to limits enforceable if necessary by resistance, but not to any limits either explicitly recognized by the law itself or enforceable by the courts.

Another Scot, John Erskine of Carnock, stated in his authoritative *Principles of the Law of Scotland* (1777) that '[l]aw is the command of a sovereign'; that '[n]o sovereign state can subsist without a supreme power, or a right of commanding in the last resort'; that unwritten or customary law 'is equally founded

[289] Blackstone (1765: 50–1).

[290] Weston (1965: 125); see also Carrithers (1977: 78), Stoner (1992: 156–7), and Jay (1994: 156 n. 147).

[291] Montesquieu (1748: 163). Montesquieu seems to have regarded juries, not the judiciary, as having 'the power of judging' in England (ibid. 157–8). On that view, the judiciary had an even less important constitutional role than juries.

[292] See Jay (1994: 160–5), and references cited therein.

[293] A. Smith (1978: 326, 433). Here and in what follows, I combine remarks made by Smith in his 1762–3 and 1766 lectures.

[294] ibid. 311; see also ibid. 315, 319.   [295] ibid. 315.

in the will of the law-giver', that is, 'the tacit consent of King and people'; and that 'the supreme power of one age cannot therefore be fettered by any enactment of a former age, otherwise it would cease to be supreme.[296]

Blackstone's description of the Parliament's sovereign law-making authority was unequivocal.

It has sovereign and uncontrollable authority . . . this being the place where that absolute despotic power, which must in all governments reside somewhere, is entrusted by the constitution of these kingdoms . . . It can, in short, do every thing that is not naturally impossible.[297]

An Act of Parliament . . . is the exercise of the highest authority that this kingdom acknowledges upon earth.[298]

It has power to bind every subject in the land . . . nay, even the king himself . . . And it cannot be altered, amended, dispensed with, suspended, or repealed, but in the same forms and by the same authority of parliament.[299]

Judicial invalidation of statutes was inconceivable to Blackstone: 'all the other powers of the state must obey the legislative power in the execution of their several functions, or else the constitution is at an end'.[300] The judges had no authority to reject even a statute whose main object was unreasonable, because 'that were to set the judicial power above that of the legislature, which would be subversive of all government'.[301]

De Lolme observed that 'it is a fundamental principle with the English lawyers, that Parliament can do every thing, except making a Woman a Man, or a Man a Woman'.[302] In discussing 'the Legislative Power' he also claimed that by its 'bare will' it can 'give being to the laws' and 'also annihilate them', and that it 'can change the Constitution, as God created the light'. The only way of restraining this power, he reasoned, was to divide it: if it were undivided, it would be as impossible to restrain it as to move the earth.[303]

In *The Principles of Moral and Political Philosophy* (1785), published in numerous editions and used at Cambridge as a standard undergraduate textbook, William Paley reiterated the familiar argument that, because there cannot be an infinite series of appeals, 'there necessarily exists in every government a power from which the constitution has provided no appeal; and which power, for that reason, may be termed absolute, omnipotent, uncontrollable, arbitrary, despotic'. The person or assembly with that power was called the sovereign or supreme power, and also the legislature, of the state.[304] 'When laws are made, courts of justice, whatever be the disposition of the judges, must abide by them; for the

---

[296] Erskine (1777: Bk. 1, Tit. I, 1, 4, and 16). Erskine also said that natural law was immutable, but ultimate authority to interpret that law is necessarily vested in the supreme power.

[297] Blackstone (1765: 156).   [298] ibid. 178.   [299] ibid.

[300] ibid. 49.   [301] ibid. 91.

[302] De Lolme (1796: 130). For the possible origins of this aphorism, see Chapter 4, n. 86, above. Parliament could, however, require that for legal purposes a man be deemed to be a woman.

[303] ibid. 213–14.   [304] Paley (1785: 360).

legislature being necessarily the supreme power of the state, the judicial and every other power is accountable to that.'[305]

Paley argued that every custom and law was subject to alteration for the benefit of the community, including

[t]he family of the prince, the order of succession, the prerogative of the crown, [and] the form and parts of the legislature . . . These points are wont to be approached with a kind of awe; they are represented to the mind as principles of the constitution settled by our ancestors, and, being settled, to be no more committed to innovation or debate; as foundations never to be stirred . . . Such reasons have no place in our system.[306]

Supposedly unalterable 'fundamentals' of the constitution were so vague and indeterminate, they served only 'to embarrass the deliberations of the legislature, and afford a dangerous pretence for disputing the authority of the laws'.[307]

Blackstone's successor to the Vinerian Chair, Sir Robert Chambers, was equally forthright in asserting parliamentary sovereignty. According to him, '[t]he powers of Parliament are always said by lawyers to be unlimited and uncontrolled'. 'As parliament unites, either in person or by representation, all the powers that can possibly subsist in a community, it necessarily possesses supreme jurisdiction, and consequently an unlimited and irresistible authority.'[308] He went on to dispel a common confusion:

[W]e must always carefully distinguish *juridical* from *moral* power, or authority from justice. Some men have been perplexed by a position that Parliament has a right to do what is not right to be done. A position undoubtedly true in its proper sense, and meaning no more than that the supreme authority is necessarily judge of its own actions, and though, by human infirmity liable to error, and by human depravity capable of injustice, has a *civil* right to obedience from its subjects . . . But this is not to be understood as implying any confusion of right and wrong, for the supreme power though unaccountable to any sublunary tribunal may yet violate the laws of God . . . [which] whenever violated will find their vindication in another state.[309]

The same distinction was drawn by Richard Wooddeson, who succeeded Chambers in the Vinerian Chair. Although he agreed that 'no human authority can rightfully infringe . . . natural or divine law', he rejected as 'dangerous' the dicta of Justices Coke and Hobart which seemed to suggest that judges can declare statutes to be void. 'We must distinguish between right and power, between moral fitness and political authority. We cannot expect that all acts of legislators will, or can be, entirely good, ethically perfect; but, if their proceedings are to be decided upon by their subjects, government and subordination cease', which is a greater evil to the community than the occasional injurious law.[310] He suggested that Parliament could not totally alienate its own power, and could 'discover no

---

[305] ibid. 401–2.   [306] ibid. 342–3.   [307] ibid. 337; see also ibid. 339.
[308] Chambers (1986: i. 137, 140).   [309] ibid. 140. Emphases in original.
[310] Wooddeson (1842: i. 32).

assignable bounds to legislative authority, considered abstractly, from the mere moral right of its proceedings'.[311]

Chambers favoured a utilitarian interpretation of natural law: 'the sole object of natural law is the happiness of man in this life', and it is 'manifested by its conformity to reason, and by its utility to his creatures'.[312] 'Society implies in its nature an interest common to many individuals, a pursuit of the highest degree of happiness that can be obtained and enjoyed', and '[t]o the happiness of the whole, it will frequently be necessary to sacrifice the happiness of a part'.[313] In emphasizing the importance of evaluating actions and laws according to their effects on human happiness, he concurred with Jeremy Bentham. Bentham agreed with Blackstone that '[i]n Great Britain . . . the sovereignty is in the King, Lords, and Commons in Parliament assembled: it would hardly be possible for that complex body to issue any order the issuing of which would not be looked upon as an act of legislation'.[314] But he was scornful of Blackstone's natural law theorizing, and his criticisms eventually led to the almost total eclipse of the idea of natural rights in British political thought. Utilitarianism in the nineteenth century became 'almost synonymous with progressive political and social thought', and even rival philosophies 'were not framed in terms of the doctrine of the rights of man'.[315] But Parliament's sovereign power was not released from all moral limitations.[316] It was held to be governed by the principle of utility, which, according to Austin, was an injunction of divine law.[317]

7. American Revolutionary Constitutional Theory

British constitutional orthodoxy was well known to Americans. In the *Federalist Papers*, James Madison observed that 'the British Constitution fixes no limit whatever to the discretion of the legislature'; 'in Great Britain . . . it is maintained that the authority of the Parliament is transcendent and uncontrollable as well with regard to the Constitution as the ordinary objects of legislative provision. They have accordingly, in several instances, actually changed, by legislative acts, some of the most fundamental articles of the government.'[318] In his *Lectures on the Law*, James Wilson explained that 'no such thing as a constitution, properly so called, is known in Great Britain. What is known, in that kingdom, under that name . . . is the creature and the dependent of the legislative power . . . The omnipotent authority of parliament is the dernier resort.'[319] The anti-federalist writer 'Brutus' noted that English judges 'in no instance assume the authority to

[311] ibid. 34.   [312] Chambers (1986: i. 88, 85, respectively).
[313] ibid. 89.   [314] Bentham (1782: 5).   [315] H. L. A. Hart (1983: 183).
[316] I disagree with J. C. D. Clark (1994: 90–1) on this point.   [317] Austin (1954: 37 ff.).
[318] Hamilton *et al.* (1961: no. 53, 259 and 331).
[319] J. Wilson, *Lectures on the Law* (1790), in R. G. McCloskey (ed.), *The Works of James Wilson* (Cambridge, Mass., 1967: i. 309), quoted in Snowiss (1990: 72); see also Beer (1993: 189).

set aside an act of parliament under the idea that it is inconsistent with their constitution. . . . [They] are under the control of the legislature, for they are bound to determine according to the laws passed by them.'[320] These commonplaces of British constitutional practice were also alluded to by American judges shortly after the revolution.[321]

Many American dissidents did not dispute either the philosophical thesis that a sovereign authority necessarily governs every independent state, or Parliament's claim to constitute that authority within Britain. Even their decision to repudiate its claim to sovereignty over themselves was arrived at slowly and reluctantly. John Witherspoon, who taught many of the future leaders of the American Revolution, acknowledged that 'in every government there is a supreme irresistible power lodged some where . . . To this power is the final appeal in all questions . . . [although] if the supreme power wherever lodged, come to be exercised in a manifestly tyrannical manner, the subjects may certainly if in their power, resist and overthrow it'.[322] Gordon Wood argues that this theory was a 'powerfully persuasive assumption' that 'pervaded the arguments of the whole Revolutionary generation'.[323]

The potent influence in America of both the philosophical theory of sovereignty, and the legal doctrine of parliamentary sovereignty, is illustrated by the writings of James Otis, who attempted to combine both of them with natural law ideas. In his famous pamphlet *The Rights of the British Colonies Asserted and Proved*, Otis declared that an Act of Parliament contrary to God's immutable natural laws of equity and justice would be 'void', and that '[w]hen such mistake is evident and palpable . . . the judges of the executive courts have declared the act "of a whole Parliament void"'.[324] But in the same pamphlet, he also stated that

[t]he power of Parliament is uncontrollable but by themselves, and we must obey. They only can repeal their own acts. There would be an end of all government if one or a number of subjects or subordinate provinces should take upon them so far to judge of the justice of an act of Parliament as to refuse obedience to it. . . . Therefore let the Parliament

---

[320] 'Brutus' (1787–8: 438; Essay XV, 20 March 1788).

[321] In *VanHorne's Lessee v Dorrance*, Justice Patterson stated '[t]hat in England . . . where there is no written constitution, . . . the parliament is omnipotent, and can mould the constitution at pleasure': (1795) 2 U.S. (2 Dall.) 304, 314, and see also ibid. 307–8. In *Eakin v Raub*, Justice Gibson noted that 'in England, the constitution, resting on principles consecrated by time, and not in an actual written compact, and being subject to alteration by the very act of the legislature, is consequently no separate and distinct criterion by which the question of constitutionality may be determined': (1825) 12 Sergeant & Rawles (Pa.) 330, 347.

[322] J. Witherspoon, 'Of Civil Society', in *The Works of the Rev. John Witherspoon* (2nd edn., Philadelphia, 1802: iii. 436–8), quoted by J. C. D. Clark (1994: 122).

[323] G. S. Wood (1969: 345). See also J. C. D. Clark (1994: 99, 93–110), and Corwin (1925: 517). Of course, this was not true of everyone. The Boston Legislative Council, for example, declared that there could be no such thing as supreme or unlimited authority except for that of God himself: quoted by Bailyn (1967: 221).

[324] Otis (1764: 454–5); see also ibid. 476–7.

lay what burdens they please on us, we must, it is our duty to submit and patiently bear them till they will be pleased to relieve us.[325]

He made similar remarks in his subsequent *Vindication of the British Colonies*: for example, that '[i]t is certain that the Parliament of Great Britain has a just, clear, equitable, and constitutional right, power, and authority to bind the colonies by all acts wherein they are named. Every lawyer, nay every tyro, knows this . . . This is involved in the idea of a supreme legislative or sovereign power of a state',[326] and that 'the mother state justly asserts the right and authority to bind her colonies where she really thinks the good of the whole requires it; and of this she remains the supreme judge'.[327]

Like Locke, Defoe, Bolingbroke, Blackstone, and Burke, Otis believed that Parliament was bound by natural law but also legally sovereign. But his attempt to reconcile these two principles, unlike theirs, was confused by his explicit claim that the courts could declare Acts of Parliament void. Bernard Bailyn suggests that Otis was referring not to judicial review in the modern sense, but to a kind of advisory function.[328] Otis said that '[i]f the supreme legislature errs, it is informed by the supreme executive in the King's court of law', and then the invalidity of a statute contrary to natural law is 'adjudged by the Parliament itself when convinced of their mistake. Upon this great principle Parliaments repeal such acts as soon as they find they have been mistaken.'[329] As Bailyn puts it, if a court should judge a statute to be contrary to natural law, it should say so in plain words, to enable Parliament to correct what must be presumed to be a mistake; but if Parliament should choose to ignore its advice, that would be the end of the matter.[330]

Alexander Hamilton, who was heavily influenced by Blackstone, was another leading American dissident who at one time believed in both natural law and legislative sovereignty.[331] He said that when human laws denied 'the essential rights of any society, they defeat the proper end of all laws, and so become null and void',[332] but also asserted that 'in every government, there must be a supreme absolute authority lodged somewhere', 'a supreme power, to which all the members of that society are subject; for, otherwise . . . that is no government at all'.[333] He was able to accept both propositions because, like Blackstone, he held natural law to be enforceable by extra-legal means.

When the first principles of civil society are violated, and the rights of a whole people are invaded, the common forms of municipal law are not to be regarded. Men may then

---

[325] ibid. 448.   [326] Otis (1765: 555–6).
[327] ibid. 563; see also ibid. 565 and 573–5, discussed by Bailyn (1965: i. 547–51, 122).
[328] Bailyn (1967: 179–80).   [329] Otis (1764: 454–5).
[330] Bailyn (1965: i. 416–17); see also ibid. 100–2, 121–2. See also Bailyn (1967: 176–80, 186, 205–8), and G. S. Wood (1969: 262–4).
[331] Stourzh (1970: 21–2).   [332] Hamilton (1775: 136).
[333] ibid. 97–8; see also Stourzh (1970: 53–4).

betake themselves to the law of nature . . . There are some events in society, to which human laws cannot extend; but when applied to them lose all their force and efficacy.[334]

It was only much later, in the 1780s, that Hamilton became the most influential early advocate of the novel idea of judicial review.[335]

Few Americans disputed Parliament's claim to possess sovereign power within Britain, because few denied that it represented those who lived there.[336] What they did deny was that it represented them, and this forced them to look elsewhere for the sovereign power which, they often conceded, necessarily existed even in their own communities. Their initial complaint was that Parliament's attempt to tax them was an illegitimate innovation, a breach of customary arrangements and constitutional principles. They distinguished legislation from taxation, arguing that although the former was a function of sovereignty, the latter was the 'free gift' of those who paid it, and therefore required the assent of their elected representatives. It followed that even if Parliament possessed absolute legislative authority within the empire, it could not tax the colonists: it could not make a gift of moneys on behalf of people whom it did not represent.[337] As we have seen, that distinction was overwhelmingly rejected by all but a handful of British politicians.[338]

At about the same time, some Americans attempted to draw a broader and more radical distinction, to establish that Parliament had supreme legislative authority over 'external' matters such as trade, common to Britain and its colonies, but none at all over matters of 'internal' colonial governance, which were the exclusive concern of local legislatures. The question was not the existence of legislative sovereignty, but its divisibility. It was argued that sovereignty was divided between the imperial and the local legislatures, both being supreme and uncontrollable within their respective domains.[339] Parliament remained the 'supreme and overruling authority' in all matters of concern to the whole imperial commonwealth, as Stephen Hopkins, the Governor of Rhode Island, put it in 1765.[340] Hamilton seems to have initially held this view.[341]

Attempts to draw this distinction were eventually regarded as failures. According to Gordon Wood, by the early 1770s many Americans felt compelled to accept the orthodox theory that sovereignty was indivisible.[342] Because they agreed that sovereignty was 'all or nothing', unlimited or non-existent, they concluded that the British Parliament had no legitimate authority over them.[343] The logic of the theory of sovereignty was turned against the British: combined with

---

[334] Hamilton (1775: 136).
[335] The development of Hamilton's later views is described in Stimson (1990: ch. 6).
[336] G. S. Wood (1969: 347–8); see also J. C. D. Clark (1994: 7, 99).
[337] Morgan (1968: 165–8).
[338] William Pitt was one of that handful. He said that '[t]axation is no part of the governing or legislative power': quoted in ibid. 177.
[339] Bailyn (1967: 216).   [340] [Hopkins] (1765: 512).   [341] Stourzh (1970: 16–17).
[342] G. S. Wood (1969: 350).   [343] ibid. 350–4.

the principle of representation, it indicated that legislative sovereignty in the colonies rightfully belonged exclusively to the colonial legislatures. 'The Americans thus acknowledged their "submission to the authority of our Provincial Legislatures in the same manner as the people in Great-Britain acknowledge the power of parliament over them . . ." '.[344] James Madison later wrote that '[t]he fundamental principle of the Revolution was, that the Colonies were coordinate members with each other and with Great Britain, of an empire united by a common executive sovereign [the King], but not united by any common legislative sovereign. The legislative power was maintained to be as complete in each American Parliament, as in the British Parliament.'[345]

At first, the Americans felt no reason to distrust their own legislatures. They had inherited the traditional English confidence in the wisdom and justice of parliaments, elected on a regular basis, and had yet to envisage any superior method for protecting their rights. As Samuel Johnston, a North Carolina Whig, said in 1776, 'there can be no check on the representatives of the people in a democracy, but the people themselves', and this was best effected 'by having their elections very frequent, at least, once in a year'.[346] In the same year, the republican writer 'Demophilus' declared that '[w]hile all kinds of governmental power reverts annually to the people, there can be little danger of their liberty'.[347] Professor Rakove describes this as a basic assumption of the period in which the new state constitutions were adopted.[348] It remained influential during the adoption of the federal Constitution. At the Pennsylvania Convention, Benjamin Rush said that liberty depended on 'a pure and adequate representation' in the legislature, rather than on a bill of rights.[349] Alexander Hamilton observed in the *Federalist Papers* that 'bills of rights are, in their origin, stipulations between kings and their subjects', and therefore 'according to their primitive signification, they have no application to constitutions, professedly founded upon the power of the people and executed by their immediate representatives and servants'. The fact that government was established by the people was 'a better recognition of popular rights than volumes of those aphorisms which make the principal figure in several of our State bills of rights and which would sound much better in a treatise of ethics than in a constitution of government'.[350]

But during the war with Britain, Americans began to distrust their legislatures. As had happened in England during the 1640s, the extraordinary demands of wartime mobilization led to the enactment of legislation curtailing rights,

[344] ibid. 352.
[345] G. Hunt (ed.), *The Writings of James Madison*, vi. 373, quoted by Schuyler (1963: 196).
[346] Quoted in G. S. Wood (1969: 273).
[347] 'Demophilus', *The Genuine Principles of the Ancient Saxon, or English Constitution* (Philadelphia, 1776: 24), quoted by Rakove (1991: 115).
[348] Rakove (1991: 115), and see also ibid. 102, 108–9, and 116–17; see also Sosin (1989: 191).
[349] Quoted in Sandel (1996: 34).
[350] A. Hamilton in Hamilton *et al.* (1961: no. 85, 512–13).

especially to property, which would never have been contemplated in peace-time.[351] This generated grievances that rapidly eroded the earlier trust in representative legislatures, and enhanced the attractiveness of a novel idea: that popular conventions, invested with an authority superior to that of ordinary legislatures, should establish constitutions limiting the powers of all other governmental institutions.[352] Wood describes this as 'an extraordinary invention', 'entirely different from what any other people ever had'.[353]

The reduction of constitutional principles to written form was in itself a crucial development, as many at the time appreciated. As Justice William Patterson put it in 1795, '[i]t is difficult to say what the constitution of England is; because, not being reduced to written certainty and precision, it lies entirely at the mercy of the Parliament . . . there is no written constitution, no fundamental law, nothing visible, nothing real, nothing certain, by which a statute can be tested'. In America, on the other hand, '[e]very State in the Union has its constitution reduced to written exactitude and precision'.[354] James Iredell said that a constitution should be 'not . . . a mere imaginary thing, about which ten thousand different opinions may be formed, but a written document to which all may have recourse'.[355] Henry St George Tucker stated that a constitution in America was not an 'ideal thing, but a real existence . . . in a visible form'; 'its principles can be ascertained from the living letter, not from obscure reasoning or deductions only'.[356]

But the adoption of written constitutions was not enough by itself to change ingrained attitudes towards legislative sovereignty. Their adoption by popular conventions gave concrete, practical form to the previously abstract, theoretical idea that the power of an elected legislature ultimately belonged to the people it represented, who alone were truly sovereign. As long as there was no lawful, institutional method for 'the people' to express its collective will, otherwise than by electing legislators, then the will of the legislature had to be accepted as the will of the people, or at least as the most accurate evidence of it. Previous colonial constitutions had often been described as fundamental laws that only the people could alter, but since elected legislatures, and they alone, represented the people, it was difficult to deny that they could alter those constitutions on the people's behalf.[357]

---

[351] See Rakove (1991: 122–4).   [352] G. S. Wood (1969: 306–7, 328–9, 342–3, 364–5, 383).
[353] ibid. 342, 354. See also Stourzh (1988: 47–8).
[354] *VanHorne's Lessee v Dorrance* (1795) 2 U.S. (2 Dall.) 304, 308. In 1825, Judge Gibson said that '[t]he principles of a written constitution are more fixed and certain . . . than principles which depend on tradition and the vague comprehension of the individuals who compose the nation': *Eakin v Raub* (1825) 12 Sergeant & Rawles (Pa.) 330, 354.
[355] 'Letter to Richard Spaight', in McRee (ed.), *Correspondence of Iredell*, ii. 174, quoted by Snowiss (1990: 26); see also Iredell's later remarks in *Calder v Bull* (1798) 3 U.S. (3 Dall.) 386, 399, quoted in Snowiss (1990: 70).
[356] *Kamper v Hawkins* (1793) 1 Va. Cases 20, 78, quoted in Snowiss (1990: 26).
[357] G. S. Wood (1969: 273–6). The same was true of new state constitutions established between 1776 and 1780. Enacted by those states' ordinary legislatures, they were widely regarded as being subject to change by those same legislatures in the future. Only after 1780 were popular conventions used. See Sandel (1996: 31–2).

To have done so would have been to deny to every generation except that of the constitution's founders any lawful right to alter the constitution, which would have been anathema to progressive thinking. Such was the opinion of Thomas Jefferson, for example, who argued that a constitution had the same status as any other law, and could be altered by the ordinary legislature.[358] That is how the first new state constitutions in the 1770s were regarded. Even when they included bills of rights, these were phrased, and treated in practice, as moral exhortations that did not impose legally enforceable limits to legislative authority.[359] According to Donald Lutz, 'it was not until well after 1789 that bills of rights were, for the most part, considered beyond legislative alteration'.[360]

The new idea of popular conventions, specially convened to create or to alter constitutions, offered a method by which the people could control their legislatures. But not all Americans found this plausible. Noah Webster argued that a constitutional convention was 'a body of men chosen by the people in the manner they choose the members of the legislature, and commonly composed of the same men; but at any rate they are neither wiser nor better. The sense of the people is no better known in a convention, than in a legislature.' The people had to be represented in assemblies, and whether they were called conventions or legislatures made no difference: there was no good reason to give authority to a convention to make a constitution, but withhold authority from the legislature to alter it. Webster argued, along the same lines as Henry Parker had in 1642, that elected legislatures could be trusted: '[t]he people will choose their legislature from their own body—that legislature will have an interest inseparable from that of the people—and therefore an act to restrain their power in any article of legislation, is as unnecessary as an act to prevent them from committing suicide'. Moreover, they had to be trusted: to have 'unlimited power to do right', a legislature also had to have 'unlimited power to do wrong'.[361]

Webster's objections did not prevail. But not even the adoption of constitutions by specially convened conventions, both regarded as superior in authority to ordinary legislatures, was enough by itself to establish the principle that judges could legitimately invalidate legislation.[362] A second conceptual innovation was needed before most people, including many lawyers, could be weaned from traditional habits of thought. At first, it was often argued that if legislators violated a constitution adopted by the people, the only lawful remedies (that is, short of armed rebellion) were for the people to dismiss them at the next election, and for juries to refuse to apply their laws in the meantime. John Adams, along with many others, thought of juries, rather than judges, as the protectors of the people's liberties.[363] The Virginia Bill of Rights, adopted in 1776, explicitly declared that it was for the people to determine whether their 'inherent rights' were

---

[358] Stimson (1990: 95, 98).   [359] Lutz (1980: 60–8).   [360] ibid. 68.
[361] N. Webster, 'Government', *American Magazine*, 1 (1787–88), quoted in G. S. Wood (1969: 379, 381–2).
[362] G. S. Wood (1969: 292).   [363] Stimson (1990: 84).

violated.[364] In 1787, Richard Spaight dismissed the very idea of judicial review as 'absurd': instead of being governed by their own representatives, the people would be subject to the will of a few judges, a despotism more insufferable than that of any European monarchy.[365] Even James Madison said that authorizing the judiciary to override the legislature's understanding of the meaning of the Constitution 'makes the Judiciary Department paramount in fact to the Legislature, which was never intended and can never be proper'.[366]

'Brutus', one of the ablest of the anti-federalists who opposed the new federal Constitution, strongly objected to the prospect of judicial review, on the ground that judges 'independent of the people, of the legislature, and of every power under heaven ... will generally soon feel themselves independent of heaven itself'.[367] 'Brutus' argued that the people's only remedy for violations of the constitution by their rulers was to remove them, and that this remedy was not available in the case of judicial review.

A constitution is a compact of a people with their rulers; if the rulers break the compact, the people have a right and ought to remove them and do themselves justice; but in order to enable them to do this with the greater facility, those whom the people choose at stated periods, should have the power in the last resort to determine the sense of the compact; if they determine contrary to the understanding of the people, an appeal will lie to the people at the period when the rulers are to be elected, and they will have it in their power to remedy the evil; but when this power is lodged in the hands of men independent of the people, and of their representatives, and who are not, constitutionally, accountable for their opinions, no way is left to control them but *with a high hand and an outstretched arm*.[368]

Richard Spaight insisted that the only proper remedies for a legislative violation of fundamental law were elections and, if that failed, revolution.[369] James Iredell, a proponent of judicial review, took pains to rebut what he called 'the great argument' that if the legislature violated the constitution 'the only remedy is, either by a humble petition that the law may be repealed, or a universal resistance of the people'.[370] As late as 1825, Chief Justice John Gibson of Pennsylvania, in a profound critique of judicial review, conceded that in extreme circumstances even judges might be justified in participating in revolution, but denied that this entailed that they had any constitutional authority to review

[364] ibid. 120–1.

[365] R. Spaight, 'Letter to James Iredell', 12 August 1787, quoted in G. S. Wood (1969: 461).

[366] J. Madison, *Observations on Jefferson's Draft of a Constitution for Virginia*, quoted and discussed in Snowiss (1990: 97). For other expressions of the same or similar views, see ibid. 39, and G. S. Wood (1969: 161, 301–2, 304, 455, 459). Madison's views are discussed in Sosin (1989: 227, 235, 240–1, 245–6), Stimson (1990: 121), and Snowiss (1990: 90–9).

[367] 'Brutus' (1787–8: 438; Essay XV, 20 March 1788).

[368] ibid. 442. Emphasis in original.

[369] Spaight, *Letter to James Iredell*, 2 August 1787, discussed in Sosin (1989: 219–20), and quoted in Snowiss (1990: 33).

[370] J. Iredell, 'To the Public', in McRee (ed.), *Correspondence of Iredell*, ii. 147, quoted in Snowiss (1990: 34).

legislation on a regular basis. Discussing an earlier judgment in which Justice William Paterson had argued that judges would have no option but to declare void any attempt by the legislature to abolish such fundamental rights as trial by jury, the electoral franchise, or religious liberty, Gibson observed that these were 'examples of monstrous violations of the constitution':

[A]ny of these would be such a usurpation of the political rights of the citizens, as would work a change in the very structure of the government; or, to speak more properly, it would itself be a revolution, which, to counteract, would justify even insurrection; consequently, a judge might lawfully employ every instrument of official resistance within his reach. By this, I mean, that while the citizen should resist with pike and gun, the judge might co-operate with *habeas corpus* and *mandamus*. It would be his duty, as a citizen, to throw himself into the breach, and if it should be necessary, perish there; but this is far from proving the judiciary to be a *peculiar organ*, under the constitution, to prevent legislative encroachment on the powers reserved by the people; and this is all that I contend it is not.[371]

Gibson's views exemplify the traditional Anglo-American understanding of the relationship between legislatures and fundamental law.

Alexander Hamilton first argued in favour of judicial review in 1784, in a case before the New York Mayor's Court, but his argument was rejected by Mayor Duane, who, paraphrasing Blackstone, asserted that should the legislators 'think fit positively to enact a law, there is no power which can control them'.[372] Rather than impugning the legislature's sovereignty, Duane interpreted the statute in question very restrictively. But even this aroused the anger of the New York Assembly, which formally resolved that the Mayor's reasoning 'is in its tendency subversive of all law and good order', because 'if a Court . . . may take it upon them to dispense with, and act in direct violation of a plain and known law of the State, all other Courts either superior or inferior may do the like; and therewith will end all our dear bought rights and privileges, and the Legislatures become useless'.[373] The Rhode Island Legislature condemned several judges merely for entertaining an argument that a statute might be invalid for violating the right to trial by jury: the judges were accused of attempting to 'abolish the legislative authority', and three were denied reappointment.[374]

Several states experimented with non-judicial mechanisms for ensuring legislative compliance with constitutional limitations. Pennsylvania and Vermont both established a Council of Censors, to be elected every seven years, to inquire into violations of their state constitutions, order impeachments, recommend the repeal of statutes, and convene conventions to make constitutional amendments.[375] New York created a Council of Revision, including the Governor,

---

[371] *Eakin v Raub* (1825) 12 Sergeant & Rawles (Pa.) 330, 356.
[372] Stimson (1990: 113–15), discussing *Rutgers v Waddington* (1784). See also Snowiss (1990: 19–20).
[373] Stimson (1990: 115). See also Snowiss (1990: 19–20).   [374] Stimson (1990: 116).
[375] G. S. Wood (1969: 232, 308, 339, 407–8, 438–41, 444–5). This idea had been proposed by John Adams in his *Thoughts on Government* (1776): see Stimson (1990: 70).

Chancellor, and Supreme Court judges, armed with a limited but not final veto over legislation deemed to be inconsistent 'with the spirit of [the] constitution'. The Council was regarded as a political and advisory body, not a court of law. Similar institutions were proposed in other states, and at the Constitutional Convention in Philadelphia that proposed the new federal Constitution for ratification by the states.[376] James Wilson and James Madison supported judicial review at that Convention only after a majority rejected their proposal for a Council of Revision, armed with a power of veto that could be overridden by a special Congressional majority.[377] Even then, Madison's support appears to have been limited to 'cases of a Judiciary nature', in which legislation directly encroached upon the judicial function itself, rather than in all cases arising under the Constitution, and whether a majority of his fellow delegates supported a broader power of judicial review is still unclear.[378]

According to Gordon Wood, acceptance of judicial review required a revolutionary clarification in the American understanding of law and politics, which did not begin until the 1780s.[379] A long-standing ambivalence towards law and judicial power had to be resolved. A widespread desire for legal certainty, and hostility towards broad judicial discretion, coexisted uneasily with an inherited faith in natural law, equity, and judicial 'reason', which by contemporaneous British lights was somewhat old-fashioned.[380] The novel idea of judicial review eventually caught on because new, written constitutions were adopted in a climate in which that old-fashioned jurisprudence remained influential.[381] The idea developed slowly, and its originality was often commented on at the time. In a letter to Madison, Alexander White described it as 'a novelty in politics'.[382] 'Brutus', the anti-federalist who strongly opposed it, complained that it would place the judiciary 'in a situation altogether unprecedented in a free country'.[383] James Iredell, who endorsed it, described it as 'new in the annals of mankind' because it was contrary to the prevailing theory 'of the necessity of the legislature being absolute in all cases'.[384] According to Stimson, even its strongest supporters, such as Hamilton, sometimes 'showed a reluctance, and an apparent disingenuousness, by refusing to recognise it openly', which has helped keep historians guessing about their true intentions ever since.[385] Well after the establishment of the new Constitution, judicial review continued to meet widespread opposition.[386] Thomas Jefferson maintained that each branch of the government had an equal right to

---

[376] Stimson (1990: 116–17); G. S. Wood (1969: 433, 455, 552).

[377] Sosin (1989: 240–1); Stimson (1990: 134).

[378] Wright (1942: 18 n. 24); Sosin (1989: 245–6, 253), on Madison's position, and ibid. 244, 254, on that of the delegates as a whole.

[379] G. S. Wood (1969: 304–5, 462–3).   [380] ibid. 292–305.   [381] ibid. 456–63.

[382] A. White (1788: 233).   [383] 'Brutus' (1787–8: 418; Essay XI, 31 January 1788).

[384] J. Iredell, 'To the Public', in McRee (ed.), *Correspondence of Iredell*, ii. 145, quoted in Snowiss (1990: 46–7).

[385] Stimson (1990: 124).

[386] In 1807–8, the Ohio legislature impeached judges for holding its Acts void: Thayer (1893: 134). See also the powerful dissent of Justice Gibson in *Eakin v Raub* (1825) 12 Sergeant & Rawles (Pa.) 330, although by 1845, Gibson had changed his mind: Snowiss (1990: 187–8).

After the Revolution

decide for itself what its constitutional duties were, regardless of the opinions of the others.[387] In 1820 he rejected the notion of judicial review as 'a very dangerous doctrine indeed, and one which would place us under the despotism of an oligarchy'.[388]

One justification offered for judicial review was the sovereignty of 'the people', who had supposedly adopted the Constitution.[389] Judicial review does not presume a superiority of the judicial to the legislative power, explained Alexander Hamilton, '[i]t only supposes that the power of the people is superior to both'.[390] According to Madison, '[t]he people were in fact, the fountain of all power... They could alter constitutions as they pleased.'[391] James Wilson agreed: the people 'always retain the right of abolishing, altering, or amending their constitution, at whatever time, and in whatever manner, they shall deem it expedient'.[392] This followed from the fact that 'in our governments, the supreme, absolute, and uncontrollable power remains in the people. As our constitutions are superior to our legislatures; so the people are superior to our constitutions.'[393] As another Federalist put it, the power of the people was 'paramount to every constitution, inalienable in its nature, and indefinite in its extent'.[394] It has been argued that just as the British venerated the judgment of Parliament, Madison and Wilson regarded the will of the people as sovereign 'because it was the conclusion of the rational deliberation of the members of the extended republic. And their conclusions, while by no means infallible, were more likely to be in accord with what the higher law required of government than those of any other human collectivity.'[395]

J. C. D. Clark claims that '[s]overeignty in the United States therefore proved to be as transcendent and absolute, as despotic and uncontrollable as in the United Kingdom; the final irony of the American Revolution was that Sir William Blackstone's analysis prevailed in the end'.[396] But this is doubtful, because the people of the United States have never possessed a sovereign legal power to amend their Constitution, or indeed any direct, unmediated law-making power

---

[387] Stimson (1990: 101). Jefferson had earlier supported judicial review, or at least, a moderate version of it: see Snowiss (1990: 94).

[388] Thomas Jefferson, 'Letter to William Charles Jarvis', 28 September 1820, reprinted in Jefferson (1899: x. 160).

[389] Sosin (1989: 265–26).   [390] Hamilton *et al.* (1961: no. 78, 467–8).

[391] Farrand (1937: ii. 476).

[392] J. Wilson, *Lectures on Law* (1790) in R. G. McCloskey (ed.), *The Works of James Wilson* (Cambridge, Mass., 1967: i. 770), quoted in Kammen (1988: 30–1).

[393] ibid. See also Beer (1993: 323, 338, and 366). Wilson's theory of sovereignty is discussed in Jezierski (1971).

[394] Quoted in Morgan (1988: 281). In *Kamper* v *Hawkins*, Judge St George Tucker justified judicial review in Virginia on the ground that the state's Constitution had been created by 'a power which can supersede all law, and annul the constitution itself—namely, the *people*, in their *sovereign, unlimited*, and *unlimitable* authority and capacity': (1793) 1 Va. Cases 20, 74, quoted in Snowiss (1990: 29); emphasis in original. Justice Patterson said much the same thing in *VanHorne's Lessee v Dorrance* (1795) 2 U.S. (2 Dall.) 304, 308.

[395] Beer (1993: 366).   [396] J. C. D. Clark (1994: 140); see also Wood (1969: 599).

at all.[397] Article V of the Constitution requires that any amendment first be proposed by a two-thirds majority of either both Houses of Congress or the state legislatures, and then passed by three-quarters of either the state legislatures or special state conventions. As the only procedure by which the Constitution can be lawfully amended, this was adopted specifically to prevent a nation-wide majority of 'the people' being able to override sectional interests of particular states, and especially less populous states. Thornton Anderson says that during the Convention debate leading to the adoption of Article V, '[t]he idea of a single national body politic whose people were the source of supreme power, and therefore of the supreme law, was not even a debatable position'.[398] As Henry Monaghan explains, 'the American Constitution rested on *two* pillars: namely, "We the People" (nationally understood) *and* the several states (i.e., "We the People" thereof) as independent political communities'.[399] This is what Federalists such as Wilson probably meant by the 'sovereign power' of 'the people'; if not, they did not represent general opinion.[400]

Samuel Beer argues that the American founders had two kinds of sovereignty in mind, one to overthrow and reconstitute governments, which was unlimited by human law, and the other to exercise governmental powers according to the laws conferring and controlling them. Both kinds of sovereignty were exercised by the people of the United States.[401] If this is the case, then the two powers the founders attributed to the people would seem to be, first, an extra-legal, Lockean power to dissolve governments and establish new ones in their place, and secondly, a political power to control government as established in the United States that is far too diffuse, divided, and indirect to deserve the label 'sovereign'. Beer says that the Americans 'conceded the British point by granting the existence of a human law-making power unlimited by man-made law'.[402] But they only conceded part of the British point. The British tended to believe not only that that the people necessarily possessed an extra-legal, and therefore legally unlimited, power to overthrow established governments, but that within every established government the legislature necessarily possessed a legally unlimited power to make laws. The Americans rejected the second belief, and by the Constitution they established, proved that it was false.

8. The Reform Movement in Britain

In Britain, the idea that the people rather than Parliament were sovereign became increasingly popular in the last few decades of the eighteenth century,

---

[397] Monaghan (1996: 121–2).   [398] Anderson (1993: 160).

[399] Monaghan (1996: 129), and see also ibid. 138–9.

[400] On Wilson, see ibid. 152–3 and 159. See also ibid. 165–8 on the dubious concept of 'the people'.

[401] Beer (1993: 336).   [402] ibid.

even among members of the ruling classes, until it was discredited by the excesses of the French Revolution. Radical Whig reformers advocated constitutional changes to enhance the power of the people, including universal suffrage, equal representation, and annual Parliaments. Some argued that if Parliament did not agree to reform, a popular assembly or convention could be convened to initiate change.[403]

Several of these reformers denied that Parliament was omnipotent, because they thought it was bound by inviolable rights of the people it was supposed to represent. Richard Price said that nothing could be more absurd than the doctrine that parliaments were omnipotent, because '[t]hey possess no power beyond the limits of the trust for the execution of which they were formed'. The only real omnipotence was that of the people, 'where all legislative authority originates'.[404] In 1777, John Wilkes said in Parliament that the omnipotence of Parliament was 'a false and dangerous doctrine' because '[g]overnment is only a trust from the people for their good, and in several instances, so far from possessing an absolute power, we ought to acknowledge, that we have no power at all'. Fundamental rights such as trial by jury could not be abolished 'unless the body of the people expressly declare otherwise, after free and full consideration'.[405] But as previously noted, Price believed that the rights of the people were enforceable by popular resistance, and not by judicial review. In modern terminology, he believed that the people were sovereign in a moral or political, but not in a legal, sense.[406]

Another leading reformer, Thomas Paine, acknowledged that under existing constitutional arrangements, Parliament was legally sovereign. Fascinated by recent developments in America, in which he took part, he denied that England had a genuine constitution. A genuine constitution, he argued, was something adopted by a people for the regulation and control of its government, which had never been done in England.[407] Instead of a constitution, England had 'the universal supremacy and the omnipotence of parliament'.[408] 'From the want of a constitution in England to restrain and regulate the wild impulse of power, many of the laws are irrational and tyrannical', and the existing system of government was 'despotic', because those who are elected 'possess afterwards, as a parliament, unlimited powers'.[409]

---

[403] Dickinson (1977: 224–5).

[404] Price (1776: 10). For other statements along similar lines, see Dickinson (1976: 205 n. 46; 207 n. 56).

[405] Cobbett (1806–20: xix. 570). Obadiah Hulme said that no more dangerous doctrine could be admitted than that Parliament had the right to alter the first principles of the constitution, because then 'they may mould it into what shape they please; and, in the end, make us slaves, by law': [Obadiah Hulme] *An Historical Essay on the English Constitution* (London, 1771: 141), quoted by Dickinson (1976: 207).

[406] See text to nn. 252–3, above.

[407] Paine (1791: 93–4, 151–2; 1792*a*: 204–5; and 1792*b*: 374).

[408] Paine (1791: 151). Original emphasis removed.   [409] Paine (1792*a*: 208, 206).

The reformers never looked to the common law or the judges to control the power of Parliament. They realized that the 'ancient rights of Englishmen', recognized by the common law, protected the property and privileges of the élite, at the expense of the rights of ordinary people. Therefore, they appealed to natural rights, ascertained by reason, rather than to pre-existing legal rights, established by precedent.[410] Moreover, democrats such as Thomas Paine could not have regarded any part of the common law as immutable. He dismissed the very possibility that any law could be immutable, on the ground that this would be inconsistent with the equal right of every generation to order its own affairs, as well as impossible to enforce. This argument, which had been made by Milton and Locke in the previous century, was popular in eighteenth century debates.[411] Paine argued that '[e]very age and generation must be free to act for itself, in all cases, as the ages and generations which preceded it'; '[t]hat which may be thought right and found convenient in one age may be thought wrong and found inconvenient in another'; 'although laws made in one generation often continue in force through succeeding generations, yet they continue to derive their force from the consent of the living'.[412]

There never did, nor never can exist a parliament, or any description of men, or any generation of men, in any country, possessed of the right or the power of binding or controlling posterity to the 'end of time,' or of commanding forever how the world shall be governed, or who shall govern it; and therefore all such clauses, acts, or declarations, by which the makers of them attempt to do what they have neither the right nor the power to do, nor the power to execute, are in themselves null and void.[413]

Jeremy Bentham later made much the same argument, attacking what he called 'the fallacy of irrevocable laws'.[414] No generation could possess sufficient knowledge of the future to enable it to enact a law that would never require amendment. As long as laws continue to enhance the public welfare, they are retained for that reason, without any need for the pretence that they are unalterable; indeed, the fallacy of irrevocability is typically invoked by those desperate to protect laws for which they can provide no good justification. 'The aggregate body of the

[410] Dickinson (1977: 240–4).
[411] Locke had argued that just as no adult is bound by a contract made on his behalf when he was a child by his father, so too, no one is bound by the form of government established by his forefathers: Locke (1690: 345–6; II: 115–16). In 1717, during debate over the Peerage Bill, John Toland insisted that the legislature in any age had as much right to make new laws as any previous one, and that 'to enact a law for posterity, is no more, than recommending a thing to their choice; since if they think there's a reason for it, they can no more be divested of the power to repeal any law enacted by their ancestors, than we are of repealing such laws as have been enacted by ours': Toland (1717: 10). In 1772, Edmund Burke questioned the wisdom and competence of any legislature that attempted to enact a fundamental law 'to disable itself from executing its own functions . . . [and] to prevent it from adapting itself to its own opinions, however clear, or to its own necessities, however urgent': Cobbett (1806–20: xvii. 277–8).
[412] Paine (1791: 61, 65, 64, respectively). Original emphasis removed. [413] ibid. 61.
[414] Larrabee (1952: ch. III). Bentham publicly advocated democratic reform only late in his career; the evolution of his thinking on the subject is described in Hart (1982: 66–71).

living' should not 'remain forever in subjection to an inexorable tyranny exercised, as it were, by the aggregate body of the dead'.[415] Moreover, the living cannot be compelled to obey the dead, unless they are deceived by the fallacy in question.[416]

Paine called for a democratically elected national convention to establish a constitution on behalf of the people of England, which would function as a superior law limiting the ordinary institutions of government.[417] If a genuine constitution were created by the sovereign people, Parliament as a subordinate legislature would be denied the power to alter it. But even so, the constitution could not be made immutable: the people could not alienate their own sovereign power to alter it in the future. Paine did not reject the orthodox theory of sovereignty: he wanted sovereignty to be democratized along American lines, to be acknowledged as belonging to the people rather than Parliament.[418] Moreover, there is no evidence that if that had happened, and a constitution had been adopted, Paine would have wanted judges to have the ultimate power to interpret and enforce it. Judges should be subordinate to the legislature, he believed, so that they did not become domineering or dangerous.[419] In a pamphlet written in 1776, he endorsed the establishment of the Pennsylvanian Council of Censors, an elected body charged with enforcing constitutional limitations.[420]

Major John Cartwright, recently described as 'the father of radicalism' and 'one of the most influential of the reformers', once proposed that Britain adopt the American system of judicial review.[421] But, according to Dickinson, this 'found little favour with other reformers'.[422] Bentham rejected it because it gave too much power to judges, and argued that the most effective check on Parliament's authority was the risk of popular disobedience or resistance. He acknowledged that, in a particular case, it might be beneficial for judges to have a controlling power over an Act of Parliament. 'A public and authorised debate on the propriety of the law is by this means brought on. The artillery of the tongue is played off against the law, under cover of the law itself. An opportunity is gained of impressing sentiments unfavourable to it, upon a numerous and attentive audience.'

Still what benefit would, from the *general* tendency of such a doctrine, and such a practice in conformity to it, accrue to the body of the people is more than I can conceive . . . Give to the Judges a power of annulling its [Parliament's] acts; and you transfer a portion of the supreme power from an assembly which the people have had *some* share, at

---

[415] ibid. 56.   [416] ibid. 57.   [417] Paine (1791: 91–2, 93–4; 1792b: 377–84).
[418] S. Holmes (1995: 144).   [419] H. H. Clark (1961: p. liv).
[420] T. Paine, *Four Letters on Interesting Subjects* (1776), discussed in Claeys (1989: 50–1). On the Pennsylvanian Council of Censors, see n. 375, above.
[421] J. A. W. Gunn (1983: 304, 254).
[422] Dickinson (1976: 208–9; and 1977: 223). J. G. A. Pocock (1984: 44) says that 'the sovereignty of Parliament became an unstated premise of Anglo-Scottish political discourse, which not even the most radical critic proposed to reject or replace'; and see also Pocock (1985: 74, 84).

least, in choosing, to a set of men in the choice of whom they have had not the least imaginable share: to a set of men appointed solely by the Crown.[423]

By 1823, Cartwright himself had abandoned the idea of judicial review, and proposed instead the creation of a Council of Elders, authorized merely to advise Parliament as to the constitutionality of proposed legislation, with no power either to reject or invalidate it.[424] Anyway, in previously advocating a system of judicial review, he assumed that it was not already part of the Constitution.

Most British reformers 'sought the restoration of a balanced constitution through parliamentary reform. They wanted a better constitution by way of a better Parliament'.[425] Their object was not to limit Parliament's powers, but to make it more accountable to the people.[426] Joseph Priestley expressed confidence that, if the House of Commons were made a truly representative body, 'every other reform could be made without any difficulty whatever'.[427] Richard Price agreed that, provided the Commons justly represented the people, government by King, Lords, and Commons 'is the perfection of government'.[428]

Priestley maintained that 'our only proper sovereign is the Parliament'.[429] He argued that in a large state, in which all the people cannot be assembled, deputies must be appointed to act in their name, and 'the whole power of the community must necessarily, and almost irreversibly, be lodged in the hands of these deputies'.[430] In England, 'the power of the state is lodged in the king, lords and commons', as the deputies of the people.[431] 'No maxims or rules of policy can be binding upon them, but such as they themselves shall judge to be conducive to the public good. Their own reason and conscience are their only guide, and the people, in whose name they act, their only judge.'[432] In cases of extreme tyranny, the people could take up arms, and attempt to rescind the authority of their deputies. In cases of less egregious oppression, they could present a remonstrance to the legislature, or if necessary, disobey particular laws; but if these methods were unsuccessful, 'there is no method left, until an opportunity offers of choosing honester deputies . . . in order to obtain the repeal of an oppressive law'.[433]

The reformers' goal was eventually largely realized. The electoral reforms achieved in the nineteenth century made it possible to reconcile, at least to the

---

[423] Bentham (1776: 100–1, esp. n. l).

[424] J. Cartwright, *English Constitution Produced and Illustrated* (1823), discussed in Weston (1965: 223–6).

[425] Toohey (1978: 153).

[426] Paul Langford (1991: 154) says that '[i]t was . . . the subjection of the people which worried some of the new, radical Whigs of the 1770s and 1780s . . . The thrust of their argument, as of much so-called republican argument later, in the 1790s, was not that Parliament must abandon its power but that its members must be rendered fully accountable for their exercise of it by electoral reform'.

[427] Priestley (1791*b*: 107).   [428] Price (1776: 20).

[429] Priestley (1791*a*: 168 n. I). Original emphasis removed.   [430] Priestley (1771: 10–11).

[431] Priestley (1803: lect. XLIV, 261) and Priestley (1771: 11).   [432] Priestley (1771: 11).

[433] ibid. 27–8, 36–7.

satisfaction of the vast majority of Britons, the legal sovereignty of Parliament and the political sovereignty of the people, and to that extent, the constitutional theories of eighteenth century conservatives and radicals. The sovereignty of Parliament was preserved, but given a new, or rather, a renewed justification, in that the reforms made more plausible a claim that had been frequently made since the fourteenth century: that Parliament represented the entire community.

8

The Nineteenth Century

By the beginning of the nineteenth century, the doctrine of parliamentary sovereignty had come to be taken for granted by British lawyers and political theorists. In 1830, Samuel Taylor Coleridge stated that

[t]he Omnipotence of Parliament, in the mouth of a lawyer, and understood exclusively of the restraints and remedies within the competence of our Law-courts [as opposed to resistance by the nation as a whole], is objectionable only as bombast. It is but a puffing pompous way of stating a plain matter of fact ... [W]ithin the sphere of the Courts *quic-quid Rex cum Parliamento voluit, Fatum sit* [whatever the King with Parliament has decided, let it be Fate]![1]

In 1825, Sydney Smith enthusiastically endorsed Bentham's argument that no law could be made unalterable by subsequent generations. 'The sovereign power, at any one period, can only form a blind guess at the measures which may be necessary for any future period.' 'The despotism of Nero or Caligula ... would be more tolerable than an irrevocable law', because the despot might be induced to relent, whereas deceased legislators could never be 'awakened from the dust in which they repose'. It would be absurd if some men could make 'irrevocable laws for men who toss their remains about with spades, and use the relics of these legislators, to give breadth to broccoli'.[2]

Frost, it is true, cannot be put off by Act of Parliament, nor can Spring be accelerated by any majority of both Houses. It is however quite a mistake to suppose that any alteration of any of the Articles of Union is as much out of the jurisdiction of Parliament, as these meteorological changes ... [Parliament] can have no other criterion of wrong and right than that of public utility.[3]

In a study of the royal prerogative, published in 1830, John Allen stated that 'the sovereign authority of the commonwealth ... is vested, not in the King singly, but in the King, Lords, and Commons jointly'.[4] Two years later, John Austin adopted the slightly unorthodox position that sovereignty was held jointly by the King, the Lords, and the electors, rather than the members, of the House of Commons.[5] But he added that the electors delegated their share of the sovereign power, other than their power of election, to their representatives 'absolutely and unconditionally', so that '[d]uring the period for which those members are

---

[1] Coleridge (1976: 97; ch. XI) (first published 1830).   [2] S. Smith (1825: 371).
[3] ibid.   [4] Allen (1849: 159) (these words are also in the 1830 edition).
[5] Austin (1954: 228–31). Joseph Priestley had previously expressed a similar opinion: see Priestley (1965: 200).

elected ... the sovereignty is possessed by the king and the peers, with the members of the commons' house'.[6] Although the electors delegated their power to their representatives subject to a tacit trust, that it should not be used to defeat the purposes for which it was delegated, the terms of the trust were 'general and vague', and enforceable only by moral, and not legal, sanctions.[7] Legally, therefore, the House of Commons could 'concur with the king and the peers in defeating the principal ends for which it is elected and appointed. It might concur, for instance, in making a statute ... which would annihilate completely the actual constitution of the government, by transferring the sovereignty to the king or the peers from the tripartite body wherein it resides at present'.[8]

The Professor of English Law and Jurisprudence at King's College, London, Professor John James Park, observed in 1832 that the British Constitution had no fundamental laws that could not be changed in the same way as ordinary laws.[9] He quoted the following words from a recent American book:

This is admitted by English jurists to be the case in respect to their own constitution, which, in all its vital parts, may be changed by an act of parliament; that is, the king, lords, and commons, may, if they think proper, abrogate and repeal any existing laws, and pass any new laws in direct opposition to that which the people contemplate and revere as their ancient constitution. No such laws can be ... declared void by the courts of justice as unconstitutional.[10]

Alexis de Tocqueville noted in the 1830s that the Parliament in England 'has an acknowledged right to modify the Constitution', which therefore 'may undergo perpetual changes'. 'Consequently', he added, 'a law emanating from the three powers of the State can in no case be unconstitutional'.[11]

In *Stockdale v Hansard* (1839), the Attorney-General, Sir John Campbell, a future Chief Justice and Lord Chancellor, attempted to persuade the Court of Queen's Bench that the House of Commons had supreme jurisdiction to decide the existence and extent of its own privileges, and that the Court was bound to accept its decisions. In the course of his argument, he adverted to the authority of Parliament as a whole. He asserted that 'the Parliament of England being sovereign and supreme, the appeal from all courts of justice is to Parliament', and it would be 'a gross absurdity to suppose that an act done by Parliament could be questioned in an inferior tribunal'.[12] He acknowledged that Parliament might conceivably abuse its 'unlimited power', for example, by abolishing the House of Commons, or changing the religion of the country against the wishes of the people.[13] But possibilities of this kind were unavoidable: 'wherever there

---

[6] Austin (1954: 229).   [7] ibid. 231.   [8] ibid. 229–30.   [9] Park (1832: 14–15).
[10] ibid. 20, quoting from William Rawle, *View of the Constitution of the United States* (Philadelphia, 1829).
[11] Tocqueville (1838: 80 and 81; ch. 6); by 'unconstitutional' he must have meant 'unlawful'.
[12] *Stockdale v Hansard* (1839), in MacDonell (1891: iii. 771, 761–2).
[13] ibid. 777.

is a paramount power, there is some possibility of abuse; and paramount power must be lodged somewhere'.[14] Even in a 'balanced government', in which this power was divided and distributed among various departments of state, it was impossible for the law to provide a remedy for all abuses.[15] This was true, for example, of the Crown's prerogative powers, of the House of Lords' power of judicature as the final court of appeal, and of the Attorney-General's powers to prevent or terminate legal proceedings.[16] 'The constitution cannot, by anticipation, provide a legal remedy for the act of abuse, as it supposes that power, which is conferred for the public good, will be constitutionally and beneficially exercised.'[17] If Parliament did grossly abuse its powers, '[r]esistance is the only remedy; revolution has begun; society is destroyed; the constitution must be reconstructed'.[18]

The Court of Queen's Bench rejected the Attorney-General's main argument, that an assertion of privilege by the House of Commons was not subject to review by the courts. But the judges agreed that the power of Parliament as a whole was sovereign and unchallengeable: indeed, that is why they rejected his main argument. Lord Chief Justice Denman said that '[t]he supremacy of Parliament ... appears to me to completely overturn' the argument, because the House of Commons was only a part of Parliament. 'That sovereign power can make and unmake the laws; but the concurrence of the three legislative estates is necessary: the resolutions of any one of them cannot alter the law'; the Attorney-General's argument was therefore 'abhorrent to the first principles of the constitution of England'.[19] 'Parliament is said to be supreme; I most fully acknowledge its supremacy', the Chief Justice added. 'I am far from believing that the judges ever had, or ought to have, by law, the smallest power over Parliament ... The independence of Parliament is the corner stone of our free constitution.'[20] In response to the proposition 'that the courts of law are inferior courts to the Court of Parliament and to the Court of the House of Commons, and cannot form any judgment as to the acts and resolutions of their superiors', Justice Patteson said: 'I admit fully that the Court of Parliament is superior to the courts of law ... but the House of Commons by itself is not the Court of Parliament'.[21] No 'body of men, however exalted, except the three branches of the legislature concurring, should, by passing a resolution that they have the power to do an act illegal in itself, be able to bind all persons whatsoever, and preclude them from enquiring into the existence of that power and the legality of that act'.[22] Justice Coleridge, like the Attorney-General, adhered to Locke's and Blackstone's theory, that the authority of Parliament is subject only to extra-legal limits, enforceable by revolution. He declined to 'waste time by examining those extreme cases', in which 'according to the theory of the Constitution, even its [Parliament's] so called omnipotence is limited', because they were 'cases wisely not specified,

---

[14] ibid. 784. [15] ibid. 784, 777. [16] ibid. 777. [17] ibid. 784. [18] ibid. 777.
[19] ibid. 850. [20] ibid. 851–2. [21] ibid. 910. [22] ibid. 909.

nor in terms provided for, because they are beyond the Constitution, and, when they unhappily arise, resolve society in its original elements'.[23]

Lord Denman subsequently published a defence of the Court's decision in the *Edinburgh Review*, in which he again contrasted the authority of Parliament as a whole with that of the House of Commons acting alone. In every state, he said, there is necessarily 'an ultimate arbitrary power without appeal', which in Britain is exercised by the Queen, Lords, and Commons. 'The constitution has lodged the sacred deposit of sovereign authority in a chest locked by three different keys, confided to the custody of three different trustees.' He complained that the House of Commons, like the Crown before 1688, claimed 'to enjoy the privilege of striking off the other two locks, when, for any purpose of its own, it wishes to lay hands on the treasure'.[24]

The decision in *Green v Mortimer* (1841)[25] is occasionally said to be inconsistent with the doctrine of parliamentary sovereignty, but has been shown to be 'no more than a proper application of the normal rules of statutory interpretation'.[26] In *Middleton v Anderson* (1842), Lord Mackenzie said: 'We sit here as a Court created by Parliament, the organ of Parliament, and must judge according to what appears to be the will of Parliament, or resign our office. I have felt no call to any such martyrdom and shall certainly adhere to my duty of obedience to Parliament.'[27]

Sir Thomas Erskine May, in the first edition of his *Treatise on the Law, Privileges, Proceedings and Usage of Parliament* (1844), asserted that within the United Kingdom and its foreign possessions the legislative authority of Parliament was subject to no limits 'other than those which are incident to all sovereign authority—the willingness of the people to obey, or their power to resist'. He pointed out that it was bound by no fundamental charter or constitution, and therefore 'has itself the sole constitutional right of establishing and altering the laws and government of the empire'. '[M]any laws may be unjust, and contrary to sound principles of government: but Parliament is not controlled in its discretion, and when it errs, its errors can only be corrected by itself.'[28]

In 1848, Sir Fortunatus Dwarris, partly paraphrasing Blackstone, described Parliament as 'the highest authority which this kingdom acknowledges upon earth. It has power to bind every subject in the land . . . It can do no wrong.'

Statutes of the realm . . . are the declared will of the supreme power in the state, which, unless they are repugnant to the law of God, all subjects are bound to obey. Created by an exercise of the highest authority which the constitution of this country acknowledges,

---

[23] ibid. 930.   [24] [Denman] (1846: 40).

[25] (1861) 3 L.T. 642, cited in Walker (1985: 280 n. 39), and *Building Construction Employees and Builders' Labourers Federation of N.S.W. v Minister for Industrial Relations* (1986) 7 N.S.W.L.R. 372, 403 *per* Kirby J.

[26] Wallington (1974: 688); this is hardly surprising, since judgment was given by Lord Chancellor Campbell.

[27] *Middleton v Anderson* (1842) 4 D. 957 at 1010, quoted in Mitchell (1964: 66).

[28] May (1844: 29, 30–1).

they cannot be dispensed with, altered, amended, suspended, or repealed, but by the same authority of Parliament by which they were made.[29]

In the same year, the second edition of Henry John Stephen's *New Comment-aries on the Laws of England* repeated, word for word, Blackstone's discussion of the sovereign authority of Parliament.[30]

In 1861, James Fitzjames Stephen wrote that it could 'very easily be seen how exactly' John Austin's definition of sovereignty applied to the King, Lords, and Commons. Attempts to bind the sovereign itself were 'simply futile', he insisted, referring to the articles of Union between England and Scotland as an example. Although they declared the established Churches of England and Scotland to be fundamental conditions of the union,

no one can doubt that the existing Parliament of Great Britain could, if it pleased, abolish both or either, and such an abolition would be legal in the strict sense of the word. It is equally true that, against the sovereign so defined, no one has legal rights. A man's right not to be put to death is the most important and beneficial of all rights, yet a bill of attainder—an act of parliament for cutting off the head of a person convicted of no crime—is just as good law as any bill whatever.[31]

An Australian judge said in 1862 that the United Kingdom Parliament had 'unlimited' and 'despotic' powers over its subjects.[32] In *The Institutions of the English Government* (1863), Homersham Cox described 'the need of some supreme power in every civil community for the protection of the rights of its members', and noted that '[t]he supreme legislative power of the British Empire is by its constitution given to Parliament'.[33] He classified the judicial power as a branch of the executive power, confined by the principle of the separation of powers to the interpretation and execution of the laws.[34] As for the authority of Parliament, he quoted Blackstone on its having 'absolute despotic power', and Sir Edward Coke on its having a 'transcendent' jurisdiction. He insisted that in *Dr Bonham's* case, Coke 'refers to cases of obvious mistakes in Acts of Parliament, and . . . does not assert any power of the judges to control the *clearly manifested* intention of the legislature'.[35]

John Stuart Mill argued, in 1865, that 'the ideally best form of government is that in which the sovereignty, or supreme controlling power in the last resort, is vested in the entire aggregate of the community; every citizen . . . having a voice in the exercise of that ultimate sovereignty'.[36] He argued that Britain enjoyed such a form of government, because 'unwritten maxims', or 'constitutional morality', modified the law of the Constitution, and made the House of Commons

---

[29] Dwarris (1848: 523, 528–9).   [30] H. J. Stephen (1848: ii. 313–14).
[31] [J. F. Stephen] (1861: 471).
[32] *Dill v Murphy* (1862) 1 W. and W. (L.) 342, 362 *per* Molesworth J.
[33] Cox (1863: 1, 8).   [34] ibid. 5–7.   [35] ibid. 8–9; emphasis in original.
[36] J. S. Mill, *Considerations on Representative Government* (1865), in Mill (1963–77: xix. 371, 403).

'the real sovereign of the State', 'destined to control as sovereign the enactment of laws and the administration of the general affairs of the nation'.[37] The 'most important liberty of the nation, [was] that of being governed only by laws assented to by its elected representatives'.[38] Much earlier, in 1831, he had observed that the revolution of 1688 'overthrew the doctrine of divine right; put an end to the political influence of the Catholic Church; and established the omnipotence of Parliament'.[39]

W. E. Hearn wrote in 1867 that:

It is now universally conceded that the authority of Parliament in matters of legislation is unlimited. Parliament cannot indeed make an unjust or wicked action to be other than unjust or wicked: but it can make such an action not illegal. It cannot make murder or any other crime unlawful, for such an attempt would involve a contradiction in terms: but it can except any given act from the definition of murder.[40]

In fact, the doctrine was not universally conceded. Thomas Anstey, a former Member of Parliament who had held judicial office in India, published a critique of Blackstone's account of the doctrine in 1867. Anticipating recent criticisms, he erroneously argued that it was a 'new and startling dogma', inspired by Hobbes and invented by Blackstone, that was inconsistent with the Lockean principles cherished by Englishmen.[41]

At about the same time, Walter Bagehot published 'the most celebrated and compelling account of the working of the political system in Victorian Britain'.[42] He observed that 'everybody now understands, that there must be a supreme authority, a conclusive power, in every State on every point somewhere. The idea of government involves it—when that idea is properly understood.' While the American Constitution divided that ultimate power, and vested it in different organs for different purposes, 'the English Constitution . . . has only one authority for all sorts of matters'.[43] 'The English Constitution, in a word, is framed on the principle of choosing a single sovereign authority, and making it good'.[44] Although Bagehot erroneously attributed this authority to the House of Commons alone, because he greatly exaggerated the extent to which the power of the House of Lords had declined, he clearly endorsed the notion of legislative sovereignty.[45] Whatever the question, 'no matter whether it concerns high matters of the essential Constitution or small matters of daily detail . . . a new House of Commons

[37]   ibid. 422–3, 434.   [38]   ibid. 432.
[39]   J. S. Mill, *Letter to the Examiner* (2 January 1831: 8), in Mill (1963–77: xxii. 224).
[40]   Hearn (1867: 50).
[41]   Anstey (1867: 312, 317–18). As well as citing the usual authorities, such as Coke and Holt, and misinterpreting Locke and Burke, Anstey cited some prize cases in which Parliament's authority to override international law might seem to have been questioned (ibid. 331–4). But at that time, prize courts had an anomalous and uncertain status within the British legal system: whether their duty was to apply international law, or domestic law, in cases of inconsistency between the two, was not free of doubt until the early twentieth century. See Colombo (1926: 4–7, 14–18).
[42]   Jenkins (1996: 5).   [43]   Bagehot (1964: 214–15).   [44]   ibid. 220.
[45]   On this aspect of Bagehot's argument, see Jenkins (1996: 11–12).

can despotically and finally resolve' it; 'when sure of the popular assent, and when freshly elected, it is absolute, it can rule as it likes and decide as it likes'.[46] Elections constituted the 'regulating wheel' whereby the Constitution controlled this power: '[i]t does not impair the authority of Parliament as a species, but it impairs the power of the individual Parliament. It enables a particular person outside Parliament to say, "You Members of Parliament are not doing your duty . . . I will appeal from Parliament No.1 to Parliament No.2." '[47] Bagehot was confident that, subject to two minor deficiencies, Parliament accurately represented 'corporate public opinion'; 'it pours out in characteristic words the characteristic heart of the nation'.[48]

C. D. Yonge observed in 1868 that '[t]he first principle of the Constitution is the omnipotence of Parliament'.[49] Justice Willes asserted in 1871 that 'Acts of Parliament . . . are the law of the land; and we do not sit here as a court of appeal from parliament . . . We sit here as servants of the Queen and the legislature . . . The proceedings here are judicial, not autocratic, which they would be if we could make laws instead of administering them.'[50] In 1872, Chief Justice Cockburn and Justice Blackburn said: 'There is no judicial body in the country by which the validity of an act of parliament can be questioned. An act of the legislature is superior in authority to any court of law . . . and no court could pronounce a judgment as to the validity of an act of parliament'.[51]

In 1880, Sheldon Amos claimed that 'in one sense Parliament can do anything, because it can pass a law which by the existing Constitution must be recognised in every Court of Justice in the land'.[52] In the same year, Alpheus Todd asserted that because Parliament needed 'entire freedom of action . . . to legislate for the public welfare',

by the law of England the Imperial Parliament is regarded as omnipotent and supreme in all matters upon which it may undertake to legislate; and . . . no court of law would venture to question the right of Parliament to legislate in any case or upon any question, or presume to assert that any act of the Imperial Parliament was *ultra vires*. It is equally certain that a Parliament cannot so bind its successors by the terms of any statute, as to limit the discretion of a future Parliament . . .[53]

In 1882, Leslie Stephen wrote that 'lawyers are apt to speak as though the legislature were omnipotent, as they do not need to go beyond its decisions. It

---

[46] Bagehot (1964: 219–20).

[47] ibid. 222. Bagehot referred to this as an 'extrinsic' as opposed to a 'intrinsic' check on Parliament: ibid. 224.

[48] ibid. 176 and 177.

[49] C. D. Yonge, *The Life and Administration of the Second Earl of Liverpool* (London, 1868: iii. 340), quoted in Kenyon (1986: 322).

[50] *Lee v The Bude and Torrington Junction Railway Company* (1871) L.R. 6 C.P. 576, 582.

[51] *Ex parte Canon Selwyn* (1872) 36 J.P. 54, quoted in Phillips (1987: 51).

[52] Amos (1880: 15). He went on to add that nevertheless there were political limits to the powers of Parliament, determined by the force of popular opinion (ibid. 15–16).

[53] Todd (1880: 192).

is, of course, omnipotent in the sense that it can make whatever laws it pleases
. . .'.[54] Herbert Spencer detested the doctrine of parliamentary sovereignty, but
acknowledged in 1884 that it was 'the great political superstition of the present',
'common to Tories, Whigs, and Radicals'.[55] In *Bradlaugh v Gossett* (1884), Justice
Stephen said: 'There is no legal remedy . . . for oppressive legislation, though it
may reduce men practically to slavery'.[56]

After the extension of the franchise, the principal justification for the doctrine of parliamentary sovereignty was Parliament's democratic function of
expressing the will of the people.[57] But as we have seen, other justifications, also
perpetuating older themes, continued to be advanced. Dicey argued that in
extraordinary situations of internal disorder or war, legal rights must sometimes
be violated to protect the public interest from irreparable harm. The executive
might have to break the law 'for the sake of legality itself', and then seek an
Act of Indemnity from Parliament.[58] Such an Act, legalizing illegality, was 'the
highest exertion and crowning proof of sovereign power'.[59]

As James Bryce advised the House of Commons in 1886

[t]here is no principle more universally admitted by constitutional jurists than the absolute omnipotence of Parliament. This omnipotence exists because there is nothing beyond
Parliament or behind Parliament . . . [W]e represent the whole British nation, which has
committed to us the plenitude of its authority, and has provided no method of national
action except through our votes.[60]

[54] Stephen (1907: 137) (first published in 1882).
[55] Spencer (1884: 151–2); see also ibid. 254–5.
[56] *Bradlaugh v Gossett* (1884) 12 Q.B.D. 271, 285.
[57] See e.g. Dicey (1964: 83).   [58] ibid. 411–13.
[59] ibid. 50; see also ibid. 232–7.
[60] *Hansard's Parliamentary Debates* (3rd ser.), vol. 305, 1218–19 (1886).

9

Historical Conclusions

The sovereignty of Parliament evolved from that of the medieval English King. The King was said to be subject to law, but the law was mainly unwritten custom, and since he was the source of all temporal jurisdiction and judgment, he could not be legally compelled to observe it. The only available method of restraining a lawless King was political rather than legal. He was widely believed to be obligated to seek the advice and consent of his magnates, in matters affecting their interests. But if they failed to persuade him to obey the law, they could only resist, or, as a last resort, attempt to depose him. They knew that the common law offered them no remedy, because it was his law, and its judges were his judges. Since there were no judicial means of compelling the King to obey the law when he acted against his magnates' wishes, obviously there were no such means when he acted with their consent. There was no authority within the realm able to oppose the King and his magnates when they were united. The possibility of a legal challenge to the validity of whatever laws they might choose to make would have been unthinkable.

Parliament evolved from the medieval tradition of baronial counsel and consent. Participation in law-making was gradually extended from the barons to representatives of counties and towns. By the late fourteenth century, Parliament had become the most authoritative institution in the realm in temporal matters, apart from the monarchy itself. As the King's highest court, it was an instrument of royal government, but was also believed to represent the entire community and to express its collective counsel and consent. Every subject was deemed to consent to its acts. For that reason, when affairs of the highest importance, including the deposition of kings, needed to be authoritatively settled, parliamentary validation was invariably sought. The Lords and Commons both looked to Parliament, rather than inferior courts, to redress their most serious grievances. In temporal matters, it exercised omnicompetent authority, including what we now classify as administrative, legislative, and judicial powers. Its ability to change the law was obvious and frequently acknowledged. It was accepted that statutes could be repealed only by subsequent statutes, even when the former were believed to have been enacted by the parliament of a usurper. Its authority was agreed to be subordinate to the law of God, but inferior courts had no authority to invalidate its acts on that ground. The only human institution that claimed such an authority was the Church, headed by the Pope, with respect to purely spiritual matters.

In the 1530s, the Reformation Parliament transferred ultimate authority over the Church in England from the Pope to the King. Consequently, the King in

Parliament could legislate with respect to spiritual as well as temporal matters, and was, in practice, fully sovereign. That sovereignty was demonstrated by the enactment of many statutes dealing with matters of fundamental constitutional and religious importance, such as the succession to the throne, the royal prerogative, property rights, and ecclesiastical government and doctrine. Whatever private reservations they may have held, judges and bishops dutifully enforced these statutes without questioning their validity. Even when Tudor monarchs regarded earlier statutes as contrary to God's law, they ensured that they were formally repealed by Parliament, rather than simply ignored on the ground that they were null and void. Government officials, lawyers, and learned authors frequently attested to Parliament's omnicompetent and unchallengeable authority.

But the nature of Parliament and its authority was the subject of disagreement. Was it 'the King, in Parliament', or a composite institution, 'the King-in-Parliament'? Royalist theories maintained that statutes were made by the King alone, exercising his God-given authority with the consent of his subjects. Parliamentarian theories held that the King, Lords, and Commons exercised a shared legislative power on behalf of the whole community. These theories agreed on many points: for example, that every community needs a final decision-maker, entrusted with unchallengeable authority to make and declare law; that this decision-maker could not be bound by human laws, because they might have to be overridden in an emergency; and that everyone was obligated to obey its decisions, unless they were manifestly contrary to the law of God, in which case passive disobedience only was permitted. The question that divided them was whether this final, unchallengeable decision-maker was the King alone, or the King, Lords, and Commons in Parliament.

Royalists maintained that it was the King alone, who was appointed by God, and was more trustworthy than any other person or body, because he had been raised to a station above self-interest, and infused with special wisdom and love for his subjects. But they agreed that his authority was highest when he made laws with the consent of his subjects in Parliament. The making of laws in Parliament was the most absolute—the most unchallengeable—of his powers, standing at the pinnacle of his divinely ordained authority. His judges, whom he appointed to enforce his laws, had no authority to question their validity. Some royalists held that his legislative power was nevertheless limited: he could not alienate or restrict his God-given authority, or change the course of its descent after his death. But their view was not far removed from the doctrine of parliamentary sovereignty. The King was both fully sovereign, and 'at his highest' in Parliament, and the only limits to his sovereignty were those inherent in its divine source and inalienable nature.

Parliamentarians believed that final, unchallengeable authority was shared by the King, Lords, and Commons in Parliament, who together represented the entire community. Parliament was often said to represent the Church as well, because the community and the Church were one and the same. Consequently, its authority extended to the interpretation of the word of God. Its decisions embodied not only the consent, but also the combined wisdom of the community; if not actually infallible, it was more trustworthy than any other decision-maker. As the highest court in the land, it was not subject to the laws that bound inferior courts, let alone to their interpretations of those laws. The authority of Parliament and that of the common law were one and the same: the reason of the community. As the voice of the community, Parliament was the supreme interpreter of the common law, and could override even fundamental legal principles if reason required. Since declaring law and making law were both matters of reason, they were ultimately indistinguishable. Parliament alone could be trusted never to violate the rights of the people: it was their foundation and chief protector. The judges of inferior courts were ineligible to play that role, because the King's powers of appointment and dismissal made them unduly susceptible to his influence.

Even before the 1640s, many statesmen and lawyers described Parliament's legislative authority as legally unlimited. During the civil war, royalist and parliamentarian theorists explicitly agreed on that score. What the royalists vehemently denied was that the two Houses could exercise that unlimited authority without the actual assent of the King, who could be deemed a party to their decisions *ex officio*. Parliamentarians insisted that since sovereignty belonged to the whole community rather than a single person, it could be exercised by the two Houses alone, in an extreme emergency threatening the safety of the community.

During the interregnum, the Levellers and the Army often proposed that legislative authority be subjected to legal limits, to be ratified by an agreement of the people. But influential republicans, such as Milton and Harrington, disagreed. Milton argued, as many would do in the following century, that every generation possesses the same unfettered right as its fallible predecessors to alter its laws and even its method of governance.

When the monarchy was restored in 1660, so was the sovereignty of the King in Parliament. But the idea that its authority was limited by fundamental laws was probably more popular after the Restoration than it had been before. An understandable yearning for security and stability must have enhanced its appeal. Moreover, Sir Edward Coke's ambiguous dictum in *Dr Bonham's* case had gained some currency, owing to its being invoked by some lawyers who were punished by the two Houses during the civil war. After the Restoration, most of those who appealed to fundamental laws were monarchists, seeking to protect the succession and prerogatives of the Crown from statutory interference. But not all monarchists took that approach. Most of them adhered to the old royalist theory that the King's sovereign authority was absolute, and denied that it was limited by any laws other than God's.

Some unpopular judicial decisions, widely condemned as unduly partial towards the King's interests, discredited the idea that Parliament's authority was limited by judicially enforceable laws. Parliament's sovereignty was enthusiastically endorsed by leading Whig lawyers during the Exclusion Crisis, on the ground it needed unlimited power to be able to defend the nation in unexpected emergencies. The best known Whig theorist, John Locke, argued that the legislature was entrusted by the people with limited authority. But he held the limits to be enforceable only by armed rebellion, leading to the dissolution of the Constitution. No means of legal enforcement were available because, while the Constitution remained intact, the legislature was superior to all other organs of government. This thesis, that the supreme power recognized by the Constitution, that of the legislature, was subordinate to a power outside the Constitution, that of the people, became very popular during the next century.

After the Revolution of 1688, Parliament's sovereign power was used to control both the royal succession and the prerogatives of the Crown, which some royalists had previously deemed sacrosanct. Parliamentary sovereignty was central to the ideology of Court Whigs, and by 1702, was endorsed by most establishment Tories as well. The ideologies of the two parties converged, the Tories adopting the Whig theory that legislative sovereignty belonged to the King, Lords, and Commons in Parliament, and the Whigs agreeing with the Tories that 'the people' could have only an indirect and strictly limited role in public decision-making. A refusal by the people to trust and obey their representatives in Parliament would spell anarchy.

The Union of England and Scotland, in 1707, was brought about by statutes that included provisions declaring certain institutions to be permanently unalterable, but this had little noticeable impact on the English doctrine of parliamentary sovereignty, which eventually came to be accepted by Scottish lawyers as well. Even those who regarded these provisions as legally unalterable did not believe that they were judicially enforceable; like Locke, they regarded them as enforceable only by rebellion. Indeed, throughout the eighteenth century, those who seem to have questioned Parliament's sovereignty, such as the Country party in the early decades, and democratic reformers later on, envisaged limits enforceable by the people, through resistance if necessary, rather than by judicial review. When their views are translated into modern terminology, they are consistent with parliamentary sovereignty. Indeed, that terminology was adopted in order to accommodate their concerns. Customary limits to Parliament's sovereignty, enforceable by political rather than legal methods, came to be described as constitutional, but not legal, limits.

While those who denied that Parliament's legal authority was unlimited were not proposing judicially enforceable limits, those of the opposite opinion agreed that it was subject to moral limits, enforceable in extraordinary cases by resistance. Eighteenth century statesmen and lawyers developed Locke's insights into a sophisticated defence of the thesis that the people's right to resist parliamentary tyranny was a moral and not a legal right. It was unnecessary for the law to recognize any limits to Parliament's authority, because the people had never in the past, and would not in the future, need any legal pretext to resist tyranny.

And it was undesirable for the law to do so, because moral limits were so abstract and vague, that it was more likely that they would be interpreted too broadly, inciting unjustified resistance, than that Parliament would violate them.

In the second half of the century, almost all politicians, lawyers, and political theorists agreed that Parliament possessed a legally unlimited legislative authority within Britain. This was generally admitted even by the dissident Americans who denied that it had unlimited authority over them. The theory of legislative sovereignty was so influential that they cast it off only with great difficulty, inventing in the process a whole new system of government, in which their legislatures were limited by written constitutions, adopted by special conventions, and enforceable by the judiciary. But this novel method of controlling legislatures found little favour in Britain, even among those who advocated radical constitutional reform. The reformers pinned their hopes on universal suffrage, equal representation, and more frequent elections. They did not trust the common law or the judges to protect their freedoms, and rejected the very idea of immutable laws on the ground that no generation had any right to shackle its descendants. Their goal was not to limit Parliament's powers, but to make it more accountable to the people. Eventually that goal was realized, thereby reconciling, at least to the satisfaction of most Britons, the legal sovereignty of Parliament and the political sovereignty of the people. But even by the beginning of the nineteenth century, parliamentary sovereignty had become a rarely questioned assumption of British constitutional thought, an apparently necessary truth.

In 1871, Justice Willes denied that the courts had any authority 'to act as regents over what is done by parliament'.[1] It seems that this has always been the opinion of a large majority of the political nation, including lawyers and judges. Reviewing the position since the twelfth century, Holdsworth asserted that 'it is clear that it has never been the view of the common lawyers that the common law was a fundamental law which Parliament could not change'.[2] Although many lawyers maintained that Parliament was bound by natural or divine law, there is no evidence of substantial support in any period for the notion that the judiciary rather than Parliament possessed ultimate authority to interpret and enforce that law. The idea that courts could invalidate statutes contrary to fundamental principles of common law appeared briefly in the seventeenth century, but did not enjoy substantial influence either then or since. If the doctrine of parliamentary sovereignty was a dogma, it was not Dicey's dogma, but that of the political nation as a whole.[3]

But of course, the doctrine never was a dogma, in the sense of an unreasoned article of faith. The lawyers, statesmen, and political theorists, whose ideas

---

[1] *Lee v The Bude and Torrington Junction Railway Company* (1871) L.R. 6 C.P. 576, 582.

[2] Holdsworth (1925: 42).

[3] cf. Walker (1985: 276–84) and Allan (1993: 1, 69, 135). Note that Dicey himself described the doctrine as 'the one fundamental dogma of English constitutional law': Dicey (1964: 145); and see also ibid. 70.

contributed to its evolution over many centuries, were not fools. They accepted the doctrine for many reasons, not all compatible with one another. These include the ideas that:

1. as a matter of either logical or practical necessity, there had to be a single, ultimate, and unlimited law-making power in the kingdom;
2. with the consent of his subjects in Parliament, the King exercised an absolute power to make law, conferred by and subject only to God;
3. Parliament was the highest court in the land, the authority of last resort from which no appeal was possible, which could make new laws as well as interpret and apply old ones;
4. if its authority were limited, Parliament might be unable to take extraordinary measures needed to protect the community in emergencies;
5. every generation must be equally free to make and change its laws, as contemporary circumstances might require;
6. all subjects were represented in Parliament, and were therefore deemed to consent to its acts and to be estopped from disputing them;
7. Parliament's decisions reflected the collective wisdom of the entire community, which, if not infallible, was far superior to that of any other agency in the state;
8. the ability of the King, Lords, and Commons to check and balance one another was the best possible safeguard against tyranny;
9. judges could not to be trusted with authority to nullify Parliament's judgments; and
10. to limit Parliament's powers to prevent it from abusing them would be to adopt a cure much more dangerous than the highly improbable disease of parliamentary tyranny.

Judges in Britain, Australia, and New Zealand are sometimes invited to repudiate the doctrine of parliamentary sovereignty.[4] It is said that '[t]his would not be at all revolutionary. What is revolutionary is talk of the omnicompetence of Parliament.'[5] This is false. There can be no doubt that for many centuries there has been a sufficient consensus among all three branches of government in Britain to make the sovereignty of Parliament a rule of recognition in H. L. A. Hart's sense, which the judges by themselves did not create and cannot unilaterally change. That is what is meant by saying that the rule is a 'political fact'. At the fundamental level of a rule of recognition there is no difference between legal and political facts.[6]

Judicial repudiation of the doctrine would amount to an attempt unilaterally to alter that political fact. This would be a dangerous step for the judges to take. Britain has enjoyed relative stability since 1689 partly because the great

---

[4] Of course, the doctrine applies in Australia only in a heavily qualified form: Australian Parliaments are sovereign only within limits imposed on them by superior constitutional enactments.

[5] Edwards (1996: 76).   [6] See Chapter 10, Section 2, below.

constitutional conflicts of the seventeenth century were largely settled then. What was achieved, at a terrible cost, was 'a relatively sharp demarcation between the "is" and the "ought"—a fairly clear and shared definition of what, in the normative terms of law, the political framework was, leaving people free to dispute whether it ought to be such and to contend about what should be done within it'.[7] That shared definition cannot now be repudiated by judges, without risk of renewed uncertainty and disputation.

In any event, judges cannot justify taking that step on the ground that it would revive a venerable tradition of English law, a golden age of constitutionalism, in which the judiciary enforced limits to the authority of Parliament imposed by common law or natural law. There never was such an age.

[7] Gray (1992: 191).

10

The Philosophical Foundations of Parliamentary Sovereignty

1. Parliamentary Sovereignty and Legal Philosophy

The historical evidence demonstrates that for several centuries, at least, all three branches of government in Britain have accepted the doctrine that Parliament has sovereign law-making authority. But in spite of this evidence, some critics argue that the doctrine is not part of British law. It is easy to understand why someone might regard the doctrine as undesirable, and advocate its demise by a constitutional reform such as the adoption of a Bill of Rights. But how can critics argue that no such reform is needed, because the doctrine is not currently part of the law? One of them admits that 'it is hard to question . . . [the] doctrine without appearing to lose touch with practical reality. Until very recently, it was almost unthinkable that the courts would ever refuse to apply an Act of Parliament'.[1] How can the most senior officials of British government, including judges, have been so wrong for so long about the foundations of the legal system they administer?

Legal questions are usually answered on the basis of unquestioned assumptions about the foundations of the legal system in question. When those assumptions are questioned, it can be difficult to know where to turn for answers. What could possibly constitute the foundations of a legal system other than the actual practices and beliefs of the people who administer it? To answer that question, it is necessary to consult recent philosophical reflection on the nature of law and our knowledge of it.

2. Law as the Foundation of Law-Making Authority

Until relatively recently, legal philosophy in Britain was dominated by the Hobbesian theory that at the foundation of every legal system there is a 'sovereign', who is the creator of all law and whose power is therefore above the law. This theory seemed plausible for various reasons. Perhaps most importantly, it seemed that for every law there had to be a law-maker. Some law-makers, such as municipal councils, which make by-laws, exercise an authority conferred on

---

[1] Allan (1993: 16). Another leading critic acknowledges that '[i]t has become a constitutional commonplace' (Detmold 1985: 253).

them by a higher law, made by a superior law-maker. But since there cannot be an infinite regress of laws, and of law-makers, it seemed reasonable to postulate the existence in every legal system of an ultimate law-maker, or sovereign—a legally 'uncaused cause' of all the laws of the system in question. In the case of divine and natural law, God is the putative sovereign. In the case of human law, it might be a monarch, an oligarchy, or a representative assembly, this being a question of fact whose answer varies from one legal system to another. The important point is that whatever the identity of the sovereign, it is by definition above, and uncontrolled by, human law. Otherwise the sovereign would be subject either to a superior human law-maker, or to a human law not made by any human law-maker, which are both contradictions in terms. Or so it seemed, especially in Britain, where the King in Parliament appeared to fit the definition of a sovereign.[2]

But this theory did not fit the facts. Critics such as H. L. A. Hart pointed out that in many legal systems, there is no sovereign in the Hobbesian sense of the term. For example, in many countries the supreme legislature is not sovereign because its powers are limited by a written constitution, and those able to amend the constitution are not sovereign either, because their authority is also conferred and controlled by its provisions. Even monarchies, in countries without a written constitution, are often governed by laws that determine who has the right to succeed to the throne, which the monarchs themselves are not able to amend.[3] At the foundations of all these legal systems are laws that were created by human beings, but not by sovereigns (in the Hobbesian sense of the term).

Fundamental human laws can come into existence either by express agreement among the members of a community, or at least the most powerful of them, as in the case of the adoption of a written constitution, or by the gradual development of customs, as in the case of rules of succession governing traditional monarchical systems. In both cases, the continued existence of such laws depends on their being accepted as binding, at least by people who are able to force others to comply with them. To accept that such a law is binding is to have what Hart called the 'internal point of view' towards the law: it is to believe that there are good reasons for insisting that it be obeyed, and for criticizing those who fail to obey it.

Hart argued that for a legal system to exist, its most fundamental laws must be accepted as binding by its most senior officials, and the system as a whole must be generally obeyed, for whatever reason, by those subject to it. Indeed, the most fundamental laws of any legal system simply are whatever laws are accepted as binding, and routinely applied in administering the system, by its most senior officials. The most important of these laws is a 'rule of recognition', which specifies the criteria that determine what other laws should be recognized as members of the system or, in other words, as valid laws. While the existence, as valid laws, of all the other laws of the system depends on their satisfying those

---

[2] Jennings (1959: 148).   [3] Hart (1961: ch. 4).

criteria, the existence of the rule of recognition itself depends on its being accepted as binding by the most senior officials of the system, and on their decisions being generally obeyed by everyone else. Those officials must adopt the internal point of view, but ordinary citizens need not.[4]

According to Hart, the content of the rule of recognition, in any legal system, is entirely a matter of fact. It is whatever rule that system's most senior officials, including its judges, do in fact accept and apply in identifying valid laws of the system, irrespective of its merits from the perspective of political morality. That we might regard as morally repugnant the rule of recognition actually accepted and applied by the most senior officials of some legal system cannot alter the fact that it is a fundamental law of that system. If it confers sovereign law-making authority upon some person or institution, their unworthiness to exercise such authority cannot diminish the fact that they have it. Denying that fact would be as futile as denying that Hitler was Chancellor of Germany, because of the iniquity of his actions.

In Britain, the most senior legal officials, including judges, have for a very long time recognized as legally valid whatever statutes Parliament has enacted, and have often said that they are bound to do so. In applying Hart's theory to the British legal system, the case for regarding the sovereignty of Parliament as a central component of its rule of recognition seems clear cut, as Hart himself apparently believed.[5] Fear that Parliament might one day grossly abuse its authority might be a good reason to change the rule, but that is a different matter.

3. The Common Law as the Foundation of Law-Making Authority

According to Hart's theory, Parliament's sovereignty is established by fundamental law. It is often argued that this fundamental law must be common law, which was made by judges and can therefore be legitimately modified or overruled by them. 'It is for the judges . . . to say what they will recognize as valid and binding legislation. They invented the doctrine of parliamentary sovereignty; they have the power to curb their own invention.'[6]

This argument usually proceeds by a process of elimination. The doctrine was not, and logically could not have been, originally established by statute. Any Parliament that enacted a statute purporting to confer sovereign power on itself would be begging the question, since the validity of that statute would depend on the very power it purported to confer.[7] But '[i]f the powers do not come from

---

[4] ibid., chs. 5 and 6. The qualification 'most senior' is my own, not Hart's. Low level government employees are more like ordinary citizens, in terms of their relationship to the most fundamental rules of the legal system.

[5] ibid. 144–8.

[6] Brazier (1998: 155). Rishworth (1997*b*: 299) describes this notion as a 'consistent theme' in Sir Robin Cooke's thinking. See also Kirby (1997: 341).

[7] Fitzgerald (1966: 111).

statute, then they must be part of the common law, for our legal system knows no sources of law other than these two'.[8] On this view, the common law is 'the ultimate constitutional foundation',[9] and Britain has a 'common law constitution'.[10]

Judges have always had power to decide what the common law is, and are now generally believed to be able to change it. They can modify or overrule even well settled doctrines of the common law, if they are persuaded that those doctrines either were unjust all along, or have become incompatible with contemporary circumstances or values. Trevor Allan argues that they must be able to change even fundamental doctrines of a constitutional nature. 'As a constitutional framework . . . the common law is self-evidently adaptable to new insights and fresh demands . . . [and] must be developed with imagination to meet the needs of modern constitutionalism.'[11] He is confident that 'British courts are on the threshold of giving us a reinvigorated constitution at common law',[12] and recommends that in doing so, they repudiate the doctrine of parliamentary sovereignty. As he summarizes the whole argument:

[L]egislation obtains its force from the doctrine of parliamentary sovereignty, which is itself a creature of the common law and whose detailed content and limits are therefore matters of judicial law-making. (It could hardly, without circularity, be a doctrine based on statutory authority.) Parliament is sovereign because the judges acknowledge its legal and political supremacy.[13]

Professor William Wade has even claimed that '[i]n this one fundamental matter it is the judges who are sovereign'.[14]

It is possible to take this argument one step further, by contending that the doctrine of parliamentary sovereignty has never been firmly established at common law. Judicial statements expressly affirming it are all obiter dicta, because none were strictly necessary for the decision of the case at hand. Since judges first began making those statements, in the late nineteenth century, no outrageously undemocratic or evil statute has been enacted, and therefore it has never been necessary for them to hold that such a statute would be legally valid. If such a statute were enacted, they would be able to distinguish it from all the other statutes they have previously accepted as valid, and hold that it is invalid. In doing so, they would merely be exercising their undoubted power to distinguish earlier decisions, and repudiate erroneous obiter dicta.[15] As Allan explains, '[i]t is not . . .

---

[8] Munro (1987a: 103). See also Bradley (1989: 30), Walker (1988: 153–5), Detmold (1985: 229–30; and 1989a: 96).

[9] Dixon (1957: esp. 242); Detmold (1985: 97). Dixon was a distinguished Chief Justice of the High Court of Australia.

[10] Allan (1993: 4); see also Allan (1996: 146).   [11] Allan (1993: 10).

[12] Allan (1996: 146).

[13] Allan (1993: 10); see also ibid. 282, and Allan (1997: 445, 448–9).

[14] Wade (1989: 33).

[15] Jennings (1959: 160), Dike (1976: 296–7), Detmold (1985: 254; 1989a: 96–7, 178–9), Walker (1988: 145), Bradley (1989: 50), and Wilson (1997: 115–16).

in the common law tradition to define such a point conclusively in advance; but it is the responsibility of common law judges to reserve the right to reject a statute which is sufficiently abhorrent'.[16]

Now, it is true that Parliament did not, and could not, confer sovereign authority on itself by statute. But it is less often noted that for similar reasons the doctrine of parliamentary sovereignty cannot be a product of judicial law-making. The argument that it is judge-made consists of four steps: first, that there are only two kinds of law in Britain, statute law and common law; secondly, that the doctrine could not have been established by statute, because that would have been question-begging; thirdly, that it must therefore be a matter of common law; and fourthly, that the common law is judge-made law.

The argument fails because of the conjunction of the first and fourth steps. To say both that there are only two types of law in Britain, statute law and common law, and that the common law has been made by judges, is to say that all law in Britain has been deliberately made, either by Parliament, or by the judges. But if so, what could be the legal source of the judges' authority to make the common law? It could not be statute, because that would create a vicious circle (since the point of the argument is that Parliament's authority to enact statutes was conferred by the judges). The only alternative consistent with the argument is to think that the judges conferred authority on themselves. But that would be just as question-begging as the discredited idea that Parliament conferred authority on itself by statute.

The source of these logical difficulties is the Hobbesian assumption that every law, including those conferring authority on Parliament, and on the judges, must originally have been deliberately made by someone, and if it was not Parliament, then it must have been the judges. That assumption leads to the question-begging conclusion that either Parliament, or the judges, originally conferred legal authority on themselves. But the truth is that the judges are no more qualified than Parliament to be regarded as a Hobbesian sovereign, ultimately responsible for the creation of all law. The authority of either Parliament, or the judges, or both, must be based on laws that neither was solely responsible for creating. Those more fundamental laws are what H. L. A. Hart called the 'secondary rules' of the legal system, comprising rules of recognition, change, and adjudication. A necessary condition for the existence of such rules is a consensus among the most senior officials of the legal system, in all three branches of government, legislative, executive, and judicial. This avoids the question-begging that is implicit in any one branch of government purporting to confer law-making authority on itself. Parliament's sovereignty was not created by the judges alone, and its continued existence depends only partly, and not solely, on their willingness to accept it.

A common mistake in the interpretation of Hart's theory is to think that the rule of recognition is constituted by the practices and convictions of the

---

[16] Allan (1996: 161); see also Allan (1997: 445).

judiciary alone.[17] This is clearly not what Hart meant in the first edition of *The Concept of Law*.[18] In describing the rule of recognition, he continually referred to its being constituted by the practices of legal officials in general: it 'rests simply on the fact that it is accepted and used as such a rule in *the judicial and other official* operations of a [legal] system whose rules are generally obeyed'.[19] The reason why Hart insisted that no legal system can exist unless its officials adopt the internal point of view towards its most fundamental rules, and particularly its rule of recognition, is that 'the characteristic unity and continuity of a legal system' depends on the acceptance of 'common standards of legal validity'.[20] He pointed out that if only some judges accepted the sovereignty of Parliament, and they made no criticisms of those who did not, ordinary citizens would sooner or later be faced with contradictory legal directives. The legal system would disintegrate into chaos. But this reasoning extends to all of the most senior officials of the system: the same disastrous consequences would flow from a rift between the judiciary as a whole, and the other branches of government.

Hart explicitly acknowledged this point when discussing events in South Africa in the 1950s. At that time, 'the legislature acted on a different view of its legal competence and powers from that taken by the courts, and enacted measures which the courts declared invalid'. The legislature then established a special appellate 'court' to overrule the regular courts, but the latter declared that this too was invalid. As Hart concluded

[h]ad this process not been stopped . . . we should have had an endless oscillation between two views of the competence of the legislature and so of the criteria of valid law. The normal conditions of official, and especially of judicial, harmony, under which alone it is possible to identify the system's rule of recognition, would have been suspended.[21]

At other times and places, he observed, judges sometimes decide disputed questions of fundamental constitutional law, even concerning uncertainties in the rule of recognition itself, and their decisions are accepted as authoritative. But this is not because they necessarily have authority to do so. Indeed, he noted that it 'seems paradoxical' that courts can exercise 'creative powers which settle the ultimate criteria by which the validity of the very laws, which confer upon them jurisdiction as judges, must itself be tested'.[22]

The truth may be that . . . they get their authority to decide them accepted after the questions have arisen and the decision has been given. Here all that succeeds is success . . . Where this is so, it will often in *retrospect* be said, and may genuinely appear, that there always was an 'inherent' power in the courts to do what they have done. Yet this may be a pious fiction, if the only evidence for it is the success of what has been done.[23]

---

[17] McCormick (1978: 56) has cautioned against this mistake.

[18] Hart (1994: 266–7) says that 'the rule of recognition is treated in my book as resting on a conventional form of judicial consensus', but this misrepresents the position he adopted in the first edition of the book.

[19] Hart (1961: 117), emphasis added, and ibid. 109–14, *passim*.   [20] ibid. 113.

[21] ibid. 118–19.   [22] ibid. 148.   [23] ibid. 149–50, emphasis in original.

   In other words, as long as they do not disagree too strongly with the judges'
decision, other legal officials may be willing to accept that it has resolved the
constitutional disagreement, thereby retrospectively vindicating the judges' presumption of authority to resolve it.

   It follows that there is no logical or practical necessity that judges have authority to determine and enforce limits to the authority of other branches of government. They may have it, but only if other senior legal officials have agreed
that they do. The existence of rules allocating decision-making authority at that
fundamental level depends on official consensus. For example, the immediate
trigger of civil war in 1642 was a dispute between the two Houses of Parliament
and the King concerning their respective constitutional authority. Neither the King
nor the two Houses would have accepted that the judges had authority to resolve
their dispute, since both claimed to possess an authority superior to the judges'.
The King regarded them as his servants, bound to enforce his laws, while the
two Houses regarded inferior courts as subject to their own superior jurisdiction.
As Philip Hunton reluctantly concluded at the time, because there was 'no legal
constituted judge' capable of authoritatively resolving the disagreement, subjects
had to make a moral choice as to whom to support in a civil war.[24]

   Another example is the dispute between the House of Commons and the Court
of Queen's Bench, concerning the proceedings in *Stockdale v Hansard* (1839),
as to which of them had superior jurisdiction to judge the existence and extent of the House's privileges.[25] No official consensus with respect to the matter
had ever been reached. When the Court rejected the House's claims that it had
superior jurisdiction, and that one of its privileges was threatened by those proceedings, many members of the House were outraged. The Attorney-General, Sir
John Campbell, asserted that the judgment was 'totally contrary to law . . . and
a flagrant usurpation of power by the Court of Queen's Bench'.[26] The dispute was
fortunately defused, when the Court acquiesced in the House's imprisonment for
contempt of two sheriffs who executed the Court's judgment, and Parliament
enacted a statute that confirmed the particular privilege claimed by the House.[27]
But in his autobiography, Campbell suggested that the dispute could have produced 'a convulsion unexampled in our history': if the House had committed the
judges themselves for contempt, the Crown would have been forced 'to determine on which side the army should be employed, and for a time we must have
lived under a military government'.[28] The House has still not conceded the courts'
jurisdiction to be the final arbiter of its privileges.[29]

   This philosophical objection to regarding the doctrine of parliamentary
sovereignty as judge-made is corroborated by history. The idea that the judges,

---

[24] P. Hunton, *A Treatise of Monarchy* (1643), in Wootton (1986: 210–11).

[25] *Stockdale v Hansard* (1839) 9 Ad. and E. 1; 112 E.R. 1112.

[26] *The Parliamentary Debates (Hansard)*, 3rd Ser., vol. 48, 365–6 (17 June 1839).

[27] *Sheriff of Middlesex's case* (1840) 11 Ad. and E. 273; Parliamentary Papers Act 1840.

[28] Hardcastle (1881: ii. 129).   [29] De Smith and Brazier (1994: 331).

who were always subordinate to the King and Parliament, conferred authority on their superiors, is historically absurd. As George Winterton has forcefully argued, Parliament's sovereignty was established by political struggle, not judicial decision.[30] When Parliament asserted its authority in novel and controversial ways, for example, to destroy papal jurisdiction in the sixteenth century, and to control the prerogatives of the Crown in the seventeenth century, the judges were virtually compelled by political circumstances to acquiesce—although in the second case, only after many of them were impeached, and their decisions overturned by statute.

It follows that either the first or the fourth steps of the fallacious argument previously criticized must be rejected. Either parliamentary sovereignty is a matter of neither statute law nor common law, or it is a common law doctrine that was not made by the judges. The second alternative is certainly arguable. The term 'common law' is now somewhat ambiguous. Until relatively recently, it meant customary law, which judges discovered and enunciated but did not make, whereas today, it usually means judge-made law. It is wrong to describe the doctrine of parliamentary sovereignty as a matter of common law in the modern sense of judge-made law.[31] But it can be described as a matter of common law in the old sense of the term, meaning a custom that the courts have recognized, but did not create, and therefore cannot unilaterally change. It is indeed a creature of custom—or at least, of custom among senior legal officials—that gradually evolved from the sovereignty of the medieval King.

Nevertheless, it might help prevent confusion if the doctrine were not described as one of common law, because its nature and status are so different from those of all other common law doctrines, as we understand them today. As Winterton has argued, '[i]t is, in fact, *sui generis*, a unique hybrid of law and political fact deriving its authority from acceptance by the people and by the principal institutions of the state, especially parliament and the judiciary'.[32] Even those who argue that it is a common law doctrine would presumably agree that it is *sui generis*. This is because, as long as it continues to be accepted, Parliament can change, repeal, or codify the rest of the common law. Parliament through codification can remove ordinary doctrines from the common law, and from further judicial law-making. If the same were true of the doctrine of parliamentary sovereignty itself, Parliament could prevent the courts from modifying or rejecting it. But that consequence would not be acceptable to those who argue that,

---

[30] Winterton (1981: 273). See also Winterton (1976: 592; 1996: 136) and Joseph (1993: 455–6).

[31] Wilson (1997: 111) argues that it would be socially beneficial if the doctrine were regarded as a creature of common law, which judges can therefore change. He concedes that this would be 'somewhat romantic', requiring 'both a degree of imagination and some sleight of hand', but argues that 'the courts do not operate on the basis of real history . . . [but] assumed, conventional, one might even say consensual, history in which historical events and institutions often have a symbolic value' (ibid. and 128–9). I would suggest that it is unwise to base constitutional doctrines on historical falsehoods.

[32] Winterton (1996: 136).

because it is a common law doctrine, it is amenable to judicial law-making. In fact, there are sound logical reasons for denying that Parliament can unilaterally change, repeal, or codify the doctrine. If Parliament could not have established it in the first place, without begging the question, how could it now have authority to change, repeal, or codify it? If it is the source of Parliament's authority to enact statutes, it must logically be superior to statute.[33] On the other hand, since the judges could not have established it in the first place, it must be equally true that they have no authority unilaterally to change or reject it.[34]

It does not follow that the doctrine of parliamentary sovereignty cannot be changed. There are many examples of fundamental legal rules changing as a result of official consensus changing. In the Australia Act 1986 (UK), the United Kingdom Parliament relinquished its authority to alter Australian law. If it attempted to resume that authority by repealing the Act, Australian courts would almost certainly refuse to accept the validity of the repeal, even if this meant repudiating the doctrine of parliamentary sovereignty that they themselves accepted many years ago.[35] But this change in the allegiance of Australian courts is part of a change in the allegiance of all senior legal officials, and citizens, in Australia, and would therefore be universally accepted there as legitimate. Indeed, a refusal by Australian courts to subscribe to that general change in allegiance would provoke political conflict between them and the other branches of government.

Another example, involving essentially the same process in reverse, is the way in which a nation can surrender its independence by merging with a larger political entity. This may be the future in store for Britain, if it ever comes to be generally accepted by British legal officials that Parliament has lost its authority to withdraw Britain from the European Community. That point has not yet been reached, because if Parliament were tomorrow to legislate to terminate Britain's membership of the Community, British courts would almost certainly acquiesce. It follows that Parliament still retains ultimate legal sovereignty, even though the rules governing its exercise of that sovereignty have changed. They have changed because Parliament, by enacting section 2(4) of the European Communities Act 1972, and the courts, by the way they have applied that section, have overturned the former assumption that Parliament cannot control the form in which future legislation must be enacted.[36] This is itself an example of a change in official

[33] Wade (1955: 187).

[34] In a justly famous article, Professor William Wade wobbles on this point. He rightly says that the doctrine of parliamentary sovereignty is a common law rule only 'in one sense', because it is also an 'ultimate political fact' (ibid. 188–9). But he also says that the doctrine 'lies in the keeping of the courts', and that it cannot be 'altered by any authority outside the courts'—which erroneously suggests that the courts have an exclusive right to alter it (ibid. 189). As an 'ultimate political fact', the doctrine cannot be changed either by the courts, or by Parliament, alone.

[35] 'Even if' because it has always been arguable that the doctrine permitted the Imperial Parliament to abdicate its powers with respect to an external territory such as Australia: see e.g. Anson (1886).

[36] In *R v Secretary of State for Transport, ex parte Factortame Ltd (No. 2)* [1991] A.C. 603, the House of Lords accepted that section 2(4) required the courts not to apply statutory provisions that are inconsistent with directly applicable laws of the Community.

consensus changing the rule of recognition: in effect, Parliament and the courts have tacitly agreed that as long as Parliament does not repudiate Britain's treaty obligations with Europe in express and unambiguous language, the courts will not apply statutory provisions that violate those obligations. But that former assumption was not entailed by the concept of parliamentary sovereignty: a Parliament that can only effectively legislate if it uses a particular form of words, to ensure that its intentions are unmistakable, is still free to legislate whenever it wishes to do so.[37]

Of course, a change in a fundamental legal rule has to start somewhere: someone has to initiate the requisite change in the official consensus that constitutes it. Parliament can do so, by enacting legislation such as the Australia Act, or the European Communities Act, provided that the courts are willing to accept the change. Alternatively, the courts can initiate change, provided that the other branches of government are willing to accept it. An example of this is the way in which the courts today are increasingly subjecting the exercise of royal prerogatives to judicial review. In past centuries, this would have been vehemently opposed by the executive branch of government, and blocked by legislation. The courts have been permitted to expand their authority to control the exercise of power by the executive government only because its attitudes, as well as their own, have changed.[38]

It is sometimes suggested that any change in the fundamental rules of a legal system, brought about by a change in official consensus, must be described as 'extra-legal' or even 'revolutionary'.[39] This is debatable. There are important differences between abrupt changes to fundamental legal rules, imposed on many senior officials through their coercion or removal from office, and gradual changes resulting from a voluntary change of mind on their part in response to broader social developments. In the latter case, it may be appropriate to say that the rules have evolved legally. Be that as it may, there is nothing necessarily wrong with one group of officials attempting to initiate change in the fundamental rules of their legal system. But great caution is needed. If significant numbers of other officials are unlikely to agree with them, the result may be conflict endangering the stability of the system. In the language of the eighteenth century, this might tend towards dissolution of the Constitution. A unilateral rejection by British courts of the doctrine of parliamentary sovereignty is unlikely to be meekly accepted by the other branches of government. Instead, they are likely to condemn it as an illegitimate attempt to alter the currently accepted balance

---

[37] See Chapter 2, text to nn. 32–3, above.
[38] It could be argued that the royal prerogative has always been a matter of common law, and therefore subject to the law-making authority of the courts. But the position tacitly agreed among legal officials in earlier centuries was that the authority of the courts was strictly limited to deciding whether or not the Crown possessed a claimed prerogative, and did not extend to the manner in which it exercised it.
[39] Wade (1955: 188–91).

of power, in favour of the courts.[40] By unsettling what has for centuries been regarded as settled, the courts would risk conflict with the other branches of government that might dangerously destabilize the legal system.

Trevor Allan denies that the present partial integration of Britain's legal system with that of Europe was brought about by the judges alone, guided by their own political ideals. It is the result of their accepting 'that Parliament and people had chosen to join such a supra-national entity, understanding and accepting the legal and political consequences'.[41] If Parliament's authority is to be subjected to substantive constitutional limits, the same procedure should be followed. According to Allan, '[i]f it is possible to recognise limits on the power of Parliament to enact legislation which conflicts with European Community law, even if only to the extent of requiring express wording, it is equally possible to countenance other limits on parliamentary sovereignty which reflect the demands of constitutional principle'.[42] But his own argument suggests that this should be possible only if Parliament and the people so choose, understanding and accepting the legal and political consequences.

4. Legal Principles as the Foundation of Law-Making Authority

Hart's theory of law, so effective in its criticisms of the Hobbesian theory, has itself been powerfully criticized by Ronald Dworkin. Hart argued that legal rules, rather than sovereigns, constitute the foundations of legal systems. Dworkin argues that legal principles, rather than rules, do so. Applying law is fundamentally a matter of interpreting principles, rather than obeying rules, and this necessarily involves value judgments. This theory has been argued to cast doubt on the doctrine of parliamentary sovereignty.[43]

The differences between Hart's and Dworkin's theories of law are clearest in 'hard cases', where relevant legal rules are ambiguous, vague, inconsistent, or simply lacking, and consequently do not provide a clear answer to a legal dispute. According to Hart, judges in these cases must exercise discretion, decide the dispute according to their own assessment of justice or public policy, and in doing so, make new law. On his view, judges also make new law, according to their own moral judgments, when they overrule common law doctrines laid down in earlier cases. But Dworkin objects that in all these cases judges do not step

---

[40] The White Paper 'Rights Brought Home: The Human Rights Bill' (24 October 1997), which accompanied the Human Rights Bill 1997 (UK), asserts that 'a general power over the decisions of Parliament' is something 'which under our present constitutional arrangements they [the courts] do not possess, and would be likely on occasions to draw the judiciary into serious conflict with Parliament' (para. 2.13).

[41] Allan (1997: 445).   [42] ibid. 448.

[43] Allan (1993: esp. at 130–4), but also at ibid. 7–12, 44–7, and 282–90. See also Craig (1993: 325–8).

outside the law, and resort to moral or political judgments. If the relevant legal rules do not provide a clear answer in a hard case, judges look 'behind' the rules, to the principles that underlie and justify them. For example, they resolve ambiguities in rules by reference to the principles that the rules are supposed to serve. The law includes not only rules, but their underlying principles, and in addition, more abstract principles that in turn underlie them, provided that all these rules and principles fit together in a coherent whole. If a particular principle or rule is incompatible with deeper principles, it must be rejected as a mistake. This is what happens when judges overrule common law doctrines laid down in earlier cases: they do not radically change the law, but merely correct an error in the application of deeper legal principles.[44]

Trevor Allan argues that Dworkin's theory applies to the most fundamental constitutional rules of the legal system, including what Hart calls the rule of recognition. The rule of recognition is not an arbitrary axiom. It is accepted by legal officials for reasons—because they believe that it serves deeper principles of political morality. It therefore cannot be the ultimate foundation of the legal system, because those principles are also part of the system and more fundamental than the rule. In Britain, therefore, 'the fundamental rule that accords legal validity to Acts of Parliament is not itself the foundation of the legal order, beyond which the lawyer is forbidden to look. That fundamental rule derives its legal validity from the underlying moral or political theory to which it belongs.'[45] It follows that constitutional rules, including the rule of recognition, must be rejected as mistakes if they are inconsistent with those deeper principles. According to Allan, this is how the doctrine of parliamentary sovereignty should be treated.

But there is a problem here. It is not obvious that Dworkin's theory of the common law is equally applicable to constitutional law. His theory must be shown to fit the facts, rather than the facts distorted to fit the theory. It is not an a priori truth that every legal rule in every legal system is subordinate to deeper legal principles that are judicially enforceable. In so far as it is true of particular legal systems or parts of legal systems, it is a contingent truth, which depends on the practices of their officials. Dworkin himself presents his theory as the best 'interpretation' of how judges in common law legal systems do in fact decide hard cases, and claims that it is confirmed by the way they themselves describe their reasoning.[46] His theory is plausible as an interpretation of the common law, because in applying and changing it judges speak and act as if they are guided by fundamental principles. Indeed, Dworkin has arguably breathed new life into the traditional theory of the common law, which dominated legal thought for many centuries until losing ground to more sceptical theories in recent times.[47]

---

[44] See the discussion in Chapter 2, text to nn. 21–3.   [45] Allan (1993: 265–6).
[46] Dworkin (1977: ch. 4, esp. 86–7, 112, 115–16; and 1986: chs. 1, 3, and 7).
[47] For accounts of Sir Edward Coke's strikingly Dworkinian conception of the common law, see Gray (1980: 28–40; and 1992: 158–64, esp. 162–3).

But the doctrine of parliamentary sovereignty is not a matter of common law, at least in the modern sense of the term, and is quite unlike ordinary common law rules.[48]

Whether Parliament's legislative authority is limited by judicially enforceable principles therefore depends, not on a priori premises, but on the practice of British legal officials, including judges. But for centuries, they have accepted the legal validity of every statute that Parliament has enacted, and have often said that they are legally bound to do so. Allan must demonstrate that judicial authority to invalidate statutes is implicit in the practice of British legal officials, even though they have constantly asserted that it is not. To do so, he must show that they are mistaken about the true nature of their own practice. This is not impossible. He can resort to Dworkin's argument that a legal practice must be 'interpreted' in order to be properly understood, and that this may expose mistakes among the beliefs of legal officials about their practice.

Hart conceived of legal practices as matters of fact, which can be objectively ascertained and described even though they are constituted not only by the behaviour of officials, but also by their reasons for engaging in it, at least in so far as those reasons constitute rules. But Dworkin emphasizes the existence of obscurities and inconsistencies among the reasons that motivate officials, which produce uncertainties and disagreements about what they should do. To resolve those uncertainties and disagreements, their practice must be interpreted, rather than merely described. The object of interpretation is to make the best possible sense of their practice, by identifying, among all the possible reasons for participating in it, those that provide the strongest possible justification for doing so.[49] The best interpretation must satisfy two requirements. First, it must be consistent with most of the behaviour commonly recognized as part of the practice. It would be unrealistic to require that it be consistent with all of that behaviour, because behaviour motivated by partly obscure and inconsistent reasons is unlikely to be completely consistent. Secondly, it must provide a better justification of the practice than any other interpretation that satisfies the first requirement. In constructing such a justification, some of the reasons that officials have given for their behaviour, along with some of the behaviour itself, will be shown to be inconsistent with the reasons that best justify the practice, and therefore mistaken. Even rules traditionally accepted as part of the practice may have to be rejected as erroneous.[50] The officials themselves should accept this, and revise their understanding of their practice accordingly. In this way, interpretation may cause a practice to be clarified and corrected, but not fundamentally changed.[51]

---

[48] See Section 3, above. The British constitution includes common law rules, such as those governing the royal prerogative, and to that extent it may be plausible to think of it as partly based on the principles that underlie those rules: see N. MacCormick, 'Institutional Morality and the Constitution', in MacCormick and Weinberger (1986: 171–88).

[49] Dworkin (1986: chs. 2, 3). [50] ibid. 1986: 47, 66. [51] Postema (1987: 292–3).

Allan purports to interpret the British Constitution. Like Dworkin, he argues that interpretation involves evaluation, and is partly creative.[52] But, again like Dworkin, he concedes that moral ideals are relevant only to the extent that they are consistent with the practices of existing, contingent institutions.[53] He therefore appeals to the actual behaviour of British legal officials, and to the underlying reasons, or principles, that justify it.[54] His aim is to show that the doctrine of parliamentary sovereignty is mistaken because it is inconsistent with some aspects of that behaviour, and with those principles.

His main argument is that the doctrine of parliamentary sovereignty is inconsistent with the principles that justify judicial obedience to statutes. Judges obey statutes because they believe that they are required to do so by principles of justice, the rule of law, democracy, and most fundamentally, equal citizenship.[55] It follows that Parliament's law-making authority is conferred, and limited, by those principles.[56] They are consistent with it having very great, but not unlimited, authority. For example, the principle of democracy could not possibly justify judicial obedience to a statute that undermined democracy. 'Judicial obedience to the statute . . . could not coherently be justified in terms of the doctrine of parliamentary sovereignty, since the statute would violate the political principle which the doctrine itself enshrines.'[57] For the same reason, Allan implicitly denies that even the people themselves, voting in referendums, could possess a legally unlimited authority to make laws: the judges would be justified in preventing them from violating the most fundamental principles of the law.[58]

This is a more sophisticated version of the theory that Parliament's authority is a matter of common law, whose interpretation is the responsibility of the courts. According to Allan, Parliament's authority ultimately derives from deeper principles, which turn out to be indistinguishable from the deepest principles of the common law. The law is a matter of reason rather than arbitrary will because it is grounded in these principles. It is the responsibility of the judges to ascertain and apply the law, and therefore, its deepest principles. They must reject as mistaken any rule that is inconsistent with those principles, and the doctrine of parliamentary sovereignty is such a rule.

Allan has been strongly influenced by Michael Detmold, the leading Australian critic of the doctrine of parliamentary sovereignty, whose theory is in many respects similar. Detmold, too, argues that the whole of the law, including Parliament's law-making authority, is ultimately based on deep common law principles; that the deepest of them is a principle of equal citizenship; and that judges

---

[52] Allan (1993: 9).   [53] ibid. 21. See also Allan (1997: 444–5).

[54] For further discussion, see Sections 5 and 6, below.

[55] On equality, Allan (1996: 151–2, 165; and 1993: 290).

[56] Allan (1993: 130).   [57] ibid. 282.

[58] This is implicit in his denial that the Australian Constitution can lawfully be amended in violation of fundamental principles of freedom and justice: Allan (1996: 158, 159, 164).

would be legally bound to declare invalid any statute (or constitutional amend-ment endorsed by a majority of voters) inconsistent with it.[59]

5. The Practice of British Officials

In this section, I will examine Allan's contention that some aspects of the behaviour of British legal officials are inconsistent with the doctrine of parlia-mentary sovereignty. Then, in the next two sections, I will examine his argu-ment that the underlying reasons or principles that justify their behaviour are inconsistent with it.

Allan relies partly on the way British judges sometimes interpret statutory pro-visions restrictively, even to the extent of distorting their literal meanings, in order to protect fundamental common law principles. He claims that this shows that 'the legislative will must be tempered with (judicial) reason'.[60] Although this is a matter of interpretation, Allan argues that the distinction between interpreting and applying statutes is one of degree rather than kind.[61] 'Questions of interpreta-tion merge imperceptibly into questions of validity.'[62] If judges were to refuse to apply a statute, because it violated a fundamental common law principle, that would merely be an extreme example of the kind of 'interpretation' they have always practised.[63] '[T]he traditional role of the common law in defence of jus-tice and liberty . . . is radically inconsistent with a notion of unlimited legislat-ive supremacy.'[64]

This is not persuasive because, as Allan acknowledges, when judges interpret statutes restrictively, in order to protect important common law principles, they invariably claim to be giving effect to Parliament's implicit intention.[65] This was just as true in earlier centuries as it is today. Allan quotes Sir Edward Coke's dictum that 'the surest construction of a statute is by the rule and reason of the common law'.[66] But Coke also said that 'every statute ought to be expounded according to the intent of them that made it', and seems to have regarded this as the fundamental rule of interpretation.[67] It can be traced at least as far back as the fifteenth century: Chrimes reports that it was 'certainly established by the second half of the fifteenth century', and by Henry VIII's reign was 'sufficiently established to be clearly stated several times from the bench'.[68] Non-literal or

---

[59] See Detmold (1996; and 1985: 256). Some of Detmold's main arguments are discussed in Sec-tion 8, below.
[60] Allan (1993: 17).   [61] ibid. 65; see also ibid. 267, and Detmold (1989a: 179–80).
[62] Allan (1997: 447).   [63] Allan (1993: 267); see also Dike (1976: 291).
[64] Allan (1993: 17).   [65] ibid. 13, 65, 266–7, and 277.
[66] 1 Co. Inst. 272b, quoted by Allan (1993: 15).
[67] 4 Co. Inst. 330, discussed in MacKay (1924: 236–7).
[68] Chrimes (1936: 293–4). The rule was affirmed by Lord Chancellor Ellesmere, Plowden, and Selden, as well as Coke: on early English authorities, see Berger (1986: 299–308; and 1989: 1059–65).

'equitable' interpretations of statutes were justified on that basis. 'Equity is a construction made by the judges', Coke said, 'that cases out of the letter of a statute, yet being within the same mischief . . . shall be within the same remedy . . . and the reason hereof is, for that the law-makers could not possibly set down all cases in express terms'.[69] The same justification was given when cases within the letter of a statute were excepted out of it: 'because the text is contrary to reason . . . therefore they took it that the intent of the maker of the statute could not be according to the letter'.[70] The judges quite reasonably took the view that 'injustice . . . is not to be presumed in a Parliament'.[71]

The judges' claim to be giving effect to Parliament's implicit intention when interpreting statutes non-literally need not be a disingenuous rationalization, nor the concept of legislative intention an artificial or fictional 'construct of reasoning in accordance with common law principles'.[72] To think otherwise is to think that for many centuries, judges have been either confused or lying when they have made that claim. But there is no reason to think so, other than the curious modern scepticism about the existence of legislative intentions.[73] Despite occasional suggestions that collective intentions are mythical entities that cannot really exist, it is obvious that they can. We see them in action when we watch team sports, and hear them when we listen to orchestras.[74] If legislation were never the product of collective intentions within legislatures, it would be a quite mysterious phenomenon. Moreover, those intentions are often matters of public knowledge, owing to the publicity given to the policies of the political parties that secure the enactment of legislation.[75] That is why the courts were sometimes able and willing to take those intentions into account, when interpreting legislation, even when they refused to consult published parliamentary debates.[76]

Although legislators usually attempt to be very explicit in framing laws, implications are unavoidable. This is partly because of human error, which causes deficiencies in expression that can be corrected by implication when it is obvious what Parliament 'really meant to say'. More important are implications that result not from any misuse of language, but from the inescapable dependence of every communication on background assumptions that are necessarily left unexpressed. It is impossible to make explicit all the background knowledge that is essential to properly understand any communication, because every item that is expressly mentioned necessarily depends on others that are taken for granted. Even if it were possible to expressly mention all of them, the result of doing so

---

[69] 1 Co. Inst. 24*b*.

[70] *Fulmerston v Steward* (1 and 2 Philip and Mary) 1 Plow. 101, 109–10; 75 E.R. 160, 172. See also *Earl of Leicester v Heydon* (13 Eliz.) 1 Plow. 348, 398; 75 E.R. 582, 602–3; *Partridge v Strange and Croker* (6 and 7 Ed. VI) 1 Plow. 77, 82; 75 E.R. 123, 130; and *Stradling v Morgan* (2 Eliz.) 1 Plow. 199, 205; 75 E.R. 305, 315.

[71] *Hill v Grange* (3 and 4 Philip and Mary) 1 Plow. 164, 175; 75 E.R. 253, 270. See also *Stowell v Lord Zouche* (4 and 5 Eliz.) 1 Plow. 353, 361–5, 75 E.R. 536, 549–54.

[72] Allan (1993: 15), quoting Dyzenhaus (1991: 95).   [73] See Goldsworthy (1995: 459–60).

[74] Searle (1990: 401).   [75] Marmor (1992: 164–5).   [76] Goldsworthy (1995: 450–1).

would be so prolix and convoluted that it would be very difficult to read, let alone to understand. Moreover, it would be counter-productive to waste one's own time, and that of one's intended audience, by expressly stating what should be obvious to them. For all these reasons, 'the express words of every Act have the shadowy accompaniment of a host of implicit statements'.[77] Judges are therefore often justified in claiming that by interpreting statutory language restrictively, so that it does not disturb common law principles, they are giving effect to Parliament's implicit intention.

It must be admitted that in many cases, what the judges describe as Parliament's implicit intention is a counter-factual rather than an actual intention, a matter of what Parliament would have intended if it had anticipated the problem.[78] The courts in these cases exercise a kind of equitable power, to prevent inadvertent harshness in the application of statutes, which Parliament has implicitly delegated to them or, at least, tacitly consented to. It must also be admitted that in some other cases, the judges' claim to be faithful to Parliament's implicit intention has been a 'noble lie', used to conceal judicial disobedience. But such cases are relatively rare, and the fact that the lie is felt to be required indicates that the judges themselves realize that their disobedience is, legally speaking, illicit. The lie also preserves Parliament's freedom, after reconsidering its position, to override the judges by enacting new legislation expressing its intention more clearly.

Judges who interpret a statute by presuming that Parliament did not intend to violate an important common law principle do not deliberately flout the doctrine of parliamentary sovereignty unless they know that there is clear, admissible evidence that it did intend to do so. And even if they do know this, they do not openly flout the doctrine unless they admit that they know it. There are very few, if any, cases in which they have done so.

A second aspect of official behaviour that Allan relies on is the expectation that constitutional conventions will be adhered to, even by Parliament in the exercise of its legislative authority. These conventions are constituted by general agreement among government officials that, for reasons of political morality, they should exercise, or refrain from exercising, their legal powers in particular ways. Conventions protect important principles, such as representative government, the separation of powers, and the rule of law. They are usually distinguished from laws on the ground that they are not judicially enforceable: the sanction for violating conventions is said to be political rather than legal. Allan argues that this distinction is 'artificial', and therefore mistaken. Consequently, the courts could justifiably hold these conventional limits to be judicially enforceable legal limits.[79] But the distinction between law and convention is not artificial. It is a distinction between standards that judges have generally acknowledged authority

[77] Bennion (1992: 3). For fuller discussion, see Goldsworthy (1994: 150–66; and 1995: 454–6).
[78] Allan (1993: 93) describes this counter-factual intention as 'imaginary'.
[79] ibid. 1993: 72, 244, 253, 263, 283.

to enforce, and others that they do not. There are many sensible reasons why government officials might agree that certain customary standards of behaviour are obligatory but not judicially enforceable. For example, they might prefer those standards to be flexible and fluid, capable of being waived in exceptional situations, and of evolving in response to changing circumstances and community values. Allan is right to point out that many imaginary statutes would be a clear violation of constitutional conventions: for example, statutes plainly infringing the independence of the judiciary, or basic rights such as free speech or equality.[80] But he produces no evidence that there has been any change in the conventional understanding of legal officials that judges have no authority to declare such statutes legally invalid. It is very likely that an attempt by British judges to invalidate a statute on such a ground would be angrily resisted by the legislative and executive branches of government, precisely because it would be contrary to that understanding.

6. Official Consensus as the Foundation of Law-Making Authority

The actual behaviour of British legal officials provides Allan with little support. But there is more to be said for his argument that the underlying principles that best justify that behaviour cannot be reconciled with the doctrine of parliamentary sovereignty. In this and the next section I will respond to that argument.

The methodology that Dworkin recommends for 'interpreting' legal practices is not entirely clear. The interpreter is required to identify the principles that, in her opinion, best justify the behaviour of legal officials. This might seem to involve interpreting official behaviour as if it were motivated by principles endorsed by the interpreter, even if they would be disowned by the officials themselves.[81] But if a social practice consists of behaviour motivated by reasons, then to make the best sense of the practice is to make the best sense of the whole package, and not the behaviour alone. To disconnect the behaviour from the reasons that actually motivate those who engage in it, and provide it with a justification that they would disown, is to propose a new practice rather than to interpret theirs. The role of the interpreter who seeks to understand a practice must be to clarify and harmonize the reasons or principles that motivate its participants, in ways that they are capable of recognizing as enhancing their own understanding of their practice.[82] Dworkin himself has recently explained that '[j]udges must not read their own convictions into the Constitution . . . They must regard themselves as partners with other officials, past and future, who together elaborate a coherent constitutional morality, and they must take care to see that what they contribute

---

[80] See Marshall (1984: 9, 201).
[81] Dworkin (1986: 52–3, 54–5, 58, 64–5), discussed in Postema (1987: esp. 287–9, 290–1, 296).
[82] Postema (1987: esp. 288–9, 308–19).

fits with the rest.'[83] This is required by an important objective of interpretation, which is to enable legal officials to act with 'integrity', by applying the same set of principles to all members of their community. If judges were to interpret the law according to their own personal moral convictions, rather than those of the legal community to which they belong, their interpretations would be more likely to differ from one another, and litigants to be subjected to different principles.

Provided that Allan's interpretive methodology is construed in this way, as an attempt to clarify and harmonize the principles actually accepted by British legal officials, the following critique of his argument can be regarded as an 'internal' one, which accepts, at least for the sake of argument, his methodology. In other words, my critique can be regarded as proposing a rival interpretation of British legal practice, which vindicates Hart's thesis that British law is ultimately based on rules, even though officials accept them only because they also accept deeper principles of political morality. The best interpretation of their practice may show that they have good reasons for regarding those principles as non-justiciable and extra-legal.[84]

It must be admitted that it would be surprising if principles such as democracy, justice, and the rule of law justified the judicial enforcement of whatever statutes Parliament might choose to enact, including ones that egregiously violate those very principles. But for two main reasons, it does not follow that the doctrine of parliamentary sovereignty is a mistake, which legal officials themselves, upon reflection, should realize they cannot really accept. The first reason is that the doctrine of parliamentary sovereignty does not entail that judges should actually enforce such statutes. It maintains that Parliament has legal authority to enact them, and that judges have a legal duty to enforce them, but not that judges would be morally justified in enforcing them. Legal validity and authority are not the same as moral validity and authority. Judges may have a legal but not a moral duty to enforce an evil statute.[85] The second reason is that Parliament's legal authority is justified partly by other principles, which are essential to the justification of any kind of ultimate legal authority. To recognize any kind of ultimate legal authority is necessarily to trust that it will not be abused, and to take the risk that it will be. If that kind of trust is in principle justifiable, partly because it is unavoidable, then a doctrine that reposes it in a democratically elected legislature must surely be justifiable. But these reasons must be more fully explained.

Principles of morality are not self-executing. They only have practical consequences when someone identifies, interprets, and acts on them. People notoriously disagree about what the most fundamental principles of morality are, and

---

[83] Dworkin (1996: 10); and see also nn. 158–9, below.

[84] It is, of course, possible for a Dworkinian interpretation of a legal practice to arrive at non-Dworkinian conclusions as to the nature of the practice and the legal duties of judges within it: Dworkin (1986: ch. 4) provides an example of such an interpretation.

[85] See the discussion in the next section.

what they require people to do in specific circumstances. The most important function of a legal system is to enable people to co-operate with one another despite those disagreements, not (*per impossibile*) by achieving unanimity, but by authoritatively deciding how they should behave even if they continue to disagree. To serve this function a legal system must include officials who are accepted as having authority to make such decisions.[86] In modern societies, their authority is law-making authority, because translating abstract principles of morality into concrete prescriptions is what law-making is all about. Ideally, all members of the community, citizens and officials alike, would accept the authority of their law-makers, and would have good reasons for doing so. But as Hart showed, it is possible for a legal system to exist, and maintain order effectively, even if only its most senior officials, for bad reasons, do so, as long as they can compel the rest of the community to obey them.

It is important to be clear about what is required for a legal system to exist and maintain order effectively. It is not necessary that its law-makers have *de jure*, or morally legitimate, authority. But it is necessary that they have some measure of *de facto* authority, which is authority that is believed to be morally legitimate. Hart's thesis is that at the very least, they must have *de facto* authority among the other senior officials of the system, including its judges. Having this kind of *de facto* authority to make laws is a necessary, even if it is not a sufficient, condition for having *legal* authority to make them.[87] Someone may have morally legitimate authority to tell other people what they must do, but cannot have legal authority to make laws unless senior legal officials, at the very least, accept that she has it.

Unless they are irrational, legal officials, like citizens, believe that authority is legitimate only because they believe that there are good reasons—sound principles of political morality—for doing so. Those principles determine the existence of *de jure*, or morally legitimate, authority. But for the reason just explained, they do not by themselves establish the *de facto* authority that is required for a legal system to exist. The main problem that law is needed to resolve is that of chronic disagreements about what moral principles require, and those disagreements can extend to the question of who should be recognized as having morally legitimate authority to resolve them. Although a legal system is needed to settle disagreements about moral principles, it can do so only if there is sufficient agreement about some of them, at least among people powerful enough to coerce dissenters, to maintain its *de facto* authority to do so. This means that a legal system cannot be based on principles of political morality alone. It requires extensive agreement, at least among senior legal officials, as to how disagreements about those principles should be resolved. It is significant that even a

[86] This co-ordinating function of law is emphasized in much recent jurisprudential literature: see, for example, Finnis (1980: 245–52), Postema (1982), and Coleman (1982).

[87] This should be accepted even by those who believe that having *de jure* authority is also a necessary condition for having legal authority (which I deny).

judicial system cannot function effectively unless some judges have a *de facto* decision-making authority superior to that of others. If judges disagree about the law, it is a practical necessity that some of them accept the opinions of others as authoritative. Thus, the judges of lower courts must accept the decisions of higher courts as authoritative, and within the highest court, dissenting judges must accept the decisions of a majority as authoritative, even if they rightly believe those decisions to be wrong.

Legal officials, including judges, accept that other officials have legitimate authority to make certain kinds of decisions, because they believe that there are principles of political morality that justify their doing so. It is therefore correct to say that, in one sense, law is necessarily based on principles of political morality, or 'reason'.[88] But it is more accurate to say that it is necessarily based on the beliefs of senior legal officials about principles of political morality—on *their* reason, rather than reason *per se*.[89] Moreover, it is not based exclusively on the moral beliefs, or reason, of judges. As Hart pointed out, a rule of recognition is necessarily constituted by a general consensus among the most senior officials of a legal system, legislative, executive, and judicial, and not by the beliefs and values of any single group of them. This is because without such a consensus, a viable legal system can be neither established nor maintained.

Furthermore, it does not follow from the fact that a legal system is necessarily based on legal officials' beliefs about principles of political morality, that those principles should be regarded as legal principles. For at least two reasons, it may be reasonable, or even necessary, to distinguish between the law, and the principles of political morality that motivate legal officials to participate in its creation and enforcement.

First, it is possible for fundamental legal rules to be accepted by different officials for different reasons. A legal system based on such rules can function effectively as long as disagreements among officials about underlying principles do not undermine their acceptance of the rules. In the sixteenth and seventeenth centuries, for example, officials agreed that what the King in Parliament enacted was law, but for different reasons. Some believed that statutes were enacted by the King alone, albeit with his subjects' consent, whereas others believed that the King, Lords, and Commons exercised a shared legislative power on behalf of the community.[90] When officials believe that different and incompatible principles justify the most fundamental rules of law, it seems inapt to describe them as legal principles, because then the law would be incoherent. As far as possible, those principles are best ignored by the legal system, because once introduced into legal debate, they may spark destabilizing disputes among officials. Such a system rests on what has been called an 'incompletely theorised agreement': an

---

[88] Both Detmold and Allan speak of the common law being ultimately a matter of 'reason': Detmold (1989*b*: *passim*) and Allan (1993: 15).

[89] Contra Detmold (1985: 199; and 1989*a*: 95).

[90] See Chapter 4, Section 3, and Chapter 5, Section 1, above.

agreement that is sufficient for practical purposes, but might be jeopardized by any attempt to achieve a deeper agreement about underlying principles.[91]

Secondly, even if all legal officials subscribe to the same underlying principles, they may lack the essential qualities that characterize law. I have argued that our concept of law excludes norms, such as purely customary or moral norms, that are neither enforced by the courts, nor incorporated in a formally enacted legal instrument.[92] The principles of political morality that underlie a legal system may fail to qualify as legal principles on this ground.

Although the moral authority of all legal institutions is necessarily limited by principles of political morality, it is impossible to provide legal mechanisms for the enforcement of all such limits. There cannot be an infinite regress of limits together with legal institutions charged with enforcing them. At least one institution, charged with enforcing limits to some other institution's authority, must be trusted voluntarily to exercise its own authority responsibly. It would be impossible to construct a workable system of 'checks and balances' in which every institution was subject to limits that were fully enforceable by some other institution. If the judiciary were authorized to invalidate legislation for exceeding constitutional limits, some other institution would have to be authorized to invalidate its judgments to ensure that it did not exceed that authority. But then, yet another institution would have to be given authority to override that institution's judgments, and so on. Among a finite number of institutions this would inevitably lead to circularity. If none of them could be trusted voluntarily to exercise their own authority responsibly, and all limits had to be constantly enforced, it would also lead to an endless cycle of disagreements, because no institution's decisions would be final and conclusive. In practice, such a system would be workable only if some of the institutions routinely deferred to the judgments of at least one of the others, which would have to be trusted to exercise its authority responsibly.

There is no law of nature that legislatures can never be trusted voluntarily to comply with the deeper principles that confer, and limit, their moral authority, and that instead, judges must always be trusted with ultimate authority to interpret and enforce those principles.[93] As we have seen, whether judges have such authority depends on whether other senior officials have agreed, or can be persuaded to agree, that they do.[94] In Britain, senior legal officials have long denied that the judges have authority to enforce the moral principles and constitutional conventions that are thought to bind Parliament.

We do not usually describe principles of political morality as legal principles if they are not judicially enforceable. We might be prepared to do so if they were written, relatively clear, and set out in a formally enacted legal instrument. But the principles that interest Allan are not of that kind. They have not been incorporated

---

[91] Sunstein (1996).   [92] See Chapter 2, Section 1, above.
[93] This is accepted even by natural lawyers: see George (1996: 331).
[94] See text to nn. 17–29, above.

in any formally enacted legal instrument. Indeed, Allan acknowledges that they are necessarily abstract and imprecise. 'Since future events are unknown, the constitutional limits to legislative power cannot be definitively stated', he says. They 'are embedded in a more fundamental constitutional morality . . . [and] attempts at formal definition are bound to fail'.[95] This is surely for a reason well known in earlier centuries. Particular legal rules and institutions should not be regarded as immutable, because it is impossible accurately to foresee what changes may be justified in response to unpredictable future developments. Each generation must be equally free to reform the law as it deems appropriate. In the seventeenth century, it was said that 'it is the privilege of God's laws only to bind unalterably'.[96] Today, we would say that this is the privilege of fundamental moral principles only, such as justice, democracy, and the rule of law. For example, the rule of law may require that legal disputes be decided by independent judges, but not that the present structure and jurisdictions of courts be preserved for all time.

As well as being abstract and imprecise, these fundamental moral principles are inherently defeasible: situations can be envisaged in which each one is outweighed or overridden by one or more of the others. Even the most basic human rights, to life, liberty, and property, can be overridden in unusual circumstances. Opinions can differ as to whether it is better to entrust elected legislators, or judges, with ultimate authority to weigh up competing moral principles, and decide which of them ought to prevail. But in either case, their decisions will depend on controversial judgments of political morality. For that reason, even when such principles are set out in a judicially enforceable Bill of Rights, it can be argued that they are better described as moral or political, rather than as legal, principles. On one view, the effect of a Bill of Rights is that judges are legally required to interpret and enforce principles of political morality, rather than principles of law.[97] Even if this view is rejected, and these abstract principles are classified as legal, this is because they have been reduced to writing, formally enacted in a legal document, and made judicially enforceable. If, as in Britain, none of these conditions obtains, it is merely confusing to describe the various principles that motivate official allegiance to the legal system as legal, rather than moral or political, principles. It is confusing because, given the close relationship between our concept of law and judicial enforcement, it may erroneously suggest that the principles *must* be judicially enforceable, after all.[98] But it is fallacious to argue that

---

[95] Allan (1993: 270, 286).

[96] C. Herle, *A Fuller Answer to a Treatise Written by Doctor Ferne* (December 1642: 17), quoted in Judson (1932: 265).

[97] This is the view of so-called 'exclusive' legal positivists, such as Joseph Raz, which is opposed by 'inclusive' legal positivists as well as non-positivists: see Waluchow (1994).

[98] See Chapter 2, Section 1, on this close connection. T. B. Smith (1957: 114) is therefore wrong to argue that because the supposedly unalterable provisions of the Acts of Union of 1707 should be regarded as 'fundamental law', they must be judicially enforceable. Even if his premise is correct, it is not illogical for a legislature to bind itself by limitations that are not judicially enforceable, as he concedes in T. B. Smith (1961: 209).

principles must be judicially enforceable, because they motivate official allegiance to the legal system and therefore deserve to be called 'legal'. Whether particular principles are judicially enforceable depends on official consensus, not verbal classification.

It can be argued that in unusual cases, principles such as democracy might be judicially enforceable. For example, if the British Parliament enacted a statute providing that thereafter it was bound to follow a special procedure in order to enact other statutes of a certain kind, but later passed a statute of that kind by some other procedure, the judges might be asked which of the two statutes was legally binding.[99] This would be a 'hard case', which the doctrine of parliamentary sovereignty would not clearly resolve because it is arguably consistent with a decision either way. As in other hard cases, the judges would have to look 'behind' the doctrine, to the underlying principles that are supposed to justify it. They would have to decide which decision would be more consistent with underlying principles such as democracy and fairness.[100] But this does not establish either that these principles are legal principles, or that the judges have authority to invoke them to limit Parliament's authority in 'easy' cases. As for the first point, the preceding argument suggests that judicial resort to such principles to decide a hard case would exemplify Hart's thesis, that judges must sometimes exercise a law-making discretion, by reaching beyond the law to principles of political morality. As for the second point, the judges' legal authority to decide the hard case would depend on other senior legal officials, and especially current Members of Parliament, accepting it.[101] They would almost certainly do so, for two reasons: first, the issue would be a genuinely hard one, in which reasonable legal arguments could be made on both sides, and secondly, the issue would need to be peacefully settled, and there would be no better method of doing so than by judicial decision.[102] But it simply does not follow that in an easy case, in which the doctrine of parliamentary sovereignty is neither ambiguous nor uncertain, other senior officials would accept that the judges had authority to overrule the doctrine, and invalidate a statute on the ground that it is inconsistent with deeper principles.

7. The Argument From Extreme Cases

By far the most popular argument against the doctrine of parliamentary sovereignty is that no one could possibly be obligated to obey, and therefore

---

[99] Arguably, British judges have already been asked to decide just this question, with respect to the validity of statutes inconsistent with laws of the European Community, and therefore with the European Communities Act 1972 (UK). See the text to nn. 36–7, above.

[100] Allan (1993: 265–6).

[101] For the reasons given in the text to nn. 17–29, above.

[102] Although the House of Commons was not moved by these considerations in 1839, when it refused to accept the validity of the decision in *Stockdale v Hansard*: see nn. 25–8, above.

Parliament could not possibly have authority to enact, a statute that is blatantly and egregiously unjust or undemocratic. F. A. Mann, for example, invites us to imagine a statute depriving Jews of their nationality, prohibiting Christians from marrying non-Christians, dissolving marriages between blacks and whites, or confiscating the property of all red-haired women. 'Is it really suggested that English judges would have to apply and would in fact apply such a law? Do not evade the issue, do not avoid the legal test by asserting that, as we all hope and believe, no English parliament would ever pass such a statute.'[103]

Allan also resorts to improbable, extreme examples. He insists that the courts could not possibly be justified in obeying a 'wicked' statute, which 'seriously contradicted the fundamental tenets of our political morality', such as one requiring all blue-eyed babies to be killed, depriving a large section of the population of the right to vote, or authorizing officials to inflict punishment for whatever reason they should choose.[104] Because it leads to the opposite conclusion, the doctrine of parliamentary sovereignty is an 'absurdity' that is 'bereft of any rational justification'.[105]

One difficulty with this argument is that, although it may show that it is unreasonable for officials to believe that Parliament has unlimited law-making authority, it does not overcome the fact that they do so. That fact is sufficient to establish that, as a matter of law, Parliament has unlimited authority, even if in this respect the law is unreasonable. But this difficulty can be surmounted if it can be shown that legal officials cannot really mean what they say, because it is inconsistent with deeper principles to which they are committed. It is here that Dworkin's idea that legal practices must be 'interpreted' as a whole, rather than simply taken as given, is so useful. I myself once made use of it:

> [I]t is not clear that British judges do in fact accept the rule of unlimited Parliamentary sovereignty. They may say they do, but they may be mistaken: they may be misinterpreting their own practices. Consider the blue-eyed babies Act [requiring that all blue-eyed babies be killed]. Judicial endorsements of the rule of unlimited Parliamentary sovereignty imply that were such an Act to be passed, the judges would be bound to enforce it. But would they in fact believe themselves bound to do so? More importantly for our purposes, do they now believe that they would be bound to do so? If, as we are surely entitled to assume, they are reasonable people, the answer to both questions must be no. If so, then the rule of unlimited Parliamentary sovereignty must be either a mistake, or an exaggeration of a more qualified truth. Both are genuine possibilities. If a mistake, it may be the quite understandable result of bad philosophy: classical legal positivism. If an exaggeration, it is equally understandable and possibly justifiable as a 'noble lie': since Parliament is unlikely to enact truly evil laws, why not ignore unnecessary complications and say that whatever Parliament enacts is necessarily valid? But whatever the reason for their misrepresenting it, the rule which judges really accept is surely the rule on which

---

[103] Mann (1978: 513).

[104] Allan (1993: 130, 282, 285, respectively). Others who rely on the argument from extreme cases include Brookfield (1995: 54–6), and Wilson (1997: 115–16).

[105] Allan (1996: 156, 160; see also 1993: 18, 77; 1997: 449), and Brookfield (1995: 55).

they are actually prepared to act, rather than the rule on which they merely say or imply that they are prepared to act. Thus, it can be argued that the alleged rule of unlimited Parliamentary sovereignty is a misinterpretation of the traditional deference of British judges to Parliament. That deference must really be based on Parliament's having vast, but not unlimited, authority. For them to accept this, and consequently modify their conception of Parliament's sovereignty, would constitute not a change in their practice, but an improvement in their understanding of it.[106]

The fatal flaw in this argument is that it treats moral and legal authority, and moral and legal obligation, as equivalents.[107] It would be unreasonable to believe that a morally fallible legislature could have unlimited moral authority to enact laws, and that people would therefore have a moral obligation to obey whatever laws it might enact, no matter how undemocratic or unjust they might be. If legal authority to enact laws were the same as moral authority, then it would also be unreasonable to believe that such a legislature could have unlimited legal authority to enact laws. But there are good reasons for distinguishing between moral and legal authority, and between moral and legal obligation. They are reasons for thinking that a morally fallible legislature could have unlimited legal authority, despite having only limited moral authority, to enact laws. It follows that the doctrine of parliamentary sovereignty is not an absurdity, which legal officials cannot really accept.

It is not a logical or practical necessity that Parliament should have ultimate legal authority to decide what the law is. But it is a practical necessity that *some* institution have ultimate authority to decide any legal question that may arise, even if it is a different institution with respect to different types of questions. Otherwise the decisions of legal institutions would be no more than recommendations as to what the law is, and could not resolve disagreements between people with passionately opposed views. In the seventeenth century, this was often put in terms of obedience. 'Appeals must not be infinite', said one author. 'There must be some supreme power, in whose final determination (be it *right*, or be it *wrong*) all inferiors must acquiesce and submit, otherwise, no controversies could be decided; nay, there could be no government, nothing but disorder and confusion in the world.'[108] This goes too far. What is necessary is that on any legal question there must be an ultimate authority whose decisions are accepted as authoritatively stating the law, even if they are disobeyed because they are unjust.

If the judges rather than Parliament had this ultimate authority, we would be in the same predicament. Their decisions would have to be accepted as lawful even by people who, rightly or wrongly, believe them to be unjust. And because

---

[106] Goldsworthy (1990: esp. 482–3).

[107] The larger thesis of the article just cited depends on interpreting 'internal' legal statements of validity as fully committed moral statements. I have been persuaded by Holton (1998) that that interpretation is erroneous.

[108] *The Royal Apology: Or, An Answer To the Rebels Plea* (London, T. B. for Robert Clavel, 1684: 35–6), quoted in Houston (1991: 79). Emphasis in original.

judges, like legislators, are morally fallible, we would still face the danger of occasional, possibly egregious, injustice.[109] To adapt the words of Dudley Digges the younger, 'we cannot have any absolute security; in all governments it is necessary to trust somebody. . . . if you are weary of democracy you know the way to cast it off by placing judicial guardians over your Parliament, but have you any greater assurance than before? *Quis custodiet ipsos custodes?*'[110] In other words, if it is useful to ask whether a statute requiring that blue-eyed babies be killed could possibly be valid, it is equally useful to ask whether a judicial decision that a blue-eyed baby be killed could possibly be valid. And if a negative answer to the former question justifies judges having authority to invalidate statutes, a negative answer to the latter question must justify officials other than judges having authority to invalidate judicial decisions. But who might they be, and to whom would we turn if *they* declared that blue-eyed babies must be killed? Such reasoning produces either a vicious circle, or an infinite regress, of authority to overrule egregiously unjust decisions. In practice, the chain of legal authority, and the availability of legal methods of overruling egregiously unjust decisions, must at some point come to an end. At that point, whichever institution has ultimate authority to decide a question must be trusted to exercise it responsibly. By itself, 'the possibility of the abuse of power, is no objection against that power . . . for there can be no power at all, which is not accompanied with some trust; and there is no trust, but it possibly (morally speaking) may be broken'.[111]

Decision-making by legislatures composed of ordinary people, elected by their fellow citizens, is undeniably imperfect. But judges, too, are fallible: courts, like legislatures, decide questions by majority vote, and the majority are not always right. Indeed, it can be argued that with respect to rights, judges are not as well placed as legislators to make wise decisions. Because rights are never absolute, but must be weighed against competing rights and interests, one person's complaint that his or her right has been violated usually raises questions about the interests of other members of the community, who may not be represented in court. Parliament is often more able to gather all relevant facts, consult widely with all affected parties, and arrive at an overall balance or compromise of the competing interests at stake. There are, of course, important arguments on the other side: judges are arguably more trustworthy than elected legislators because they are more able to think calmly and impartially about difficult moral problems, independently of popular prejudices. But whether or not this is so depends on difficult factual and normative questions, whose answers can vary from one country to another, depending on culture, social structure, and political organization. That the doctrine of parliamentary sovereignty facilitated massive

---

[109] Anyone who doubts this should read the infamous judgment of the American Supreme Court in the 'Dred Scott' case: *Scott v Sandford* (1857) 60 US (19 How.) 393.

[110] Adapted from Digges (1643: 81 and 79, respectively), discussed in Chapter 5, text to n. 70, above.

[111] Solicitor-General Finch, in *The East-India Co v Sandys* ('*The Great Case of Monopolies*') (1684), in Howell (1816–28: x. 407).

injustice in South Africa, for example, is not a good reason for concluding that it should be repudiated in Britain.[112] It may have impeded the ability of South African judges to obstruct an unrepresentative and unjust legislature, but it does not follow that judges elsewhere should be encouraged to obstruct representative and generally just legislatures.[113] In many other countries, judicial supremacy has been used to impede progress towards justice and democracy.[114]

But the question is not simply whether judges are likely to make better decisions than legislators, however that is to be measured. Who has the right to decide some question may not depend solely on who is more likely to decide it rightly. One of the most fundamental of all rights is that of ordinary people to participate, on equal terms, in the political decision-making that affects their lives as much as anyone else's.[115] To respect that right is to respect their intelligence and virtue. Moreover, democracy aspires to develop important civic virtues: to reduce feelings of powerlessness, enhance self-confidence and self-respect, and promote education, a broadening of horizons, and an appreciation of other points of view. It is hoped that by doing so, it fosters co-operation and harmony, a sense of membership within, and responsibility to, the community, and a more willing acceptance of collective decisions.[116] Moreover, it is often argued that people have a special obligation to accept the decisions of a democratic procedure in which they have an equal right to participate.[117] Richard Hooker argued that '[a] law is the deed of the whole body politic, whereof if you judge yourselves to be any part, then is the law even your deed also'.[118] Although this may be an exaggeration, some modern philosophers agree with it: 'If I am a genuine member of a political community, its act is in some pertinent sense my act, even when I argued and voted against it . . . On no other assumption can we intelligibly think that as members of a flourishing democracy we are governing ourselves.'[119]

As Robert Dahl has observed, '[t]he democratic process is a gamble on the possibilities that a people, in acting autonomously, will learn how to act rightly'.[120] Judicial review has been criticized for having the opposite effect on the political and moral capacity of legislators and citizens: by making them not ultimately responsible for respecting one another's rights, it may make them irresponsible.[121] Be that as it may, genuine and lasting respect for the rights of others cannot be imposed by judicial fiat: it is most likely to emerge from the dialogue and compromise that characterize politics in a democracy.

At this point, it may be objected that no matter who has ultimate legal authority, it cannot be absolute, for the very reason we have mentioned: the danger of occasional, egregious, injustice. People can be bound to obey laws (or judicial

---

[112] The case of South Africa is discussed in Dyzenhaus (1991).   [113] See Bakan (1992).
[114] Mandel (1998).   [115] A point made very forcefully in Waldron (1993).
[116] Goldsworthy (1992: 172–3).   [117] See e.g. Singer (1974).
[118] Hooker (1888: i. 164; 'Preface').
[119] Dworkin (1996: 22). See also Detmold (1989*b*: 461): 'What charges them [criminals] is their community, and since it is their community its laws are their laws in the fundamental sense'.
[120] Dahl (1989: 192).   [121] See Lazare (1996: 152), discussing Thayer (1893: 155–6).

decisions) that they believe are unjust, but only up to a point. Officially sanctioned injustice can be so extreme that the reasons in favour of obedience are overridden. In a sufficiently extreme case, people might be morally entitled or even obligated to resort to violence rather than to suffer or permit such injustice. Furthermore, legal officials such as judges might be morally bound to help them. As Chief Justice John Gibson of Pennsylvania argued in 1825, a truly 'monstrous' violation of the citizens' rights

> would justify even insurrection; consequently, a judge might lawfully employ every instrument of official resistance within his reach. By this, I mean, that while the citizen should resist with pike and gun, the judge might co-operate with *habeas corpus* and *mandamus*. It would be his duty, as a citizen, to throw himself into the breach, and if it should be necessary, perish there.[122]

But this does not prove that judges possess legal authority to invalidate legislation. What judges might be morally entitled or even bound to do in an extraordinary emergency may differ from what they are legally authorized to do. It does not follow from the fact that judges must decide for themselves whether or not they can enforce a statute with a clear conscience, that if they decide they cannot do so, they have authority to hold that the statute is legally invalid. If it did, it would also follow that bailiffs, police officers, and prison warders have authority to declare that judicial decisions are legally invalid. Judges no less than Parliament rely on the co-operation of other officials for the enforcement of their decisions: they do not step down from the bench and personally enforce them. Bailiffs, police officers, and prison warders must decide for themselves whether or not they can in good conscience enforce judicial decisions, but it does not follow that they have legal authority to invalidate those decisions. The same is true of ordinary citizens. They must decide for themselves whether or not they ought morally to obey statutes, judicial decisions, or other official directives. But it does not follow that a citizen has any legal authority to declare those statutes, decisions, or directives invalid.

Allan suggests that this does follow. His interpretation of the rule of law 'places ultimate responsibility on each individual, taking account of political morality as he understands it, to determine finally for himself what the law requires'.[123] If a citizen disagrees with a judicial decision, 'only judicial arrogance' would insist on 'identifying the content of legal duties with judicial pronouncements'.[124] '[I]t does not follow that the [citizen's] legal obligation is necessarily to be identified with the court's account of it.'[125] The citizen might be right in believing that his interpretation of the law is more accurate than the court's.[126] Moreover, 'a citizen is *legally entitled*, and morally bound, to act on the basis of his own best understanding of what the law requires. . . . Even . . . resistance to decisions of the highest court of appeal may be morally (*and legally*) justified'.[127]

---

[122] *Eakin v Raub* (1825) 12 Sergeant and Rawles (Pa.) 330, 356.   [123] Allan (1993: 120).
[124] ibid. 111.   [125] ibid. 114.   [126] ibid. 113–19.   [127] ibid. 125, my emphasis.

Allan is to be commended for his consistency. He maintains not only that the courts might be legally entitled to disregard statutes that they believe are unlawful, but also that citizens might be legally entitled to disregard judicial decisions that they believe are unlawful. But this makes him vulnerable to the objection that, since he is clearly wrong about citizens, he is probably wrong about courts as well.

No legal system could function effectively if judicial decisions concerning citizens' legal obligations were no more legally authoritative than the opinions of the citizens themselves. Consider a judicial decision regarded by a citizen as legally erroneous. Allan says that the citizen might be legally, and not just morally, justified in resisting the decision. But if so, then the judges would not be legally justified in ordering bailiffs or police officers to enforce it, and if they did, those officials would be legally bound to defy them and to defend the citizen. Moreover, in the absence of some higher, more authoritative, decision-maker, everyone concerned would have to be guided by their own judgments of the legal issues involved. Citizens' and officials' legal obligations would be as interminably debatable as their moral obligations, and there would be as many equally authoritative opinions as there are citizens and officials, many of them inconsistent with one another. The law would be indistinguishable from anarchy: instead of their legal disagreements being authoritatively resolved by judges, citizens and officials would be left to fight them out in the streets.

Anarchy can only be avoided if some officials have legal authority superior to that of others, and citizens, to decide what legally ought to be done, an authority sufficient to make their decisions, rather than dissenting opinions, legally enforceable. Allan concedes that 'as a practical matter, the courts will have the last word', in the sense that their opinions will be enforced, and that perhaps 'for practical purposes all must (ultimately) submit to the court's authority'.[128] But there can be no justification for judicial decisions being routinely enforced, rather than the contrary opinions of dissenting citizens, unless the former are legally more authoritative than the latter. Citizens and subordinate officials may rightly believe a particular decision to be wrong—perhaps even so wrong that it morally ought not to be obeyed—but that cannot affect its legal authority. From their point of view, there is necessarily a conceptual difference between the requirements of law and those of morality. But if so, then it is also possible for a legislature to have a decision-making authority superior to that of judges, in which case there is a conceptual difference between legal and moral requirements from their point of view as well.

It might be objected that there is a difference between judges, on the one hand, and bailiffs, police officers, and prison warders, on the other. Judges are recognized by law as having authority to decide what the law is, whereas those other officials are not. But to make that argument would be to concede that the

[128] ibid. 111 and 117.

crucial question is what legal authority particular officials have. It is true that British judges have authority to declare what the law is, and this includes much greater authority than most other officials, or citizens, have, to change the law according to their moral convictions. In common law cases, for example, judges in superior courts have considerable authority to do so. It is also true that judges are often able to exceed their authority, and change the law while pretending not to. But their legal authority to change the law is not unlimited. Because they are bound by the doctrine of parliamentary sovereignty, judges do not have legal authority to decide that statutes are invalid on the ground that they are unjust or undemocratic. That judges might be morally bound to disobey a statute, in an extraordinary case, does not alter that fact. In deciding whether or not they are morally justified in obeying legally valid statutes, they merely do what every government official, and citizen, must necessarily do.[129]

Michael Detmold rightly insists that judging is a practical rather than a theoretical activity. Its object is not the advancement of knowledge of the law for its own sake, but the termination of disputes, by deciding what the disputants ought to have done, and requiring them to rectify any wrongdoing.[130] But all legal officials, from the highest to the lowest, are engaged in practical rather than theoretical activities. Judges may order people to be imprisoned, but court bailiffs, police officers, and prison warders carry out their orders. The practical nature of the judges' decisions does not entail that they necessarily have ultimate decision-making authority, any more than the practical nature of other legal officials' decisions entails that they have it. A legal system is ultimately based on an allocation of decision-making authority, whereby some officials are authorized to enunciate rules or principles to govern the practical reasoning of other officials, and citizens. The practical reasoning of those other officials is guided by theoretical reasoning aimed at identifying, interpreting, and applying those rules and principles in a consistent fashion. Which officials have ultimate authority within the system to enunciate those rules and principles is a contingent question, which depends on agreement among the most senior officials. But whoever they are, the system cannot function effectively unless their legal authority to do so is accepted by other officials, be they bailiffs or judges. From the point of view of those other officials, as well as citizens, there is necessarily a difference between legal and moral obligation.

Questions of legal validity are ultimately determined, not by the moral convictions of judges alone, but by rules or principles that are necessarily accepted

[129] Detmold distinguishes judges from bureaucrats on the ground that democracy requires the latter to be 'bound not by reason, but by the will of the government' (Detmold 1985: 231–2). But elsewhere he says that no human being can submit to the will of another except as his reason determines, or, in other words, escape 'the ultimate sovereignty of his own reason': Detmold (1989a: 95 and 109); see also (1985: 239). It follows that bureaucrats, no less than judges, must decide for themselves whether they should obey the legislature.

[130] This is the most fundamental point made in all of Detmold's jurisprudential writings: see Detmold (1984: 198; 1985: ch. 14; 1989a: 94; 1989b).

by senior legal officials collectively. The creation and maintenance of law depends on there being a consensus, at least among senior officials, concerning the most fundamental rules that allocate decision-making authority. Compromise is required to sustain such a consensus: it cannot be perfectly consistent with every individual official's opinion concerning the morally ideal allocation of authority. Individuals who find the consequences of that consensus morally unacceptable, either in general or in a particular instance, can refuse to help implement it. They can refuse to accept appointment to legal office, or if they have already done so, they can either resign, or refuse to apply a particular, abhorrent law. If a sufficient number of officials were to refuse to obey laws, the consensus that constitutes the fundamental rules of the system might be destroyed, and the constitution dissolved. Nevertheless, no official can truthfully say that the legal validity of laws is determined by his or her personal moral ideals, rather than by rules or principles established by general consensus.[131] That is why, from the point of view of individual officials as well as citizens, legal validity differs from moral validity.

It must be conceded that if, in an extreme case, judges were morally justified in disobeying an evil statute, they might also be morally justified in pretending that the statute was legally invalid. This is because any means of resisting tyranny, including lying about the law, might be justified. Moreover, if the judges were to help defeat a tyrannical legislature by lying about its legal authority, they might in the process change the rule of recognition underlying their legal system, and their lie might become true. But it would not follow that it was true all along.

The maxim 'hard cases make bad law' can be used to reinforce this argument. The meaning of the maxim is that legal rules should be framed with ordinary rather than extraordinary cases in mind, because it is better to achieve satisfactory results in the vast majority of cases that are likely to arise, even at the risk of unsatisfactory decisions in a small number of very unlikely cases (the 'hard' cases), rather than vice versa.[132] It may not be possible to qualify a rule, so that it could achieve satisfactory results in those unlikely cases, without damaging its actual results in many other cases.

Consider a rule prohibiting police from torturing suspected criminals. In almost all conceivable cases such a rule is preferable to one that permits the torture of suspects. But a hard case might arise if the police captured a terrorist whom they knew had hidden a nuclear weapon, set to explode within an hour, in a major city. They might be morally justified in torturing him, in order to prevent the deaths of millions of innocent people. But it does not follow that the rule should be amended, to authorize the police to torture suspects in emergency

---

[131] The argument in Goldsworthy (1990) is flawed in that it erroneously suggests that legal validity depends on the moral convictions of the judiciary, rather than on rules or principles endorsed by senior legal officials in general.

[132] In this context, the term 'hard cases' does not have the same meaning it has in the debate between Hart and Dworkin: see the text to nn. 43–4, above.

situations. Such an amendment would be extremely undesirable, because of the danger that the police would interpret that authority too broadly, and inflict torture when it was unjustified. That some action might be morally justified in an extraordinary emergency does not entail that a legal rule authorizing that action is justified.[133]

Another example of the same principle concerns the ability of juries to acquit defendants who have clearly violated a law, if the jurors believe that law to be unjust.[134] Their ability in effect to nullify the law is often applauded as an important safeguard against tyrannical laws or oppressive prosecutions, and there are many historical examples of its use for those purposes. This example differs from that of police torture, in that the law provides no means for reviewing or remedying a jury's decision to nullify a law. But it does not follow that juries have, let alone that they should be told that they have, any legal right to do so. In the United States, the courts have refused to require judges to instruct juries, or even to permit counsel to advise them, that they have the ability to nullify a law. To the contrary, juries are routinely instructed that they are required to follow the directions of the trial judge on questions of law. This is explicitly because of the fear that if juries were instructed that they had a right to nullify the law, they might make excessive use of it, thereby damaging both the rule of law and democratic decision-making.[135] As the Court of Appeals has explained, '[t]he danger of articulating discretion to depart from a rule, [is] that the breach will be more often and casually invoked'.[136] 'The jury system provides flexibility for the consideration of interests of justice outside the formal rules of law. . . . But it is subject to the overriding consideration that what is tolerable or even desirable as an informal, self-initiated exception, harbors grave dangers to the system if it is opened to expansion and intensification through incorporation in the judge's instruction.'[137] 'What makes for health as an occasional medicine would be disastrous as a daily diet.'[138] The courts have therefore achieved an equilibrium 'with the jury acting as a "safety valve" for exceptional cases, without being a wildcat or runaway institution'.[139]

This reasoning is very similar to that of eighteenth century lawyers, who conceded that resistance to unjust laws might be a legitimate weapon of last resort in extraordinary cases, but warned against recognizing the existence of a legal right of resistance on the ground that it would invite anarchy.[140] As Josiah Tucker put it, 'the English constitution does not point out those [extraordinary] cases, for fear mankind should make a bad use of such an interpretation . . . [and] deem

---

[133] Detmold (1984: 217–18) draws this distinction very clearly; but for criticism of his use of it, see Goldsworthy (1986: 15–17).
[134] Allan (1993: 118–20) attempts to use this example to support his theory.
[135] For a very recent discussion of US case law, see Crispo *et al.* (1997).
[136] *United States v Dougherty* (1972) 473 F.2d 1113, 1135.   [137] ibid. 1137.
[138] ibid. 1136.   [139] ibid. 1134–6.   [140] See Chapter 7, Section 3, above.

that to be legal liberty, which in truth and reality is no better than . . . lawless anarchy'.[141]

For the same reason, judicial defiance of Parliament might be morally legitimate in an extraordinary case, but not something that should be recognized as lawful. This may be why, even when British judges are suspected of disobeying Parliament, they do not do so openly.[142] The consequences of the doctrine of parliamentary sovereignty are generally beneficial: democratic decision-making is facilitated, and reasonably just statutes are enacted. Unjust statutes are sometimes enacted, but they are rarely obviously and egregiously unjust. Occasional injustice is a price that must be paid for democracy—as indeed for any decision-making procedure, since none can be guaranteed never to produce unjust laws. It is possible to imagine 'hard cases', involving statutes so outrageously unjust that morally they ought not to be obeyed, even by judges. But it does not follow that the doctrine of parliamentary sovereignty ought to be abandoned, and the judges authorized to invalidate outrageously unjust statutes. They might interpret that authority too broadly, and invalidate statutes that are not outrageously unjust. Chief Justice Gibson of Pennsylvania recognized this. Although he argued that judges might be justified in using their judicial powers to help the citizenry resist a truly 'monstrous' injustice, he denied that this proved that judges possessed legal authority to invalidate legislation on a regular basis.[143] What judges might be morally entitled or even bound to do in an extraordinary emergency may differ from what they should be legally authorized to do. As Sir Matthew Hale explained, 'the method and modelling of governments are to be fitted to what is the common and ordinary state of things . . . [a]nd it is a madness to think that the model of laws or government is to be framed according to such circumstances as very rarely occur'.[144]

In a healthy democratic society, cases of clear and extreme injustice are rare; in most cases, whether or not a law violates some basic right is open to reasonable arguments on both sides. The whole point of having a democracy is that in these debatable cases the opinion of the majority rather than of an unelected élite is supposed to prevail.[145] The price that must be paid for giving judges authority to invalidate a few laws that are clearly unjust or undemocratic is that they must also be given authority to overrule the democratic process in a much larger number of cases where the requirements of justice or democracy are debatable. The danger of excessive judicial interference with democratic decision-making might be worse than that of parliamentary tyranny, given the relative probabilities of their actually occurring.[146]

---

[141] Tucker (1781: 421–2).   [142] See Section 5, above.

[143] *Eakin v Raub* (1825) 12 Sergeant and Rawles (Pa.) 330, 356.   [144] Hale (1924: 512).

[145] For a very powerful argument to this effect, see Waldron (1993).

[146] 'The actual Constitution does not forbid every ghastly hypothetical law, and once you begin to invent doctrine that does, you will create an unconfinable judicial power' (Bork 1990: 234).

An additional consideration is that it is unlikely that a judicial declaration of invalidity would be effective in extreme situations such as those imagined by Mann and Allan.[147] As Lord Irvine has suggested, a government determined to enact evil laws could probably be defeated only on the political battlefield, and not in the courts: it is 'romanticism to believe that a judicial decision could hold back what would, in substance, be a revolution'.[148] A government and Parliament prepared to flout minimum standards of justice or democracy are unlikely to have sufficient respect for the rule of law to meekly submit to judicial correction. They are more likely to use their powers to appoint, dismiss, and threaten judges, in order to reduce them to submission. The argument from extreme cases is therefore open to the further objection that in those cases, the proposed remedy of judicial invalidation would probably be useless anyway.

Allan is therefore wrong to say that the question is '[w]hether or not judicial allegiance to statute would be justified in extreme or unusual situations'.[149] That is an easy question, and the answer is that it would not be justified. But it does not follow that the law should recognize that the courts have authority to invalidate statutes. Nor does it follow that the law already recognizes that they have such authority. Allan concedes that the doctrine of parliamentary sovereignty 'expresses a conclusion of political principle which sufficiently captures the (legal and political) duty of the courts for most practical purposes'.[150] 'In almost all likely circumstances' the judges' commitment to democracy 'will demand respect for the legislative measures adopted by Parliament as the representative assembly'.[151] Other critics of the doctrine agree.[152] But if so, the real question is whether the judiciary should claim a legal authority that will undermine democratic decision-making in many cases that are certain to arise, in order to provide a remedy for extreme situations that are very unlikely to arise, and which would probably be useless if they did.

It can reasonably be argued, given their record in the United States, that judges are almost certain to interpret such an authority too broadly. Even in the interpretation of a written constitution, as case after case is decided, a vast coral reef of judicial interpretation gradually accumulates around provisions limiting legislative power. Each decision may extend the judges' authority only slightly, but the eventual cumulative effect is a massive expansion far beyond what was originally intended. For entirely understandable reasons, the temptation to stretch their authority to remedy what they perceive to be injustice can be 'more than judicial flesh and blood' can withstand.[153] If this a problem when judges enforce a written Bill of Rights, it could be much worse if they were to enforce unwritten common law rights, which they themselves could identify and define, on a case

---

[147] See text to nn.103–4, above.   [148] Irvine of Lairg (1996a: 77).
[149] Allan (1993: 286).   [150] ibid.   [151] ibid. 282; see also ibid. 130.
[152] Lord Woolf of Barnes, *Parliamentary Debates, Fifth Series*, vol. 572, House of Lords, 5 June 1996, col. 1273, and Brookfield (1995: 56).
[153] Wade and Forsyth (1994: 306).

by case basis. Even if they attempted to invalidate only obviously unreasonable or irrational legislation, they would almost certainly interpret those vague concepts broadly. They would do so with the best of intentions, and not for self-interested or other base motives. There is a powerful temptation to reject as not only mistaken, but clearly mistaken and therefore unreasonable, value judgments that differ from one's own. This is especially true of judges who, by virtue of their position, symbols of office, and unchallenged authority, are constantly exposed to 'the intoxicating notion that they may be wiser, more dispassionate and sure-footed than their fellow men'.[154]

Allan and Detmold deny that it is possible to state in advance of actual cases the appropriate limits to Parliament's legitimate authority. 'Since future events are unknown, the constitutional limits to legislative power cannot be definitively stated. They remain to be refined and tested in future instances.'[155] Allan brushes aside the difficulties that would be faced by judges determining those limits, on the ground that such difficulties 'are the ordinary concerns of common law adjudication'.[156] But there are many situations in which clear rules are desirable, even though future events cannot be known. A clear and definite rule on some question may be worthwhile, even though it might turn out to have undesirable consequences in very unlikely future circumstances. It may be much better than leaving the matter to the vagaries of common law adjudication. With respect to who should have ultimate authority to decide controversies concerning competing moral principles, the best clear rule may be the doctrine of parliamentary sovereignty.

It follows that the doctrine of parliamentary sovereignty is not irrational. To the contrary, the principles of political morality underlying it are arguably preferable to those that Allan prefers. This is because, in some communities, a legal system in which unelected judges have authority to invalidate statutes, on the basis of their own assessment of abstract and controversial principles of political morality, may be morally inferior to a system in which a democratically elected legislature has ultimate authority to decide what those principles require. Be that as it may, the doctrine is vindicated even by Dworkin's theory of law, because the principles preferred by Allan are inconsistent with the practice of British legal officials. It is worth repeating that a genuine interpretation of a legal practice must be guided, not by principles external to the practice that are endorsed by the interpreter, but by internal principles that are accepted by legal officials collectively.[157] Adapting Dworkin's words to the British context, the principle of integrity in law requires that judges 'must not deploy moral principles, no matter how much they are personally committed to such principles, that cannot be defended as consistent with the general history of past . . . decisions and the general structure of . . . political practice'.[158] 'Judges must defer to general, settled understandings about the character of the power the [c]onstitution assigns them';

---

[154] McCluskey (1987: 1).   [155] Allan (1993: 270), Detmold (1996: 48).
[156] Allan (1993: 76).   [157] See text to n. 83, above.   [158] Dworkin (1996: 319).

they must 'find the best conception of constitutional moral principles . . . that fits the broad story of [Britain's] historical record'.[159] Allan's theory is inconsistent with that general structure and historical record.[160]

8. Further Arguments

Michael Detmold has put forward further arguments to show that judges necessarily have authority to invalidate statutes. I have left these until now because, in assessing them, it is useful to draw upon some of the main points previously made.

Detmold rejects what he concedes is the 'conventional' opinion, that 'the absolutely fundamental law' in Britain is 'the law of Parliament', and in Australia, 'the law of the constitution'. He argues that in both cases the fundamental law is, instead, 'the decisions of superior courts'—'the law of the courts'.[161] One reason for this is that the superior courts have 'self-validating jurisdictional power', which is power to determine the extent of their own jurisdictions. This means that if they judge that they have jurisdiction to make a decision, that judgment is binding on other officials even if it is wrong.[162] It follows that their decisions are legally valid even if made in excess of jurisdiction, until such time as the law is changed, and therefore at any particular moment they constitute 'the ultimate point in the legal system'.[163]

Now, it is true that a decision of a superior court that exceeds its jurisdiction is usually regarded as legally valid and binding, unless and until it is set aside by a higher court. It follows that if the supreme court itself exceeds its jurisdiction, the legal validity of its decision cannot be authoritatively impugned. This is partly because there is, by definition, no higher court that can enforce the limits to its jurisdiction. For the practical reasons previously explained, the supreme court must be trusted voluntarily to comply with those limits.[164] If lower courts, or other legal officials, were at liberty to ignore its decisions on the ground that they were in excess of jurisdiction, then as Detmold puts it, 'there would be no settled foundation of . . . law'.[165] 'Only when the question has been decided by an institution with a self-validating jurisdictional power . . . is there complete finality, a complete foundation of law'.[166]

But while other legal officials usually take this view if they believe that a superior court has made an error, despite conscientiously attempting to comply

---

[159] ibid. 11.   [160] See Craig (1993: 327).
[161] Detmold (1989a: 93).   [162] ibid. 14, 19, and 27–8.
[163] ibid. 93. By 'jurisdiction' I mean what Detmold calls 'jurisdiction as office', as opposed to 'jurisdiction as power': see ibid. 11–29.
[164] See text to nn. 92–3 and 110–11.   [165] Detmold (1989a: 90).
[166] ibid. 104. In this respect, Detmold's position is somewhat similar to mine, although he believes that 'self-validating jurisdictional power' can belong only to superior courts, and not to legislatures: ibid. 106. Also, he regards this as a matter of logical necessity, whereas I do not.

with the limits to its jurisdiction, they might not do so if they believed that the court had deliberately and egregiously violated those limits. In that case, they might think that the court itself had undermined the settled foundations of law, and ought to be resisted even at the risk of further undermining them. That was the reaction of many members of the House of Commons, after the Court of Queen's Bench in *Stockdale v Hansard* rejected the House's claim that the defendant was protected by parliamentary privilege, of which the House itself was the only competent judge.[167] The Attorney-General, Sir John Campbell, asserted that 'if this was an unlawful judgment it should be resisted by all possible means', and later that it 'was totally contrary to law . . . and a flagrant usurpation of power by the Court of Queen's Bench'.[168]

Nevertheless, it is extremely difficult to overturn the decisions of a supreme court that violates the trust reposed in it. For example, if British judges, contrary to the doctrine of parliamentary sovereignty, were to hold a statute invalid, Parliament might be unable to overturn their decision merely by enacting a further statute, because they might hold that statute to be invalid too. Parliament might have to demand that the judges be dismissed, and replaced with more compliant ones willing to overrule their predecessors' decision.

But it does not follow that the fundamental law of any legal system consists of the decisions of its supreme court. To describe them as fundamental law because they are not subject to appeal or review is to commit the logical fallacy of confusing finality with either infallibility or omnipotence.[169] Detmold concedes that the jurisdiction of a supreme court can be limited, and if it is, the law that limits it is surely more fundamental than the court's decisions. The 'conventional view' would therefore seem to be correct: that in Australia, that more fundamental law is 'the law of the constitution', and in Britain, 'the law of Parliament'.[170]

Detmold appears to believe that because law is essentially a practical, rather than a theoretical, enterprise—concerned with how people are obligated to act —the important question is what is fundamental law for practical, rather than theoretical, purposes. And since a supreme court's decisions are legally valid, even if they exceed its jurisdiction, then for the practical purpose of how people are obligated to act they are the fundamental law.[171] But this is wrong. He concedes that such a court is required to endeavour conscientiously to abide by the limits to its jurisdiction: it cannot legitimately take the view that because its decisions will be recognized as valid even if it does not, it is at liberty to ignore those limits.[172] If so, then from its point of view, those limits are of crucial practical, and not merely theoretical, importance. Perhaps from other points of view,

---

[167] (1839) 9 Ad. and E. 1; 112 E.R. 1112.
[168] *The Parliamentary Debates (Hansard)*, 3rd Ser., vol. 48, 362 and 365–6 (17 June 1839). The defendant could have appealed to the House of Lords, but the House of Commons also objected to the Lords being the ultimate judges of its privileges.
[169] Hart (1961: 138–44). See also Chapter 2, text to n. 18, above.
[170] See n. 161, above.   [171] Detmold (1989a: 94, and 104–7).   [172] ibid. 26.

the law, for practical purposes, is whatever the supreme court says it is. But from the court's own point of view, it is not: the court itself is bound to regard the law that limits its jurisdiction as more fundamental than its own decisions. And how can a court's decisions be truly fundamental if the court itself is bound to think otherwise?

Detmold does not need to rely on this dubious argument, based on superior courts' decisions being valid even if they are in excess of jurisdiction. This is because he believes that superior courts have jurisdiction to invalidate legislation (or even, in Australia, a constitutional amendment) that violates the fundamental right of individuals to 'equal respect'.[173] On this view, a superior court that invalidates such legislation does not make a decision that is valid notwithstanding that it is erroneous. Its decision is legally correct as well as valid.

One of Detmold's arguments is that legislation is a matter of will, the common law is a matter of reason, and reason is necessarily superior to will.[174] 'Reason is always ultimate over will', because whether or not one should submit to someone else's will is inescapably a question to be decided by one's own reason.[175] Therefore 'reason is ultimate over any sovereign', and 'this establishes the power of judicial review in the court, for reason is the province of the court and will is the province of the parliament'.[176] 'It is this logical status of reason which establishes that the judicial power (or the process of the common law) is the ultimate foundation of a commonwealth.'[177]

There are at least two problems with this argument. One is that, as Detmold concedes, statutes are enacted for reasons, and are therefore 'matters of reason' in at least one sense of the term.[178] Legislators pass laws requiring people to behave in certain ways for the same reason that judges at common law order people to behave in certain ways: because they believe that those people ought to do so.[179] At one point, Detmold argues that the 'critical thing . . . is that a court, though not a parliament, is bound by reason'.[180] But he surely cannot mean this. No one is entitled to act contrary to reason. He has since insisted that legislation is subject to the requirement that it must not discriminate between people unless there is a rational ground—something recognizable as a reason—for doing so. So parliaments are bound by reason after all.[181]

The second problem is that judicial decisions, like statutes, are 'matters of will' in so far as they are binding on other legal officials who disagree with the

[173] Detmold (1996). Detmold previously argued that the most fundamental right was 'radical autonomy' (Detmold 1989a: 1–2, 5, and 102–10). That change of mind does not affect my disagreement with him.
[174] Detmold (1985: 199, 230–6, 239; and 1989b: 440).
[175] Detmold (1985: 239, 256; and 1989a: 95).
[176] Detmold (1985: 256, 239, respectively).   [177] ibid. 257.
[178] Detmold (1989b: 441).
[179] Or at least, legislators ought to pass laws only for that reason, but again, the same is true of judges making orders.
[180] Detmold (1985: 241, 230–1).   [181] Detmold (1996: 43).

reasoning behind them. Detmold seems to recognize this when he concedes that a court's judgment for the plaintiff 'has the status of a legitimate act of will' because 'if it merely had the status of reason the defendant might for ever contest it'.[182] The same is true of the ratio, or reason, for the court's judgment, which necessarily transcends the particular parties in question. This constitutes a rule or principle binding on lower courts in subsequent cases of the same kind—that is, cases that cannot be rationally distinguished—even if those courts believe that the ratio was wrong.[183] In Detmold's terminology, the common law is not pure, self-executing reason, but 'instituted reason'. Its 'particular doctrines' are 'particular decisions of reason . . . attributable to the will of their authors, and in so far as they are argued to be legally significant by virtue of their being instituted (willed), their legitimacy must be in issue'.[184]

Both statute law and common law are therefore 'instituted reason'. Both result from the reasoning of their makers, and both are binding on other officials (including judges) even if they disagree with that reasoning.[185] It is true that people should accept decisions they disagree with only if they believe that there are good reasons for doing so. It follows that judges should obey statutes only if they believe that there are good reasons for doing so. But then, legislators and other officials should obey judicial decisions only if they believe that there are good reasons for doing so. It does not follow either that those officials have legal authority to invalidate judicial decisions, or that judges have legal authority to invalidate statutes. There is no logical or practical necessity that the instituted reason of judges must be legally superior to the instituted reason of legislators. It is therefore question-begging to equate, as Detmold does, 'reason' with 'the common law' and 'judicial power'.[186] Whose 'instituted reason' is supreme within a legal system is determined by agreement among all those whose acceptance of its authority is essential to maintaining it. In Britain, the 'reason of the community' was traditionally thought to be most authoritatively expressed by Parliament.[187] '[P]ublic reason', said John Milton, is 'enacted reason in a free Parliament'.[188]

Detmold also argues that there is a crucial distinction between a court refusing to apply a statute on the ground that the statute is unreasonable, and its

---

[182] Detmold (1985: 241).

[183] Detmold disagrees with this. He maintains that the only part of a court's judgment that is authoritatively binding is its settlement of the particular dispute in question: no general rule or principle expressly or implicitly laid down in the course of that settlement can bind subsequent courts (Detmold 1989b: 449–50). But the orthodox view is that a judgment lays down a rule or principle that is binding on inferior courts in all cases of the same kind (i.e. that cannot be rationally distinguished). In technical terms, Detmold accepts the principle of *res judicata* but not that of *stare decisis*.

[184] Detmold (1985: 199–200).

[185] Detmold (1989b: 445) claims that a judicial precedent is 'intrinsically reasonful', and 'is liable to be overruled or not followed (void or null) by virtue of its lack of reason'. But a judicial precedent cannot be overruled or not followed by a lower court in a case of the same kind (one that is not rationally distinguishable), and so to that extent it is like a statute.

[186] Detmold (1985: 199, 256).   [187] See Chapter 5, esp. Sections 3 and 4, above.

[188] J. Milton, *Eikonoklastes*, in Milton (1953–82: iii. 360).

refusing to do so on the ground that its applying the statute would be unreasonable. This is because for various reasons (stability, democracy, and so on) it is not necessarily unreasonable for a court to apply a statute that is unreasonable.[189] Detmold concedes that the legislature has authority to decide what statutes it is reasonable to enact, but insists that the judiciary necessarily has authority to decide what statutes it is reasonable for it to apply. If a court were to refuse to apply a statute on the ground that the statute was unreasonable, it would be usurping the authority of the legislature. But if it were to refuse to do so on the ground that it would be unreasonable for it to apply the statute, it would be deciding a question that only it can, and indeed must, decide.[190] Detmold goes so far as to claim that because these two decisions are different, a judicial decision that it would be unreasonable for it to apply a statute would 'not in any sense challenge the legislative decision' to enact the statute.[191] The court would be deciding a question that Parliament itself had not decided.[192] This suggests that it should not lead to any conflict between the two branches of government.

But there are at least two problems with this argument. First, the difference between the two kinds of decisions would usually be one of degree, not kind. A decision that it would be unreasonable to apply a statute is most likely to be based on a judgment that the statute is so extraordinarily unreasonable (either in general or in its application to a particular group of individuals) that the usual reasons for applying even an unreasonable statute are overridden. Therefore, such a decision would be inconsistent with the legislature's decision that the statute was a reasonable one to enact, and could provoke conflict between the two branches. Secondly, although it is true that judges must necessarily decide whether or not it is reasonable for them to apply a statute, it does not follow that they have legal authority to refuse to do so, for the reason explained on the previous page. Whether or not they have legal authority to do so is determined, not by their decisions alone, but by general agreement among the most senior legal officials of the legal system.

Another of Detmold's arguments is that the foundation of law is the right of every individual to be treated as an autonomous moral agent, that no legislature can 'speak for' or have 'constitutional responsibility for' that right, and therefore that it is the function of the courts to do so.[193] It follows that legislatures deal with the good of the community as a whole, and courts with that most fundamental right of individuals.[194] This is because that right is logically 'prior to the conception of Parliament's power', in that it cannot be established by any legislative enactment: 'no written (legislated) statement of power, can ever

[189] Detmold (1989*a*: 101).   [190] ibid. 1989*a*: 101; and 1989*b*: 445.
[191] Detmold (1989*a*: 101).   [192] ibid. 106. See also Detmold (1989*b*: 453).
[193] Detmold (1989*a*: 1–2, 103, and 6). Detmold (1996) now describes this fundamental right as a constitutional right to 'equal respect', rather than a human right to 'radical autonomy', but this presumably does not affect the argument discussed in the text.
[194] Detmold (1989*a*: 5 and 102).

be the fundamental source of the protection of human rights'.[195] But the most fundamental rights of individuals are also logically prior to the authority of the judiciary, in the sense that they cannot be established by any judicial decision. So this consideration by itself fails to establish the distinction that Detmold seeks to draw between legislative and judicial functions.

He also argues that the most fundamental difference between those functions is that 'legislation deals in universals (classes of cases) whilst adjudication decides particular cases'. He claims that '[u]niversals do not contain particulars', and therefore that '(universal) legislation is not the decision of all its (contained?) particular cases'. No matter how carefully a universal is defined, whether or not a particular case 'comes within' it is necessarily a further question that must be decided by a court.[196] Therefore, a judicial decision that a statute should not be applied in a particular case cannot conflict with Parliament's decision in enacting the statute. 'Parliament has only decided the (universal) rule . . . it has not decided the particular case'.[197] But this is puzzling. It is true that, in enacting a universal rule, Parliament might overlook or fail to foresee a legitimate objection to its application in some particular case, and on that ground, a court might reasonably hold that Parliament could not have intended it to be applied in that case, which is excepted from the rule by implication.[198] But otherwise, it is difficult to understand why, if a universal is a 'class of cases', all the cases that belong to the class do not automatically, without the need for any judicial decision, 'come within' it. Moreover, it is difficult to make any sense of what Parliament is doing, in enacting a universal rule, if it is not declaring that, subject to implied exceptions, the rule should be applied in all the particular cases that come within its terms.

9. The Alleged Necessity of Judicially Enforceable Constitutional Rights

Why is the doctrine of parliamentary sovereignty now being subjected to these criticisms? It may be because the United States model of judicial review has become so influential that many people believe it is not only desirable, but essential, for the preservation of human rights and democracy. It is not clear why this belief has lately become so prevalent, since there is little if any evidence that the United States is a more just and democratic society than other Western nations whose constitutions do not include judicial review.[199] As Robert Dahl has observed:

No one has shown that countries like the Netherlands and New Zealand, which lack judicial review, or Norway and Sweden, where it is exercised rarely and in highly restrained

---

[195] ibid. 5.　　[196] ibid. 101–2. See also Detmold (1989*b*: 454–63).

[197] Detmold (1989*a*: 106).　　[198] See text to nn.77–8, above.

[199] For an interesting comparison of the United States and Britain in this respect, see Lazare (1996: ch. 9).

fashion, or Switzerland, where it can be applied only to cantonal legislation, are less democratic than the United States, nor, I think, could one reasonably do so.[200]

Nevertheless, the assumption that it is essential for courts to have ultimate legal
authority to protect democratic and other rights has become commonplace in legal
discourse. Sir John Laws, for example, argues that '[i]t is a condition of democracy's preservation that the power of a democratically elected government—or
Parliament—be not absolute. The institution of free and regular elections, like
fundamental rights, has to be vindicated by a higher-order law.'[201] Recent decisions of the High Court of Australia, purporting to discover an implied freedom
of political speech in the federal Constitution, are based on the same assumption. The judges argued at length that freedom of political speech is essential to
representative democracy, which is true, but simply assumed that therefore judicial enforcement of the freedom is also essential, which is demonstrably false.
It is demonstrably false because Australia had an effective representative
democracy for nearly a century, as did Canada until 1982, and as many other
Western nations still do, in the absence of such a judicially enforceable freedom.[202]

Another reason for recent criticisms of parliamentary sovereignty is an
influential conception of the ideals of 'constitutionalism' and 'the rule of law'.
For some people, these ideals require legislative power to be subject to constitutional limits enforceable by an independent judiciary. Allan, for example,
insists that it is 'ultimately impossible to reconcile . . . the rule of law with the
unlimited sovereignty of Parliament . . . An insistence on there being a source of
ultimate political authority, which is free from all legal restraint . . . is incompatible with constitutionalism'.[203] And Sir John Laws insists that 'the need for a
higher-order law is dictated by the logic of the very notion of a government under
law'; it would be 'self-contradictory' for Britain to have no higher-order law,
'unless we are to say that the power of Parliament is not legal power at all'.[204]

But it is question-begging to assume that a constitution such as Britain's, so
deeply rooted in tradition, necessarily conforms to contemporary understandings
of a priori principles, especially when those understandings are inspired by the
United States model of government, which was a radical departure from British
tradition.[205] Moreover, if 'the rule of law' required that the authority of every
institution be subject to legal limits enforceable by some other institution, it would
be a chimerical ideal that could never be realized in practice. As we have seen,
in any legal system, at least one institution must ultimately be trusted to adhere
to whatever principles are believed to limit its authority.[206] Moreover, those principles must be abstract and flexible, to ensure that government can respond appro-
priately to all the exigencies of changing circumstances. That is why a judicially

---

[200] Dahl (1989: 189–91), emphasis added.   [201] Laws (1995: 85).
[202] For further discussion, see Goldsworthy (1997: 372–4).   [203] Allan (1993: 16).
[204] Laws (1995: 85 and 88).
[205] On the question-begging nature of this aspect of Allan's argument, see Winterton (1996: 136–7).
[206] See text to nn. 92–3, above.

enforceable Bill of Rights consists of abstract and flexible principles of political morality, whose 'interpretation' is indistinguishable from moral and political philosophy. It is not obvious that a judiciary, charged with weighing up and applying abstract moral principles in concrete cases, is any more bound by 'the rule of law' than is a sovereign legislature, responsible for translating the same moral principles into legislation. The judiciary may be better at making moral judgments, and therefore more trustworthy, but that is beside the present point. If in both cases decisions are governed by abstract moral principles, what reason is there to describe the judiciary, but not the legislature, as 'ruled by law'?

Judicial review of the validity of legislation is not an essential prerequisite for the protection of human rights and democracy in every legal system committed to those ideals. It may be essential in some, but not in all. This depends on the culture, social structure, and political organization in which each system operates. It can certainly be argued that in most legal systems judicial review would improve the protection of human rights and democracy. The question for countries such as the United Kingdom, Australia, and New Zealand, is whether or not it would be desirable for that reason. That question is currently being debated by those who favour, and those who oppose, the adoption of a judicially enforceable Bill of Rights. Although many of the arguments in this chapter bear on that important debate, they are not intended to resolve it: there is much more to be said on both sides.[207] This chapter is intended merely to defend the orthodox understanding that the doctrine of parliamentary sovereignty is currently part of the constitutional law of all three countries, albeit in a heavily modified form in Australia. If it were not, there would be no need to debate the merits of a Bill of Rights: judges would already have authority to invalidate legislation that they regard as inconsistent with fundamental rights. Since they do not already have that authority, proponents of judicial review must persuade us that they ought to. To give judges that authority would require a fundamental constitutional change in all three countries, which should be brought about by consensus, rather than judicial fiat. That is surely a requirement of democracy itself. I have argued in this chapter that it is also a requirement of law.

---

[207] See Goldsworthy (1992) for a contribution to that debate.

References

Note: EEB refers to the microfilm collection *Early English Books 1641–1700*, published by University Microfilm Inc., Ann Arbor, Michigan. References to works that I have read only on microfilm include the reel number.

ADDISON, J. (1716) (1979 edn.), *The Freeholder*, J. Leheny (ed.) (Oxford: Clarendon Press).
ALLAN, T. R. S. (1993), *Law, Liberty and Justice: The Legal Foundations of British Constitutionalism* (Oxford: Clarendon Press).
—— (1996), 'The Common Law as Constitution: Fundamental Rights and First Principles', in C. Saunders (ed.), *Courts of Final Jurisdiction: the Mason Court in Australia* (Sydney: Federation Press), 146–66.
—— (1997), 'Parliamentary Sovereignty: Law, Politics, and Revolution', *Law Quarterly Review*, 113: 443–52.
ALLEN, C. K. (1964), (7th edn.), *Law in the Making* (Oxford: Clarendon Press).
ALLEN, J. (1849) (2nd edn.), *Inquiry Into the Rise and Growth of the Royal Prerogative in England* (New York: Burt Franklin).
ALLEN, J. W. (1928) (rev. edn. 1957), *A History of Political Thought in the Sixteenth Century* (London: Methuen & Co.).
—— (1938), *English Political Thought 1603–1644* (London: Methuen).
ALLOTT, P. (1979), 'The Courts and Parliament: Who Whom?' *Cambridge Law Journal*, 38: 79–117.
AMOS, S. (1880), *Fifty Years of the English Constitution 1830–1880* (London: Longmans, Green & Co.).
An Exact Collection of all Remonstrances, Declarations [etc.] . . . and other Remarkable Passages between the King's most Excellent Majesty, and His High Court of Parliament (1643) (London: for Edward Husbands, T. Warren, R. Best).
ANDERSON, T. (1993), *Creating the Constitution: The Convention of 1787 and the First Congress* (Pennsylvania: Pennsylvania State University Press).
ANONYMOUS (1642a), *An Appendix to the late Answer, Printed by His Majesties Command, or, Some Seasonable Animadversions Upon the Late Observator* (London) (EEB Reel 1447: 22).
—— (1642b), *A Disclaimer and Answer of the Commons of England* (London: printed for G.M.) (EEB Reel 244: E. 100, no. 23).
—— (1642c), *England's Absolute Monarchy or Government of Great Britaine* (London: Thomas Bankes) (EEB Reel 245: E. 107, no. 3).
—— (1642d), *A Miracle: An Honest Broker* (London: s.n.) (EEB Reel 266: E. 246, no. 34).
—— (1642e), *Questions Resolved, and Propositions Tending to Accommodation Between the King and Both Houses of Parliament* (London: s.n.) (EEB Reel 247: E. 118, no. 38).
—— (1642f), *The Second Part of Vox Populi* (London: n.s.) (EEB Reel 248: E. 124, no. 34).
—— (1643), *The Subject of Supremacie* (London: Ben Allen) (EEB Reel 245: E. 106, no. 1).

Anonymous (1697), *A Letter to a Friend, in Vindication of the Proceedings Against Sir John Fenwick by Bill of Attainder* (London: Samuel Heyrick) (EEB Reel 766: 14).

Anson, W. R. (1886), 'The Government of Ireland Bill', *Law Quarterly Review*, 2: 427–43.

Anstey, T. (1867), 'On Blackstone's Theory of the Omnipotence of Parliament', *Juridical Society Papers*, 3: 305–38.

Arnold, M. S. (1977), 'Statutes As Judgments: The Natural Law Theory of Parliamentary Activity in Medieval England', *University of Pennsylvania Law Review*, 126: 329–43.

Ashcraft, R. (1986), *Revolutionary Politics and Locke's Two Treatises of Government* (Princeton: Princeton University Press).

Ashton, R. (1982), 'From Cavalier to Roundhead Tyranny, 1642–9', in Morrill (1982), 185–207.

—— (1989) (2nd edn.), *The English Civil War: Conservatism and Revolution* (London: Weidenfeld & Nicolson).

—— (1994), *Counter-Revolution: The Second Civil War and its Origins, 1646–8* (New Haven and London: Yale University Press).

Atiyah, P. S., and Summers, R. S. (1987), *Form and Substance in Anglo-American Law: A Comparative Study of Legal Reasoning, Legal Theory and Legal Institutions* (Oxford: Clarendon Press).

Atkins, R. (1689) (reprinted in 1973, London: Scholarly Resources Inc.), *The Power, Jurisdiction and Privilege of Parliament, and the Antiquity of the House of Commons Asserted* (London: Timothy Goodwin).

[Atterbury, F.] (1710), *The Voice of the People, No Voice of God* (n.p.).

Austin, J. (1954), *The Province of Jurisprudence Determined, and the Uses of the Study of Jurisprudence*, H. L. A. Hart (ed.) (London: Weidenfeld & Nicholson).

Bacon, F. (1858–74), *The Works of Francis Bacon*, J. Spedding, R. L. Ellis, and D. D. Heath (eds.) (London: Longman & Co.), 14 vols.

—— (1861–74), *The Letters and Life of Francis Bacon*, J. Spedding (ed.) (London: Longman & Co.), 7 vols. (vols. 8–14 of Bacon (1858–74)).

—— (1985), *The Essayes or Counsels, Civil and Moral*, Michael Kiernan (ed.) (Oxford: Clarendon Press).

Bagehot, W. (1964), *The English Constitution* (London: C. A. Watts & Co.).

Bailyn, B. (ed.) (1965), *Pamphlets of the American Revolution* (Cambridge, Mass.: The Belknapp Press of Harvard University Press).

—— (1967), *The Ideological Origins of the American Revolution* (Cambridge, Mass.: The Belknapp Press of Harvard University Press).

Bakan, J. (1992), 'Some Hard Questions About the Hard Cases Question', *University of Toronto Law Journal*, 42: 504–16.

Baker, J. H. (ed.) (1978), *The Reports of Sir John Spelman* (London: Selden Society), 2 vols.

—— (1990), (3rd edn.), *An Introduction to English Legal History* (London: Butterworths).

—— (ed.) (1994), *Reports from the Lost Notebooks of Sir James Dyer* (London: Selden Society), 2 vols.

Baumer, F. Le Van (1937) 'Christopher St. German', *American Historical Review*, 42: 631–51.

—— (1940) (reissued 1966, New York: Russell & Russell), *The Early Tudor Theory of Kingship* (New Haven: Yale University Press).

BAXTER, R. (1994), *A Holy Commonwealth*, W. Lamont (ed.) (Cambridge: Cambridge University Press).

BEER, S. H. (1993), *To Make A Nation: The Rediscovery of American Federalism* (Cambridge, Mass.: Harvard University Press).

BENNION, F. A. R. (1992) (2nd edn.), *Statutory Interpretation* (London: Butterworths).

BENTHAM, J. (1776) (new edn. 1988), *A Fragment on Government*, J. H. Burns and H. L. A. Hart (eds.) (Cambridge: Cambridge University Press).

—— (c.1782) (new edn. 1970), *Of Laws in General*, H. L. A. Hart (ed.), in *The Collected Works of Jeremy Bentham*, J. H. Burns (ed.) (London: The Athlone Press).

BERGER, R. (1969), 'Doctor Bonham's Case: Statutory Construction or Constitutional Theory?' *University of Pennsylvania Law Review*, 117: 521–45.

—— (1986), ' "Original Intention" in Historical Perspective', *George Washington Law Review*, 54: 296–337.

—— (1989), 'The Founders' Views—According to Jefferson Powell', *Texas Law Review*, 67: 1033–96.

BERTIE, W. (Earl of Abingdon) (1778), *Thoughts on the Letter of Edmund Burke, Esq., to the Sheriffs of Bristol, on the Affairs of America* (Oxford), reprinted in P. H. Smith (1972), 193–230.

BIGONGIARI, D. (ed.) (1953), *The Political Ideas of St. Thomas Aquinas* (New York: Hafner Publishing Company).

BLACK, A. (1988), 'The Conciliar Movement', in Burns (1988), 573–87.

BLACKALL, O. (1705), *The Subjects Duty: A Sermon*, 8 March 1704 (London: J. Leake).

BLACKSTONE, W. (1765), *Commentaries on the Laws of England, Book the First: The Rights of Persons* (Oxford: Clarendon Press).

BLYTHE, J. M. (1992), *Ideal Government and the Mixed Constitution in the Middle Ages* (Princeton: Princeton University Press).

BODIN, J. (1962) (reprint of 1606 translation), *The Six Books of the Commonweale*, K. D. McRae (ed.) (Cambridge, Mass.: Harvard University Press).

—— (1992), *On Sovereignty, Four Chapters from The Six Books of the Commonweale*, J. H. Franklin (ed. and trans.) (Cambridge: Cambridge University Press).

BOGDANOR, V. (1996), *Politics and the Constitution: Essays on British Government* (Aldershot, England: Dartmouth).

BORK, R. (1990), *The Tempting of America* (New York: Simon & Schuster).

BOUDIN, L. B. (1932), *Government By Judiciary, Vol. 1* (New York: Russell & Russell).

BOYER, A. D. (1997), ' "Understanding, Authority, and Will": Sir Edward Coke and the Elizabethan Origins of Judicial Review', *Boston College Law Review*, 39: 43–93.

BRACTON, H. de (1968–77), *De legibus et consuetudinibus angliae*, G. E. Woodbine (ed.), S. E. Thorne (trans.) (Cambridge, Mass.: Belknapp Press of Harvard University Press and Selden Society).

BRADLEY, A. W. (1989), 'The Sovereignty of Parliament—In Perpetuity?' in J. Jowell and D. Oliver (eds.), (2nd edn.), *The Changing Constitution* (Oxford: Clarendon Press), 25–52.

—— and EWING, K. D. (1997), (12th edn.), *Constitutional and Administrative Law* (London and New York: Longman).

BRAMHALL, J. (1643), *The Serpent-Salve, or, A Remedie for the Biting of an Aspe* (s.n.) (EEB Reel 15: 19).

BRAZIER, R. (1998) (2nd edn.), *Constitutional Reform: Reshaping the British Political System* (Oxford: Oxford University Press).

BREDVOLD, L. I., and Ross R. G. (eds.) (1960), *The Philosophy of Edmund Burke* (Ann Arbor: The University of Michigan Press).

BREWER-CARIAS, A. R. (1989), *Judicial Review in Comparative Law* (Cambridge: Cambridge University Press).

BROOKFIELD, F. M. (1995), 'Parliament, the Treaty, and Freedom—Millennial Hopes and Speculations', in P. A. Joseph, (ed.), *Essays on the Constitution* (Wellington: Broker's), 41–60.

BROUGHAM, H. (1830), 'Review of *Inquiry into the Rise and Growth of the Royal Prerogative in England*, by James Allen', *Edinburgh Review*, 52: 139–57.

BROWN, A. L. (1981), 'Parliament, 1377–1422', in Davies and Denton (1981), 109–40.

—— (1989), *The Governance of Late Medieval England 1272–1461* (London: Edward Arnold).

BROWNING, R. (1982), *Political and Constitutional Ideas of the Court Whigs* (Baton Rouge, La.: Louisiana State University Press).

'BRUTUS' (1787–8), *Essays of Brutus*, in H. J. Storing (ed.) (1981), *The Complete Anti-Federalist, Vol. 2* (Chicago: University of Chicago Press), 358–452.

BRYCE, J. (1889) (2nd edn.) *The American Commonwealth* (London: Macmillan).

BUCK, A. R. (1990), 'The Politics of Land Law in Tudor England, 1529–1540', *Journal of Legal History*, 11: 200–17.

BURGESS, G. (1992*a*), 'The Divine Right of Kings Reconsidered', *English Historical Review*, 107: 837–61.

—— (1992*b*), *The Politics of the Ancient Constitution: An Introduction to English Political Thought 1603–1642* (Basingstoke: Macmillan).

—— (1994), 'On Hobbesian Resistance Theory', *Political Studies*, 42: 62–83.

—— (1996), *Absolute Monarchy and the Stuart Constitution* (New Haven and London: Yale University Press).

BURKE, E. (1765), *Tracts Relating to the Popery Laws*, in Burke (1981–98), ix (1991), *The Revolutionary War 1794–1797 & Ireland*, R. B. McDowell (ed.), 434–82.

—— (1774), *Speech on American Taxation*, in Burke (1981–98), ii (1981), *Party, Parliament, and the American Crisis 1766–1774*, P. Langford (ed.), 406–63.

—— (1777), *Letter to the Sheriffs of Bristol*, in Burke (1981–98), iii (1996), *Party, Parliament, and the American War 1774–1780*, W. M. Elofson and J. A. Woods (eds.), 288–330.

—— (1788), *Speech on the Opening of the Impeachment of Warren Hastings*, in Burke (1981–98), vi (1991), *India, The Launching of the Hastings Impeachment, 1786–1788*, P. J. Marshall (ed.), 313–73.

—— (1981–98), *The Writings and Speeches of Edmund Burke*, P. Langford (general ed.), (Oxford: Clarendon Press).

BURN, R. (1763), *Ecclesiastical Law* (London: H. Woodfall & W. Strahan).

BURNET, G. (1897–1900), *A History of My Own Time, Part One, The Reign of Charles II*, O. Airy (ed.) (Oxford: Clarendon Press), 2 vols.

BURNS, J. H. (1962), 'Bolingbroke and the Concept of Constitutional Government', *Political Studies*, 10: 264–76.

—— (ed.) (1988), *The Cambridge History of Medieval Political Thought c.350–c.1450* (Cambridge: Cambridge University Press).

—— (ed.) (1991), *The Cambridge History of Political Thought 1450–1700* (Cambridge: Cambridge University Press).

BUTTERFIELD, H. (1931), *The Whig Interpretation of History* (London: Bell).

CAENEGEM, R. C. van (1995), *An Historical Introduction to Western Constitutional Law* (Cambridge: Cambridge University Press).

CAMDEN, W. (1984), *Remains Concerning Britain*, R. D. Dunn (ed.) (Toronto: University of Toronto Press).

CAMPBELL, J. L. (1857) (4th edn.), *Lives of the Lord Chancellors, and the Keepers of the Great Seal of England* (London: John Murray).

—— (1874) (3rd edn.), *The Lives of the Chief Justices of England* (London: John Murray).

CANNING, J. P. (1988), 'Law, Sovereignty and Corporation Theory, 1300–1450', in Burns (1988), 454–76.

CAPPELLETTI, M. (1971), *Judicial Review in the Contemporary World* (Oxford: Clarendon Press).

CARMICHAEL, D. J. C. (1990), 'Hobbes on Natural Right in Society: The Leviathan Account' *Canadian Journal of Political Science*, 23: 3–21.

CARPENTER, D. A. (1996), *The Reign of Henry III* (London and Rio Grande: The Hambledon Press).

CARRITHERS, D. W. (1977), 'Introduction', to C. Montesquieu, *The Spirit of Laws*, D. W. Carrithers (ed.) (Berkeley: University of California Press), 1–88.

CARTWRIGHT, J. (1776), *American Independence, the Interest and Glory of Great Britain*, reprinted in P. H. Smith (1972), 125–92.

CHALMERS, G. (1777), *Second Thoughts: Or, Observations upon Lord Abingdon's Thought on the Letter of Edmund Burke, Esq. to the Sheriffs of Bristol* (London).

CHAMBERS, R. (1986), *A Course of Lectures on the English Law Delivered at the University of Oxford 1767–1773*, T. M. Curley (ed.) (Madison: University of Wisconsin Press).

CHARLES I, KING OF ENGLAND (1642), *His Majesties Answer to the Declaration of Both Houses Concerning Hull* (London: printed for S.E.) (EEB Reel 1279: 16).

CHODOROW, S. (1972), *Christian Political Theory and Church Politics in the Mid-Twelfth Century: The Ecclesiology of Gration's Discretum* (California: University of California Press).

CHRIMES, S. B. (1936) (1966 reprint), *English Constitutional Ideas in the Fifteenth Century* (New York: American Scholars Publications).

—— and BROWN, A. L. (eds.) (1961), *Select Documents of English Constitutional History 1307–1485* (London: Adam & Charles Black).

CHRISTIANSON, P. (1984), 'Young John Selden and the Ancient Constitution, c.1610–18', *Proceedings of the American Philosophical Society*, 128: 271–315.

—— (1991), 'Royal and Parliamentary Voices on the Ancient Constitution c.1604–1621', in Peck (1991), 71–95.

—— (1993), 'Ancient Constitutions in the Age of Sir Edward Coke and John Selden', in E. Sandoz (ed.), *The Roots of Liberty, Magna Carta, Ancient Constitution, and the Anglo-American Tradition of Rule of Law* (Columbia and London: University of Missouri Press), 89–146.

—— (1996), *Discourse on History, Law, and Governance in the Public Career of John Selden, 1610–1635* (Toronto: University of Toronto Press).

CHRISTIE, W. D. (ed.) (1859), *Memoirs, Letters and Speeches of Anthony Ashley Cooper, First Earl of Shaftesbury, Lord Chancellor, Volume 1* (London: John Murray).

CLAEYS, G. (1989), *Thomas Paine: Social and Political Thought* (Boston: Unwin Hyman).

CLARK, H. H. (ed.) (1961), *Thomas Paine: Representative Selections* revised edn. (New York: Hill & Wang).

CLARK, J. C. D. (1994), *The Language of Liberty 1660–1832: Political Discourse and Social Dynamics in the Anglo-American World* (Cambridge: Cambridge University Press).

CLARKE, M. V. (1931), 'Forfeitures and Treason in 1388', *Transactions of the Royal Historical Society, Fourth Series*, 14: 65–94.

COBBETT, W. (1806–20), *Cobbett's Parliamentary History of England* (London: R. Bagshaw/Longman), 36 vols.

COKE, E. (1628) (18th edn. corrected, 1823), *The First Part of the Institutes of the Laws of England* (London: J. & W. T. Clarke).

—— (1641) (5th edn., 1671), *The Second Part of the Institutes of the Laws of England* (London: E. & R. Brooke).

—— (1644), *The Fourth Part of the Institutes of the Laws of England Concerning the Jurisdiction of the Courts* (London: M. Flesher).

COLEMAN, J. (1982), 'Negative and Positive Positivism', *Journal of Legal Studies*, 11: 139–64.

COLERIDGE, S. T. (1976), *On the Constitution of the Church and State, According to the Idea of Each*, J. Colmer (ed.), in *The Collected Works of Samuel Taylor Coleridge*, K. Coburn (general ed.) (London: Routledge & Kegan Paul), x.

COLLINSON, P. (1997), 'The Monarchical Republic of Queen Elizabeth I', in Guy (1997a), 110–34.

COLOMBO, C. J. (1926), *A Treatise on the Law of Prize* (London: Sweet and Maxwell).

COOKE, R. (1988), 'Fundamentals', *New Zealand Law Journal*, 158–65.

COOPER, J. P. (1983), *Land, Men and Beliefs: Studies in Early-Modern History*, G. E. Aylmer and J. S. Morrill (eds.) (London: Hambledon Press).

COPE, E. S., and COATES, W. H. (eds.) (1977), *Proceedings of the Short Parliament of 1640* (London: Royal Historical Society).

COQUILLETTE, D. R. (1992), *Francis Bacon* (Edinburgh: Edinburgh University Press).

CORWIN, E. S. (1925), 'The Progress of Constitutional Theory between the Declaration of Independence and the Meeting of the Philadelphia Convention', *American Historical Review*, 30: 511–36.

—— (1955), *The 'Higher Law' Background of American Constitutional Law* (Ithaca, NY and London: Great Seal Books).

COX, H. (1863), *The Institutions of the English Government* (London: H. Sweet).

CRAIG, P. (1991), 'Sovereignty of the United Kingdom Parliament after *Factortame*', *Year Book of European Law*, 11: 221–55.

—— (1993), 'Public Law, Sovereignty and Citizenship', in R. Blackburn (ed.), *Rights of Citizenship* (London: Mansell Publishing Ltd.), 307–32.

CRISPO, L. W., SLANSKY, J. M., and YRIARTE, G. M. (1997), 'Jury Nullification: Law Versus Anarchy', *Loyola of Los Angeles Law Review*, 31: 1–61.

CROMARTIE, A. (1995), *Sir Matthew Hale 1609–1676* (Cambridge: Cambridge University Press).

CROSS, C. (1969), *The Royal Supremacy in the Elizabethan Church* (London: George Allen & Unwin Ltd.).

—— (1977), 'Churchmen and the Royal Supremacy', in F. Heal and R. O'Day (eds.), *Church and Society in England: Henry VIII to James I* (London and Basingstoke: Macmillan), 15–34.

DAHL, R. (1989), *Democracy and Its Critics* (New Haven: Yale University Press).

DAICHES, D. (1977), *Scotland and the Union* (London: John Murray).

DALLISON, C. (1648), *The Royalist's Defence* (London) (EEB Reel 91: 3).

DALRYMPLE, J. (Viscount of Stair) (1693) (2nd edn.). The Institutions of the Law of Scotland (Edinburgh: The Heir of Andrew Anderson) (EEB Reel 1732: 22).

DALY, J. (1978), 'The Idea of Absolute Monarchy in Seventeenth Century England', *Historical Journal*, 21: 227–250.

—— (1979a), 'Cosmic Harmony and Political Thinking in Early Stuart England', *Transactions of the American Philosophical Society*, Part 7, 69: 1–41.

—— (1979b), *Sir Robert Filmer and English Political Thought* (Toronto: Toronto University Press).

DAVIES, R. G., and DENTON, J. H. (eds.) (1981), *The English Parliament in the Middle Ages* (Manchester: Manchester University Press).

DEFOE, D. (1701), *Legion's Memorial to the House of Commons*, reprinted in D. Defoe, (1965), *Daniel Defoe*, J. T. Boulton (ed.) (London: B. T. Batsford), 83–5.

—— (1702a), *The Original Power of the Collective Body of the People of England, Examined and Asserted* (London).

—— (1702b), *Legion's New Paper: Being A Second Memorial to the Gentlemen of a Late House of Commons* (London).

—— (1786), *The History of the Union Between England and Scotland, with an Introduction by J. L. De Lolme* (London: John Stockdale).

DE LOLME, J. L. (1796) (new edn.), *The Constitution of England, or, An Account of the English Government* (London: G. G. & J. Robinson).

[DENMAN] (1846), 'Parliament and the Courts', *Edinburgh Review*, 83: 1–47. (Denman is named as the author in Houghton (1966: i. 495)).

DERRETT, J. D. M. (1964), 'The Trial of Sir Thomas More', *English Historical Review*, 79: 449–77.

—— (1979), 'The Affairs of Richard Hunne and Friar Standish', in More (1963–87), ix, *The Apology*, J. B. Trapp (ed.), 215–46.

DE SMITH, S., and BRAZIER, R. (1994) (6th edn.), *Constitutional and Administrative Law* (London: Penguin Books).

DETMOLD, M. J. (1984), *The Unity of Law and Morality: A Refutation of Legal Positivism* (London: Routledge & Kegan Paul).

—— (1985), *The Australian Commonwealth: A Fundamental Analysis of Its Constitution* (Sydney: Law Book Company).

—— (1989a), *Courts and Administrators: A Study in Jurisprudence* (London: Weidenfeld & Nicolson).

—— (1989b), 'Law as Practical Reason', *Cambridge Law Journal*, 48: 436–71.

—— (1996), 'Australian Constitutional Equality: The Common Law Foundation', *Public Law Review*, 7: 33–51.

DEWAR, M. (1982), 'Introduction', in Sir Thomas Smith, *De Republica Anglorum*, M. Dewar (ed.) (Cambridge: Cambridge University Press).

DICEY, A. V. (1964) (10th edn.), *Introduction to the Study of the Law of the Constitution*, E. C. S. Wade (ed.) (London: Macmillan).

288   *References*

DICEY, A. V. and RAIT, R. S. (1920), *Thoughts on the Union Between England and Scotland* (London: Macmillan).

DICKINSON, H. T. (1976), 'The Eighteenth-Century Debate on the Sovereignty of Parliament', *Transactions of the Royal Historical Society, Fifth Series*, 26: 189–210.

—— (1977), *Liberty and Property, Political Ideology in Eighteenth Century Britain* (London: Weidenfeld & Nicolson).

—— (1985), *British Radicalism and the French Revolution 1795–1815* (Oxford: Basil Blackwell).

DIGGES, D. (1643) (1978 reprint, New York and London: Garland Publishing Inc.), *The Unlawfulness of Subjects taking up Armes Against Their Soveraigne in what case soever* (Oxford).

DIKE, C. (1976), 'The Case Against Parliamentary Sovereignty', *Public Law*, 283–97.

DISNEY, W. (1681), *Nil Dictum quod non dictum prius, or the Case of the Government of England Established by Law* (London: A.B. for F.T.) (EEB Reel 350: 17).

DIXON, O. (1957), 'The Common Law as an Ultimate Constitutional Foundation', *Australian Law Journal*, 31: 240–54.

DOE, N. (1989), 'Fifteenth-Century Conceptions of Law, Fortescue and Pecock', *History of Political Thought*, 10: 257–80.

—— (1990), *Fundamental Authority in Late Medieval English Law* (Cambridge: Cambridge University Press).

DRAPER, T. (1996), *A Struggle For Power: The American Revolution* (New York: Random House).

DUNHAM, W. H., Jr. (1964), 'Regal Power and the Rule of Law: A Tudor Paradox', *Journal of British Studies*, 3 (2): 24–56.

—— (1987), 'Parliament, English', in Strayer (1982–9), ix, 422–34.

—— and PARGELLIS, S. (eds.) (1938), *Complaint and Reform in England 1436–1714* (New York: Oxford University Press).

—— and WOOD, C. T. (1976), 'The Right to Rule in England: Depositions and the Kingdom's Authority, 1327–1485', *American Historical Review*, 81: 738–61.

DWARRIS, F. (1848), *A General Treatise on Statutes* (London: William Benning & Co.).

DWORKIN, R. (1977), *Taking Rights Seriously* (Cambridge, Mass.: Harvard University Press).

—— (1986), *Law's Empire* (London: Fontana).

—— (1996), *Freedom's Law: The Moral Reading of the American Constitution* (Oxford: Oxford University Press).

DYZENHAUS, D. (1991), *Hard Cases in Wicked Legal Systems: South African Law in the Perspective of Legal Philosophy* (Oxford: Clarendon Press).

ECCLESHALL, R. (1978), *Order and Reason in Politics, Theories of Absolute and Limited Monarchy in Early Modern England* (Oxford: Oxford University Press).

EDWARDS, J. G. (1970a), 'The *Plena Potestas* of English Parliamentary Representatives', in Fryde and Miller (1970), *i: Origins to 1399*, 136–49.

—— (1970b), '"Justice" in Early English Parliaments', in Fryde and Miller (1970), *i: Origins to 1399*, 279–97.

EDWARDS, R. A. (1996), '*Bonham's* Case: The Ghost in the Constitutional Machine', *Denning Law Journal*, 63–90.

E. F. (1679), *A Letter from a Gentleman of Quality to His Friend, Relating to the Point of Succession to the Crown* (London: s.n.).

ELTON, G. R. (1964), 'The Tudor Revolution: A Reply', *Past and Present*, 29: 26–49.

—— (1965), 'A Revolution in Tudor History?' *Past and Present*, 32: 103–9.

—— (1972), 'The Rule of Law in Sixteenth-Century England', in A. J. Slavin (ed.), *Tudor Men and Institutions: Studies in English Law and Government* (Baton Rouge, La.: Louisiana State University Press), 265–94.

—— (1973), *Reform and Renewal: Thomas Cromwell and the Common Weal* (London: Cambridge University Press).

—— (1974*a*–92), *Studies in Tudor and Stuart Government and Politics* (Cambridge: Cambridge University Press).

—— (1974*b*), ' "The Body of the Whole Realm": Parliament and Representation in Medieval England', in Elton (1974*a*–92), ii: *Parliament/Political Thought*, 19–61.

—— (1974*c*), 'A High Road to Civil War?' in Elton (1974*a*–1992), ii: *Parliament/ Political Thought*, 164–82.

—— (1974*d*), 'The Divine Right of Kings', in Elton (1974*a*–1992), ii: *Parliament/ Political Thought*, 193–214.

—— (1974*e*), 'The Political Creed of Thomas Cromwell', in Elton (1974*a*–1992), ii: *Parliament/Political Thought*, 215–35.

—— (1977), *Reform and Reformation, England 1509–1558* (London: Edward Arnold).

—— (1981), Review of A. B. Ferguson, 'Clio Unbound', *History and Theory*, 20: 92–100.

—— (1982) (2nd edn.), *The Tudor Constitution, Documents and Commentary* (Cambridge: Cambridge University Press).

—— (1986), *The Parliament of England 1559–1581* (Cambridge: Cambridge University Press).

—— (1991) (3rd edn.) *England under the Tudors* (London and New York: Routledge).

—— (1992), '*Lex Terrae Victrix*: The Triumph of Parliamentary Law in the Sixteenth Century', in Elton (1974*a*–1992), iv: *Papers and Reviews 1983–1990*, 37–57.

ERSKINE, J. (1777) (5th edn.), *The Principles of the Law in Scotland, In the Order of Sir George MacKenzie's Institutions of that Law* (Edinburgh: John Balfour).

ERSKINE-HILL, H., and STOREY, G. (eds.) (1983), *Revolutionary Prose of the English Civil War* (Cambridge: Cambridge University Press).

FARRAND, M. (ed.) (1937) (1966 reprint of 2nd edn.), *The Records of the Federal Convention of 1787* (New Haven and London: Yale University Press).

FAULKNER, R. K. (1981), *Richard Hooker and the Politics of Christian England* (Berkeley: University of California Press).

FERGUSON, A. (1776), *Remarks on a Pamphlet Lately Published by Dr. Price*, reprinted in Peach (1979), 253–60.

FERGUSON, A. B. (1965), *The Articulate Citizen and the English Renaissance* (Durham, NC: Duke University Press).

FIGGIS, J. N. (1922) (2nd edn.), *The Divine Right of Kings* (Cambridge: Cambridge University Press).

FILMER, R. (1991), *Patriarcha and Other Writings*, J. P. Sommerville (ed.) (Cambridge: Cambridge University Press).

FINCH, H. (1678) (1st edn. published in 1627), *Law, or a Discourse thereof, in Four Books* (London: Richard & Edward Atkins).

FINNIS, J. M. (1980), *Natural Law and Natural Rights* (Oxford: Clarendon Press).

FITZGERALD, P. J. (1966) (12th edn.) *Salmond on Jurisprudence* (London: Sweet & Maxwell).

FORSYTH, C. (1996), 'Of Fig Leaves and Fairy Tales: The Ultra Vires Doctrine, the Sovereignty of Parliament and Judicial Review', *Cambridge Law Journal*, 55: 122–40.

FORTESCUE, J. (1949), *De Laudibus Legum Angliae*, S. B. Chrimes (ed.) (Cambridge: Cambridge University Press).

—— (1980), *De Natura Legis Naturae* (New York and London: Garland Publishing).

FOSTER, E. R. (ed.) (1966), *Proceedings in Parliament 1610* (New Haven and London: Yale University Press), 2 vols.

FOX, A., and GUY, J. A. (1986), *Reassessing the Henrician Age: Humanism, Politics and Reform 1500–1550* (Oxford: Basil Blackwell).

FRANKLE, R. J. (1985), 'Parliament's Right to Do Wrong: The Parliamentary Debate on the Bill of Attainder Against Sir John Fenwick, 1696', *Parliamentary History*, 4: 71–85.

FRANKLIN, J. H. (1973), *Jean Bodin and the Rise of Absolutist Theory* (Cambridge: Cambridge University Press).

—— (1978), *John Locke and the Theory of Sovereignty, Mixed Monarchy and the Right of Resistance in Political Thought of the English Revolution* (Cambridge: Cambridge University Press).

—— (1991), 'Sovereignty and the Mixed Constitution, Bodin and His Critics', in Burns (1991), 298–328.

FRYDE, E. B., and MILLER, E. (eds.) (1970), *Historical Studies of the English Parliament* (Cambridge: Cambridge University Press).

FUKUDA, A. (1997), *Sovereignty and the Sword: Harrington, Hobbes, and Mixed Government in the English Civil Wars* (Oxford: Clarendon Press).

FUSSNER, F. S. (1957), 'William Camden's "Discourse Concerning the Prerogative of the Crown"', *Proceedings of the American Philosophical Society*, 101: 206 ff.

GALLOWAY, B. (1986), *The Union of England and Scotland 1603–1608* (Edinburgh: John Donald).

GARDINER, S. (1933) (reprinted 1970, Westport, Conn.: Greenwood Press), *The Letters of Stephen Gardiner*, J. A. Muller (ed.) (Cambridge: Cambridge University Press).

GARDINER, S. R. (ed.) (1906), (3rd edn.), *The Constitutional Documents of the Puritan Revolution 1625–1660* (Oxford: Clarendon Press).

GARRETT, J. (1980), *The Triumphs of Providence: The Assassination Plot, 1696* (Cambridge: Cambridge University Press).

GEORGE, R. P. (1996), 'Natural Law and Positive Law', in R. P. George (ed.), *The Autonomy of Law: Essays on Legal Positivism* (Oxford: Clarendon Press), 321–34.

GOLDIE, M. (1983), 'John Locke and Anglican Royalism', *Political Studies*, 31: 61–85.

—— (1991), 'The Reception of Hobbes', in Burns (1991), 589–615.

—— (1997), 'Restoration Political Thought', in L. K. J. Glassey (ed.), *The Reigns of Charles II and James VII & II* (New York: St Martin's Press), 12–35.

GOLDSWORTHY, J. (1986), 'Detmold's *The Unity of Law and Morality*', *Monash University Law Review*, 12: 8–26.

—— (1987), 'Manner and Form in the Australian States', *Melbourne University Law Review*, 16: 403–29.

—— (1990), 'The Self-Destruction of Legal Positivism', *Oxford Journal of Legal Studies*, 10: 449–86.

—— (1992), 'The Constitutional Protection of Rights in Australia', in G. Craven (ed.), *Australian Federation, Towards the Second Century* (Melbourne: Melbourne University Press), 151–76.

—— (1994), 'Implications in Language, Law and the Constitution', in G. Lindell (ed.), *Future Directions in Australian Constitutional Law* (Sydney: Federation Press), 150–84.

—— (1995), 'Marmor on Meaning and Interpretation', *Legal Theory*, 1: 439–64.

—— (1997), 'Constitutional Implications and Freedom of Political Speech: A Reply to Stephen Donaghue', *Monash University Law Review*, 23: 362–74.

GOODHART, A. L. (1958), 'The Rule of Law and Absolute Sovereignty', *University of Pennsylvania Law Review*, 106: 943–63.

GOODWIN, J. (1643), *Os Ossorianum, or A Bone for a Bishop to Pick* (London: Henry Overton) (EEB Reel 244: E. 96, no. 1).

GOUGH, J. W. (1955), *Fundamental Law in English Constitutional History* (Oxford: Clarendon Press).

—— (1962), 'Flowers of the Crown', *English Historical Review*, 77: 86–93.

G. P. (1690), (George Philips, alias George Petyt) *Lex Parliamentaria: or, A Treatise of the Laws and Customs of the Parliaments of England* (London: T. Goodwin).

GRAVES, M. A. R. (1985), *The Tudor Parliaments, Crown, Lords and Commons, 1485–1603* (London and New York: Longman).

GRAY, C. M. (1972), 'Bonham's Case Reviewed', *Proceedings of the American Philosophical Society*, 116: 35–68.

—— (1980), 'Reason, Authority, and Imagination: The Jurisprudence of Sir Edward Coke', in P. Zagorin (ed.), *Culture and Politics From Puritanism to the Enlightenment* (Berkeley: University of California Press), 25–66.

—— (1992), 'Parliament, Liberty, and the Law', in Hexter (1992*a*), 155–200.

GREENBERG, J. (1991), 'Our Grand Maxim of State, "The King Can Do No Wrong"', *History of Political Thought*, 12: 209–28.

GREENE, J. P. (1986), 'From the Perspective of Law: Context and Legitimacy in the Origins of the American Revolution', *The South Atlantic Quarterly*, 85: 56–77.

GREENLEAF, W. H. (1964), *Order, Empiricism and Politics: Two Traditions of English Political Thought 1500–1700* (London: Oxford University Press).

GRIFFITHS, R. A. (1984), 'The Later Middle Ages', in K. O. Morgan (ed.), *The Oxford Illustrated History of Britain* (Oxford: Oxford University Press), 166–222.

GUNN, J. A. W. (1983), *Beyond Liberty and Property: The Process of Self-Recognition in Eighteenth-Century Political Thought* (Kingston and Montreal: McGill-Queen's University Press).

GUNN, S. J. (1995), *Early Tudor Government 1485–1558* (Basingstoke: St Martin's Press).

GUY, J. A. (1985*a*), *Christopher St German on Chancery and Statute* (London: Selden Society).

—— (1985*b*), 'Law, Lawyers and the English Reformation', *History Today*, 35 (November): 16–22.

—— (1986*a*), 'Thomas More and Christopher St German: The Battle of the Books', in Fox and Guy (1986), 95–120.

—— (1986*b*), 'Scripture as Authority: Problems of Interpretation in the 1530s', in Fox and Guy (1986), 199–220.

—— (1987*a*), 'Introduction', in More (1963–87), x: *The Debellation of Salem and Bizance* (1987), J. A. Guy, R. Keen, C. H. Miller, and R. McGugan (eds.), pp. xv–xciv.

—— (1987*b*), 'The Later Career of Christopher St. German (1534–1541)', in More (1963–87), x: *The Debellation of Salem and Bizance* (1987), J. A. Guy, R. Keen, C. H. Miller, and R. McGugan (eds.), 393–417.

GUY, J. A. (1988), *Tudor England* (Oxford: Oxford University Press).

—— (1992), 'The "Imperial Crown" and the Liberty of the Subject: The English Constitution from Magna Carta to the Bill of Rights', in Kunze and Brautigam (1992), 65–87.

—— (1993), 'The Henrician Age', in Pocock (1993), 13–46.

—— (ed.) (1995a), *The Reign of Elizabeth I: Court and Culture in the Last Decade* (Cambridge: Cambridge University Press).

—— (1995b) 'Introduction—The 1590s: the Second Reign of Elizabeth I?' in Guy (1995a), 1–19.

—— (1995c), 'The Elizabethan Establishment and the Ecclesiastical Polity', in Guy (1995a), 126–49.

—— (1996), 'Tudor Monarchy and Political Culture', in Morrill (1996), 219–38.

—— (ed.) (1997a), *The Tudor Monarchy* (London and New York: Arnold).

—— (1997b), 'Tudor Monarchy and its Critiques', in Guy (1997a), 78–109.

GWYN, P. (1990), *The King's Cardinal: The Rise and Fall of Thomas Wolsey* (London: Barrie & Jenkins).

HAIGH, C. (1993), *English Reformations: Religion, Politics and Society under the Tudors* (Oxford: Clarendon Press).

HALE, M. (1796), *The Jurisdiction of the Lords House of Parliament, Considered According to Antient Records*, F. Hargrave (ed.) (London: T. Cadell).

—— (1924), 'Reflections by the Lord Chief Justice Hale on Mr Hobbes his Dialogue of the Law', reprinted in Holdsworth (1903–72), v: 500–513.

HALLER, W. (1979), *Tracts on Liberty in the Puritan Revolution, 1638–1647, Vol. 2* (New York: Octagon Books).

HAMBURGER, P. A. (1994), 'Revolution and Judicial Review: Chief Justice Holt's Opinion in *City of London v Wood*', *Columbia Law Review*, 94: 2091–153.

HAMILTON, A. (1775), *The Farmer Refuted, or, A More Impartial and Comprehensive View of the Dispute Between Great-Britain and the Colonies*, reprinted in H. C. Syrett (ed.) (1961), *The Papers of Alexander Hamilton, Vol 1: 1768–1778* (New York and London: Columbia University Press), 81–165.

—— MADISON, J., and JAY, J. (1961), *The Federalist Papers*, C. Rossiter (ed.) (New York: New American Library).

HANSON, D. W. (1970), *From Kingdom to Commonwealth: The Development of Civic Consciousness in English Political Thought* (Cambridge, Mass.: Harvard University Press).

HARDCASTLE, HON. MRS. (1881), *Life of John, Lord Campbell* (London: John Murray), 2 vols.

HARDING, A. (1973), *The Law Courts of Medieval England* (London and New York: George Allen & Unwin Ltd.).

HARPSFIELD, N. (1932), *Life and Death of Sir Thomas Moore*, E. V. Hitchcock (ed.) (London: Oxford University Press).

HARRIS, I. (1994), *The Mind of John Locke: A Study of Political Theory in its Intellectual Setting* (Cambridge: Cambridge University Press).

HARRIS, T. (1990), '"Lives, Liberties and Estates": Rhetorics of Liberty in the Reign of Charles II', in T. Harris, P. Seaward, and M. Goldie (eds.), *The Politics of Religion in Restoration England* (Oxford: Basil Blackwell), 217–41.

—— (1993), *Politics Under the Later Stuarts: Party Conflict in a Divided Society 1660–1715* (London and New York: Longman).

HARRISS, G. L. (1963), 'Medieval Government and Statecraft', *Past and Present*, 25: 8–39.

—— (1965), 'A Revolution in Tudor History?' *Past and Present*, 31: 87–94.

—— (1981), 'The Formation of Parliament, 1272–1377', in Davies and Denton (1981), 29–60.

HART, H. L. A. (1961), *The Concept of Law* (Oxford: Clarendon Press).

—— (1982), *Essays on Bentham: Jurisprudence and Political Theory* (Oxford: Clarendon Press).

—— (1983), *Essays in Jurisprudence and Philosophy* (Oxford: Clarendon Press).

—— (1994) (2nd edn.) *The Concept of Law* (Oxford: Clarendon Press).

HARTLEY, T. E. (ed.) (1981), *Proceedings in the Parliaments of Elizabeth I* (Leicester: Leicester University Press).

HAVIGHURST, A. F. (1950), 'The Judiciary and Politics in the Reign of Charles II (Part II, 1676–1685)', *Law Quarterly Review*, 66: 229–52.

—— (1953), 'James II and the Twelve Men in Scarlet', *Law Quarterly Review*, 69: 522–46.

HAWKINS, M. (1973), 'The Government, its Role and its Aims', in Russell (1973), 35–65.

HEARN, W. E. (1867), *The Government of England, Its Structure, and Its Development* (Melbourne: George Robertson).

HELMHOLZ, R. H. (1986), 'The Sons of Edward IV: A Canonical Assessment of the Claim That They Were Illegitimate', in P. W. Hammond and R. Horrox (eds.), *Richard III: Loyalty, Lordship and Law* (London: Richard III and Yorkist History Trust), 91–103.

HENSHALL, N. (1992), *The Myth of Absolutism: Change and Continuity in Early Modern European Monarchy* (London and New York: Longman).

HERLE, C. (1642), *A Fuller Answer to a Treatise Written by Doctor Ferne* (London: John Bartlet) (EEB Reel 266: E. 245 no. 3).

—— (1643), *An Answer to Doctor Ferne's Reply* (London: Thomas Brudenell for N.A.) (EEB Reel 245: E. 102, no. 3).

HEUSTON, R. F. V. (1979) (2nd edn.), *Essays in Constitutional Law* (London: Stevens & Sons).

HEXTER, J. H. (1986), 'The Apology', in R. Ollard and P. Tudor-Craig (eds.), *For Veronica Wedgwood These: Studies in Seventeenth-Century History* (London: Collins), 13–44.

—— (ed.) (1992*a*), *Parliament and Liberty: From the Reign of Elizabeth to the English Civil War* (Stanford, Calif.: Stanford University Press).

—— (1992*b*), 'Parliament, Liberty, and Freedom of Elections', in Hexter (1992*a*), 21–55.

HEYLYN, P. (1643), *The Rebells Catechisme* (Oxford: n.s.) (EEB Reel 234: E. 35, no. 22).

HEYRICKE, R. (1646), *Queen Esthers Resolves: Or a Princely Pattern of Heaven-Born Resolution* (London: Luke Fawne) (EEB Reel 1505: 7).

HILL, C. (1965), *Intellectual Origins of the English Revolution* (Oxford: Clarendon Press).

HINTON, R. W. K. (1960), 'English Constitutional Theories From Sir John Fortescue to Sir John Eliot', *English Historical Review*, 75: 410–25.

HOAK, D. (1996), 'The Anglo-Dutch Revolution of 1688–89', in Hoak and Feingold (1996), 1–26.

—— and M. FEINGOLD (eds.), (1996) *The World of William and Mary: Anglo-Dutch Perspectives on the Revolution of 1688–89* (Stanford, Calif.: Stanford University Press).

HOBBES, T. (1968), *Leviathan*, C. B. Macpherson (ed.) (Harmondsworth: Penguin Books).

HOGG, P. W. (1992) (4th edn.), *Constitutional Law of Canada* (Toronto: Carswell).

HOLDSWORTH, W. S. (1903–72), *A History of English Law* (London: Methuen), 18 vols.

HOLDSWORTH, W. S. (1921), 'The Prerogative in the Sixteenth Century', *Columbia Law Review*, 21: 554–71.

—— (1925), *Sources and Literature of English Law* (Oxford: Clarendon Press).

—— (1946a), *Essays in Law and History*, A. L. Goodhart and H. G. Hanbury (eds.) (Oxford: Clarendon Press).

—— (1946b), 'Central Courts of Law and Representative Assemblies in the Sixteenth Century', in Holdsworth (1946a), 37–70.

—— (1946c), 'The Influence of the Legal Profession on the Growth of the English Constitution', in Holdsworth (1946a), 71–90.

HOLLINGWORTH, R. (1643), *An Answer to a Certain Writing* (London: Luke Fawne) (EEB Reel 239: E. 67, no. 5).

HOLINSHED, R. (1807) (1965 reprint), *Holinshed's Chronicles of England, Scotland, and Ireland*, H. Ellis (ed.) (New York: AMS Press Inc.).

HOLMES, G. S. (1993), *The Making of a Great Power: Late Stuart and Early Georgian Britain 1660–1722* (London and New York: Longman).

HOLMES, S. (1995), *Passions and Constraint: On the Theory of Liberal Democracy* (Chicago and London: University of Chicago Press).

HOLT, J. C. (1981), 'The Prehistory of Parliament', in Davies and Denton (1981), 1–28.

HOLTON, R. (1998), 'Positivism and the Internal Point of View', *Law and Philosophy*, 17: 597–625.

HOOD PHILLIPS, O. (1975), 'Self-Limitation by the United Kingdom Parliament', *Hastings Constitutional Law Quarterly*, 2: 443.

HOOKER, J. (1977), *Parliament in Elizabethan England: John Hooker's 'Order and Usage'*, V. F. Snow (ed.) (New Haven and London: Yale University Press).

HOOKER, R. (1888) (7th edn., 1977), *The Works of Mr Richard Hooker*, J. Keble (ed.) (Hildesheim: Georg Olms Verlag).

[HOPKINS, S.] (1765), *The Rights of Colonies Examined*, reprinted in Bailyn (1965), i: *1750–1776*, 507–22.

HOUGHTON, W. E. (1966), *The Wellesley Index to Victorian Periodicals 1824–1900* (Toronto: University of Toronto Press).

HOUSTON, A. C. (1991), *Algernon Sidney and the Republican Heritage in England and America* (Princeton: Princeton University Press).

HOWELL, T. B. (ed.) (1816–28), *A Complete Collection of State Trials* (London: Longman), 34 vols.

HUNT, T. (1682), *Mr. Hunt's Postscript for Rectifying some Mistakes in some of the Inferior Clergy, Mischievous to our Government and Religion* (London: n.s.) (EEB Reel 816: 8).

HUNTON, P. (1643), *A Treatise of Monarchy* (London: Richard Baldwin) (EEB Reel 637: 5).

—— (1644), *A Vindication of the Treatise of Monarchy* (London: John Bellamy for G.M.) (EEB Reel 235: E. 39, no. 12).

Ingulph's Chronicle of the Abbey of Croyland (1893), H. T. Riley (trans.) (London: George Bell & Sons).

Irvine of Lairg, Lord (1996a), 'Judges and Decision-Makers: The Theory and Practice of *Wednesbury* Review' *Public Law*, 59–78.

—— (1996b), 'Response to Sir John Laws 1996', *Public Law*, 636–8.

JACOB, E. F. (1961), *The Fifteenth Century 1399–1485* (London: Oxford University Press).

JACOB, M. C., and JACOB, J. R. (eds.) (1984), *The Origins of Anglo-American Radicalism* (London: George Allen & Unwin).

JAFFE, L. L., and HENDERSON, E. G. (1956), 'Judicial Review and the Rule of Law', *Law Quarterly Review*, 72: 345–64.

JAMES I, KING OF ENGLAND (1616) (1918 reprint), *The Political Works of James I* (Cambridge: Harvard University Press).

JAMES VI AND I (1994), *Political Writings*, J. P. Sommerville (ed.) (Cambridge: Cambridge University Press).

JAY, S. (1994), 'Servants of Monarchs and Lords: The Advisory Role of Early English Judges', *The American Journal of Legal History*, 38: 117–96.

JEFFERSON, T. (1899), *The Writings of Thomas Jefferson*, P. L. Ford (ed.) (New York: G. P. Putnam's Sons).

JENKINS, T. A. (1996), *Parliament, Party and Politics in Victorian Britain* (Manchester: Manchester University Press).

JENNINGS, W. I. (1959) (5th edn.), *The Law and the Constitution* (London: University of London Press).

JEZIERSKI, J. V. (1971), 'Parliament or People: James Wilson and Blackstone on the Nature and Location of Sovereignty', *Journal of the History of Ideas*, 32: 95–106.

JOHNSON, R. C., KEELER, M. F., COLE, M. J., and BIDWELL, W. B. (eds.) (1977), *Commons Debates 1628* (New Haven: Yale University Press), 3 vols.

JOHNSON, S. (1770), *The False Alarm*, reprinted in Johnson (1977), x: *Political Writings*, 317–45.

—— (1775), *Taxation No Tyranny*, reprinted in Johnson (1977), *x: Political Writings*, 411–55.

—— (1977), *The Yale Edition of the Works of Samuel Johnson*, D. J. Greene (ed.) (New Haven and London: Yale University Press).

JOLLEY, N. (1975), 'Leibniz on Hobbes, Locke's *Two Treatises* and Sherlock's *Case of Allegiance*', *Historical Journal*, 18: 21–35.

JONES, J. R. (1991), 'James II's Revolution: Royal Policies, 1686–92', in Jonathan I. Israel (ed.), *The Anglo-Dutch Moment: Essays on the Glorious Revolution and its World Impact* (Cambridge: Cambridge University Press), 47–71.

—— (ed.) (1992a), *Liberty Secured? Britain Before and After 1688* (Stanford, Calif.: Stanford University Press).

—— (1992b), 'The Revolution in Context', in J. R. Jones (1992a), 1–52.

JONES, N. L. (1982), *Faith By Statute, Parliament and the Settlement of Religion 1559* (London: Royal Historical Society).

—— (1995), 'Parliament and the Political Society of Elizabethan England', in D. Hoak (ed.), *Tudor Political Culture* (Cambridge: Cambridge University Press), 226–42.

JONES, W. J. (1971), *Politics and the Bench: The Judges and the Origins of the English Civil War* (London: George Allen & Unwin).

JORDAN, W. K. (1942), *Men of Substance: A Study of the Thought of Two English Revolutionaries, Henry Parker and Henry Robinson* (Chicago: University of Chicago Press).

JOSEPH, P. A. (1993), *Constitutional and Administrative Law in New Zealand* (Sydney: Law Book Company).

JUDSON, M. A. (1932), 'The Development of the Theory of Parliamentary Sovereignty From 1640 to 1649' (unpublished Ph.D. thesis, Radcliffe College).

—— (1949), *The Crisis of the Constitution: An Essay in Constitutional and Political Thought in England 1603–1645* (New Brunswick, NJ: Rutgers University Press).

KAMMEN, M. (1988), *Sovereignty and Liberty: Constitutional Discourse in American Culture* (Madison: University of Wisconsin Press).

KANTOROWICZ, E. H. (1957), *The King's Two Bodies: A Study in Mediaeval Political Theology* (Princeton, NJ: Princeton University Press).

KAVANAGH, P. (1995), 'The Deposition of Edward II', *Australian Journal of Law and Society*, 11: 205–41.

KEIR, D. L. (1936), 'The Case of Ship-Money', *Law Quarterly Review*, 52: 546–74.

KENYON, G. T. (1873), *The Life of Lloyd, First Lord Kenyon* (London).

KENYON, J. P. (ed.) (1969), *Halifax: Complete Works* (Harmondsworth: Penguin Books).

—— (1977), *Revolution Principles: The Politics of Party 1689–1720* (Cambridge: Cambridge University Press).

—— (ed.) (1986) (2nd edn.), *The Stuart Constitution 1603–1688: Documents and Commentary* (Cambridge: Cambridge University Press).

KERN, F. (1939) (3rd edn., 1956), *Kingship and Law in the Middle Ages*, S. B. Chrimes (trans.) (Oxford: Basil Blackwell).

KIRBY, M. D. 'Lord Cooke and Fundamental Rights', in Rishworth (1997*a*), 331–54.

KISHLANSKY, M. (1982), 'Ideology and Politics in the Parliamentary Armies, 1645–9', in Morrill (1982), 163–83.

—— (1996), *A Monarchy Transformed: Britain 1603–1714* (London: Penguin).

KNAFLA, L. A. (1977), *Law and Politics in Jacobean England: The Tracts of Lord Chancellor Ellesmere* (Cambridge: Cambridge University Press).

KNIGHTS, M. (1994), *Politics and Opinion in Crisis, 1678–81* (Cambridge: Cambridge University Press).

KUNZE, B. Y., and BRAUTIGAM, D. D. (eds.) (1992), *Court, Country and Culture: Essays on Early Modern British History in Honor of Perez Zagorin* (Rochester, NY: University of Rochester Press).

LABAREE, L. W. (ed.) (1959–97), *The Papers of Benjamin Franklin* (New Haven: Yale University Press), 33 vols.

LACEY, D. R. (1969), *Dissent and Parliamentary Politics in England, 1661–1689: A Study in the Perpetuation and Tempering of Parliamentarianism* (New Brunswick, NJ: Rutgers University Press).

LAKE, P. (1988), *Anglicans And Puritans? Presbyterianism and English Conformist Thought from Whitgift to Hooker* (London: Unwin Hyman).

LAMBARDE, W. (1957), *Archeion, or a Discourse upon the High Courts of Justice in England*, C. H. McIlwain and P. L. Ward (eds.) (Cambridge, Mass.: Harvard University Press).

LAMONT, W. (1991), *Puritanism and the English Revolution, Vol. 1: Marginal Prynne, 1600–1669* (Aldershot, Hampshire: Gregg Revivals).

LAMPSON, E. T. (1941), 'Some New Light on the Growth of Parliamentary Sovereignty—Wimbish versus Taillebois', *American Political Science Review*, 35: 952–60.

LANGFORD, P. (1991), *Public Life and the Propertied Englishman 1689–1798* (Oxford: Clarendon Press).

LAPSLEY, G. T. (1951), *Crown, Community and Parliament in the Later Middle Ages: Studies in English Constitutional History* (Oxford: Blackwell).

LARRABEE, H. A. (ed.) (1952), *Bentham's Handbook of Political Fallacies* (New York: Thomas Y. Cromwell Co.).

LAUD, W. (1695), *The History of the Troubles and Trial of Archbishop Laud* (London: Chiswell).

LAWS, J. (1995), 'Law and Democracy', *Public Law*, 72–93.

—— (1996), 'The Constitution, Morals and Rights', *Public Law*, 622–35.

LAWSON, G. (1657) (2nd edn.), *Politica Sacra et Civilis, Or, A Model of Civil and Ecclesiastical Government* (London: J. S.).

LAZARE, D. (1996), *The Frozen Republic: How the Constitution is Paralyzing Democracy* (New York, San Diego, London: Harcourt Brace & Co).

LEHMBERG, S. E. (1977), *The Later Parliaments of Henry VIII, 1536–1547* (Cambridge: Cambridge University Press).

L'ESTRANGE, R. (1662), *A Memento, Directed to all Those that Truly Reverence the Memory of King Charles the Martyr . . . The First Part* (London: Henry Brome).

—— (1679), *The Free-born Subject, or, the Englishman's Birthright* (London: Henry Brome) (EEB Reel 500:19).

LEVACK, B. P. (1987), *The Formation of the British State: England, Scotland, and the Union 1603–1707* (Oxford: Clarendon Press).

—— (1994), 'Law, Sovereignty and the Union', in R. A. Mason (ed.), *Scots and Britains: Scottish Political Thought and the Union of 1603* (Cambridge: Cambridge University Press), 213–37.

LEVINE, M. (1973), *Tudor Dynastic Problems, 1460–1571* (London & New York: Allen & Unwin).

LEWIS, E. (ed.) (1954), *Medieval Political Ideas* (New York: Alfred A. Knopf).

—— (1964), 'King Above Law? *"Quod Principi Placuit"* in Bracton', *Speculum*, 39: 240–69.

LIEBERMAN, D. (1989), *The Province of Legislation Determined: Legal Theory in Eighteenth Century Britain* (Cambridge: Cambridge University Press).

LIND, J. (1776), *Three Letters to Dr. Price, Containing Remarks on His Observations on the Nature of Civil Liberty,* reprinted in Peach (1979), 235–44.

LLOYD, H. A. (1991), 'Constitutionalism', in Burns (1991), 254–97.

LOADES, D. M. (1979), *The Reign of Mary Tudor: Politics, Government and Religion in England, 1553–1558* (London: Ernest Benn Ltd.).

—— (1997), *Tudor Government: Structures of Authority in the Sixteenth Century* (Oxford: Blackwell Publishers).

LOBBAN, M. (1991), *The Common Law and English Jurisprudence 1760–1850* (Oxford: Clarendon Press).

LOCKE, J. (1689) (1983 edn.), *A Letter Concerning Toleration*, J. Tully (ed.) (Indianapolis: Hackett Publishing Company).

—— (1690) (1988 student edn.), *Two Treatises of Government*, P. Laslett (ed.) (Cambridge: Cambridge University Press).

—— (1997), *Political Essays*, M. Goldie (ed.) (Cambridge: Cambridge University Press).

LOCKWOOD, S. (1991), 'Marsilius of Padua and the Case for the Royal Ecclesiastical Supremacy', *Transactions of the Royal Historical Society, Sixth series*: 89–119.

—— (ed.) (1997), *Sir John Fortescue, on the Laws and Governance of England* (Cambridge: Cambridge University Press).

LUTZ, D. S. (1980), *Popular Consent and Popular Control: Whig Political Theory in the Early State Constitutions* (Baton Rouge La., and London: Louisiana State University Press).

McCluskey, Lord (1987), *Law, Justice and Democracy* (London: Sweet & Maxwell).

McCormick, N. (1978), *Legal Reasoning and Legal Theory* (Oxford: Clarendon Press).

—— and Weinberger, O. (1986), *An Institutional Theory of Law, New Approaches to Legal Positivism* (Dordrecht: Reidel).

MacDonell, J. (ed.) (1891) (1970 reprint, London: Professional Books Ltd.), *Reports of State Trials, New Series* (London: Eyre and Spottiswoode), 8 vols.

McIlwain, C. H. (1910) (reissued 1962, Hamden, Conn.: Archon Books), *The High Court of Parliament and Its Supremacy: An Historical Essay on the Boundaries Between Legislation and Adjudication in England* (New Haven: Yale University Press).

—— (1942), 'Book Review [of Thorne (1942)]', *Harvard Law Review*, 56: 148–50.

MacKay, R. A. (1924), 'Coke—Parliamentary Sovereignty or the Supremacy of the Law?' *Michigan Law Review*, 22: 215–47.

McKenna, J. W. (1979), 'The Myth of Parliamentary Sovereignty in Late-Medieval England', *English Historical Review*, 94: 481–506.

MacKenzie, G. (1684), *Jus Regium, Or the Just and Solid Foundations of Monarchy* (London: Richard Chiswell) (EEB Reel 845: 22).

Mackie, J. D. (1952), *The Earlier Tudors 1485–1558* (London: Oxford University Press).

MacKinnon, J. (1896), *The Union of England and Scotland: A Study of International History* (London: Longmans Green & Co).

Mackworth, H. (1701), *A Vindication of the Rights of the Commons of England* (London: J. Nutt).

Maitland, F. W. (1908) (reprinted 1963), *The Constitutional History of England* (Cambridge: Cambridge University Press).

Mandel, M. (1998), 'A Brief History of the New Constitutionalism, or "How We Changed Everything So That Everything Would Remain the Same"', *Israel Law Review*, 32: 250–300.

Mann, F. A. (1978), 'Britain's Bill of Rights', *Law Quarterly Review*, 94: 512–33.

Marmor, A. (1992), *Interpretation and Legal Theory* (Oxford: Clarendon Press).

Marshall, G. (1957), *Parliamentary Sovereignty and the Commonwealth* (Oxford: Clarendon Press).

—— (1984), *Constitutional Conventions: The Rules and Forms of Political Accountability* (Oxford: Clarendon Press).

Marshall, J. (1994), *John Locke: Resistance, Religion and Responsibility* (Cambridge: Cambridge University Press).

Martin, J. (1992), *Francis Bacon, the State, and the Reform of Natural Philosophy* (Cambridge: Cambridge University Press).

May, T. E. (1844) (reissued in 1971, Dublin), *A Treatise on the Law, Privileges, Proceedings and Usage of Parliament* (London: Butterworths).

—— (1893) (10th edn.), *A Treatise on the Law, Privileges, Proceedings and Usages of Parliament* (London: William Clowes & Sons).

Mendle, M. (1973), 'Politics and Political Thought 1640–1642', in Russell (1973), 219–45.

—— (1985), *Dangerous Positions, Mixed Government, the Estates of the Realm, and the Making of the Answer to the XIX Propositions* (Alabama: University of Alabama Press).

—— (1989), 'The Ship Money Case, *The Case of Shipmony*, and the Development of Henry Parker's Parliamentary Absolutism', *Historical Journal*, 32: 513–36.

—— (1995), *Henry Parker and the English Civil War: The Political Thought of the Public's Privado* (Cambridge: Cambridge University Press).

MIDDLETON, K. W. B. (1954), 'New Thoughts on the Union Between England and Scotland', *Juridical Review*, 66: 37–60.

MILL, J. S. (1963–77), *The Collected Works of John Stuart Mill*, J. M. Robson (ed.) (Toronto: University of Toronto Press), 33 vols.

MILLER, J. (1990), 'Britain', in J. Miller (ed.), *Absolutism in Seventeenth-Century Europe* (New York: St Martin's Press), 195–224.

MILSOM, S. F. C. (1956), 'Formedon Before *De Donis*', *Law Quarterly Review*, 72: 391–7.

MILTON, J. (1953–82), *Complete Prose Works of John Milton* (New Haven and London: Yale University Press), 8 vols.

—— (1991), *Political Writings*, M. Dzekzainis (ed.) and C. Gruzelier (trans.) (Cambridge: Cambridge University Press).

MITCHELL, J. D. B. (1964), *Constitutional Law* (Edinburgh: W. Green & Sons).

MOCKET, T. (1644), *A View of the Solemn League and Covenant* (London: Christopher Meredith) (EEB Reel 241: E. 80, no. 2).

MONAGHAN, H. P. (1996), 'We the People[s], Original Understanding, and Constitutional Amendment', *Columbia Law Review*, 96: 121–77.

MONTESQUIEU, C. (1748), *The Spirit of Laws*, A. M. Cohler, B. C. Miller, and H. S. Stone (eds.), (1989) (Cambridge: Cambridge University Press).

MOORE, J., and SILVERTHONE, M. (1995), 'Protestant Theologies, Limited Sovereignties: Natural Law and Conditions of Union in the German Empire, the Netherlands and Great Britain', in Robertson (1995*a*), 171–97.

MORE, T. (1963–87), *The Complete Works of St. Thomas More*, various eds. (New Haven and London: Yale University Press) 15 vols.

MORGAN, E. S. (1968), 'Colonial Ideas of Parliamentary Power 1764–1766', in J. P. Greene (ed.), *The Reinterpretation of the American Revolution 1763–1789* (New York and London: Harper & Row), 151–81.

—— (1988), *Inventing the People: The Rise of Popular Sovereignty in England and America* (New York and London: W. W. Norton & Co.).

MORRILL, J. (ed.) (1982), *Reactions to the English Civil War 1642–1649* (London: Macmillan).

—— (ed.) (1996), *The Oxford Illustrated History of Tudor and Stuart Britain* (Oxford: Oxford University Press).

MOSSE, G. L. (1947), 'Change and Continuity in the Tudor Constitution', *Speculum*, 22: 18–28.

—— (1968), *The Struggle for Sovereignty in England: From the Reign of Queen Elizabeth to the Petition of Right* (New York: Octagon Books).

MOUNT, F. (1992), *The British Constitution Now: Recovery or Decline?* (London: Mandarin).

MULLENDER, R. (1998), 'Parliamentary Sovereignty, the Constitution, and the Judiciary' *Northern Ireland Law Quarterly*, 49: 138–67.

MUNRO, C. R. (1987*a*), *Studies in Constitutional Law* (London: Butterworths).

—— (1987*b*), 'Was Parliament Born Free?' in Munro (1987*a*), 61–78.

MYERS, A. R. (1981), 'Parliament, 1422–1509', in Davies and Denton (1981), 141–84.

NEALE, J. E. (1924), 'Peter Wentworth, Part II', in Fryde and Miller (1970), *ii: 1399–1603*, 265–95. This article is a reprint of the original in *English Historical Review* (1924), 39: 175–205.

References

NEALE, J. E. (1957), *Elizabeth I and Her Parliaments 1584–1601* (London: Jonathan Cape).

NEDERMAN, C. J. (1984), 'Bracton on Kingship Revisited', *History of Political Thought*, 5: 61–77.

—— (1988), 'The Royal Will and the Baronial Bridle, the Place of the *Addicio de Cartis* in Bractonian Political Thought', *History of Political Thought*, 9: 415–29.

—— (1997), 'Kings, Peers and Parliament, Virtue and Corulership in Walter Burley's *Commentaries in VIII Libros Politicorum Aristotelis*', in C. J Nederman, *Medieval Aristotelianism and its Limits* (Aldershot: Variorum).

NENNER, H. (1977), *By Colour of Law, Legal Culture and Constitutional Politics in England 1660–1689* (Chicago: Chicago University Press).

—— (1992), 'Liberty, Law, and Property', in J. R. Jones (1992a), 88–121.

—— (1993), 'The Later Stuart Age', in Pocock (1993), 180–208.

—— (1995), *The Right to be King: The Succession to the Crown of England 1603–1714* (Chapel Hill, NC: University of North Carolina Press).

—— (1996), 'Sovereignty and the Succession in 1688–89', in Hoak and Feingold, (1996), 104–17.

—— (1997), 'The Trial of the Regicides, Retribution and Treason in 1660', in H. Nenner (ed.), *Politics and the Political Imagination in Later Stuart Britain: Essays Presented to Lois Green Schwoerer* (New York: University of Rochester Press), 21–42.

NICHOLSON, G. (1988), 'The Act of Appeals and the English Reformation', in C. Cross, D. Loades, and J. J. Scarisbrick (eds.), *Law and Government Under the Tudors* (Cambridge: Cambridge University Press), 19–30.

NOTESTEIN, W. (ed.) (1923), *The Journal of Sir Simonds D'Ewes* (New Haven: Yale University Press).

—— RELF, F., and SIMPSON, H. (eds.) (1935), *Commons Debates 1621* (New Haven: Yale University Press), 7 vols.

OAKLEY, F. (1984), *Omnipotence, Covenant, and Order: An Excursion in the History of Ideas from Abelard to Leibniz* (Ithaca, NY: Cornell University Press).

OTIS, J. (1764), *The Rights of the British Colonies Asserted and Proved*, reprinted in Bailyn (1965), i: *1750–1776*, 419–82.

—— (1765), *A Vindication of the British Colonies: Against the Aspersions of the Halifax Gentleman, in His Letter to a Rhode-Island Friend*, reprinted in Bailyn (1965), i: *1750–1776*, 554–79.

PAINE, T. (1791), *Rights of Man, Part One*, reprinted in H. H. Clark (1961), 54–165.

—— (1792a), *Rights of Man, Part Two*, reprinted in H. H. Clark (1961), 166–233.

—— (1792b), *Letter Addressed to the Addressers on the Late Proclamation*, reprinted in H. H. Clark (1961), 367–86.

PALEY, W. (1785), *The Principles of Moral and Political Philosophy*, in W. Paley (new edn. 1825), *The Works of William Paley, Vol. 4*, E. Paley (ed.) (London: C & J Rivington).

PALLISTER, A. (1971), *Magna Carta: The Heritage of Liberty* (Oxford: Clarendon Press).

PARK, J. J. (1832), *The Dogmas of the Constitution, Four Lectures . . . on the Theory & Practice of the Constitution* (London: B. Fellowes).

PARKER, H. (1642), *Observations Upon Some of His Majesties Late Answers and Expresses*, reprinted in Haller (1979), 165–213.

—— (1643a), *The Contra-Replicant, His Complaint to His Majestie* (London: s.n.) (EEB Reel 242: E. 87, no. 5).

—— (1643*b*), *The Oath of Pacification, or a Forme of Religious Accommodation Humbly Proposed Both to King and Parliament* (London: Robert Bostock) (EEB Reel 240: E. 70, no. 27).

PARKER, S. (1671), *A Defence and Continuation of the Ecclesiastical Polity* (London: by A. Clark for J. Martyn).

PATTERSON, A. (1994), *Reading Holinshed's Chronicles* (Chicago and London: University of Chicago Press).

PEACH, B. (ed.) (1979), *Richard Price and the Ethical Foundations of the American Revolution* (Durham, NC: Duke University Press).

PECK, L. L. (ed.) (1991), *The Mental World of the Jacobean Court* (Cambridge: Cambridge University Press).

—— (1993), 'Kingship, Counsel and Law in Early Stuart Britain', in Pocock (1993), 80–155.

PENNINGTON, K. (1993), *The Prince and the Law, 1200–1600: Sovereignty and Rights in the Western Legal Tradition* (Berkeley: University of California Press).

PENOVICH, K. R. (1995), 'From "Revolution Principles" to Union: Daniel Defoe's Intervention in the Scottish Debate', in Robertson (1995*a*), 228–42.

PERRY, K. (1990), *British Politics and the American Revolution* (London: Macmillan).

PETYT, W. (1739), *Jus Parliamentarium, Or, the Ancient Power, Jurisdiction, Rights and Liberties of the Most High Court of Parliament, Revived and Asserted* (London: John Nourse).

PHILLIPS, O. H. (1987) (7th edn.), *Constitutional and Administrative Law* (London: Sweet & Maxwell).

PICKTHORN, K. (1934*a*) (reprinted 1967, New York: Octagon Books), *Early Tudor Government: Henry VII* (Cambridge: Cambridge University Press).

—— (1934*b*), *Early Tudor Government: Henry VIII* (Cambridge: Cambridge University Press).

PLUCKNETT, T. F. T. (1922), *Statutes and Their Interpretation in the First Half of the Fourteenth Century* (Cambridge: Cambridge University Press).

—— (1926), 'Bonham's Case and Judicial Review', *Harvard Law Review*, 40: 30–70.

—— (1944), 'Ellesmere on Statutes', *Law Quarterly Review*, 60: 242–9.

—— (1949), *The Legislation of Edward I* (London: Oxford University Press).

—— (1960) (11th edn.), *Taswell-Langmead's English Constitutional History: From the Teutonic Conquest to the Present Time* (London: Sweet & Maxwell Ltd.).

POCOCK, J. G. A. (ed.) (1977), *The Political Works of James Harrington* (Cambridge: Cambridge University Press).

—— (1984), 'Radical Criticisms of the Whig Order in the Age Between Revolutions', in Jacob and Jacob (1984), 33–57.

—— (1985), '1776, The Revolution Against Parliament', in J. G. A. Pocock, *Virtue, Commerce, and History: Essays in Political Thought and History, Chiefly in the Eighteenth Century* (Cambridge: Cambridge University Press), 73–88.

—— (1987), *The Ancient Constitution and the Feudal Law: A Reissue with a Retrospect* (Cambridge: Cambridge University Press).

—— (ed.) (1993), *The Varieties of British Political Thought, 1500–1800* (Cambridge: Cambridge University Press).

POLLARD, A. F. (1926) (2nd edn., 1964 reprint), *The Evolution of Parliament* (London: Longmans).

POLLOCK, F. (1894), 'Sovereignty in English Law', *Harvard Law Review*, 8: 243–51.

—— (1907), 'Book Review, *De Republica Anglorum*, ed. L. Alston', *Law Quarterly Review*, 23: 221–3.

—— (1923), 'A Plea for Historical Interpretation', *Law Quarterly Review*, 39: 163–9.

—— (1929) (6th edn.), *A First Book of Jurisprudence, for Students of the Common Law* (London: Macmillan).

PORTER, H. C. (1972), 'Hooker, the Tudor Constitution, and the *Via Media*', in W. Speed Hill (ed.), *Studies in Richard Hooker* (Cleveland: The Press of Case Western Reserve University), 77–116.

POST, G. (1964), 'Book Review of M. J. Wilks, *The Problem of Sovereignty in the Later Middle Ages*', *Speculum*, 39: 365–72.

—— (1968), 'Bracton on Kingship', *Tulane Law Review*, 42: 519–602.

POSTEMA, G. (1982), 'Coordination and Convention at the Foundations of Law', *Journal of Legal Studies*, 11: 165–203.

—— (1987), ' "Protestant" Interpretation and Social Practices', *Law and Philosophy*, 6: 283–319.

POWELL, D. (1995), 'Why did James Whitelocke go to Jail in 1613? "Principle" and Political Dissent in Jacobean England', *Australian Journal of Law and Society*, 11: 169–90.

POWELL, E. (1994), 'Law and Justice', in R. Horrox (ed.), *Fifteenth Century Attitudes: Perceptions of Society in Late Medieval England* (Cambridge: Cambridge University Press), 29–41.

POWICKE, F. M. (1962) (2nd edn.), *The Thirteenth Century, 1216–1307* (London: Oxford University Press).

—— and FRYDE, E. B. (eds.) (1961) (2nd edn.), *Handbook of British Chronology* (London: Offices of the Royal Historical Society).

PRESTWICH, M. (1990), *English Politics in the Thirteenth Century* (Houndmills: Macmillan).

PRICE, R. (1776) (6th edn.), *Observations on the Nature of Civil Liberty: The Principles of Government and the Justice and Policy of the War with America* (London: E & C Dilly).

PRIESTLEY, J. (1771) (2nd edn.), *An Essay on the First Principles of Government, and on the Nature of Political, Civil and Religious Liberty,* reprinted in Priestley (1972), xxii: 1–144.

—— (1791a), *Letters to the Right Honourable Edmund Burke Occasioned by His Reflections on the Revolution in France,* reprinted in Priestley (1972), xxii: 145–244.

—— (1791b), *A Political Dialogue on the General Principles of Government,* reprinted in Priestley (1972), xxv: 81–108 .

—— (1803), *Lectures in History and General Policy,* reprinted in Priestley (1972), xxiv: 1–438.

—— (1965), *Priestley's Writings on Philosophy, Science and Politics,* J. A. Passmore (ed.) (New York: Collier Books).

—— (1972), *The Theological and Miscellaneous Works of Joseph Priestley*, J. T. Rutt (ed.) (New York: Klaus Reprint Co.), 25 vols.

PROTHERO, G. W. (ed.) (1913) (4th edn.), *Select Statutes and Other Constitutional Documents Illustrative of the Reigns of Elizabeth and James I* (London: Oxford University Press).

PRYNNE, W. (1643) (2nd edn.), *The Soveraigne Power of Parliaments and Kingdomes* (London: Michael Sparke Sen.).

QUILLET, J. (1988), 'Community, Counsel and Representation', in Burns (1988), 520–72.

RAIT, R. S. (1924), *The Parliaments of Scotland* (Glasgow: Maclehose, Jackson & Co.).

RAKOVE, J. N. (1991), 'Parchment Barriers and the Politics of Rights', in M. J. Lacey and K. Haakonssen (eds.), *A Culture of Rights: The Bill of Rights in Philosophy, Politics and Law, 1791–1991* (Cambridge: Cambridge University Press), 98–143.

RAYMOND, J. (1998), 'John Streater and *The Grand Politick Informer*', *Historical Journal*, 41: 567–74.

RAZ, J. (1979), *The Authority of Law: Essays on Law and Morality* (Oxford: Clarendon Press).

—— (1980) (2nd edn.), *The Concept of a Legal System: An Introduction to the Theory of a Legal System* (Oxford: Clarendon Press).

REID, J. P. (1977), 'In Legitimate Stirps: the Concept of "Arbitrary," the Supremacy of Parliament, and the Coming of the American Revolution', *Hofstra Law Review*, 5: 459–99.

—— (1991), *Constitutional History of the American Revolution: The Authority to Legislate* (Madison: University of Wisconsin Press).

—— (1993), *Constitutional History of the American Revolution: The Authority of Law* (Madison: University of Wisconsin Press).

REID, LORD (1972), 'The Judge as Law Maker', *Journal of the Society of Public Teachers of Law*, 12: 22–9.

RICHARDSON, H. G., and SAYLES, G. O. (1963), *The Governance of Mediaeval England, from the Conquest to Magna Carta* (Edinburgh: Edinburgh University Press).

RISHWORTH, P. (1997*a*), *The Struggle for Simplicity in Law: Essays for Lord Cooke of Thorndon* (Wellington: Butterworths).

—— (1997*b*): 'Lord Cooke and the Bill of Rights', in Rishworth (1997*a*), 295–330.

ROBERTSON, J. (ed.) (1995*a*), *A Union For Empire, Political Thought and the British Union of 1707* (Cambridge: Cambridge University Press).

—— (1995*b*), 'An Elusive Sovereignty: The Course of the Union Debate in Scotland 1698–1707', in Robertson (1995*a*), 198–227.

ROBINSON-MORRIS, M. (BARON ROKEBY) (1774), *Considerations on the Measures Carrying on With Respect to the British Colonies in North America*, reprinted in P. H. Smith (1972), 49–105.

ROPER, W. (1935), *The Life of Sir Thomas Moore, Knight*, E. V. Hitchcock (ed.) (London: Oxford University Press).

RUSHWORTH, J. (1659), *Historical Collections of Private Passages of State* (London: Thomas Newcombe for George Thomason), 3 vols.

—— (1721), *Historical Collections of Private Passages of State* (London: D. Browne, J. Walthoe, *et al.*), 8 vols.

RUSSELL, C. (ed.) (1973), *The Origins of the English Civil War* (London: Macmillan).

—— (1979), *Parliaments and English Politics 1621–1629* (Oxford: Clarendon Press).

—— (1990*a*), *The Causes of the English Civil War* (Oxford: Clarendon Press).

—— (1990*b*), 'English Parliaments 1593–1606: One Epoch or Two?' in D. M. Dean and N. L. Jones (eds.), *The Parliaments of Elizabethan England* (Oxford: Clarendon Press), 191–213.

—— (1993), 'Divine Rights in the Early Seventeenth Century', in J. Morrill, P. Slack, and D. Woolf (eds.), *Public Duty and Private Conscience in Seventeenth-Century England* (Oxford: Clarendon Press), 101–20.

RUSSELL, C. (1997), 'Thomas Cromwell's Doctrine of Parliamentary Sovereignty', *Transactions of the Royal Historical Society, Sixth series*, 7: 235–46.

RUTHERFORD, S. (1644), *Lex, Rex, The Law and the Prince: A Dispute for the Just Prerogative of King and People* (London: John Field) (EEB Reel 230: E. 11, no. 5).

SACHSE, W. L. (1975), *Lord Somers, a Political Portrait* (Manchester: Manchester University Press).

SACKS, D. H. (1992), 'Parliament, Liberty, and the Commonweal', in Hexter (1992*a*), 85–121.

ST GERMAN, C. (*c.*1532), *A Treatise Concerning The Division Between Spirituality And Temporality*, in More (1963–87), *ix: The Apology* (1979), J. B. Trapp (ed.), 177–212.

—— (1974), *Doctor and Student*, T. F. T. Plucknett and J. L. Barton (eds.) (London: Selden Society, Vol. 91).

ST JOHN, H. (VISCOUNT BOLINGBROKE) (1735) (3rd edn.), *A Dissertation Upon Parties, In Several Letters to Caleb D'Anvers, Esq.* (London: H. Haines).

—— (1749), *Letters, on the Spirit of Patriotism, on the Idea of a Patriot King* (London: A. Millar).

SALMON, J. H. M. (1959), *The French Religious Wars in English Political Thought* (Oxford: Clarendon Press).

SANDEL, M. J. (1996), *Democracy's Discontent: America in Search of a Public Philosophy* (Cambridge, Mass.: The Belknap Press of Harvard University Press).

SANDERSON, J. (1993), 'Conrad Russell's Ideas', *History of Political Thought*, 14: 85–102.

SAUL, N. (1997), *Richard II* (New Haven and London: Yale University Press).

SAYLES, G. O. (1974), *The King's Parliament of England* (New York: W. W. Norton & Co.).

SCARISBRICK, J. J. (1968), *Henry VIII* (London: Eyre & Spottiswoode).

SCARMAN, L. (1974), *English Law: The New Dimension* (London: Stevens and Sons).

SCHOCHET, G. J. (1992), 'The English Revolution in the History of Political Thought', in Kunze and Brautigam (1992), 1–20.

SCHONHORN, M. (1991), *Defoe's Politics, Parliament, Power, Kingship, and Robinson Crusoe* (Cambridge: Cambridge University Press).

SCHULZ, F. (1945), 'Bracton on Kingship', *English Historical Review*, 60: 136–76.

SCHUYLER, R. L. (1963), *Parliament and the British Empire: Some Constitutional Controversies Concerning Imperial Legislative Jurisdiction* (Hamden, Conn.: Archon Books).

SCHWOERER, L. G. (1984), 'The Contributions of the Declaration of Rights to Anglo-American Radicalism', in Jacob and Jacob (1984), 105–24.

—— (1992), 'The Coronation of William and Mary', in L. G. Schwoerer (ed.), *The Revolution of 1688–1689: Changing Perspectives* (Cambridge: Cambridge University Press), 107–30.

—— (1995), 'The Attempted Impeachment of Sir William Scroggs, Lord Chief Justice of King's Bench, November 1680–March 1681', *Historical Journal*, 38: 843–73.

SCOTT, W. (ed.) (1809–15) (reissued 1965, New York: AMS Press, 2nd edn.), *The Somers Collection of Tracts* (London: T. Cadell), 13 vols.

SEARLE, J. (1990), 'Collective Intentions and Actions', in P. R. Cohen, J. Morgan, and M. Pollack (eds.), *Intentions in Communication* (Cambridge, Mass.: MIT Press), 401.

SEAWARD, P. (1988), *The Cavalier Parliament and the Reconstruction of the Old Regime 1661–1667* (Cambridge: Cambridge University Press).

—— (1997), 'Constitutional and Unconstitutional Royalism', *Historical Journal*, 40: 227–39.

SEDLEY, SIR S. (1995), 'Human Rights: A Twenty-First Century Agenda', *Public Law*, 386–400.

—— (1997), 'The Common Law and the Constitution', in Lord Nolan of Brasted and Sir S. Sedley, *The Making and Remaking of the British Constitution* (London: Blackstone Press).

SELDEN, J. (1696) (2nd edn.), *Table Talk, being the Discourse of John Selden Esq.* (London: Jacob Tonson).

SHARP, A. (1983), *Political Ideas of the English Civil Wars 1641–1649: A Collection of Representative Texts with a Commentary* (London and New York: Longman).

SHEPARD, M. (1936), 'The Political and Constitutional Theory of Sir John Fortescue', in C. Wittke (ed.), *Essays in History and Political Science in Honor of Charles Howard McIlwain* (Cambridge, Mass.: Harvard University Press), 289–319.

SHERIDAN, C. (1779) (2nd edn.), *Observations on the Doctrine Laid Down by Sir William Blackstone Respecting the Extent of the Power of the British Parliament, Particularly with relation to Ireland* (London: J. Almon, J. Didsley, and E. and C. Dilly).

SHERINGHAM, R. (1660) (3rd edn.), *The Kings Supremacy Asserted* (London: for Jonas Hart and Charles Morden) (EEB Reel 898:13).

SHETREET, S. (1976), *Judges on Trial* (Amsterdam: North-Holland Publishing Co.).

SIDNEY, A. (1704) (2nd edn.), *Discourses concerning Government* (London: J. Darby).

SIMMONS, R. C., and THOMAS, P. D. G. (eds.) (1982–7), *Proceedings and Debates of the British Parliaments respecting North America 1754–1783* (New York and London: Kraus International Publications), 6 vols.

SINGER, P. (1974), *Democracy and Disobedience* (New York and London: Oxford University Press).

SKINNER, Q. (1978), *The Foundations of Modern Political Thought* (Cambridge: Cambridge University Press).

SLAVIN, A. J. (1992), 'The Tudor State, Reformation and Understanding Change: Through the Looking Glass', in P. A. Fideler and T. F. Mayer (eds.), *Political Thought and the Tudor Commonwealth: Deep Structure, Discourse and Disguise* (London and New York: Routledge), 223–53.

SMITH, A. (1978), *Lectures on Jurisprudence*, R. L. Meek, D. D. Raphael, and P. G. Stein (eds.) (Oxford: Clarendon Press).

SMITH, D. L. (1992), 'The Struggle for New Constitutional and Institutional Forms', in J. Morrill (ed.), *Revolution and Restoration: England in the 1650s* (London: Collins and Brown), 15–34.

—— (1994), *Constitutional Royalism and the Search For Settlement, c.1640–1649* (Cambridge: Cambridge University Press).

SMITH, P. H. (ed.), (1972), *English Defenders of American Freedoms 1774–1778: Six Pamphlets Attacking British Policy* (Washington: Library of Congress).

SMITH, S. (1825), 'Review of *The Book of Fallacies: from Unfinished Papers of Jeremy Bentham*', *Edinburgh Review*, 42: 367–89.

SMITH, SIR T. (1583) (1906 reprint), *De Republica Anglorum*, L. Alston (ed.) (Cambridge: Cambridge University Press).

SMITH, T. B. (1957), 'The Union of 1707 as Fundamental Law', *Public Law*, 99–121.

—— (1961), *British Justice: The Scottish Contribution* (London: Stevens).

SMITH, T. B. (1962), *A Short Commentary on the Law of Scotland* (Edinburgh: W. Green & Son Ltd.).

—— (1987), 'Constitutional Law, Fundamental Law', in *The Laws of Scotland, Stair Memorial Encyclopaedia, Vol. 5* (Edinburgh: Butterworths), 137–62.

SNOWISS, S. (1990), *Judicial Review and the Law of the Constitution* (New Haven and London: Yale University Press).

[SOMERS, J.] (1697), *A Letter, Ballancing the Necessity of Keeping a Land-Force in Times of Peace with the Dangers that may Follow on it* (London?: s.n.).

SOMMERVILLE, J. P. (1983), 'Richard Hooker, Hadrian Saravia, and the Advent of the Divine Right of Kings', *History of Political Thought*, 4: 229–45.

—— (1986), *Politics and Ideology in England 1603–1640* (London and New York: Longman).

—— (1990), 'Oliver Cromwell and English Political Thought', in J. Morrill (ed.), *Oliver Cromwell and the English Revolution* (London and New York: Longman), 234–58.

—— (1991), 'Absolutism and Royalism', in Burns (1991), 347–73.

—— (1992), *Thomas Hobbes: Political Ideas in Historical Context* (Houndmills: Macmillan).

—— (1996*a*), 'The Ancient Constitution Reassessed: The Common Law, the Court and the Languages of Politics in Early Modern England', in M. Smuts (ed.), *The Stuart Court and Europe: Essays in Politics and Political Culture* (Cambridge: Cambridge University Press), 39–64.

—— (1996*b*), 'English and European Ideas in the Early Seventeenth Century: Revisionism and the Case of Absolutism', *Journal of British Studies*, 35: 168–94.

SOSIN, J. M. (1989), *The Aristocracy of the Long Robe: The Origins of Judicial Review in America* (New York: Greenwood Press).

SPELMAN, J. (1642*a*), *Certain Considerations upon the Duties both of Prince and People,* (Oxford: Leonard Lichfield) (EEB Reel 1390: 11).

—— (1642*b*), *A View of a Printed Book Intituled Observations Upon His Majesties Late Answers and Expresses* (Oxford: Leonard Liechfield) (EEB Reel 266: E. 245, no. 22).

—— (1644) *The Case of Our Affaires in Law, Religion* (Oxford: H. H. for W. W.) (EEB Reel 233: E. 30, no. 14).

SPENCER, H. (1884) (1969 reprint), *The Man versus the State*, D. Macrae (ed.) (Harmondsworth: Penguin).

SPUFFORD, P. (1967), *Origins of the English Parliament* (London: Longmans).

State Tracts: Being a Farther Collection of Several Choice Treatises Relating to the Government, From the Year 1660 to 1689 (1692) (London: Richard Baldwin).

STEPHEN, H. J. (1848) (2nd edn.), *New Commentaries on the Laws of England* (London: Henry Butterworth).

[STEPHEN, J. F.] (1861), 'English Jurisprudence', *Edinburgh Review*, 114: 456–86. (Stephen is named as the author in Houghton (1966: i. 511).)

STEPHEN, L. (1907), *The Science of Ethics* (London: John Murray).

—— and LEE, S. (eds.) (1917), *The Dictionary of National Biography* (Oxford: Oxford University Press), 22 vols.

STEPHENSON, C., and MARCHAM, F. G. (eds.) (1972) (revised edn.), *Sources of English Constitutional History* (New York: Harper & Row), 2 vols.

STIMSON, S. C. (1990), *The American Revolution in the Law: Anglo-American Jurisprudence Before John Marshall* (London: Macmillan).

STONER, J. R. (1992), *Common Law and Liberal Theory: Coke, Hobbes and the Origins of American Constitutionalism* (Lawrence, Kan.: University Press of Kansas).

STOURZH, G. (1970), *Alexander Hamilton and the Idea of Republican Government* (Stanford, Calif.: Stanford University Press).

—— (1988), '*Constitution*: Changing Meanings of the Term from the Early Seventeenth to the Late Eighteenth Century', in T. Ball and J. G. A. Pocock (eds.), *Conceptual Change and the Constitution* (Lawrence, Kan.: University Press of Kansas), 35–54.

STOUT, H. S. (1974), 'Marsilius of Padua and the Henrician Reformation', *Church History*, 43: 308–18.

STRAYER, J. R. (ed.) (1982–9), *Dictionary of the Middle Ages* (New York: Charles Scribener's Sons), 13 vols.

STUBBS, W. (1897) (5th edn.), *The Constitutional History of England in its Origins and Development* (New York: Barnes & Noble).

SUNSTEIN, C. (1996), *Legal Reasoning and Political Conflict* (New York: Oxford University Press).

SWIFT, J. (1701) (reissued 1967), *A Discourse of the Contests and Dissentions Between the Nobles and the Commons in Athens and Rome*, F. H. Ellis (ed.) (Oxford: Clarendon Press).

—— (1708*a*), *The Sentiment of a Church-of-England Man, With Respect to Religion and Government*, reprinted in Swift (1957), 1–25.

—— (1708*b*), *Remarks upon a Book Intitled, The Rights of the Christian Church Asserted*, reprinted in Swift (1957), 65–107.

—— (1957), *Bickenstaff Papers and Pamphlets on the Church*, H. Davis (ed.) (Oxford: Basil Blackwell).

—— (1966), *The Examiner and Other Pieces Written in 1710–11*, H. Davis (ed.) (Oxford: Basil Blackwell).

TAFT, B. (1984), 'That Lusty Puss, the Good Old Cause', *History of Political Thought*, 5: 447–68.

TALBERT, E. W. (1962), *The Problem of Order: Elizabethan Political Commonplaces and an Example of Shakespeare's Art* (Chapel Hill, NC: University of North Carolina Press).

TANNER, J. R. (1930) (1961 reprint), *Constitutional Documents of the Reign of James I, 1603–1625* (Cambridge: Cambridge University Press).

TATE, C. N., and VALLINDER, T. (eds.) (1995), *The Global Expansion of Judicial Power* (New York: New York University Press).

THAYER, J. B. (1893), 'The Origin and Scope of the American Doctrine of Constitutional Law', *Harvard Law Review*, 7: 129–56.

THOMAS, P. D. G. (1975), *British Politics and the Stamp Act Crisis: The First Phase of the American Revolution, 1763–1767* (Oxford: Clarendon Press).

THOMSON, M. A. (1938), *A Constitutional History of England 1642 to 1801* (London: Methuen).

THORNE, S. E. (1938), 'Dr. Bonham's Case', *Law Quarterly Review*, 54: 543–52.

—— (ed.) (1942), *A Discourse Upon the Exposicion & Understandinge of Statutes* (San Marino, Calif.: Huntington Library).

—— (1985), *Essays in English Legal History* (London: Hambledon Press).

TIERNEY, B. (1963*a*), 'Bracton on Government', *Speculum*, 38: 295–317.

—— (1963*b*), ' "The Prince is Not Bound by the Laws", Accursius and the Origins of the Modern State', *Comparative Studies in Society and History*, 5: 378–400.

Tierney, B. (1982), *Religion, Law and the Growth of Constitutional Thought 1150–1650* (Cambridge: Cambridge University Press).

Tocqueville, A. de (1838), *Democracy in America*, H. Reeve (trans.) (London: Saunders & Otley).

Todd, A. (1880), *Parliamentary Government in the British Colonies* (London: Longmans, Green, and Co.).

Toland, J. (1717) (4th edn.), *State Anatomy of Great Britain* (London: John Philips).

Toohey, R. E. (1978), *Liberty and Empire: British Radical Solutions to the American Problem 1774–1776* (Lexington, Ky.: The University Press of Kentucky).

Tuck, R. (1979), *Natural Rights Theories: Their Origin and Development* (Cambridge: Cambridge University Press).

—— (1982), ' "The Ancient Law of Freedom": John Selden and the Civil War', in Morrill (1982), 137–61.

—— (1993), *Philosophy and Government 1572–1651* (Cambridge: Cambridge University Press).

Tucker, J. (1781), *A Treatise Concerning Civil Government* (London: T. Cadell).

Tully, J. (1991), 'Locke', in Burns (1991), 616–52.

—— (1993), *An Approach to Political Philosophy: Locke in Contexts* (Cambridge: Cambridge University Press).

Turner, R. V. (1968), *The King and His Courts: The Role of John and Henry III in the Administration of Justice, 1199–1240* (Ithaca, NY: Cornell University Press).

Twysden, R. (1849), *Certaine Considerations Upon the Government of England*, J. M. Kemble (ed.) (London: Camden Society).

Tyndale, W. (1848), *The Obedience of a Christian Man*, in H. Walter (ed.), *Doctrinal Treatises and Introductions to Different Portions of the Holy Scriptures* (Cambridge: Cambridge University Press), 127–344.

Ullmann, W. (1961), *Principles of Government and Politics in the Middle Ages* (London: Methuen).

Valente, C. (1998), 'The Deposition and Abdication of Edward II', *English Historical Review*, 113: 852–81.

Vile, M. J. C. (1967), *Constitutionalism and the Separation of Powers* (Oxford: Clarendon Press).

Vinogradoff, P. (1913), 'Constitutional History and the Year Books', *Law Quarterly Review*, 29: 273–84.

Wade, H. W. R. (1955), 'The Basis of Legal Sovereignty', *Cambridge Law Journal*, 172–97.

—— (1989) (revised edn.), *Constitutional Fundamentals* (London: Stevens).

—— and Forsyth, C. (1994) (7th edn.), *Administrative Law* (Oxford: Clarendon Press).

Waldron, J. (1993), 'A Right-Based Critique of Constitutional Rights', *Oxford Journal of Legal Studies*, 13: 18–51.

Walker, D. M. (1995), *A Legal History of Scotland* (Edinburgh: T. & T. Clark Ltd).

Walker, G. de Q. (1985), 'Dicey's Dubious Dogma of Parliamentary Sovereignty: A Recent Fray With Freedom of Religion', *Australian Law Journal*, 59: 276–84.

—— (1988), *The Rule of Law: Foundation of Constitutional Democracy* (Melbourne: Melbourne University Press).

Wallington, P. (1974), 'Sovereignty Regained', *Modern Law Review*, 37: 686–91.

Walter, J. (1996), 'The Commons and their Mental Worlds', in Morrill (1996), 191–218.

WALUCHOW, W. (1994), *Inclusive Legal Positivism* (Oxford: Clarendon Press).

WARREN, W. C. (1987), *The Governance of Norman and Angevin England 1086–1272* (London: Edward Arnold).

WATT, J. A. (1988), 'Spiritual and Temporal Powers', in Burns (1988), 367–423.

WATTS, J. L. (1996), *Henry VI and the Politics of Kingship* (Cambridge: Cambridge University Press).

WESTON, C. C. (1965), *English Constitutional Theory and the House of Lords 1556–1832* (London: Routledge & Kegan Paul).

—— (1991), 'England, Ancient Constitution and Common Law', in Burns (1991), 374–411.

—— and GREENBERG, J. R. (1981), *Subjects and Sovereigns: The Grand Controversy over Legal Sovereignty in Stuart England* (Cambridge: Cambridge University Press).

WHEARE, K. C. (1966) (2nd edn.), *Modern Constitutions* (London: Oxford University Press).

WHITE, A. (1788), 'Letter to Madison', 16 August, in R. A. Rutland and C. E. Hobson (eds.), (1977), *Papers of James Madison, Vol. 11: 7 March 1788–1 March 1789* (Charlottesville, Va.: University Press of Virginia), 232–4.

WHITE, S. D. (1979), *Sir Edward Coke and 'the Grievances of the Commonwealth', 1621–1628* (Chapel Hill, NC: University of North Carolina Press).

WHITELOCKE, B. (1766), *Whitelocke's Notes uppon the Kings Writt for Choosing Members of Parlement XIII Car II Being Disquisitions on the Government of England by King Lords and Commons* (London: C. Morton).

WILKINSON, B. (1949), 'The "Political Revolution" of the Thirteenth and Fourteenth Centuries in England', *Speculum*, 24: 502–9.

—— (1952a), *Constitutional History of Medieval England 1216–1399* (London: Longmans).

—— (1952b) (2nd edn.), *Studies in the Constitutional History of the Thirteenth and Fourteenth Centuries* (Manchester: Manchester University Press).

—— (1964), *Constitutional History of England in the Fifteenth Century (1399–1485)* (London: Longmans).

WILKS, M. (1963), *The Problem of Sovereignty in the Later Middle Ages* (Cambridge: Cambridge University Press).

WILLIAMS, P. (1979), *The Tudor Regime* (Oxford: Clarendon Press).

—— (1995), *The Later Tudors: England 1547–1603* (Oxford: Clarendon Press).

WILSON, G. (1997), 'Postscript: The Courts, Law and Convention', in Lord Nolan of Brasted and Sir S. Sedley, *The Making and Remaking of the British Constitution* (London: Blackstone Press).

WINTERTON, G. (1976), 'The British Grundnorm: Parliamentary Sovereignty Re-examined', *Law Quarterly Review*, 92: 591–617.

—— (1981), 'Parliamentary Sovereignty and the Judiciary', *Law Quarterly Review*, 97: 265–74.

—— (1996), 'Constitutionally Entrenched Common Law Rights: Sacrificing Means to Ends?', in C. Sampford and K. Preston (eds.), *Interpreting Constitutions, Theories, Principles and Institutions* (Sydney: Federation Press), 121–45.

WITTKE, C. F. (1970), *The History of Parliamentary Privilege* (New York: Da Capo Press).

WOLFE, D. M. (ed.) (1944), *Leveller Manifestoes of the Puritan Revolution* (New York: Thomas Nelson & Sons).

WOOD, C. T. (1975), 'The Deposition of Edward V', *Traditio*, 31: 247–86.

WOOD, C. T. (1982), 'Celestine V, Boniface VIII and the Authority of Parliament', *Journal of Medieval History*, 8: 45–62.

—— (1988), *Joan of Arc and Richard III: Sex, Saints, and Government in the Middle Ages* (New York and Oxford: Oxford University Press).

—— (1989), 'England: 1216–1485', in Strayer (1982–9), iv: 472–86.

WOOD, G. S. (1969), *The Creation of the American Republic 1776–1787* (Chapel Hill, NC: University of North Carolina Press).

WOODDESON, R. (1842), *Lectures on the Law of England* (Philadelphia: John S. Littell).

WOOLF OF BARNES, LORD (1995), 'Droit Public—English Style', *Public Law*, 57–71.

—— (1998), 'Judicial Review—The Tensions Between the Executive and the Judiciary', *Law Quarterly Review*, 114: 579–93.

WOOLRYCH, A. (1982), *Commonwealth to Protectorate* (Oxford: Clarendon Press).

WOOTTON, D. (ed.) (1986), *Divine Right and Democracy* (Harmondsworth: Penguin Books).

—— (1990), 'From Rebellion to Revolution: The Crisis of the Winter of 1642/3 and the Origins of Civil War Radicalism', *English Historical Review*, 105: 654–69.

WORMUTH, F. D. (1939) (reissued 1972, New York and London: Kennikat Press), *The Royal Prerogative 1603–1649: A Study in English Political and Constitutional Ideas* (Ithaca, NY: Cornell University Press).

WRIGHT, B. F. (1942) (1967 reprint), *The Growth of American Constitutional Law* (Chicago and London: University of Chicago Press).

YALE, D. E. C. (1972), 'Hale and Hobbes on Law, Legislation, and the Sovereign', *Cambridge Law Journal*, 31: 121–56.

YORKE, C. (1746) (2nd edn., corrected and enlarged), *Some Considerations on the Law of Forfeiture for High Treason* (London: J. Roberts).

ZAGORIN, P. (1954), *A History of Political Thought in the English Revolution* (Great Britain: Routledge & Kegan Paul Ltd.).

ZALLER, R. (1991), 'Henry Parker and the Regiment of True Government', *Proceedings of the American Philosophical Society*, 135: 255–85.

Index of Names

Index of Subjects

Lightning Source UK Ltd.
Milton Keynes UK
UKHW020626200919

350107UK00003B/58/P